A Brief History of Making

1973-1975 Malcolm gives series of adult education le losophy in the Brighton area, during which the ideas in *Making Names* gradually coalesce. When *Electra* is conceived, Malcolm gives up lecturing in order to write.

Late 1977 Malcolm submits an early draft of the book to the philosophy editor of Penguins, who sends it to a (scientist) referee. The script is at this stage largely conventional essays, with two chapters on cause and effect cast as dialogues between two eponymous characters and the final chapter consisting of a playscript of *Electra*. Both editor and referee are encouraging, in particular praising the dialogue and playscript sections. Informally it is agreed that if the whole text were rewritten in dialogue form, Penguins would be interested in its publication.

Early 1984 Having completed the rewriting, Malcolm returns to Penguins to discover that the previous editor has left and that there is no longer a philosophy department. The sociology editor now responsible states that she regards philosophical dialogues as "quite out of fashion". Malcolm submits a synopsis of the book to numerous other publishers, but none requests the script.

31st August 1984 Malcolm submits the synopsis of *Making Names* to the philosophy editor of Oxford University Press who passes it to the General Books division.

14th October 1984 On invitation from the Senior General Books Editor Henry Hardy, Malcolm sends Oxford the typescript of *Making Names*. The script is sent to Oxford philosopher and OUP Delegate Alan Ryan.

11th February 1985 Ryan reports favourably on *Making Names* (see p. vii).

18th March 1985 Hardy writes Malcolm an encouraging letter which outlines various revisions required by Oxford.

24th March 1985 Malcolm writes agreeing to revise the book, but only upon securing Oxford's firm commitment to its publication. He recounts his experience with Penguins. Hardy decides to read the script himself.

20th May 1985 Having read the script, Hardy telephones Malcolm and gives Oxford's firm commitment to the publication of *Making Names*; detailed revisions and payment of "a fair royalty" are agreed (see p. vii).

May-June 1985 In letters to Malcolm, Hardy confirms Oxford's commitment, sends Malcolm a publicity questionnaire to help OUP in marketing the book and completes an internal form specifying Malcolm's royalties and the book's format, print run and retail price.

11th July 1985 Oxford philosopher Galen Strawson is asked to act as a third reader and presents a report again recommending publication of *Making Names* (see p. vii).

16th July 1985 Hardy completes an internal OUP agenda paper marked "for Delegates 23rd July" which notes the publication of *Making Names*, specifying the book's format, print run and retail price.

17th July 1985 At an OUP editorial meeting (unminuted), Managing Director Richard Charkin, aware of Hardy's commitment to Malcolm and ignorant of *Making Names*, vetoes the book's publication. Charkin serves Hardy with a disciplinary warning preparatory to dismissal.

18th-22nd July 1985 Charkin sends Malcolm a letter rejecting *Making Names*. Ryan urges Charkin to allow the book's publication and writes Hardy a second favourable report which envisages "galloping ahead" with it. Hardy telephones Malcolm, *inter alia* dictating a letter for Malcolm to write ameliorating Hardy's position. Malcolm writes a letter declining further dealings with Oxford.

23rd July 1985 The Delegates, including Ryan, attend their Summer Vacation meeting. Hardy attends a Disciplinary Tribunal, admits making a contractual commitment to Malcolm and wins the hearing; his warning is rescinded. Hardy telephones Malcolm to persuade him, after all, to go ahead with the revision of *Making Names*, giving several further assurances. Malcolm agrees to do so only upon receipt of a written list of Oxford's requirements.

31st July 1985 Hardy sends Malcolm a detailed list of Oxford's requirements. Malcolm embarks on the revision, envisaging six months' work.

21st February 1986 Malcolm sends the revised typescript, in which all of Oxford's requirements have been fulfilled (uncontested). Meanwhile Hardy has been moved by Charkin to another OUP department and the book is now handled by a junior editor, Nicola Bion.

9th May 1986 Bion sends Malcolm a rejection letter stating that the book is undoubtedly improved, but also mentioning adverse readers' reports. Subsequently Oxford produces no readers' reports on the revised script.

17th July 1986 In pre-litigation correspondence Malcolm discloses his possession of answerphone recordings of his conversations with Hardy.

19th September 1986 Alan Ryan is invited to make a statement on the affair and to read Malcolm's further revised Chapter 9. Ryan declines both invitations, saying he can no longer give a dispassionate assessment of the book. Shortly afterwards he leaves Oxford for Princeton, USA.

23rd December 1986 Malcolm serves a writ for breach of contract on the Chancellor, Masters and Scholars of the University of Oxford.

19th April 1988 After two preliminary hearings, a dispute begins over Oxford's discovery of documents, leading to a third hearing, which Malcolm wins, with costs.

3rd August 1988 An Oxford affidavit verifies that Hardy's agenda paper on *Making Names* was circulated to all Delegates on 16th July 1985.

11th August 1988 Oxford produces further documents relating to Hardy's disciplinary hearing of 23rd July 1985.

14th September 1988 Malcolm issues a Motion claiming Oxford's contempt of Court concerning discovery of documents.

6th March 1989 At the hearing of the Motion, OUP's Chief Executive Sir Roger Elliott is ordered to produce the apparently missing records of General Books tabled at the Delegates' meeting of 23rd July 1985.

19th July 1989 Elliott denies the existence of Delegates' records.

24th August 1989 The action is set down for trial.

4th October 1989 For the first time Oxford asks to hear the recordings of the Hardy/Malcolm telephone conversations. Malcolm sends the tapes.

12th February 1990 At a pre-trial hearing six Oxford witnesses are ordered to attend the trial for cross-examination.

12th-16th March 1990 The case is tried before Deputy Judge Gavin Lightman Q.C. On opening, Oxford denies Hardy's contractual authority and Hardy denies his commitment to Malcolm. The Deputy Judge disallows Oxford's new defence and rejects Hardy's testimony. He concludes that "a clear commitment" was made by Oxford but finds no enforceable contract on the grounds that certain matters such as the book's format, print run and price had not been agreed.

18th April 1990 Malcolm appeals.

17th May 1990 Oxford responds by pleading for the first time that the Delegates' approval of *Making Names* was a condition of the contract.

21st May 1990 Oxford and its witnesses send Malcolm bills of costs totalling £25,712.99. Malcolm receives an anonymous package postmarked Cambridge containing new evidence, including agenda papers for the Delegates' meeting of 23rd July 1985.

4th September 1990 Oxford applies for security of its costs of the appeal (a further £7,500) and abandons its "Delegates' approval" defence.

28th September 1990 Oxford's security of costs application is dismissed.

12th October 1990 Malcolm receives a second package of new evidence postmarked Oxford and signed ADRASTEIA.

17th-19th October 1990 Malcolm's Appeal is heard by Lords Justices Mustill, Nourse and Leggatt. Malcolm's expert evidence (that format, print run and price are rarely stipulated in publishing contracts) is resisted by Oxford but admitted by the Court; it then goes unchallenged. Oxford is invited to make a public statement (see p.vi). Judgment is reserved.

18th December 1990 Malcolm's Appeal is allowed and an assessment of damages is ordered. An out-of-court settlement is anticipated.

12th February 1991 In the absence of any offer, Malcolm initiates proceedings for the assessment of damages.

28th March 1991 Oxford reveals that it is not in possession of a script of *Making Names*, which is now needed for assessment.

10th May 1991 Oxford appoints Harvey McGregor Q.C. leading Counsel.

21st June 1991 Oxford serves 'independent expert' affidavit evidence against *Making Names* sworn by 13 witnesses from British publishers including Penguins, Routledge, Blackwells, Macmillans, HarperCollins, Reed and The Open University, none of whom has seen the book. Alan Ryan files his first legal statement in the case, retracts his 1985 reports and describes the book as "a commercial impossibility which would have sunk without trace". Ryan has not seen *Making Names* since 1986; because he is in the USA he cannot be cross-examined.

10th & 11th July 1991 Damages assessment hearing; judgment reserved.

19th November 1991 Malcolm is awarded damages of £17,444.73.

18th December 1991 Malcolm appeals for higher damages, Oxford cross-appeals for lower damages.

February 1992 *Making Names* is printed for AKME Publications.

28th May 1992 The damages appeal is scheduled for 20th July 1992.

1st July 1992 The Court endorses an agreed settlement between Malcolm and the Chancellor, Masters and Scholars of Oxford University (terms confidential).

August 1992 *Making Names* is published in hardback.

Who Runs May Read

On 14th March 1990, during Malcolm's cross-examination of Oxford's witnesses in the High Court trial, there took place the following exchanges between Deputy Judge Gavin Lightman Q.C. and Sir Roger Elliott and Richard Charkin.

Judge Sir Roger, if you heard that some responsible officer of the Press had given a commitment to an author that the Press would publish his work, would you feel concerned if, at some later date, that commitment having been given, it were withdrawn?

Elliott Editors are not allowed to give such commitments.

Judge Supposing the individual in this case had the authority to do so, would you be concerned about it?

Elliott Well, I would be concerned if he had given such a commitment since he had no authority to give such a commitment.

Judge And that would be the basis of your response?

Elliott That would be the basis of my response because all our editors are quite clear that, while of course they must enter into negotiations with authors about their books and they must obviously be encouraging about the books, they are not in a position to enter into a commitment or sign a contract. They have to get Delegates' approval and the contracts are signed by the head of the division after that approval has been given.

Judge Now, Mr Malcolm's case is that he received a commitment. There is in fact, on the pleadings of this case, no defence raised that the individual concerned did not have the authority; that is not an issue in the case. It is accepted that if Mr Hardy did in fact enter into a contract with Mr Malcolm, then there is a contract irrespective of any absence of authority. Against this background, would you feel concerned if a commitment were given by Mr Hardy to Mr Malcolm that he would publish and was subsequently reneged on?

Elliott Well, I would be concerned of course, because it would be a serious breach of discipline within the Press.

Judge And also a serious injustice to the author?

Elliott (pause) I can see that it could be an injustice to the author... It would depend upon how long it was before the matter was put straight.

Judge Thank you. Are there any further questions you want to ask?

Malcolm No, my Lord.

and

Charkin (witness statement) Editors commission a book.

Judge Is there a distinction between encouraging an author and giving him a commitment?

Charkin I think there is a distinction, but it is a very fine distinction.

Sir Roger Elliott is now the President of the Publishers' Association.
Richard Charkin is now the Chief Executive of Reed Consumer Books.

On 19th October 1990, at the conclusion of the Appeal hearing the Court invited Oxford to make a public statement, which it did. On the next day, it circulated an amended, typed version, which reads as follows:

> **Oxford University Press has defended itself in this action to defend the status of its imprint which Mr Malcolm has coveted. Notwithstanding what has been said in the evidence, all new titles published from Oxford have to obtain the approval of the Delegates. They are particularly concerned to maintain the high academic reputation of the scholarly and pedagogical books published in the name of the University. All the evidence available on Mr Malcolm's final manuscript indicated that it did not reach the appropriate standard. Many manuscripts of greater merit have to be rejected by OUP every year.**
>
> **It was not until after court proceedings were instigated that the Senior Officers of the Press were aware, through the tape recordings, that the editor had made statements which could be interpreted as a commitment to publish. This was completely beyond his authority but we accept, as he firmly believes, that he made clear that anything he offered was subject to Delegates' approval and a final written contract.**
>
> **Having taken legal advice OUP believed that there was no binding contract, and this was borne out by the judgment of the court of first instance. It is hoped that this will be confirmed in this court.**
>
> **OUP accept that Mr Malcolm's book was not handled as it should have been, and apologize for the pain and inconvenience this may have caused. But, because of their obligation to maintain the academic standing of the Press, the Delegates were bound to oppose an action for specific performance. It is also true that certain aspects of Mr Malcolm's conduct of the litigation have only served to harden the Press's attitude.**

During the subsequent damages assessment, Oxford admitted that it had not been in possession of *Making Names* since mid-1989. Oxford never produced in evidence any adverse readers' report on the book.

Passing Judgments

"I think *Making Names* is rather good... I'm rather keen that we should have a go if it's possible. It would, I think, be a plausible general book, and it might do well as a sort of introduction to philosophy for people doing 'A' Level philosophy and people doing Open University courses. It's philosophically rather good, I think – it makes one of the shrewdest cases for a sort of Collingwoodian Idealism that I've read. I like the dialogue style. *Making Names* is well worth doing, both because it is interesting in itself, and because it's a bold attempt to do philosophy in an unusual literary format – most dialogues fall terribly flat, but Malcolm's seems to me to stand up very well for long stretches. It ought to appeal to people with a general interest in science on the one hand and literature on the other... Every so often books like Colin Wilson's *The Outsider* or Hofstadter's *Godel, Escher, Bach* (which I don't like at all, to tell you the truth) do exceedingly well, so a bit of boldness is in order. So, I hope Richard Charkin is as cheerful as he sounded on the 'phone, and that we can gallop ahead as he suggested we could. It would be nice to take a chance and win – and the so-called "downside risk" isn't too drastic if we don't."
Alan Ryan, New College, Oxford (reader's reports, 11th February & 18th July 1985)

"I have now finished reading *Making Names* and we would like to do it. I know you want a commitment sufficient to take you through the last stage of revision and that is what I'm offering. I was quite gripped by the end, I was reading with the kind of attention that one gives to a novel, which is not very usual with a philosophical work... What I think we should agree is that you have a fair royalty so that if the book is a success you will do well out of it.... As said, do get in touch if you have any queries as you work through it. Don't worry about the delay in revising the book. I'm pleased that we are going to do *Making Names* and hope that it's a terrific success."
Henry Hardy, Senior Editor, Oxford University Press (telephone call and letters to Malcolm, 20th & 21st May & 14th June 1985)

"I think *Making Names* is really quite an attractive book. It is in no way crazy. It is very easy to read. Malcolm has a real gift for informal exposition, he is very clear and he knows what he's talking about. I think *Making Names* might prove extremely effective as an introduction to philosophical problems and procedures."
Galen Strawson, St Hugh's College, Oxford (reader's report, 14th July 1985)

vii

"Now let me plunge myself into the shit along with you.... OUP's Managing Director Richard Charkin has taken strongly against *Making Names*. He does not know anything about it, he certainly has not attempted to read it at all and he has not even inquired into its contents... However he has served me with a Stage Three Disciplinary Warning preparatory to dismissal, which is *totally* ludicrous... I think he's dead wrong about this and I'm doing everything I can to convince him, if only because I have made a commitment to you which I think we should honour collectively... It has become a power struggle between him and me. There's an element of personality in here which has nothing to do with your book. Charkin would lose face by now accepting it and he's not somebody who will lose face. It is not going to get a fair hearing here now that it has been treated in this way. My commitment to the book has been strengthened by all of this."
Henry Hardy (telephone calls to Malcolm, 18th-22nd July 1985)

"I am satisfied that a clear commitment to publish *Making Names* was made by the University of Oxford. I think that Mr Malcolm has been harshly and unfairly treated. I think he had a strong, moral, though not a legal commitment. I reach this decision with great regret. After reviewing these matters, it may be that the University will have second thoughts, or at least be minded to make some kind of amends... If there was a legally enforceable contract, I would have been minded to indicate that a substantial award of damages was called for to recompense Mr Malcolm."
Deputy Judge Gavin Lightman Q.C. (High Court judgment, 16th March 1990)

"I do not know whether an outsider studying the history of this transaction and of this litigation would feel that, in his self-financed struggle with the assembled Chancellor, Masters and Scholars of the University of Oxford, Mr Malcolm has had a fair crack of the whip, I certainly do not. If the evidence adduced by the Press is to be relied upon, the project was never the subject of grave deliberation by the Delegates. Mr Charkin took the decision, not because he thought the book was no good – he had never seen it and the reports were favourable – but because he thought it would not sell. Let there be no mistake about it, the failure of this transaction was about money, not prestige. Nor does the course of the litigation give any reason to suppose that Oxford University Press had any interest but to resist the claim, no matter on what grounds, so long as they succeeded."
Lord Justice Mustill (Court of Appeal judgment, 19th December 1990)

"Mr Malcolm's only remedy is an award of damages. For my part, I would allow his appeal and order an enquiry as to damages."
Lord Justice Nourse (Court of Appeal judgment, 19th December 1990)

"It is difficult to know what the Deputy Judge meant by a 'firm commitment' other than an intention to create legal relations. Nothing short of that would have had any value whatever for Mr Malcolm. To suggest that Mr Hardy intended to induce Mr Malcolm to revise *Making Names* by giving him a valueless assurance would be tantamount to an imputation of fraud... It follows that in my judgment when Mr Hardy used the expressions 'commitment' and 'a fair royalty' he did in fact mean what he said; and I venture to think that it would take a lawyer to arrive at any other conclusion. There was therefore an enforceable contract for the publication of Mr Malcolm's book."
Lord Justice Leggatt (Court of Appeal judgment, 19th December 1990)

"The progress of Malcolm's dialogue challenges, both directly and by implication, what are taken to be the guiding principles of modern physics and cosmology, particularly in respect of particle theory. He is evidently well informed. He presents us with a sort of voyage of discovery. *Making Names* is aimed at everyone..."
Jeremy Mynott, Editorial Director, Cambridge University Press (Oxford's independent expert witness at the damages assessment hearing, 10th July 1991)

"It's been said that Russell had the rare ability to write books that were both original contributions to philosophy and at the same time introductions for beginners; it seems to me that Malcolm has something of that kind of talent. One of the most striking of his original contributions is his account and criticism of Wittgenstein's theory of universals. Another is where he takes Hume's famous argument about 'ought' and 'is' and points out that Hume himself perpetrates the kind of inference which, explicitly he is disallowing. Then there is his general monist position from which he produces a peculiar combination of both materialism and idealism. Finally, there is a striking account of the language of modern particle physics which connects it with theology; here, I find Malcolm's proposal very daring and the specific form of his argument unique. All these contributions, I think, should be of considerable interest to professional philosophers. If *Making Names* were published it would create quite a stir. It ought to see the light of day."
Professor Roy Edgley, Sussex University (Malcolm's independent expert witness at the damages assessment hearing, 10th July 1991)

"*Making Names* is an original *tour de force*. As its title forewarns us, it deals with some modish issues of semiotics, but the overall contents are more comparable to some of Bertrand Russell's later writing, effectively communicating the essentials of philosophy and scientific theorising to students and general readers. With its entertaining dialogues and its realistic, direct arguments *Making Names* should prove to be a widely popular introductory text."
R.W. Noble, Times Educational Supplement, 25th September 1992

"I very much enjoyed *Making Names* and consider it to be a valuable book. It is a comprehensive, professional text that introduces the philosophy that is taught in sixth-form colleges or polytechnics. The originality of its dialogue format makes it fun to read. Resourceful teachers will find it useful. I found it valuable because it challenges in an accessible fashion the current dogmas by which we are educated and which are too easily accepted as fact. Science is not a temple of absolutism, it is the product of individuals' creativity; it is much more like art than is generally realized. In this book, by concentrating on people, the nature of science as it is practised is well portrayed. I imagine *Making Names* may well attain a certain cult status."
Terence Kealey, affidavit testimony and The Spectator, 10th April 1993

"I was delighted to discover that *Making Names* was finally in print. You may have wondered, but I have never deviated from my view that it ought to be published, and I am very pleased that it now has been. Maybe you'll sell paperback rights?"
Henry Hardy, Wolfson College, Oxford (letter to Malcolm, 16th October 1992)

"As you are using my name to help sell your book, the least you could do is send me a copy, isn't it?"
Richard Charkin, Reed Consumer Books (full text of note to Malcolm, 22nd February 1993)

To Liz

MAKING NAMES

An Idea of Philosophy

By

Andrew Malcolm

AKME

Copyright © 1992 by Andrew Malcolm

The Author asserts his moral rights

ISBN 1 874222 01 0

A CIP catalogue record for this book
is available from the British Library

AUTHOR'S NOTE
Apart from a few short new passages
in Chapter 6, the text is almost
exactly as it was when presented
for publication in 1985/6.

First published in hardback August 1992
First published in paperback with minor
changes to Chapter 9 and with foreword
and index additions October 1993

Printed by Hobbs the Printers of Southampton

AKME Publications, Brighton, England

Contents

1

MINDS
and
BODIES

ENGLAND. An unusually hot, almost windless early morning in mid-summer. A patchwork landscape of ripe cornfields, cow-grazed pasture and dense woodland undulates gently to the horizon. From this distance the black-and-white cows that dot the grassland appear as motionless as the trees that here and there punctuate the fields' hedgerows. This abnormal stillness, combined with the intense shimmering heat and the low steady buzzing of insects, imbues the scene with an air of vaguely threatening unease.

The insects' ceaseless droning reminds us that the tranquility of this landscape is only apparent. Amongst the grasses at our feet, as the briefest inspection will reveal, are countless tiny creatures all going intently about their business: a shiny black beetle carefully making his way through a thicket of clover; baby spiders scurrying up and down the tall stems of couch grass; a furry brown caterpillar hiding in the shade of a dandelion leaf; here an ants' nest, a whole civilization of black specks busily encamped in the remains of an old tree-stump; and there, a bee, buzzing diligently from flower to flower and then suddenly away, flying quickly out of sight.

As we draw back and our view of the countryside widens into a panorama, we can see that the landscape is dotted with buildings and is criss-crossed by a number of tracks and roads. In the distance a railway line runs straight for several miles, and beyond it there is the silvery glint of a small river twisting and turning its way eastwards. At the point where the river, the railway line and two of the larger roads meet, the greenness of the countryside is marked by an irregular greyish blot, from which a sentry-like file of steel pylons can be seen carrying powerlines that loop away over the horizon to the west. The greyish blot is a fair-sized country town.

As its detail gradually comes into focus we soon realize that this is no ordinary English town. There is the usual concentration of shopping streets, office buildings and a market square at the town's centre, and the usual sprawl of cramped terraced houses, public parks, new estates and small factories surrounding it, but there are also large areas, especially along the banks of the river, where complexes of massive buildings of stone, rich with ornate masonry, fine spires and grand gateways, are set amongst spacious lawns and gardens and wooded groves. There are great chapels, shady quadrangles and some fine modern buildings too, their white stone and glass glittering fiercely in the sunshine. This, certainly, must be one of England's historic *university* cities.

Looking down upon the city, we can observe the many different patterns presented by its streets and its buildings, by the movements of its traffic and its inhabitants. Indeed, though strangers to the place, from here we are probably in a better position to map the city than are its inhabitants themselves, few of whom will ever have seen it from the air. The city, we may reflect, could be mapped in many different ways, according to one's concerns. Besides a simple layout of its streets, one could make a map, say, of how its property is owned, indicating the land and buildings under the authority of the university, those belonging to private individuals and companies, and those administered by the city council. Or one could map the city's architectural history: the new parts, the old parts and the areas where ancient, perhaps even prehistoric remains have been found. Again, notice the many old churches that are scattered about the place; in former times, a map showing the different church parishes would have been important to the citizens, while nowadays it might seem to have little significance. In everyday life of course, the townsfolk get about without the aid of maps at all, using instead the well-known landmarks, the familiar main roads, the short cuts of habit and tradition. It is therefore possible that many of them would be quite surprised to discover some of the patterns that we strangers so easily can see from here. Despite their living in the city for years on end, many of its citizens remain in general ignorance of its social and architectural evolution and without any clear perspective of either their city's history or their own lives within it.

But who needs maps or perspectives on such a beautiful day? Thanks to the strong sunshine, people in all parts of the city are awakening early and the unexpectedly hot weather has quickly become the popular topic of conversation. After an ice-cold winter and a rain-soaked spring, the long-forgotten comforts and discomforts of the summer Sun are rapidly being rediscovered. Already, child-scolding housewives are hanging out washing in tiny back-to-back gardens. On a building site tanned labourers wearing dusty shorts and floppy hats are humping bricks and preparing to start up an excavator. A knot of tourists in bright tee-shirts and sunglasses is making a breakfast-time tour round one of the colleges. Here and there within the university, the few academics and students who have stayed on during the holidays gaze blinkingly around book-lined studies and stare listlessly at paper-strewn desks; not even their old rooms' narrow leaded windows can shield them from the simple power of the bright sunlight outside. It is no good swotting on a day like this.

Along one of the narrow winding streets which lead to the market square, a young driver is dreamily steering a battered but stylish old MGA sports car. Without warning, a university man, also with things on his mind, steps out absently from one of the college gateways into the street, and into the path of the car. The early-morning tranquility is rudely shattered by a fierce squealing of brakes, a clatter of shuddering bodywork and... no thud. By a miracle there is no collision. A split-second reaction on the parts of both driver and pedestrian has avoided a potentially fatal accident. Any anger is at once forgotten in the two mens' immense relief at their lucky escape. The driver anxiously walks over to his near-victim to make sure that he is unhurt, and since the man's nerves are obviously shaken, he offers him a hand. They fall into conversation.

Driver   Phew! Close one! Are you alright?

Pedestrian   Yes, fine... Twisted my ankle on the kerb, think it's okay... Agh! Be alright in a moment... Ow! Sorry, my fault, stupid of me...

Driver   I should sit down for a bit. I know, let me give you a lift. You were heading into town?

Pedestrian   Er, yes, but...

Driver   Then hop in. I'm going to Market Square, is that okay?

Pedestrian   Oh yes, thanks, I was on my way to the Market Bookshop.

Driver   Right. No problem. Oh, don't worry about the door rattling, it's quite safe...

Pedestrian   Drop me off here if you like, you'll never be able to park in the Square.

The Rarity of Accidents

Driver Hold on, let's see... Yes, we're in luck!

Pedestrian But this is a 'Disabled Driver' space!

Driver I know, handy isn't it?

Pedestrian Hey, how come you've got a permit? You're no more disabled than I am!

Driver I can limp quite convincingly when I have to. I know lots of people who...

Pedestrian You fake!

Driver Besides, surely you qualify as disabled at the moment, after our recent little, er, encounter? Ah, you pull that knotted cord to open the door.

Pedestrian But that's not the poi... Aghh! Ow!

Driver See what I mean? Now, steady as you go... Look, come and sit by the fountain and I'll get you a glass of water. It's a natural spring, said to be good for the nerves.

Pedestrian Oh, er, yes, thanks. Good idea. Delayed shock I suppose... Phew! It's just beginning to dawn how close I was back there to being, to being... hit.

Driver Yes, we were lucky, very lucky... Here, drink this down... Better? I'll get you another... It's funny you know, when you see this square and all this activity, it seems strange that accidents aren't a lot more common than they are. Look: trucks loading and unloading, vans full of gear being unpacked, men pushing carts this way and that, already quite a few shoppers milling around, cars whizzing by, a bunch of teenagers over there showing off on their motorcycles, young mums with pushchairs, students pottering about on bikes, cats, dogs, sparrows, pigeons, a blind woman tapping her way along, an old bloke in a wheelchair, some kids playing with a football... Given all this chaos, collisions are surprisingly rare.

Pedestrian That's because *most* people are careful to avoid them.

Driver Sorry, I may have been driving a bit fast. But you did cross without looking.

Pedestrian Yes I know. Stupid. Wasn't thinking.

Driver Doesn't it ever strike you how rare accidents are? It's bad enough now, but imagine this square on a busy saturday afternoon: it *teems* with people. Oh, you get a little jostling and jockeying now and then, but hardly ever an actual collision.

Pedestrian But you talk as though people were like... like gas molecules, whizzing blindly this way and that.

Driver Gas molecules?

Pedestrian Yes, you know, rushing about randomly. The molecular behaviour of gases is my field by the way. Allow me to introduce myself: Doctor Malcolm Effect, Institute of Molecular Studies.

Driver Ah, a scientist, what a coincidence! Delighted to meet you Doctor, you could be just the man I've been looking for... So what's with these molecules of yours? What is a *molecule* exactly?

Doctor Effect Surely you've heard of molecules? They are the constituents of matter, of everything that you see around you.

Driver Everything? You, me, the buildings, the cars, the sky, the Sun? All made up entirely of molecules?

Doctor Effect Of molecules and atoms and particles, yes.

Driver Uhuh? And what makes a crowd of gas molecules so different from the crowd of people milling around this square?

Doctor Effect Well obviously, as far as their colliding with one another is concerned, molecules can't see each other like we can, can't avoid each other like we can.

Driver They have no perceptions or feelings, they do not think or choose?

Doctor Effect Exactly.

Driver So in short the big difference is that men have minds and molecules don't?

Doctor Effect That's *a* big difference, certainly.

Driver But now Doctor, how do you know that?

Doctor Effect What, how do I know that molecules don't have minds?

Driver Well... No... How do you know that human beings *do*?

What is Philosophy?

Doctor Effect   I beg your pardon?

Driver   How do you know that all the things walking around here with two arms and two legs have minds, that they can see and feel and avoid things? How do you know that they're not robots being remote-controlled from the Kremlin and the Pentagon, or fleshy machines subject to some undiscovered transmission from Outer Space?

Doctor Effect   Well, I... I... Look, it's been very kind of you to, er, to take care of me, but I think I'm okay now. If you'll excuse me, I...

Driver   Or just human beings without perceptions or feelings or thoughts or choices?

Doctor Effect   Forgive me, but I really must be going. I'm working in the labs this morning.

Driver   What about your bookshop?

Doctor Effect   Ah yes, of course...

Driver   Would you mind if I tagged along?

Doctor Effect   Oh, er, no... I suppose not.

Driver   It is a serious philosophical problem though Doctor, how one knows that there are other minds in the world, any other minds.

Doctor Effect   Ahh, so you're a *philosopher* are you? I should have realized.

Driver   Philosophy is my subject, yes. Andrew Cause, er... Professor Andrew Cause, Faculty of Logic and Linguistics.

Doctor Effect   How do you do. But I thought philosophy these days was all semantics?

Professor Cause   Accent on the last two syllables, er, give or take the odd bilabial... No, not necessarily. The old problems still persist, in new forms.

Doctor Effect   So what *is* philosophy then? I never have quite understood. I did take a philosophy of science option when I was an undergraduate, but most of the stuff I read seemed to be terribly complicated and abstruse, and not really worth the effort. It was all Greek to me.

Professor Cause   I quite agree. As far as I am concerned, most important philosophical insights are essentially simple.

Doctor Effect   Most important anything insights are essentially simple.

Professor Cause   Okay, so first insights first: what makes you think that you are at present listening to a person rather than to a sophisticated sort of tape-recorder or a cleverly programmed computer? How, in short, do you know that I have a mind? How do you know that all the people around this square have perceptions and feelings and thoughts?

Doctor Effect   Why, I can see that they have! I can see them... seeing things, reacting to things, avoiding things. I can hear them talking and laughing and replying to one another. What a daft question!

Professor Cause   You can see them moving in certain ways, you can see them performing routines, you can see them circumventing obstacles, but you can't see them *seeing*, you can't hear them *thinking*. All you can observe is their bodily behaviour, and that could be imitated by robots, it proves nothing about the existence of any *minds*... Ah, the second-hand record stall. Excuse me, I'd just like to have a look through the Coltrane section...

Doctor Effect   But I can hear them talking. I can speak their language. I can understand what they say. Their remarks and their conversation make sense to me.

Professor Cause   *My* remarks don't seem to be making much sense to you! Look Doctor, human speech is just audible utterance, just another public phenomenon. It can be imitated or reproduced by machines and by minah birds, it proves nothing about the existence or otherwise of people's perceptions or feelings or thoughts... Listen, that little record player seems to be singing away quite happily and intelligibly, yet I doubt if you would therefore want to ascribe it mentality. Mm, this guy's got taste.

Doctor Effect   But... But a record player can't actually say anything, it can't respond to us.

Professor Cause   What makes you say that? You know what would happen if I kicked it.

Doctor Effect   Yes, you'd probably get a black eye... But seriously Professor, you know what I mean. A record player cannot hold a conversation, it could not discuss a philosophical problem as you and I are doing.

White Jeans, Red Top

Professor Cause   Want to bet? Hold on... This will do: Academia Postal University Courses, Introduction to Philosophy, record 15, Dialogues on Phenomenology and Linguistic Reference, by A. Verbiage and I.E. Waffle. Twenty pence. Shall we give it a try?

Doctor Effect   No, don't bother. I can see that you're always going to...

Professor Cause   Christ! That bird over there by the bookstall! White jeans, red top. Look at the arse on it! Jesus, I could use that!

Doctor Effect   Hmm. I imagine *it* might have something to say about that idea.

Professor Cause   Excuse me Doctor, I *must* have a crack at her, I won't be a moment... Hello... Forgive me, er... D'you fancy a coffee...? English? You speak English? On holiday? Vacances? Howabout a bottle of wine by the river, vino...? A drive in the country...? I must say, I really like your, er, outfit... Hello? Hello? Oh, please yourself!

Doctor Effect   No luck I take it?

Professor Cause   Not a peep! Not so much as a hello! Isn't it marvellous! I even pinched her bum, but not a flicker!

Doctor Effect   You didn't!? You, you *animal*!

Professor Cause   Well, no, I didn't actually pinch it, but I did put my hand on it nice and firmly. Ymmm.

Doctor Effect   Oh, honestly! You can't go around...

Professor Cause   Relax Doctor, relax! I suppose she gets it all the time. In fact I think she's foreign, I don't think she understands English.

Doctor Effect   She's reading an English book.

Professor Cause   Just look at that! *Wicked* isn't it?

Doctor Effect   You're impossible. You've got a problem.

Professor Cause   I know, and I could tell you where.

Doctor Effect   That proves it though doesn't it? These doubts you profess about the existence of other people's minds are not serious doubts at all. If you seriously believed for one moment that that girl over there might be a

8

robot, you wouldn't be slavering over her like some gibbering ape. Come on.

Professor Cause I'm not sure it's her mind that I'm interested in though. In fact I think ro-bot is probably the right word.

Doctor Effect And of course if either of us had any real doubts about the existence of the other's mentality, we wouldn't be wasting time talking to one another. Ah, the bookshop. Well Professor, it really has been nice to meet you, but, er, I've erm, got a book to pick up, so...

Professor Cause As a scientist though, doesn't it worry you that you have no evidence to support your belief in the mentality of others?

Doctor Effect But I do have evidence, of course I do, I have the knowledge of *my own* mentality. I have a human body which looks and behaves in certain ways and I have my own experiences of perceiving and feeling and thinking, so when I see other human bodies looking and behaving like my own I am justified in assuming that they too have perceptions and feelings and thoughts. Now if you'll excuse me, I want the second floor, so...

Professor Cause Well that's a great argument, and coming from a scientist too! So on the basis of just one known instance you will leap to an absolutely certain and universal generalization?

Doctor Effect I... I...

Professor Cause Remember that to justify a generalization about a relationship between As and Bs one normally has to witness a great number of A-B phenomena. A few known instances of A-Bs prove very little. A single known instance of an A-B proves nothing at all.

Doctor Effect I... I...

Professor Cause You go on up Doctor, I'll have a browse through the philosophy section.

※　※　※　※　※　※　※　※　※　※　※

Doctor Effect Ah, you're still here.

Professor Cause Did you find what you wanted?

Doctor Effect Oh, yes, er, no. Look Professor, I've been thinking about this other minds business, perhaps I've...

9

Name Dropping 1: Down to Business

Professor Cause Please, let's drop this 'Professor', 'Doctor' bit shall we; just call me Andrew.

Effect Oh, er, okay... Andrew. As I was saying, perhaps I've not been expressing myself carefully enough. I'm sure that there *is* a sound argument in here somewhere and I've no doubt that you, being the philosopher, know the right way in which to expound it, so perhaps you would be so good as to provide *your* solution to the problem.

Cause You mustn't expect philosophers always to provide solutions to their problems Malcolm, it may sometimes be enough for them merely to explain what the problems are. But anyway, okay, I will do what I can. Why don't we adjourn to the Italian café on the corner. Have you had breakfast yet?

Effect I have, yes, but I suppose I could always get a coffee or something.

Cause Right then. As it happens, I anticipated that our discussion might continue, so while I was in the bookshop I took the precaution of picking up a small J.S. Mill selection; it should contain a rather useful passage.

Effect Hey! I didn't see you pay for anything back there!

Cause Didn't you? Oh well... Çiao Mario! Now Malcolm, where would you like to sit, inside or out?

Effect Outside is fine. You amaze me, d'you know that?

Cause Just a coffee? Nothing to eat?

Effect On second thoughts I'll change my mind. I'll have an ice-cream if I may.

Cause Whatever you want. The ice-cream's very good here, home-made. Mario, dammi uno cappuccino, uno doughnut e uno gelato al pistacchio, grazie.

Effect What was that?

Cause I've ordered you one of their ice-creams with nuts in it. You'll love it, I promise.

Effect Thanks.

Cause Now then... Ah, here we are: Mill's examination of Sir William

Hamilton's philosophy, a carefully expressed version of the argument you proposed earlier. I take it that if a philosopher and logician as eminent as J.S. Mill is unable to formulate such an argument soundly, then no-one can.

Effect Well *there's* a move from a single instance to a generalization if you like, but let it pass.

Cause Ahem. I quote:
I conclude that other human beings have feelings like me, because, first, they have bodies like me, which I know, in my own case, to be the antecedent condition of feelings; and because, secondly, they exhibit the acts, and other outward signs, which in my own case I know by experience to be caused by feelings. I am conscious in myself of a series of facts connected by an uniform sequence, of which the beginning is modifications of my body, the middle is feelings, the end is outward demeanor. In the case of other human beings I have the evidence of my senses for the first and last links of the series, but not for the intermediate link. I find, however, that the sequence between the first and the last is as regular and constant...

Grazie Mario... Erm...
...that the sequence between the first and the last is as regular and constant in those other cases as it is in mine. In my own case I know that the first link produces the last through the intermediate link, and could not produce it without. Experience, therefore, obliges me to conclude that there must be an intermediate link; which must either be the same in others as in myself, or a different one. I must either believe them to be alive, or to be automatons: and by believing them to be alive, that is, by supposing the link to be of the same nature as in the case of which I have experience, and which is in all other respects similar, I bring other human beings, as phenomena, under the same generalizations which I know by experience to be the true theory of my own existence.
Unquote.

Effect A bit clumsy, a bit wordy, a bit quaint, but I suppose that was the sort of thing I had in mind.

Cause Really? To me, the most interesting thing about it is that a man as highly reputed as Mill could have put his name to such a naïve and illogical and badly-written piece of reasoning. Or rather, to be strictly correct about it, how the author of such a piece could have gained such a reputation. Contacts I suppose. Anyway, as you probably know Malcolm, it is customary when evaluating an argument like this to determine firstly the truth or falsehood of its premises and secondly the validity or invalidity of its inferences, so let us begin by examining Mill's various assertions. One: other human beings have bodies like me.

Effect Hmm. Ambiguous.

Cause Exactly. Does he mean that every other human being, comma, like me, comma, has a body? If so, he is saying both very little and a great deal, for of course in that sense *every* object has a body. My car, like me, has a body. This doughnut, like me, has a body, or, as we might say, has body. Mill's written work has, or is, a body.

Effect Obviously, what Mill meant was that other people had bodies like his.

Cause In which case his assertion was simply false. We know that no two human bodies are the same. My body is nothing like that fat man's over by the fountain, at least I hope it's not. And I don't suppose Mill's bore much resemblance to the bookstall girl's. Look, she's still there.

Effect I know... By the way, what sort of a man was Mill, physically speaking?

Cause I've no idea. I did once read his autobiography, but now you come to mention it, I do not recall in it one single reference to either his own body or anyone else's; it consisted, I remember, of little more than a list of the books he'd studied and the speeches he'd made; indeed it read rather like the journal of a disembodied intellect. For all one gathered, Mill might have had two left feet or the physique of a fountain-pen or, come to that, the body of a small autobiography bound in hard green covers.

Effect But you know and I know that Mill must in fact have had a *human* body, a body pretty much like yours and mine. Okay, so not even identical twins are identical, but human bodies do resemble one another. This is just a question of how like is like.

Cause Maybe, but if so, the briefest glance around this square will confirm that the answer is: not very like at all. We don't have to consult books of strange facts to discover that human bodies come in an extraordinary variety of shapes and sizes. There are tiny babies, great strapping youths, voluptuous girls, enormously fat people, extremely thin people... Just look at that elephantine lady arm-in-arm with that shrivelled, shrimp-like man; she must be three or four times his weight. Look at the different hair-colours, eye-colours, skin-colours. Look at the characteristics of the different races: there a negroid face, there a caucasian, there an asiatic. Not to mention that greatest of all subdivisions: male and female.

Effect I'm not sure that I like the sound of this. We do all share a common human *form* Andrew, two arms, two legs, a head...

Cause Don't we share that with spider monkeys, kangaroos, fruit bats? Besides, what about that old guy in the wheelchair, and the thalidomide chap standing at the bus-stop? Think too of the times when you've been *tricked* by the human form, fooled at the waxworks museum perhaps, or caught out by a shop-window dummy. Believe it or not, I once actually apologized to a parking meter; mind you, I was a bit drunk at the time.

Effect Okay, not just a common human form then, but a common human *physiology*.

Cause Mill wrote of bodies, not physiologies. And is even this true? Which of these people has a cardiac pacemaker? Which of them depends upon an artificial kidney machine? Which is a diabetic? Do you need to know before ascribing them mentality?

Effect But they, we do all partake in a common human... *process*. We are all born of man and woman, we all grow up and live and age and die.

Cause Oh come off it Malcolm, how can you possibly tell all that just from looking at people, just from looking at these bodies? Besides, again this may be simply untrue. Women nowadays can be inseminated artificially, babies can be born in test-tubes. Who knows what the people sitting here in fifty years' time will be able to say about 'a common human process'? One must always beware, in these discussions, of depending upon statements which our ever-advancing technologies could easily prove wrong.

Effect Yes, true, they are even talking of being able to control the ageing process.

Cause Hmm. Meanwhile anyway, the nail in the coffin of Mill's first premise is presented by that vast class of genuinely human bodies that do or did look more or less like yours and mine but to which we would on no account wish to ascribe mentality, namely dead ones.

Effect And there are the cases of human beings who, through car accidents for instance, suffer brain damage but live on as... human vegetables. I suppose one would not wish to ascribe them mentality, at least not in the full sense.

Behaving Like Me

Cause While paradoxically, there are those who live on, whose mentality is evident to us long after their bodies have disintegrated. I don't suppose that J.S. Mill looks anything much by now.

Effect Surely this all goes to show that the key thing in ascribing other people mentality is their *behaviour*. This was Mill's second premise was it not, that other human bodies behave in ways similar to my own... "Because first they have bodies like me, which I know in my own case to be the antecedent condition of feelings, and because secondly..."

Cause Hold on, how does Mill know that his having a human body is the antecedent condition of having feelings? Surely, all he can claim to know is that he has a human body and that he has feelings, he cannot conclude anything about the general conditionality of having feelings.

Effect I don't see what you mean. One cannot imagine having feelings *without* having a body.

Cause Can't one? People claim to be able to imagine all sorts of things. Besides, Mill claims to know not just that having a body is the condition, but that having a *Mill-like* body, a *human* body is the condition of having feelings. Given that Mill's body was nothing other than human, how he could claim this, goodness only knows.

Effect Anyway: "because secondly, they exhibit the acts and other outward signs which in my own case I know by experience to be caused by feelings..."

Cause Hmm, 'caused by'...

Effect "I am conscious in myself of a series of facts connected by a uniform sequence, of which the beginning is modifications of my body, the middle is feelings, the end is outward demeanor."

Cause Is this true? When you react to something, which seems to be what Mill has in mind here, are you conscious of a series of anything, let alone facts? Doesn't one just react to whatever it is and that's that?

Effect Well I suppose I can and sometimes do step outside myself as it were, and watch myself behaving. I think perhaps I can become conscious of myself reacting to things, as Mill suggests.

Cause Ah, but when you become conscious of reacting to things, you are no longer simply reacting to them, and indeed you may well start to react

14

to them differently: more slowly perhaps, or absently, or differently altogether. When at the last second you tried to leap out of the way of my car,
can you honestly say that you were conscious of any series of facts, of any
three-link sequence?

Effect   But that was just a reflex-action.

Cause   Exactly, no conscious mental activity or feeling was involved.

Effect   Fright. I certainly felt fright. And then the kerb. And then a pain in
my ankle.

Cause   But can you go on to say that you were *conscious* of feeling fright,
that you had time to 'step outside yourself'? Why, you didn't even have
time to step out of the road!

Effect   It was curious, but in that split second, I did seem to stand outside
myself. My whole life sort of...

Cause   Flushed before you.

Effect   Yes, like a sort of instantaneous film, strange that.

Cause   Uhuh? The point is, the more immediate one's reaction to an event,
the less plausibly does it conform to Mill's model of a three-stage process
and the less truthfully can one claim to be conscious of any 'intermediate
link'. Further, the more automatic the reaction-behaviour, the more it
becomes predictable, the more readily it can be imitated by machines, and
the less one wants to serve it up as evidence of human *mentality*.

Effect   Kicking the record player.

Cause   Quite. And this brings us to Mill's assertion that I am conscious in
myself of a uniform sequence. Do you always react to the same stimulus in
the same way? Modern jazz once meant nothing to me; when I was little I
hated it. Now I cannot get enough.

Effect   One's reactions depend a lot on one's moods, on how one is feeling at the time. After a really good meal, the last thing I want to see is a
plateful of food, although I suppose that's just an example of a uniform
sequence that is a bit more complex.

Cause   Why aren't you eating your ice-cream Malcolm? It's melting.

Effect   Oh, er, I'm sorry, I don't like the nuts very much, you have it.

Cause Oh, okay, ta. Next, there is the third of Mill's key claims, his assertion that "the sequence between the first and last, modifications of the body and outward demeanor, is as regular and constant in those other cases as it is in mine." Mill's argument depends not only upon the assumption that *my* reactions to things are uniform and predictable, which is doubtful enough, but also upon the suggestion that *everyone else's* reactions to things are the same, which is crashingly untrue. One thing that's certain is that different people react to the same events and situations in quite different ways.

Effect But there are shared human behaviour patterns: everyone reacts to physical injury in the same way, everyone responds to danger in the same way.

Cause Not so. Some people scream, some grit their teeth. Some people run, some freeze. Some people seem to enjoy pain, some even court danger. Some people throw themselves under cars, some even deliberately crash cars that are packed with high explosive.

Effect Oh, there must be some common human functions: walking, eating, sleeping.

Cause I'm afraid not Malcolm, not even these. That bloke in the wheelchair's not growing any legs; then there was that anorexic biology student who starved herself to death; and I know my mother has terrible trouble with her sleeping. Besides, already we are almost down to *un*conscious physiological functions like food-digestion and blood-circulation, not the sort of phenomena that Mill had in mind at all. Once again, the less automatic the behaviour, the more it involves in the way of conscious mental activity like the assessing of situations and the making of choices, so the less predictable it will be and the less easy to bring under any generalization. I think you will find that if you propose any rule of the form 'Human beings in an X-type situation always behave in a Y-type way', whatever you choose for X and Y, it will always be possible to produce an example of someone who breaks the rule yet whose mentality we would not wish to deny. When it comes to other people, there are no absolute rules at all.

Effect Maybe there are no absolute rules, but nonetheless there are all sorts of very familiar patterns to which most human behaviour conforms most of the time.

Cause Even if this were true, and we could probably argue about it all day, it would not be enough. Mill writes of a constant and regular sequence; his conclusion that other human beings have feelings is absolute and admits of no exceptions. If the logic of his argument were applied to your watered-down premise, the conclusion would have to be that most human beings have feelings most of the time. Somewhat inconsistent of them.

Effect Somewhat inconsistent of you. I thought you were claiming that Mill's argument doesn't have any logic.

Cause It doesn't. Even if we were to grant the truth of all of Mill's evidently false premises, they would not add up to the conclusion he wishes to draw. Tell me Malcolm, are you familiar with the traditional distinction between inductive and deductive reasoning?

Effect If my memory serves me right, inductive reasoning is reasoning from experience and deductive reasoning is reasoning from logic.

Cause Yes, give or take. An inductive argument is an argument of the form: whenever in the past *A* has occurred, *B* has occurred, *therefore* if *A* happens *B* will happen, with the certainty of the 'therefore' depending, roughly speaking, upon the number of *A-B* instances that have been witnessed. On the other hand, the 'therefore' of *de*ductive arguments has the absolute certainty of the laws of mathematics and logic: if a triangle has equal sides it will therefore have equal angles; if all men are mortal and I am a man, I am therefore mortal.

Effect Presumably, since all our knowledge of the physical world comes to us through perception, experience and experiment, it must therefore count as *in*ductively justified knowledge.

Cause So one would think. And leaving aside questions about the source and subject-matter of our *de*ductive reasonings, it seems clear that our *in*ductive ones, however much evidence we may amass, can never match the absolute certainty of the truths of mathematics. Even a statement as uncontroversial as "the Sun will rise tomorrow" carries an element of doubt, however far-fetched. One can conceive of its not rising.

Effect We know from astrophysics that one day it won't, if that's not a contradiction in terms.

Cause One cannot, on the other hand, conceive that one day two and two will stop making four.

Effect Ah, but in particle physics these days, there is even a sense in which...

17

A Special Case?

Cause Yes yes, I'm sure there is Malcolm, but let's stick with the boring old conventions for the moment shall we, we haven't finished breakfast yet. Why don't you have a cup of coffee or something?

Effect Yes, I think I will.

Cause So, given that all our knowledge traditionally fell into one or other of these two categories, the problem for philosophers like Mill was to produce either a deductive or an inductive justification of our claim to know that others have minds. Now, take the statements "Human beings have feelings" and "Other minds exist". Do these seem to you to be statements about the world, about objective matters of fact?

Effect Well presumably, yes. That human beings have feelings is as much a fact about them as that they have arms and... as that they breathe. The existence in the world of other minds is as objective as the existence of... of tigers.

Cause As objective as the existence of unicorns?

Effect More so. Unicorns exist only in books, in imagination, but other minds, human beings with perceptions and feelings and thoughts exist *in the world*.

Cause Ah Mario, un'altro cappuccino grazie... And one can conceive, nowadays all too easily, that other minds, that other human beings might *cease* to exist. One can imagine being the sole survivor.

Effect Not for long.

Cause With an 'o-l-e' or an 'o-u-l'. So, if it is to conform to the standard of all our other knowledge concerning objective matters of fact, our justification of the existence of other minds has to be along inductive lines. This of course brings us back to the problem that each of us, you, me, Mill and everyone else, has to go on only *one* known instance of a body-mind correlation, namely our own, and that in inductive justification the evidence of a single case is scarcely *any* evidence.

Effect Perhaps we are wrong to insist that all justifications should conform to one or other of the traditional paradigms. Perhaps our knowledge of other minds is a special case.

Cause On what grounds? You're a scientist Malcolm, I bet you demand the utmost logical rigour in all of your justifications. What would you say to someone who proposed a theory of some phenomenon for which he could produce no sound evidence or argument? What would make his theory a special case? A bribe? His being your boss? His being a big name?

Effect   It does happen.

Cause   If the standards of sound reasoning can be waived, the way becomes open to all sorts of crazy claims. People would be able to say "I too am a special case: I am the only human being with feelings". Mill's argument, remember, has exactly the same logical form as: I didn't shave this morning and I love the music of John Coltrane, therefore everyone who didn't shave this morning loves the music of John Coltrane.

Effect   What's with this John Coltrane obsession?

Cause   He's only the greatest saxophonist who ever lived!

Effect   Uhuh? Well... "Experience therefore obliges me," says Mill, "to conclude that there must be an intermediate link which..."

Cause   On the contrary, experience obliges him to do nothing of the kind. Indeed, there is an old and well-respected philosophical principle known as Occam's razor which advises us to minimize our inferred entities and to substitute, wherever possible, observed matters of fact. In this context of course, the inferred entities are Mill's problematic, mysterious, unevidenced other minds and the observed matters of fact are the sequences of human behaviour. What *obliges* us to infer anything? Certainly not the laws of logic or of sound reasoning.

Effect   What obliges us to use Occam's razor? As you've admitted, you don't bother even with an ordinary one.

Cause   Why one intermediate link in a three-stage sequence? Why not one hundred intermediate links in a one-hundred-and-three-stage sequence?

Effect   A one-hundred-and-*two*-stage sequence you mean... "An intermediate link which must either be the same in others as in myself or a different one... or a different one."

Cause   Ah, now *that's* true! It must either be the same or different, a perfect piece of deductive reasoning! Bravo John Stuart!

Effect   "I must either believe them to be alive or to be automatons." Shouldn't that be automat*a*?

Cause You see, after all that, he is right back where he started. He has to *assume* what he set out to prove. He admits that he is still free to believe that other people are automata. 'Believe' he says, not 'know'. He has proved nothing at all, even to himself. Except perhaps that a logically sound justification is impossible.

Effect Hmm.

Cause And that, as you might say, is the run of the Mill argument. Grazie Mario.

Effect So what do you conclude then? Are you seriously suggesting that some or all of these people may be automata?

Cause I am seriously pointing out that we do not know that they are not automata.

Effect What? Remote-controlled from the Kremlin and the Pentagon, that bit?

Cause Why not?

Effect Because the idea's preposterous!

Cause There are those who'll tell you it's true.

Effect But Andrew, if people were being radio-controlled, we would know, we would be able to detect the transmissions.

Cause Who would? A few boffins working for MI7? Besides, who said anything about radio? When did you last read a newspaper?

Effect Come on, let's get this straight: are you seriously suggesting that some or all of the people wandering around this square have heads full of radio receivers and microcircuits rather than brains?

Cause Not necessarily, sawdust for all I know.

Effect I have it! I have an argument! I have feelings and I know that I have a human brain. It can be shown experimentally that the having of a living brain is a prerequisite of having feelings and indeed that the brain is the seat of all mentality. I know that other human beings have human brains. I am justified in concluding therefore that other human beings have feelings.

Cause   Sorry, no, no will do. Quite apart from all that dubious garble about things being shown experimentally, prerequisites, seats of consciousness and whatever else, I'm afraid that brains aren't going to be of much help to you Malcolm. First, I'll wager that in fact you've no certain knowledge whatsoever about your own brain. Ironically, the last things you can observe for yourself are the contents of your own skull. Any information about them necessarily has to come second-hand via *other people's* observations, interpretations and reports and therefore depends upon the very assumption that is in question. Likewise, all claims arising from neurological experimentation and your claim to know that all these other human skulls contain brains are also systematically second-hand and therefore doubtful. When did you in fact last look inside anyone's head?

Effect   But I'm not a neurosurgeon. The point is that I *could* inspect the contents of other people's skulls if I wanted to.

Cause   Uhuh? I believe you might find it a little tricky.

Effect   So you are seriously doubting that these people's skulls contain brains?

Cause   Human skulls are in fact inspected very rarely, by anyone. I suspect that the evidence for the assertion "All human beings have brains" is a lot weaker than it is for most other inductively justified assertions. In practice it is the other way around: we infer the working of a 'normal' human brain from its owner's display of 'normal' human behaviour; or rather, we infer the existence of a brain *ab*normality from a person's *ab*normal behaviour. One might add that if any of the skulls in this square *do* contain radio receivers, their owners may well be going to great lengths to keep them undetected.

Effect   You've been watching too many cheap movies Andrew.

Cause   Maybe you haven't been watching enough. Second, in any case, whatever physical objects and phenomena and correlations we might find if we were systematically to start inspecting people's skulls, these would never constitute knowledge of people's *feelings*, any more than Mill's observations of their sequences of bodily behaviour did.

Effect   Oh no, that's not right. There is surely a sense in which studying people's brain processes *is* studying their mental processes. Perceptions and feelings and thoughts *are* neurological phenomena.

Cause   Do you really think so? Do you really mean that? Look Malcolm, I believe it is the case that when a man is excited, a substance called adrenaline is secreted by a gland somewhere near his stomach.

Effect   Near his kidneys actually, I think.

Cause   Wherever. And that this substance then sets off various reactions in his brain, his heart, his muscles and so on. Will you say on this account when you are excited, that your excitement *is* your secretion of adrenaline or that your excitement is near your kidneys? I have no doubt that when a man feels this or thinks that or does the other, all sorts of biochemical phenomena occur in many parts of his body, including his brain, but we cannot conclude that such phenomena therefore *constitute* his feelings and thoughts and actions.

Effect   Maybe not, but don't you think that a man's brain events are special in all this, that in some sense they are... they are the *causes* of his mental experiences?

Cause   Certainly not, this is an idea that I reject passionately. I can imagine that by sticking probes into various parts of my head you may be able to make me feel irritable or excited - I doubt if you could make me feel happy - but there are plenty of other ways of doing that, you could stamp on my foot or kick my car or start shouting racist abuse at the passers-by. Another point: in all experiments which attempt to correlate brain events and mental events, the only witness to the latter can be the subject under test, so in the end the experimenter can only ask the subject what he is feeling or thinking and then take his word for it.

Effect   But all research requires integrity. To be perfectly honest with you, I think one often has more reason to doubt the integrity of the experimenter than of any subjects he may be employing.

Cause   Remember too that these 'brain events' about which we are talking so glibly are themselves highly problematic. If we were to open one of these skulls, what I assume we would in fact discover would not be a miniature sorting-office with thousands of handwritten messages flying to and fro, or a tiny fifties telephone exchange with millions of little cogs and levers clicking away, or even a mass of microscopic circuit-boards and silicon chips, but just a pinkish squishy lump measuring x and weighing y, somewhat resembling a... a large soggy doughnut.

Effect   Brains always remind me of a certain sort of sea-sponge.

Cause   The 'neurological phenomena' of which you speak are not visible, even through a microscope. They take place, I understand, at a sub-microscopic level and therefore themselves involve a mass of inference, interpretation and theory. I have no doubt that neurology is a fascinating and useful science, but I don't see how it can shed much light upon the nature of our belief in other minds. The problem of justifying this belief is precisely the same however much or little one knows about neurology and the contents of people's skulls. Would we find an accident-victim's screams any the less disturbing because we knew there were a few transistors in his head? Does a primitive tribesman who has never seen or heard of a brain and whose vocabulary perhaps includes no such word believe in the thoughts and feelings of his fellows any less certainly than we do? I don't start thinking differently about a doughnut just because I discover there's a blob of jam at its centre... Mmm.. Well, a bad analogy but a good doughnut. I think I'll have another.

Effect   Perhaps I'll have one too.

Cause   And two more coffees?

Effect   Why not? Could I have an ordinary one this time, an ordinary white coffee.

Cause   Of course... Eh Mario... er, dos café con leche por favor... er, with milk, latte, si... e dos doughnut... dos, due, two... yes, please, ta... Yes, well, anyway Malcolm, this modern appeal to neurology for answers seems to me to be just another example of the mistaken scientific assumption that the best way to discover the nature of something is to take it to bits.

Effect   And perhaps your mistaken philosophical assumption is that one can discover "the nature of our belief in other minds" as you put it, by taking *that* to bits, by trying to *analyze* it in the way you have been. Perhaps we are wrong even to be seeking a justification of this belief. Perhaps we should simply take it as... an axiom, a necessary assumption, a working principle, something we cannot help believing.

Cause   Which?

Effect   That's the thing about all this, you are just playing a game, an absurd, abstract philosophical game. Despite all this professed scepticism of other minds, neither you nor I nor Mill truly doubts that other people have perceptions and feelings and thoughts. All along you have in fact talked about other people's thoughts and feelings, and doubts, without any qualms whatsoever. Indeed, your whole argument only got going because you knew that your various points would ring bells with me, would mean something to me, would turn my mind. And although, I admit, you have perplexed me at an intellectual level, you haven't shaken my belief in the feelings of others one jot, and I don't think that anything you could say ever would.

Cause Yes I know, it's an impossibly, unreasonably stubborn little belief isn't it, that's what makes it so curious. You are right though, philosophers are posers. It is a traditional ploy of theirs to draw an innocent into their discussions by trying to induce in him doubts about some faculty or area of knowledge which normally seems quite certain: perception, memory, the future and so on. The techniques vary, but a common tactic is to attempt to weave from the threads of the many everyday questions, mistakes and trickeries one encounters a *blanket* of scepticism which throws *all* of one's previously-accepted certainties into darkness and doubt. As you say, this systematic doubting can seem like some remote, abstract, intellectual game-playing, its blanket scepticism can appear absurd, unreal, impractical: no-one *really* doubts their senses or their memories or their ability to predict. Life must go on.

Effect Right.

Cause However Malcolm, I would venture to suggest that this 'other minds' case is different in a number of important respects. Our problem, remember, stems from the fact that I have *no* first-hand knowledge of other people's perceptions or feelings or thoughts. Our conclusion was that I cannot be certain that *any* other minds exist. We did not begin with an examination of our everyday uncertainties, our doubt was systematic from the word go.

Effect Your doubt.

Cause This is where it is worth reminding ourselves of the many doubts concerning other minds that are very far from being unreal or abstract or impractical. However absurd it may seem to have doubts, or to claim to have doubts about the existence of other minds, it is not the slightest bit odd to have doubts about what is going on in them. In this sense, ignorance of other minds is not some artificial philosophical pose, but is simply a harsh fact of everyday life. "He seems well-meaning, but perhaps he is trying to trick me", "They are being very polite, but I wonder what they are really thinking" and so on.

Effect Do you genuinely doubt the existence of other minds or are you just playing an intellectual game?

Cause   Further, one's ignorance of others is not confined to doubts about their sincerity. One can always ask the question "Yes, but what *else* is he thinking?" It is tempting to put forward a Mill-type argument here: I am a human being and I know that *I* don't reveal everything that's going on in my mind, therefore...

Effect   Thank goodness for that, I'd never get a word in edgeways!

Cause   Then there are the countless everyday ways in which we fail to understand other people. It is not just that by definition I cannot feel other people's feelings or desire their desires or think their thoughts, it is also that most other people seem to have beliefs, tastes and aims in life that are quite different from my own. Most people seem to live by moral, political and religious principles which I find alien and intolerable and absurd. I mean, take us two: both English, male, middle-class; similar educations I imagine, similar social backgrounds. And yet my soul echoes to the sound of John Coltrane and to you he means nothing.

Effect   Oh these are just details surely, the gloss?

Cause   Political ideals? Religious beliefs? A gloss for which men are prepared to kill and die.

Effect   But it would be awful if everyone thought the same way about everything, if everyone had the same tastes. I don't know, I find I can usually understand other people's points of view well enough, even if I don't agree with them; it's often just a matter of trying to imagine oneself in their shoes. Your trouble is that you actually *fancy yourself* as an outsider don't you?

Cause   And your trouble is that you live in a cosy, comfortable ivory tower, safe and secluded with your fellow-scientists in some molecular fantasy-world. It's easy to be all generosity and undertsanding from a thousand feet up. How can you claim to understand the mind of a jazz musician or a jailbird or a junkie? How can you imagine living in this country with a black skin? How can you know what it's like to be a company director or a coal-miner?

Effect   I come from a mining background as a matter of fact, South Yorkshire. My father was a miner, he's retired now. My two brothers have been in the pits since they were seventeen.

Cause   Really? And you were the one that got away, the working-class bright boy who broke free from the slime, and forged a better life for himself off in university-land?

Effect Something like that I suppose, although you paint far too black a picture. Life's not so bad up there nowadays. The worst thing is the unemployment; my brothers are the lucky ones.

Cause You still keep in touch?

Effect Of course. We're always going up. Actually we are a very close family. My dad's a great character. So's Mum.

Cause What about foreigners then, do you think you can understand foreigners? An African company director, a Russian jazz musician, a Chinese coal-miner?

Effect Mainly that's just a language problem.

Cause *Just* a language problem?

Effect I believe that if one takes the trouble to find out about people's personal and social and cultural histories, one discovers that their concerns and aspirations are pretty much the same the world over.

Cause Muslim suicide bombers? Javanese head hunters? Klu Klux Klansmen?

Effect Philosophers, now there's a group I'm having a bit of trouble with. Why on earth an intelligent, able-bodied, independent young man like you should be wracking your brains over all this artificial doubting nonsense, I cannot imagine.

Cause And what about women? The female mind? Can you understand women Malcolm? Bloody hell, I wish I could!

Effect Oh I think so. I believe my wife and I have a perfect understanding of one another. This 'female mind' bit is just a mystificatory cliché, or else an excuse for sexism. Again it is simply a matter of imagination, and then of according other people some reasonable respect. Oh, I do not deny that there are many areas of ignorance about other people's minds and many occasions of genuine doubt, but these do not add up to a blanket of uncertainty, to a systematic scepticism. Take the case of sincerity: we know what it means to be deceived or fooled by someone only because we have a background experience of finding people generally honest and trustworthy.

26

Cause Is this true? When I go to the theatre, *everyone* I see is acting.

Effect Ah, but performing on a stage is behaving in a publicly-recognized, institutionalized make-believe context.

Cause I wasn't just referring to the people on stage... Again, think of life in a criminal fraternity, where everyone lives in fear of being shopped by their fellows.

Effect University-land is no Shangri-La.

Cause I can imagine... I know. And politicians: aren't politicians *systematically* to be distrusted?

Effect I'm with you there.

Cause In a police state, the wise man soon learns to trust no-one. You see, Malcolm, this is where philosophical doubts about other minds turn out to be ominously different from philosophical doubts about perception, memory and the rest. It *does* seem to be possible to suffer from systematic doubt about the sincerity of others: the condition is called paranoia. Some people, through either a political regime or a terrible childhood or just a run of bad luck do end up simply trusting no-one.

Effect Mm. My wife used to be a psychiatric nurse, she has some extraordinary stories.

Cause Uhuh? In a way, the philosopher has a lot in common with the mental patient.

Effect I am beginning to realize!

Cause Indeed, it was the fashion a few years ago to regard certain types of chronic mental patient as being heroic psycho-philosophical explorer-figures. Needless to say, none of them ever wrote anything that made any sense, it was the doctors who made all the money. There is a parallel though: both the philosopher and the mental patient dwell upon certain problematic aspects of the human psyche and situation which ordinary people normally manage to forget or ignore or live with in some way or other; both indulge their worries, pursue them, become obsessed by them. Take the Mill passage for instance: it is the work of a worried man. I've no doubt that Mill *did* believe in the existence of other people's minds, of course he did, but his inability to justify his belief genuinely troubled him, genuinely disturbed him.

A _Psychological_ Imperative

Effect   Do you really think so? How can you possibly know that?

Cause   Because of what he wrote; how he wrote it; _that_ he wrote it. Again, take solipsism, the belief that one is alone. Believing oneself to be alone is not just an artificial philosophical pose, it can be the extreme case of a widespread psychological condition, loneliness. Have you read any Descartes Malcolm, the _Meditations_, the _Discourse on Method_?

Effect   Cogito ergo sum and all that?

Cause   That's the one. Well to me, the most telling feature of Descartes' obsessive journey into doubt, which was undertaken, incidentally, in conditions of literal solitude and which ended with that resoundingly solipsist avowal "I think therefore I am", was the _haste_ with which he attempted to reconstruct some certainties once he had plumbed those awful, ignorant, lonely depths. His loony logical arguments for the existence of a God who could guarantee his beliefs read like the straw-clutchings of a desperate man. Unless of course they were just satirical sops to the churchmen, to ensure his continued publication and good health.

Effect   You seem to be suggesting that our belief in the existence of other minds has a _psycho_logical justification rather than a logical one.

Cause   Ahh! Boiling water! Towels!

Effect   What?

Cause   Nothing, sorry. Suffice it to say that we are getting warm... Ah, Mario, no grazie, mi scusi, er, a mistake, er... the bill, per favore, il conto... I know what Malcolm, why don't we drive out to the Sanity?

Effect   The _where_?

Cause   The San. The Sanitarium. The Funny Farm. The Mental Hospital. You know, it used to be called Saint Xavier's. Haven't you ever been?

Effect   Saint Saviour's? Certainly not!

Cause   To the tea-room I mean. They've got a beautiful Victorian tea-room overlooking the grounds. The Day Room they call it. I often go there, you can meet some great characters.

Effect   But aren't they... Isn't it...?

Cause   Good heavens no. I know people who throw the odd wobbly just to get a few weeks off work there. Or away from their husbands or wives. You find loads of people from the University.

Effect   How far is it?

Cause   Oh, only a few miles.

Effect   Very well then, but I must be back by eleven, I've got work to do in the labs, and I've booked the computer.

Cause   No problems Malcolm, I promise... Ah, grazie Mario, ta... Oh dear, erm... I'm not sure if I've got...

Effect   I'll get it, don't worry.

Cause   Oh, thanks. I'll do the tip.

Effect   Grazie Mario. Çiao.

*   *   *   *   *   *   *   *   *   *   *

Cause   Oh damn! Damn, damn, damn! The bastards!

Effect   Whatever's the m... Oh, a parking ticket.

Cause   Bloody pigs! Ah, I get it, someone's nicked my 'disabled' permit. Christ, that's great!

Effect   Kicking the door in's not going to help.

Cause   How bloody mean! Not only nick my permit but get me a bloody ticket to boot!

Effect   That's the price of having an open-topped car. And good God Andrew, it wasn't your permit anyway! Do calm down, it's only a fine isn't it?

Cause   Only a fine? Another bloody fine? Shit!... No, okay, you're right, you're right. Easy come, easy go. I'm sorry Malcolm, I apologize. Come on, hop in.

Effect   You don't wear a safety belt?

Cause   Hate the things.

Effect   I will if you don't mind.

Cause   It's down there under the seat. I'm afraid it may be a bit grubby and knotted up.

Effect   Yes, I see what you mean... Oh, don't wait for me, I'll sort it out on the way... You know, there's something funny about this other minds business. You talk about doubting this and doubting that, but how could I doubt that you were angry just now when you found your parking ticket? There you were, throwing your arms around, kicking things, cursing and swearing.

Cause   But I needn't have done all that need I? As you said yourself, it didn't do any good.

Effect   I saw your anger though Andrew, I witnessed it. You were angry: no doubts, no questions, no inferences about unknown intermediate links. All along you have been talking about other people's minds as though they were private streams of consciousness, permanently hidden from all but their subjects' inspection. You have characterized another person's perceptions and feelings and thoughts in such a way that they are unknown to me *by definition*. You have cast us all in the role of lonely, frustrated cinema-goers, each of us locked forever inside our own private, one-seater cinema. Yet when I saw you waving your arms around just now, *I saw you being angry*. The phrase 'being angry' *means* behaving in that sort of way.

Cause   Aha, Behaviourism! Have you read a book called *The Concept of Mind*?

Effect   I can't say I have, no.

Cause   Gilbert Ryle. There should be a copy kicking around in the back somewhere. See if you can find it: a medium-sized paperback, pretty well thumbed.

Effect   I'll try... Goodness, what a mess! It would help if you weren't screeching round corners all the time. Do you always drive like this?

Cause   Sorry Malcolm... Any luck?

Effect   Not so far... Ah, what's this? Yes, *The Concept of Mind*. It's all coming to bits. It looks like some of the pages are missing.

Cause   Don't worry Malcolm. Put it down for a moment and I'll explain the background. Behaviourism was an offspring of the early twentieth-century school of philosophy called 'Logical Positivism'. Logical Positivism, as you probably know, was itself a child of that wider philosophical movement or outlook known as 'Empiricism', an outlook which was particularly associated with Britain and whose central principle or axiom is that our main or only source of true knowledge is *observation* of the world's phenomena.

Effect   Right. Where does this buckle go Andrew?

Cause   No idea Malcolm, sorry. Empiricism, from the Greek word 'ἐμπειρία', meaning 'experience', is to be contrasted with the movement or outlook known as 'Rationalism', according to which the faculty of *reason* is our main or only source of true knowledge. From the seventeenth century onwards, empiricist philosophy and the empirical sciences arose and prospered together, each deriving strength from the other. It is clear that the empiricist philosophers, along with the logical positivists who were their heirs, were under the spell of the new sciences, with their dazzling achievements in the fields of physics, chemistry, biology, medicine, astronomy and so on. Observation and experiment, armed with mathematical analysis, were going from strength to strength, and it seemed to some as though the sciences and the scientific method, whatever that was, would soon be able to solve all the terrible problems that had always beleaguered mankind. The Palace of Crystal was about to be built.

Effect   The what?

Cause   However, despite all the marvellous advances made by his empirical sciences and despite all his wonderful new technologies, man did not appear to be improving in his moral life one jot. No Newton had come along and discovered the formulae for achieving human happiness or creating an harmonious society or bringing about world peace or producing great art. Men and women everywhere still adhered to the same old practices, still clung to the same old superstitions, still believed in the same old gods, still committed the same old crimes, still waged the same old wars, still suffered the same old evils of ignorance and poverty and disease. In short, man still seemed to be a long way from realizing all the potential apparently being offered to him by his new sciences. Logical Positivism can be seen as a reaction to this failure, an attempt finally to brush away all the old bad habits, to burn all the old non-scientific books, to eradicate all the old non-empirically-justified theories. Not only was all knowledge from now on to be modelled strictly upon the empiricist principles which had proved so successful in the new sciences, but also philosophy itself was due for a spring-clean, was to be swept thoroughly with the hard broom of logic. *Out* was to go all metaphysical speculation and system-building that was not based on the sound foundations of logic and inductive reasoning. *Out* were to go all mythologies, religions and other forms of idle superstition. If you can't prove it to be true by experiment, forget it!

Effect   Hear, hear! I give up on this seat-belt.

Cause   But now, the product needed to bring about this grand spring-clean had to be a pretty strong one, had to be a principle more rigorous and more extreme than any that had been employed by previous empiricists, and its attack had to be made at the very roots of the old problems. Accordingly, the positivists' researches were concentrated in that most fundamental of areas, language. They set about analyzing how it was that words and phrases and sentences could denote and signify and have meaning. In particular, they sought a weapon which would render all the statements of their philosophical enemies empty and meaningless. The most famous example of such a weapon is A.J. Ayer's 'Verification Principle', which originally went like this:

> We say that a sentence is factually significant to any given person, if, and only if, he knows how to verify the proposition which it purports to express – that is, if he knows what observations would lead him, under what conditions, to accept the proposition as being true, or reject it as being false.

In short: the meaning of a statement is its method of verification.

Effect   I'll drink to that.

Cause   Of course, as a cleansing fluid, the Verification Principle was marvellous. At a stroke it dissolved all religious statements and statements about gods; it dissolved all speculative metaphysical world-views and systems, such as Descartes' 'reconstruction'; it dissolved all fantasizings about after-lives and heavens and hells. All this was exposed as mere unverifiable gibberish; the spring-clean was well under way. However, this was a highly dangerous corrosive, and once out of its verificationist bottle, it soon started to attack all sorts of other statements which the positivists had not originally intended to eradicate. Mathematical statements, for a start, seemed to present a problem. Here the positivists claimed, with some plausibility, that such statements were not meaningful anyway, but were just the inevitable deductions of a self-consistent logical system; hence Russell's grand attempt to secure for mathematics a set of purely logical foundations. Less convincing were the positivist attempts to rescue the value-judgements of morality and aesthetics. They did not want to dismiss out-right all such judgements as being simply meaningless, so they tried to translate them, in one way and another, into statements of personal prefer-ence or recommendation or command.

Effect Strictly speaking, I suppose the Verification Principle renders *itself* literally meaningless too.

Cause True, and all the positivist philosophizing that goes with it. Not just the baby, but the very bathroom window goes out with the mucky old bathwater. Anyway, with regard to other minds, the positivists' problem was that the Principle adjudged all statements which purport to express propositions concerning other people's mentality to be without factual sig-nificance. "You are angry", "Most Greeks believed that the world is flat", "Philosophers think analytically" are not statements which I can verify by reference to observations since I cannot observe other people's mental states, yet they are not statements which the positivist wants to write off as meaningless. Behaviourism was the theory that tried to resolve this dilem-ma, and *The Concept of Mind* was, I suppose, its classic text... Ah, here we are Malcolm: welcome to the Sanity!

Effect I say, what a beautiful place... I never realized.

Cause You wait till you see the tea-room... There's no point in locking the car, the locks don't work anyway.

Effect Don't forget the book.

✳ ✳ ✳ ✳ ✳ ✳ ✳ ✳ ✳ ✳ ✳

Cause Great! Two teas, two flapjacks and *The Concept of Mind*!

Effect There are some pretty funny-looking people around here.

Cause Don't worry Malcolm, they're perfectly harmless... See the white-haired man scribbling away in the corner, that's Hedfor Figures, the great maths brain; mad as a hatter; set fire to his rooms during the 'flu epidemic, tried to kill all the viruses. The young guy at the table staring out of the window, he's a classics scholar, very bright, heroin case... Ah, now, the chap over there in the blazer and cravat, he's a scream, he imagines he's a famous racing driver.

Effect What does he do, rush about the place going 'brrm brrm'?

Cause Oh no, he just reminisces about his great races, talks about turbo-chargers, signs autographs occasionally. He's okay, he's fine.

Effect Uhuh?

Cause If you want to see the real nutters, the dangerous ones, you should take a look round I Ward, the North Annexe.

Effect Er, no thanks. I'll take your word for it.

Cause They're quite safe, they're kept heavily sedated. 'Sedated', that's a great word isn't it?

Effect Come on, let's get back to Ryle.

Cause Ah yes, right. Well, the object of the exercise, remember, was to 'translate' all statements that purport to concern other people's minds into some form which would render them meaningful in positivist terms. In particular, the myth which Ryle wanted to lay once and for all was the old-fashioned dualism which presented the relationship between a man's mind and his body as being, as he put it, that of a ghost in a machine. The ghost-in-the-machine dogma, according to Ryle, saw the mind as an occult non-physical spirit somehow trapped within the body and manipulating it like a mysterious kind of puppeteer.

> In opposition to this entire dogma, I am arguing that in describing the workings of a person's mind we are not describing a second set of shadowy operations. We are describing certain phases of his one career; namely we are describing the ways in which parts of his conduct are managed.

Effect Exactly! That's exactly what I've been thinking.

Cause Ryle classifies this dogma as a 'category mistake', the sort of mistake, he suggests, that is made by a foreign visitor who is shown round the city's colleges, libraries, playing fields, laboratories, faculty buildings and so on and then asks "Yes, but where is the University?"

> It has then to be explained to him that the University is not another collateral institution, some ulterior counterpart to the colleges, laboratories and offices which he has seen. The University is just the way in which all that he has already seen is organized. When they are seen and when their coordination is understood, the University has been seen... The mistake is made by someone who does not know how to wield the concept *University*. The puzzle arises from an inability to use a certain term in the English vocabulary.

Effect   I'll buy that.

Cause   Ryle's mission is therefore to demonstrate how certain words and phrases are to be used correctly, to elucidate how concepts of this category co-ordinate with concepts of that, to explain how various logical relationships are organized. In particular, as you rightly anticipated, his aim is to persuade us that certain statements which apparently purport to concern other people's private mental lives can in fact be translated perfectly and completely as statements or sets of statements which concern only their publicly observable behaviour. Ryle begins with analyses of the phrases 'knowing how' and 'knowing that'.

Effect   Here, you've underlined it:

> When a person is described by one or other of the intelligence-epithets such as 'shrewd' or 'silly', 'prudent' or 'imprudent', the description imputes to him not the knowledge, or ignorance, of this or that truth, but the ability, or inability, to do certain sorts of things.

Cause   Knowing, claims Ryle, does not consist in the acquiring and storing away of catalogues of facts and information, as though in some vast, privately-accessible filing system, but rather consists in having the capacities to *do* certain things: to answer questions, to solve problems, to perform tasks and so on. To assert of someone that they know the atomic number of carbon or that they know the city well or that they know how to drive is to assert, on the evidence of their past performances, that they would give the answer 'twelve' if asked, could guide you round the city without getting lost, and will give you a safe journey home when required.

Effect   Six.

Cause   Sorry?

Effect   The atomic number of carbon is six. Twelve is its atomic *weight*.

Cause   Ah yes, of course, I know, I always muddle them up... While Ryle categorizes knowing as a capacity or skill verb, believing, he says, is a tendency or motive verb which "operates in the same field". In other words, believing things, again, is a matter of behaving in certain ways.

Effect   Exactly. One discovers what a man believes by studying what he does, by observing his public behaviour. His statements about his beliefs are, of course, elements in that behaviour, but they are by no means the most important elements. Actions, as they say, speak louder than words.

Believing and Willing

Cause The politicians who speak of their desire for disarmament yet who order ever deadlier weapons. The generals who claim to be securing world peace yet who shelter in ever deeper underground bunkers.

Effect The philosopher who claims not to believe in other minds yet who talks for an hour to a perfect stranger.

Cause But belief is not the same as knowledge, and this presents Ryle with a problem: what is the difference between believing and knowing something to be true when both can issue in the same behaviour? What price certainty?

Effect Here:

> A man who believes that the ice is dangerously thin gives warnings, skates warily and replies to pertinent questions in the same ways as the man who knows that it is dangerously thin... da-de-da-de-da... But to say that he keeps to the edge because he knows that the ice is thin, is to employ quite a different sense of 'because' from that conveyed by saying that he keeps to the edge because he believes that the ice is thin.

Cause Hm. It's Ryle who's on thin ice here if you ask me, very thin ice. Thin ice all round I'd say. Again, acts of will, for Ryle, are not mysterious, private acts of occult string-pulling, they are simply deliberate public performances. "An effort of will" I think he says, "is a particular exercise of tenacity of purpose, occurring when the obstacles are notably great, or the counter-temptations notably strong".

Effect You seem to know this book by heart.

Cause Doing something voluntarily is not triggering some outward behaviour by means of some inward private act of volition, but is simply behaving in a certain way, in a certain context: with a smile on one's face, unconstrained by the wind or by a torturer. Inclinations, continues Ryle, such as vanity, avarice, laziness, generosity, are general dispositions to behave in certain ways; to say that someone is greedy is not to say anything categorical of him or his mind, but is a sort of hypothetical proposition about how he would behave in certain circumstances – at the buffet table perhaps, or on the stock market. Moods such as happiness or depression, Ryle classifies as behavioural dispositions which affect people only temporarily, dispositions which come and go, while feelings like a thrill of anticipation or a pang of conscience he identifies as being close relatives of bodily sensations – giddiness, headaches, pains in the... You've gone very quiet Malcolm, are you okay?

Effect   Oh, yes, fine... That young guy over there, the classics scholar, he's slumped forward and hit his head on the table. Do you think he's alright?

Cause   I don't suppose he is, but there's nothing much you or I can do about it... Agitations, agitations, being excited, grief-stricken, angry, these are characterized as being momentary or brief storms of fairly violent behaviour.

Effect   I notice you soon forgot about your parking ticket.

Cause   Don't be fooled Malcolm, I may appear to have calmed down, but if I ever spot my sticker again, someone's going to need a new windscreen.

Effect   You keep talking about being fooled Andrew, but the point is that on most occasions, there is no question, no possibility of one's being fooled. When I saw you waving your parking ticket around, screaming blue murder and kicking your car door in, it would have made no sense at all to suggest that perhaps you were *not* angry, that underneath you were pleased or that privately you were happy.

Cause   You never know, maybe I just enjoy having a good rant now and then.

Effect   Maybe, maybe, maybe! You'll always be able to cook up some kind of 'maybe' won't you? But Ryle is right: being angry *means* behaving in certain ways. Anger *is* arm-waving, anger *is* voice-raising, foot-stamping and all the rest of it!

Cause   Anger is table-thumping too, apparently.

Effect   It's not anger Andrew, it's, it's, *certainty*... I'm just trying to make you see that you can't drive this *wedge* of yours between being angry and behaving angrily. This is just misuse of the language.

Cause   Okay then, let us examine the suggestion for a moment; please stop me if you think I am misusing the language. Your thesis, and Ryle's, seem to depend crucially upon the notion of synonymy, the possibility that one sentence can, in certain or various circumstances, mean the same as another sentence or set of sentences. To take your example: "He is waving his arms and raising his voice and stamping his foot" *means* "He is angry".

Effect   In your recent context, yes.

A Little Algebra

Cause But in another context the sentence "He is angry" might be true when no arm-waving or voice-raising or foot-stamping is going on. Table-thumping and going red in the face and spluttering may suffice?

Effect I suppose so, yes.

Cause So any general formulation of the relationship between reports of people 'being angry' and descriptions of their anger-behaviour is going to be quite complex?

Effect I imagine so, yes.

Cause Hold on Malcolm, let me get a pencil and paper for this; Figures will lend me one. Excuse me a moment...

Effect Remember I've got to be back by eleven...

Cause I'm sorry that took so long, he insisted on telling me about his argument proving the necessary existence of mathematicians. Quite smart actually. Anyway, let's get some of this down. Suppose we start by dividing all the verbs and verb-phrases that are used to describe and report human activities and experiences into two categories: b-verbs, we will say, are verbs which purport to denote only episodes of observable bodily behaviour, while M-verbs are verbs which, as pre-Ryleans we would ordinarily say, report, amongst other things, people's private mental experiences.

Effect Ye-es, er, okay...

Cause I will use a small 'b' and a capital 'M' to give an indication of the suggested logical priority. We may now write, as an example of one of your proposed synonymies:

$$M_{being\ angry} \equiv f_{being\ angry} \{b_{arm\text{-}waving},\ b_{voice\text{-}raising},\ b_{foot\text{-}stamping},\ b_{face\text{-}reddening}, ...\ \&c.\}$$

where the '$\equiv$' indicates synonymy and 'f' is some as yet unspecified function. The general form of such translations would be:

$$M_g \equiv f_g \{b_{g1},\ b_{g2},\ b_{g3}, ... b_{gx}\}$$

and if we were to carry out Rylean translations of all the M-verbs in the language, we could in theory end up with our completed set of synonymies looking something like:

$$M_1 \equiv f_1 \{b_{M1,1}, \, b_{M1,2}, \, b_{M1,3}, \, \ldots\ldots\ldots\ldots b_{M1,x1}\}$$

$$M_2 \equiv f_2 \{b_{M2,1}, \, b_{M2,2}, \, b_{M2,3}, \, \ldots\ldots\ldots\ldots b_{M2,x2}\}$$

$$M_3 \equiv f_3 \{b_{M3,1}, \, b_{M3,2}, \, b_{M3,3}, \, \ldots\ldots\ldots\ldots b_{M3,x3}\}$$

.

.

.

$$M_n \equiv f_n \{b_{Mn,1}, \, b_{Mn,2}, \, b_{Mn,3}, \, \ldots\ldots\ldots\ldots b_{Mn,xn}\}$$

Note that both n and xn will be finite, as the language is finite.

Effect Hm, I suppose so. Presumably though, many of the b-verbs will crop up in more than one of the M-verb translations. Going red in the face, for example, is sometimes anger-behaviour and sometimes embarrassment-behaviour. The b-verbs on the right-hand side of the pattern are bound to criss-cross and overlap a good deal.

Cause But you do accept that the whole enterprise is feasible? Its final complexity is presumably also going to depend upon what is to count as a logically 'atomic' item of bodily behaviour. So, the question now is: what sort of a function is 'f' going to be? Take our stock example again, being angry. We have already noted that no particular item of behaviour is necessary to being angry, that a man's anger may in some circumstances be his arm-waving and foot-stamping and in others be his face-reddening and spluttering.

Effect Perhaps we should say that while no one of the b-verbs is necessary to being angry, it is necessary that *some* of the b-verbs be observed if 'He is angry' is to be true. $f_{being\ angry}$ is going to be some kind of complicated disjunction.

Cause What about people who are angry without displaying very much in the way of overt behaviour? Some people get angry but, as we say, 'bottle it up'.

Effect But 'bottling up anger' itself involves certain characteristic behaviour-patterns: trembling, turning silent and sulky, bursting out hours or days later and so on.

Cause What about people who display very little overt anger-behaviour, period?

Effect People, you mean, who are rather more philosophical about life's irritations? "Heigh-ho, another parking ticket", that sort of thing?

Cause   That's not being philosophical Malcolm, that's being rich.

Effect   Again though, the point is that 'being philosophical' *means* reacting to things in certain observable ways, or rather, it means not reacting to them very much; it means remaining calm in circumstances which would make most people excited. Perhaps we should say of such people that they simply *don't get angry*.

Cause   What about people who remain calm about things for years but whose anger finally boils up unexpectedly, as if for no reason? The long-suffering spouse who silently endures twenty years of torture but who one day rises up and murders their persecutor over a chance remark?

Effect   We should say that they were angry but that they took a long time to, er, show it... Perhaps we would say that they had been angry *subconsciously*.

Cause   Ahh.

Effect   You can't get away from it though Andrew, in the end behaviour is always the criterion. If a man displays *no* anger-behaviour, no anger-behaviour of any kind, it just cannot make any sense to suggest that he may nevertheless *be angry*.

Cause   What about all those who take their secret angers with them to their graves?

Effect   But how can you talk about a 'secret anger'? If an anger is never displayed, it cannot...

Cause   Yes, yes, okay, forget it. The point is: people can be angry in an extraordinary variety of ways.

Effect   True enough.

Cause   So f_{anger} is therefore going to be extremely weak. Weak in the sense that you are going to be able to claim very little in the way of necessity in your proposed translation of M_{anger}.

Effect   What we *can* say though is that f_{anger} must be such that at least one of the b_{anger} verbs in the disjunction must be observed for M_{anger} to be true. To be angry, a man must display *some* anger-behaviour, even if it is only, say, a momentary reddening of the face.

Cause   In which case Malcolm, howabout this: "litmus paper gets angry when it is dipped in acid".

Effect   I beg your pardon?

Cause   I am right aren't I, litmus turns red in acid?

Effect   Yes, so?

Cause   So litmus gets angry when dipped in acid. Literally meaningful and factually correct, as far as behaviourism is concerned. 'Being angry' equals 'reddening', remember?

Effect   But, but...!

Cause   I suppose if the acid were strong enough, litmus might start spluttering too!

Effect   This is preposterous! Litmus can't *do* anything, it can't behave in different ways, it can't...

Cause   It can't do all the things a human being can, but it can turn red and splutter and turn blue.

Effect   But you might as well say that litmus gets embarrassed or flushed with pride!

Cause   Indeed.

Effect   But what would be the point? Where's the distinction? How could you tell the difference?

Cause   Can we always tell the difference with human beings? I can think of occasions when someone has blushed for no apparent reason and one has asked, or wanted to ask "Why have you gone red, has something angered you, or embarrassed you?" In such circumstances, all one can do is accept the person's answer, even if it mentions only the hot weather.

Effect   I suppose it never occurs to you that it's something you've said? Tell me honestly though, you're not serious about this litmus suggestion are you? Do you really believe that litmus can get angry or embarrassed? I've heard of fertile imaginations, but this is ridiculous!

Cause   Why? You're the behaviourist Malcolm, you're the one who wants to draw up the M-verb translations. It's only a linguistic problem, only a matter of synonymy after all. Why *does* litmus go red in acid by the way?

Effect   Ah, well, now... Erm... I believe that most organic indicators are weak phenolic bases, in which, erm, an electronic resonance is set up between the molecule's base radical and its phenol ring. I think it's this resonance which gives the compound distinctive colour-absorption characteristics, erm, directly affected by protonation, acidity that is. I seem to remember that litmus is in fact a mixture of dyes, Orcinol and erm...

Cause Yes, I get the picture. There's nothing wrong with the fertility of *your* imagination apparently. Okay, so suppose a computer were programmed to shout the words "You bastard!" and start vibrating every time its paintwork is scratched, doesn't your analysis render the statement "The computer is touchy" literally meaningful and factually true?

Effect Well... I suppose such a machine *would* be touchy in a literal sense, like when we talk of electrical components being excited or of computer circuits getting overheated, but this doesn't mean that we are thereby ascribing these things... feelings.

Cause Another picture: A small Cornish fishing village. Late afternoon. A stormy lead-grey sky filled with clouds hanging thick and low. Strong, sometimes gale-force winds gusting this way and that. The sea tossing and foaming in huge waves that crash against the rocks and hurl showers of pebbles onto the flooded sea-front road. The fishing boats in the harbour are being battered into one another and some are beginning to break up. Earlier on, a fisherman and his son were drowned when a gigantic wave suddenly engulfed their tiny craft and plunged it straight to the seabed. The storm has been in full spate for a hour now and parts of the old sea-wall are beginnning to crumble under the pounding.

Effect Nasty.

Cause Right Malcolm: the sea is in a rage.

Effect Ah, well, that's just a metaphor, a figure of speech.

Cause How come? According to your own analysis, being in a rage literally means and only means behaving in certain ways. Behaviour is behaviour is behaviour: molecules, machines, litmus papers, computers, pebbles, human beings, ballpoint pens, the sea – all are in the same behaviourist boat. That was one of the main purposes of behaviourism, to deny that human beings had any special status or peculiar properties in the wider scheme of things.

Effect But attributing emotions to the sea is just being anthropomorphic.

Cause   Not at all; b-verbs are merely behaviour-descriptions, they are not anthropo-anything and they are not anything-morphic. And M-verbs, remember, are merely functions of them.

Effect   Obviously though, M-verbs properly apply only to *human* behaviour; only human beings have... have...

Cause   Minds? This is it you see, the one thing the behaviourist can *not* say is that human behaviour is special because it involves mentality, mentality in the private-streams-of-consciousness sense, because this is what he has all along been at pains to deny.

Effect   But isn't it just a matter of complexity? After all, human behaviour is much much more complicated than the behaviour of other things.

Cause   Firstly, is this true? My description of the raging sea wasn't that simple, and think what your full account of the litmus' reddening was going to be like. Human behaviour, on the other hand, can be perfectly straightforward: just try scratching a man's body or dipping a man in acid.

Effect   Oh, human behaviour can often seem straightforward enough, but we know that the physiology involved, the biochemistry, the workings of the human brain are in fact all extraordinarily comp...

Cause   Pah! You're taking things to bits again aren't you! I thought one of the things you guys had learnt is that if one starts taking things to bits one soon discovers that everything is infinitely complex?

Effect   'Frustration', I wonder if Ryle has anything to say about 'frustration'... No, it's not in the index.

Cause   There are many interesting omissions in Ryle's index. 'Interesting', there's another.

Effect   'Loving', I can't find 'loving' either.

Cause   I know what you mean.

Effect   Oh surely, he must include loving?

Cause   It is a tricky one.

Effect   Perhaps the pages are missing.

Cause   Another chapter you won't find is the one on *first-person* statements. The positivists' Verification Principle and Ryle's behaviourist analysis also render assertions like "I am angry", "I am embarrassed" or "I am feeling hot" literally meaningless.

Effect But in a sense perhaps there *is* something meaningless about first-person statements, they are peculiarly... redundant. The speaker is reporting something about himself which he presumably already knows, while others know the truth or falsehood of his statement anyway, from their observations of his behaviour.

Cause Is that always so? Could not such statements simply be answers to the question "Why are you blushing?" Could they not be letter-written confidences, or diary entries?

Effect I suppose first-person utterances can sometimes *constitute* behaviour of significance, like when someone *shouts* the sentence "I am angry", but this doesn't entail that such an utterance is some sort of first-hand report upon otherwise secret happenings in the speaker's stream of consciousness. First-person utterances, notice, are characteristically used not to report things but to *do* things: "I promise you", "I forgive you", "I believe you". Your examples likewise: "I am angry" sounds like a warning; "I am embarrassed" sounds like a plea for silence; "I am feeling hot" sounds like a signal of intended jacket-removing or window-opening.

Cause Or lemonade-ordering. Fancy one?

Effect Oh, er, no thanks, I'm not thirsty.

Cause Of course first-person utterances can do things. All utterances can do things: "You have made a mistake", "We are behaving greedily", "One third of the world's people are starving". Statements can do things because sentences can mean things. Why so mealy-mouthed Malcolm, why so begrudging with respect to the first person? Why so shy of Number One?

Effect I... I...

Cause There's something very English about all this self-effacement. Will you actually deny that you have, that you experience a private stream of consciousness?

Effect I... I...

Cause What's the matter? What are you afraid of? What are you trying to pretend? Honestly, it's like trying to get blood out of a stone!

Effect I just don't like this phrase 'private stream of consciousness'. I don't like it any more than Ryle does.

Cause Okay forget the bloody phrase! Do you have thoughts Malcolm, secret thoughts? Secret desires? Secret dislikes?

Effect I... I...

Cause Embarrassed? There's no need to be. This is it you see: Rylean analyses of M-verbs that one generally associates with characteristic or strong bodily behaviour-patterns like being angry or grief-stricken carry a certain plausibility, but the further the M-verbs under consideration come, as we might say, towards the mental end of the spectrum, like imagining or thinking or introspecting, the less convincing do the behaviourist analyses of them become.

Effect Hm... 'convincing', there's another omission.

Cause One ploy of Ryle's is to divert attention to the corresponding adverbs: naturally enough, people who behave imaginatively or thinkingly or introspectively behave in certain characteristic ways. But of course one *can* imagine and think and introspect without displaying anything at all in the way of bodily behaviour: a few minutes ago I was exercising my imagination while delivering a description of a storm-lashed fishing village; you, perhaps, were exercising yours while staring blankly out of the window.

Effect Yes, imagination, imagination... Repeatedly it strikes me that attributing mentality to others is more a matter of exercising our imagination than of evaluating our evidence.

Cause And not attributing mentality to others is failing to exercise it.

Effect Perhaps, but of course our imagination can also run away with us.

Cause As for thinking, Ryle seems to recognize only two senses: 'think' meaning 'believe that' and 'thinkingly' meaning something like 'attentively'. The existence of thinking in the sense of *cogitating* or *contemplating* or *chewing over* Ryle is loth to acknowledge.

Effect It is sometimes said that by 'thinking' is meant an operation with symbols such as, par excellence, words and sentences. 'In thinking the soul is talking to itself'. But this is both too wide and too narrow.

Cause "Both too wide and too narrow", how's that for literal significance? Of course it may be suggested that few people these days *do* seem to think or reflect or introspect about things and that most people seem to blunder routinely on without daring to pause, but this could hardly be said of Gilbert Ryle: he obviously put in a great deal of thinking, that is *cogitating*, when he wrote *The Concept of Mind*. I suppose that's what philosophy is in a way, or what it should be: public introspection.

Effect   Tell me Andrew, what about *dreaming*? How does Ryle cope with dreaming? Another missing page I presume?

Cause   One line I think: Dreaming, again, is not being at a private cinematograph show.

Effect   Is that all? I must say that for a positivist, he's very keen on claiming what things are *not*.

Cause   I believe there *was* a positivist philosopher, I forget his name, who actually claimed that 'having a dream' literally means and only means waking up in the morning, uttering the sentence "I had a dream last night" and with an honest face recounting a funny story.

Effect   You're joking?

Cause   No, seriously. It seems like something out of a dream itself, but I'm sure it was suggested.

Effect   I find dreams fascinating, don't you?

Cause   Not particularly, no.

Effect   Tell me Andrew, do you dream in colour?

Cause   Er... I'm not sure.

Effect   And do you dream sounds?

Cause   Oh yes, I think so. I dream conversations sometimes. I once dreamt I was locked in a cell with Descartes.

Effect   Really? What did he say?

Cause   I can't remember. Something like "I sleep therefore I am" I think. Then his wife came in with a tray of cakes.

Effect   A tray of cakes? How odd. Dreams are strange aren't they?

Cause So you will admit you have them?

Effect Of course.

Cause You've had dreams which you've never reported?

Effect I must have done, yes.

Cause Right! Well that's enough then isn't it? At a trice the whole behaviourist thesis has collapsed: you do have, or you have had private mental experiences.

Effect Yes, I suppose so, if it makes you any happier.

Cause If it makes *me* any happier!? It's amazing the tricks people's philosophies can play on them! All that arguing to get you to concede something that's so patently obvious! All this writing of Ryle's to persuade us of something that's so patently false, so obviously perverse!

Effect Perverse?

Cause Oh yes, for Ryle and his positivist pals don't actually *believe* that other minds don't exist, any more than you do. It's just, as you say, a philosophical pose.

Effect But Ryle doesn't say that other minds don't exist. As I understand it, he is just trying to correct certain common mistakes in the ways in which people *view* their existence, in what other minds are taken to exist *as*. He is trying to clarify certain logical relationships, for example those between the concepts we have crudely distinguished as M-verbs and b-verbs. The category-mistake made by the foreigner over the meaning of the word 'university', remember?

Cause Yes, but *that* mistake was explained with the help of just a dictionary or a moment's explanation, no philosophy was needed.

Effect Come to think of it, I know a number of places around the world where the so-called 'university' *is* little more than a single large building.

Cause Even if, pray God, our foreigner had come from a culture with educational practices quite different from our own and spoke a language which contained no words for 'college' or 'university', our explanation would still be perfectly straightforward and uncontroversial, and nothing like trying to persuade him that we don't each have our own perceptions and feelings and thoughts; no book like Ryle's would be required.

.

47

Ryle and Descartes

Effect   As a matter of fact, some quite long books have been written on the concept of a university. All by university men of course and all rather different in their...

Cause   I cannot imagine a language which used the same word for 'me' and 'you'... No, a better parallel with the man who observes another's behaviour and then asks "Yes, but what is going on in his mind?" is the visitor who is shown around the university's colleges, libraries, laboratories and so on and then asks "Yes, but where does the money come from?"

Effect   Ah, but that question could be answered quite easily, quite factually.

Cause   Could it? Are you sure? Think carefully: where would the bucks stop? In the end don't we always come up against the other minds problem, or rather against the trustworthiness problem? It is ironical: the idea which is the greatest anathema to Ryle is the picture of human relationships as being that of mysterious, ghostly intellects somehow communicating with one another via their bodies' interventions in the physical world, yet his writing and my reading of *The Concept of Mind* is a classic candidate for just such a picture: one mind trying to change another mind's view through the agency of a public object, a book.

Effect   I see all this, but nonetheless there is something very right about Ryle's thesis. Whatever you say, the only way we can know about other people's perceptions and feelings and thoughts is through our observations of their bodily behaviour.

Cause   True, but Ryle is not just pointing us out the facts of life. Make no mistake Malcolm, his conclusion is that streams of consciousness *do not exist*. Ryle identifies his arch-enemy as Descartes, to whom he attributes the ghost-in-the-machine dogma, but of course Descartes never wrote of any ghost in any machine. It is a habit of philosophers to caricature their opponents' theories so as to ridicule and dismiss them the more easily.

Effect   So I notice.

Cause   Descartes may have been a dualist, but he was a dualist who found no difficulty or contradiction in suggesting that the physical location of one's 'innermost' soul is a lump of tissue found near the centre of the brain called the Pineal Gland.

Effect   The Pineal? The sand gland?

Cause   What?

Effect   Yes, truly, very strange, when you open it up all you find is a mass of sand-like grains.

Cause   Really? Good heavens! I've always thought people have their heads in the sand, but I never realized they had sand in their heads! Well well, so the sawdust theory wasn't so far wrong after all! Incidentally, it strikes me that the Cartesian view is far more compatible with a modern neurological account of mentality than Ryle's could ever be: if, as Ryle claims, it is a mistake to regard a person's 'knowing that' as his hoarding of catalogues of facts in some great private filing system, then equally it must be a mistake for the neurologists to interpret a person's memory as being the electrochemical coding of data in their brain cells, or however the fashionable jargon has it.

Effect   Computer science does provide us with some very good models of certain aspects of the brain's architecture. The more we learn about...

Cause   No, I reckon that Ryle's true opponent in all this, or rather, his philosophical mirror-image, was not Descartes so much as *Berkeley*. Berkeley's argument, presented most entertainingly in the form of three dialogues between two fictional characters named Hylas and Philonous, analyzed the logic of perception and began by listing the various ways in which our perceptions can trick and confuse us. Very briefly, it went something like this: all that we know about the material world and its so-called physical objects we know through our perceptions; perceptions are events – 'ideas' Berkeley calls them – that can occur only in minds; what we normally refer to as 'physical objects' are therefore in fact nothing more than collections of ideas existing in minds. Neat eh?

Effect   So what happens to a physical object which no-one is perceiving?

Cause   Ah, God guarantees it. God sees it when we don't, he sees everything all the time.

Effect   That's handy.

Cause   Berkeley was a bishop you see.

Effect   Ah, that figures.

Cause   Notice the symmetry though. Both Berkeley and Ryle set out to analyze some aspect of the mind/body problem in the light of their own personal philosophical vested interest; in Berkeley's case, that of Christian theology, in Ryle's that of positivism and the scientific world-view. And both base their arguments on the perfectly correct appreciation of certain inescapable epistemological facts.

Effect   Inescapable *what* facts?

Cause   Epistemological facts. From the Greek word 'ἐπιστήμη' meaning 'knowledge'. Epistemology is the study of how we know things and is to be contrasted with Ontology, the study of what things are, which comes from 'ὄντα', 'existing things' or, interestingly, 'the present'.

Effect   Hm. That sounds like the billion-dollar distinction.

Cause   Indeed, or rather, the one that money can't buy. Anyway, for Berkeley, the key fact is that the only way we can come to know anything about the physical world and its phenomena is through our perceptions of them, while for Ryle the key fact is that the only way I can come to know anything about other people's minds is through my observations of their bodily behaviour. According to Berkeley, for a physical object to be, it must be perceived or be perceivable; according to Ryle, for a mind to be it must behave bodily or be capable of behaving bodily. And of course they are both right: an unperceivable object is as much a nonsense as a disembodied mind.

Effect   Nonsense through the looking-glass.

Cause   Snap. The trouble is that Berkeley and Ryle then go on to attempt their own mirror-image nonsense of using their key facts to *unlock* the looking-glass. They both make the mistake of concluding that one side or other of the glass can then be dispensed with. Berkeley concludes that since perceptions occur in minds, the so-called physical world is in fact nothing but a set of mental events, while Ryle concludes that since all I can see are bodies, other so-called minds are in fact nothing but functions of physical behaviour.

Effect   The correct conclusion seems to be that body and mind are inseparable, are complementary, that they only make sense in terms of one another.

Cause   If you like. Of course neither Ryle nor Berkeley outrightly *denies* that mentality or physical substance exist. To do so would be too obviously absurd, too evidently loony. So instead, the madness is smuggled tactfully, in disguise: it is suggested that we have been making a 'philosophical mistake' about mentality or about physical substance, a mistake about what they exist *as*. In this way Ryle and Berkeley also avoid having to propose any wholesale linguistic upheaval: we are not recommended to abandon our use, on the one hand of the M-verbs and on the other of the b-verbs, in our everyday vocabulary.

Effect   They could hardly do that anyway; in both cases their argument is founded on everyday usage.

Cause   Incidentally, one result of that bit of analysis that we wrote out earlier is that provided every 'logically atomic' b-verb occurs somewhere in the pattern of M-verb translations, theoretically it should be possible to work out a translation of every b-verb as a super-function purely of M-verbs. In other words it should be possible, as far as synonymies and logical relations are concerned, to describe everything in the world entirely in terms of mental events and states. Berkeley one, Ryle one. Where's that paper gone? Ah, here we are... So:

$$b_1 \equiv F_1\{M_{b1,1}, M_{b1,2}, M_{b1,3}, \ldots\ldots\ldots M_{b1,y1}\}$$
$$b_2 \equiv F_2\{M_{b2,1}, \ldots\ldots\ldots$$

Effect   Yes, yes, I can see what you're getting at, there's no need to write it all out... please.

Cause   Sorry, I thought you'd be impressed by the algebra.

Effect   Surely another conclusion from all this is that the whole distinction you have proposed between our language's b-verbs and M-verbs is a nonsense too, an artificial and illegitimate philosophical ploy. It is a ploy which has misled us, rather in the way that Ryle and Berkeley appear to have been misled, into talking of a *purely* b-verb-language or a *purely* M-verb-language: again, a nonsense reflecting a nonsense, an incompetent logician's crazy fantasy.

Cause   I agree Malcolm, I agree.

Effect   Tell me this then: if Ryle's behaviourist attempt is fundamentally nonsensical, as you claim it is, and if it in any case leaves our ordinary language untouched, what is all the fuss about? If it is illogical it must be harmless.

Cause   Not so, unfortunately. The madness of a theory has never guaranteed that men will not believe it, any more than the immorality of a course of action has ever guaranteed that men will not pursue it. Already this morning we have demonstrated how strangely philosophy can play tricks upon our understanding, how queerly it can warp our perspective.

Effect   Yes, I am certainly beginning to see that.

On the Warpath

Cause   Although the positivists have not yet been able to persuade us to drop completely all our old-fashioned and misleading ways of putting things, yet in a subtle, insidious way, the influence of their philosophy has been great. Be clear Malcolm: important philosophical changes in the ways in which people 'see' and describe the world and themselves *do* take place. Language does not remain untouched. There are plenty of ways in which the role of our M-verbs has declined over the years, even with respect to accounts of our own behaviour. Our M-language is certainly not what it used to be. This artificial distinction led, as we saw, to two complementary and equally nonsensical logical conclusions. The trouble is that nowadays we apparently find one of these conclusions less obviously nonsensical than the other.

Effect   I'm sorry, I don't follow. Which conclusion?

Cause   Well what is *your* language Malcolm, the language of scientific explanation? Is it not a *purely* b-language? Is it not an attempt to describe the world and everything in it in *purely* physical terms? Is it not a language that leaves no room for any M-vocabulary?

Effect   Oh, yes, but...

Cause   An incompetent logician's crazy fantasy?

Effect   Well no, I... erm...

Cause   Oh dear! Oh blast! I can hear Matron on the warpath.

Effect   What's the matter?

Cause   Please, I think we'd better go.

Effect   Why? We're not doing anything wrong are we?

Cause   Er, no, but I'm afraid I'm not in her good books at the moment. I, um, had a sketch with one of the girls here a few weeks ago, and I think she blames me for what...

Effect   Ahh.

Cause   Christ, she sounds in a right mood! Come on Malcolm, let's move, quickly...

Effect   Okay, okay, I'm coming, relax.

*   *   *   *   *   *   *   *   *   *   *

2

PERSONS
and
THINGS

Cause What a beautiful day!

Effect Yup.

Cause The countryside round here is fantastic isn't it?

Effect It is.

Cause Looks like a sunglasses job... Oh damn!

Effect What?

Cause I seem to have walked off with Figures' biro.

Effect We'd better go back.

Cause Oh, he won't mind. He probably won't even notice. He lives in a world of his own, that guy. Anyway, it's only a cheap one.

Effect It looks like an expensive one to me.

Cause I'll give it back next time I go, I promise... Ahh, it's great to be alive on a day like this isn't it?

Effect Uhuh.

Membership of APES

Cause   Don't worry about the clanking, it's only the silencer mounting.

Effect   Oh.

Cause   I know, let's turn left here, and we can make a little detour past Hartlands. Do you know Hartlands, the zoo place?

Effect   Oh, well, I know of it. I'm a member as a matter of fact, but I've never actually been.

Cause   You're a member?

Effect   Yes, I'm a subscriber to A.P.E.S., the Association for the Protection of Endangered Species; one of the perks is that you get membership of affiliated zoos and parks.

Cause   Does that mean we can get in free?

Effect   I believe so. I should have the card somewhere... Yes, "A member may be accompanied by one guest".

Cause   Great! I think it's normally a couple of quid. Let's pop in there, just for a few minutes; we've got time. You really ought to see it. I love the place.

Effect   As long as it's only for a few minutes. I don't want to be late.

Cause   Don't worry... So you're into the protection of endangered species are you?

Effect   I do regard it as important, yes.

Cause   Uhuh? Are philosophers on the list yet? I gather there's an acute shortage of breeding pairs. There certainly is round my way.

Effect   I'm not surprised, the way you carry on.

Cause   Ah, here we are: "Hartlands Game Reserve and Zoo Park".

Effect   Note: "Please drive carefully, wild deer".

Cause   Christ, you can say that again: three pounds fifty admission! Get ready to flash your card Malcolm...

Effect   Okay, now drive slowly, I don't want you getting me into trouble.

Cause   Oh, what a setting! Just look at those trees!

Effect   It's beautiful.

Cause   I'm amazed you've never been... Deer, look, over there...

Effect   Oh yes, loads of them... And over there, a zebra... Another... Several...

Cause   I believe they've got a couple of giraffes. And see, by the lake, flamingoes, scarlet flamingoes... Paradise isn't it?

Effect   It certainly is a lovely spot.

Cause   You wait until you see the house and the gardens. They've got monkeys, parrots, a small-mammal house... I think they've got a butterfly farm too.

Effect   Oh I would like to see that.

Cause   They did try keeping lions for a while, but they went out of control, started killing the deer.

Effect   What a shame.

Cause   I've heard that they're having a bit of trouble at the moment actually, foot-and-mouth disease or something... They have a problem with foxes too, getting into the aviary... Oh look, a pheasant! What a fine fat fellow, he'd look nice on the dinner-table!

Effect   The thing is Andrew, I just don't accept what you say.

Cause   Eh?

Effect   I don't accept what you say. I don't accept that the language of scientific explanation leaves no room for any notion of mentality.

Cause   Oh, that.

Effect   Indeed, I think that one of science's greatest achievements is its explanation of how mentality has come about.

Cause   How it has *come about*?

Effect   Yes, pull over, park on the grass for a moment and I'll try to explain.

Effect's 1st Story: Darwinian Evolution

Cause   Okay, why not, we can walk to the house from here... So what now then: Darwinian evolution, random mutation, natural selection, all that?

Effect   In a nutshell, yes.

Cause   Remind me, remind me of the story.

Effect   What, the story of evolution?

Cause   Yes, it's always worth hearing again. Just a brief outline.

Effect   Okay... Well, where does one begin?... With the formation of the Solar System I suppose: of all the condensing planets, Earth was the one blessed with the constituents, the temperature-range and the atmosphere necessary to initiate the complex interactions of organic chemistry.

Cause   *Organic* chemistry, what is that?

Effect   Organic chemistry, as opposed to inorganic, is the chemistry of the huge family of substances generated by the element Carbon. The carbon atom has a uniquely symmetrical structure which enables it to form a certain very strong kind of inter-atomic bond.

Cause   So life as we know it starts with the structure of the carbon atom?

Effect   Yes. Carbon combines with elements like oxygen, hydrogen, nitrogen and so on to produce a great variety of complex yet stable molecules. One possible account of how this process got going suggests that the water vapour, methane, ammonia and hydrogen present in the Earth's primitive atmosphere were somehow ignited by lightning flashes to produce simple amino-acids.

Cause   'One possible account', you mean this is just speculation?

Effect   Informed speculation... But yes, there are a number of theories, and many unanswered questions.

Cause   Good.

Effect   Over time, the oceans would have become hot, dilute soups of simple organic molecules which would inevitably collide, and sometimes combine, with one another. Eventually this could have led to the formation of long-chain protein molecules, some of which contain over five thousand precisely-ordered individual atoms.

56

Cause Sounds like a hell of a lot of happy accidents.

Effect Proteins have the property of *catalyzing* further complex reactions, so it has been suggested that even at this early 'macromolecular' stage, some sort of natural selectivity would have ensured that only the catalytically most efficient of the chain-molecules survived in the competition to consume the organic ingredients in the soup. This might have resulted in even more complex molecules which could themselves organize proteins into self-replication, thus forming the first primitive *cells*.

Cause Hold on, slow down, already this smells of fudge to me!

Effect I did say it *might* have resulted. There is a great deal of speculation here, I wouldn't deny it. Some scientists even believe that the first bacteria reached Earth from Outer Space.

Cause A new role for God perhaps? Our Lord's cosmic sneeze?

Effect There are some reasonable certainties though... Photosynthesis started, by means of which cells used carbon dioxide and sunlight to grow more complex substances. This process liberated oxygen which began to form an atmospheric shield against harmful radiation, in turn allowing increased cell-replication to occur. Many of these simple single-celled organisms have survived to this day and in terms of resilience and distribution are the most successful of all life-forms: some bacteria can live on just carbon dioxide; the amoeba can actually propel itself towards a food-source; algae and fungi can organize themselves into communities. These cells not only can reproduce, but also, by means of the genetic material stored in their nuclei, can pass on precise biochemical characteristics to their offspring cells, making them replicas of...

Cause Carbon copies.

Effect The next step is to *multi-celled* organisms in which different cells carry out different functions: food-digestion, oxygen-respiration, propulsion and so on. Every cell in such an organism carries the encoded genetic messages which determine the design of the whole creature and issue the particular biochemical instructions to each different type of cell within it.

Cause Come again?

Effect I'm afraid the mechanism whereby the genetic information is transmitted from cell to cell is extremely complex. Every cell nucleus contains a number of chromosomes, inside which are coiled giant molecules of nucleic acid, DNA, along which the genes determining the cell-chemistries are precisely arranged. The key to the genetic code lies in the ordering of triplets of four base molecules, which are conventionally symbolized by the letters, A, T, C, G. This allows for a language of $4^3 = 64$ possible chemical code-words to be dictated to the amino-acid radicals which... shall I go on?

Cause   No, no, forget the algebra. Tell me Malcolm, can one actually *observe* any of these phenomena?

Effect   Well, one can just about see the shapes of the chromosomes with powerful optical microscopes, yes. Beyond that, one has to go to special instruments and techniques. They can, I believe, get electron micrograph images of DNA using platinum-shadowing and...

Cause   So basically we are into a fantasy-world here?

Effect   Oh not a fantasy-world, no... We are dealing in models perhaps, in crude models. Remember, the DNA molecules we are talking about are enormous by normal chemical standards, they each contain *millions* and *millions* of precisely arranged atoms; in the case of homo sapiens' DNA it is a matter of *tens* of millions, *hundreds* of millions maybe. The mathematics is mind-boggling.

Cause   It always is when you start taking things to bits.

Effect   So, we now have firstly multi-celled organisms in which communities of chemically specialized cells live and reproduce together, performing a variety of mutually beneficial functions, and secondly a code or language in which complex genetic information can accurately be transmitted from cell to cell.

Cause   Sounds like a civilization already. I don't suppose they'd harnessed nuclear power?

Effect   Well actually, they had in a sense, in photosynthesis... Anyway, all that was now needed to get the whole evolution process going was some possibility, within the system, of the occurrence of genetic variation.

Cause   Variation? I thought the whole point of the DNA theory was that it provides a perfectly mathematical, absolutely foolproof mechanism of gene-replication?

Effect   No, in this case, not quite perfect is perfect. There has to be some way in which organisms can *develop*. It is reckoned that in Nature a mis-match, a 'random mutation' as it's called, occurs roughly once in every hundred million gene-replications.

Cause   This is what goes hay-wire when there's radioactivity about?

Effect   That's right. Another advance that greatly accelerated the possibilities of genetic variation within an organism type was the advent of sexual mechanisms of reproduction, whereby replication is achieved through the mutual fertilization of oppositely-sexed cells. With this constant genetic intermixing, an organism naturally develops a more and more efficient genetic design as the less successful versions fall by the wayside.

Cause   Sometimes literally.

Effect   Whenever a mutation results in an adaptation that improves a species' chances of survival by better enabling it to exploit available food supplies or to evade or deter potential predators or to reproduce successfully, that genetic strain will naturally tend to increase its share of the species' population. This is how, over generations, the 1.4 million or so plant and animal species on Earth have become so wonderfully adapted to survive in their various ecological niches. The achievement of Darwin was to show that this whole process could be explained without recourse to the postulation of any Godly Creator or Designer, as the result solely of natural phenomena which we can see at work around us: one, the purely chemical occurrence of random gene-mutation and two, the natural selectivity of the environment which ensures that the more highly adapted strains within a species will always prosper at the expense of the less so.

Cause   The success of a species is not necessarily a matter of its perfect adaptation though, is it? Versatility, the ability to survive in a *variety* of environments, can be much more of an asset. A species which gets too precise in its adaptive direction and dependencies can easily find itself up an evolutionary gum-tree. When the weather changes, for example.

Effect   True, of course. Species survive for all sorts of reasons. I use the word 'adaptation' in its loosest, most flexible sense...

Cause   Right, so in practice, just about anything goes, or can go.

Effect   Well, not anything, no, but a very wide variety. Anyway, as a result of these perfectly natural phenomena, the whole evolutionary process grew like, like a great tree: early on, the main trunk subdivided into...

The Oak Tree

Cause Excuse me Malcolm, but what sort of a tree? They can grow in quite different ways. An Oak? A Birch? A Weeping Willow? A Palm tree perhaps?

Effect I don't know. I suppose it depends how you draw it. Something like an oak I would imagine... The main trunk subdivided into the plant and animal kingdoms; each of these subdivided and subdivided again into a multitude of branches and sub-branches and sub-sub-branches and so on; these are the myriads of species and sub-species we know today.

Cause Forgive me again, but it's not quite like this though is it? We don't actually observe any of the tree's branches, all we can see is a mass of foliage. According to your story, for each of the million species we know today there must have been countless intermediate stages of adaptation which have, as you put it, 'fallen by the wayside'; generation upon generation of dead leaves long since rotted away. The branches you describe are like million-year time-lapse films showing the many micro-adaptations frame by frame. But of course we don't have these, what we have is a sort of instantaneous flash photo of the species that happen to be surviving now. The tree is something you are asking us to imagine, something you have *inked in*.

Effect Yes, but we do have quite a lot to go on. Apart from the many inter-relationships we can now observe, we have the evidence of fossils and skeletal remains. Also, to a limited extent we can actually witness the processes of genetic mutation and natural selection at work amongst certain animal populations today.

Cause No, wait. All we can actually *witness* are changes in the characteristics of the animals.

Effect We have already mentioned the primitive single-celled creatures, the Protozoans. Next, the Metazoans, early organisms in which different cells perform specialized functions. Then come the Coelenterates, such as the jellyfish, in which we see the appearance of a simple nervous system. Then the various kinds of worms, some of which have a primitive brain and circulation. The Arachnoids or spiders feature clearly segmented bodies, external skeleta and rudimentary eyes. The Crustaceans, the crabs and shrimps, have more complex limbs, more advanced sense organs and highly-specialized mouthparts with which they...

Cause I say, look at these goaty chaps... I wonder why they're all penned in like this.

Effect Mm. Seems a bit... unnecessary.

Cause I guess they don't mix with the deer.

Effect I wonder what they are... Ibex?

Cause That's a bird isn't it?

Effect No, you're thinking of Ib*is*.

Cause Onyx perhaps... Oh no, that's the green marble isn't it...

Effect Quartz.

Cause Quartz? I haven't heard of a goat called a Quartz. I thought that was a kind of watch.

Effect No no, onyx is a kind of quartz, it's not a marble. You were thinking of Oryx, but Oryx are antelopes, they're much larger.

Cause Hyrax maybe?

Effect Hyrax!? Hyrax are tiny creatures Andrew, about the size of rabbits! I tell you, they're Ibex.

Cause Oh what the hell, they're goats! Ibex, Oryx, Hyrax, how we love to give things names don't we, to catalogue them, to pin them down, to pen them in... But you boys know better than that, don't you eh? Ouch! Vicious bugger! Tried to bite me!

Effect They're not just names Andrew, they mark distinctions that are there in Nature. Though no two members of any species are *identical*, each species shares precisely-defined anatomical and physiological characteristics. And of course, only members of the same species can successfully breed together.

Cause Can or do?

Effect Er... can, I suppose. Can or do, what's the difference?

Cause All the difference, all the difference in the world, I would have thought. I think you will find that the zoological definition of the term 'species' refers to how animals, as a matter of fact, *do* interbreed. It leaves it open to speculation whether they do what they do out of choice, and what might happen if they chose differently.

What is a Species?

Effect But it could be shown experimentally that...

Cause Could it? All sorts of funny things go on, especially in laboratories, where animals are held captive, all cooped up. Necessity is the mother of invention. And I'm not just talking about controlled cross-breeding...

Effect Did you know they've actually managed to clone a sheep-goat, a so-called 'chimera'?

Cause Yes I saw it on TV, a real half-and-half; poor thing doesn't know which way to turn! Apparently they've found some method of artificially separating the...

Effect Oh, *artificially*, maybe. But I'm talking about natural interbreeding, interbreeding in the wild.

Cause I gather there's a lot of pretty strange business in the wild too, wherever *that* is. Howabout this one: the Herring Gull and the Lesser Black-backed Gull are two quite different species, each with highly distinctive markings. In Britain, members of the different species do not interbreed, but in certain gull colonies in certain parts of Europe they sometimes do, producing identifiable and fertile hybrids; gulling the gulls. The interbreeding and the hybrids are comparatively rare, so the two species remain apparently distinct, but if gulls' mating fashions were to change...

Effect Yes, that is an interesting one.

Cause Can't the species' formation be seen as determined more by animals' sexual tastes and their communities' geographical isolations than by any supposed impossibilities of successful reproduction? Besides, how successful is successful? Didn't you say that a genetic mutation occurs only once in a hundred million replications? I'm afraid that when it comes down to it you may find neither the word 'species' nor the species themselves can be defined at all precisely.

Effect But the species *are* defined! Look: these are Ibex, those are Fallow Deer. the Ibex are stocky, they have large curved horns, woolly coats and characteristic beards. The Deer are more finely built, they have smooth dappled reddish coats and their males have palmated antlers... Ibex, Fallow Deer.

Cause Exactly! In the end, as in the beginning, you tell me what you see, you go by appearances. And of course the animals themselves do likewise.

The word 'species', you may be interested to learn, comes from the Latin verb 'specio', I look.

Effect Words evolve too Andrew.

Cause Yes, but how? Put it another way: is evolution continuous or is it stepwise?

Effect How do you mean?

Cause Well, as you describe it, the process of adaptation can only occur very slowly, mutation-by-mutation. When species B evolves from species A, the reproductive line from A to B must remain continuous and unbroken for the development to succeed. And not merely unbroken, for presumably the breeding populations of the intermediate forms will have to be of a fair size if the necessary random mutations are to occur.

Effect Yes, but in some circumstances, where there are sharp geographical demarcations or when there is a sudden change in climate, dramatic developments can in fact take place quite rapidly, over just a generation or two. It all depends.

Cause But in the history of any A-B development, however slow or rapid, surely there can be no moment when Bs or B-forms suddenly become definitively different from As and A-forms?

Effect Yes... No... There must be reproductive cut-off points. The answer is: evolution is continuous *and* stepwise. It all depends what development you are looking at, and how closely you are looking...

Cause Yes.

Effect So: Crustaceans... Insects. The Insects are really a kingdom within a kingdom, in themselves numbering almost a million different species, displaying an extraordinary variety of adaptations and together constituting the most successful and resilient group of animals on Earth. The winged insects were the first creatures to master flight. Some insects, like the butterflies, undergo remarkably complex life-cycles. Others, like the ants and the bees, congregate in huge colonies or swarms and participate in highly organized social behaviour-patterns. The Insects' dramatic evolution was crucially dependent upon their development of a horny exo-skeleton which provided protection against the harmful radiations that penetrated the Earth's early atmosphere.

The Garden Grows

Cause Blessed are the chitinous: for they shall reinherit the Earth.

Effect In the sea came the Molluscs, limpets, snails, squids, which are soft-bodied, often shelled creatures with advanced muscular control. Echinoderms, starfishes for example, developed bony internal skeletons, an advantage that was later to be most dazzlingly exploited by the Vertebrates or backboned animals.

Cause Ah, here we are. Now just look at that gaff!

Effect It's a fine house.

Cause And what a garden! What fantastic flowers! That's one thing I miss, living in town.

Effect Really? You must come out to our place sometime, we've got a big, a nice garden. er...

Cause Uhuh? Country mansion is it? Bit flash?

Effect Oh no, it's only a cottage, but it's...

Cause Comfortable. I know.

Effect Oh look, a peacock!

Cause Another! Another!

Effect The Vertebrates, yes... The Vertebrates have developed in comparatively recent geological time and form another highly versatile and successful group of species. Although the different classes display an extraordinary range of adaptations, in fact they are all variations on a single common skeletal structure. In their early stages of growth, the embryos of all the different species, from the Halibut to Homo Sapiens, are virtually indistinguishable.

Cause I know adults who seem to have remained so.

Effect The earliest vertebrates were the Fishes, who for millions of years battled with one another for mastery of the seas and rivers, developing into the thousands of superb adaptations we know today. Next, the Amphibians like frogs and newts who are the descendants of the first fish that crawled from the sea and struggled to survive on land. Then, the Reptiles, such as tortoises, crocodiles, snakes, which are cold-blooded, shelled-egg-laying vertebrates fully adapted for life on land. At one time, a number of reptile monster-species, the dinosaurs and their contemporaries, were the dominant group of land animals; it is thought that their reign was ended by the prolonged Ice Age or some other great climatic catastrophe. The Birds are warm-blooded descendants of the reptiles which became adapted for flying. The Mammals are...

Cause Hang on, that was a bit of a jump wasn't it, "the birds descended from the reptiles"? Just like that!?

Effect 'Ascended' I suppose it should be. It didn't happen overnight, obviously. Some of the more primitive birds do still display certain reptilian features: a somewhat reptilian skull; vestigial reptilian claws at the ends of their wings; areas of scaly reptilian skin; and of course, all birds are egg-layers.

Cause Come off it Malcolm, how did crocodiles ever manage to fly? I'd give pigs better odds!

Effect Oh, there were plenty of reptiles that had taken to walking upright, on their hind legs. The crucial development was the adaptation of feathered, wing-like forelimbs from scaly, food-gathering ones.

Cause Not to mention a lot of nerve, a craving to make history and a sense of humour.

Effect No honestly Andrew, there is evidence for all of this: there is the famous fossil Archaeopteryx, the earliest true bird. Archaeopteryx has a genuine reptilian skeleton with teeth and a long tail, and genuine avian feathers on aerodynamic wings.

Cause Oh, haven't you heard, it's a fake, a trick!

Effect What!?

Cause That fossil is a fake. It was done by hand. It's been proved; I read about it in the papers. It was all a con-trick pulled way back by some German scientist and his son. They made a fortune, must have laughed all the way to the bank! Well dead now of course. Brilliant stroke eh?

Effect Well... I... Are you sure? Anyway, it doesn't change the fact that the birds must have evolved from the reptiles.

Cause How though? There is, you might say, a quantum-leap here. The change from scales to feathers would have needed millions of mutations and taken yillions of years, yet until a feathered fore-limb could lift the animal off the ground, it would have been worse than useless. I suppose there might have been an intermediate, gliding-out-of-trees stage, but for a long time before that, the reptiles with partly- or half-formed wings would have gone down like lead balloons in the evolution-show.

Effect   Not necessarily. Feathers are also very good insulators.

Cause   But why, one wants to ask, did a scale ever *start* turning into a feather? One has visions of generation after generation of hapless reptiles, or rather, of generation after generation of *breeding pairs* of hapless reptiles, whose particular madness consisted of flapping their arms and throwing themselves off cliffs, until one day, after n million years of trying, one of the pairs had a soft landing!

Effect   There are still, it is true, many great gaps in our knowledge. Many of the crucial links in many of the evolutionary chains, including our own, are still missing.

Cause   'Cells', 'chains', 'missing links': from molecules to men, our pre-occupation with bondage seems inescapable. I tell you one thing Malcolm: *we* would never have made successful birds.

Effect   We have though Andrew: with our brains and our hands we have built hang-gliders, aeroplanes, even spacecraft; men have dared fly to the outermost atmosphere, and beyond.

Cause   Pshaw! I wonder what a crocodile dreams...

Effect   Anyway, whether you like it or not, there evolved from the reptiles a class of warm-blooded, feathered, egg-laying flying vertebrates which again displayed a dazzling range of adaptations. Some birds have even 're-adapted' to become flightless swimmers like penguins, or flightless land-dwellers like ostriches.

Cause   Tell me this then: why did that peacock evolve such beautiful tail-feathers? After all, they are quite useless.

Effect   Oh no, not true. He uses them in courtship, to attract a mate. And to frighten would-be predators.

Cause   Yes, one often hears this sort of thing. But given that he's got them, of course he's going to use them, who wouldn't? And given that he uses them in courtship, one can understand that the more extravagant they get, the more reproductively successful will be that strain. But this is all explanation after the event, explanation with the benefit of tailsight, it is all a 'whatever happened had to happen' pan-gloss. My question was: *why did those tail-feathers evolve in the first place?* No-one using your random mutation/natural selection theory would have predicted that *that* sort of thing would evolve. The pressures of your naturally selective, survival-of-the-fittest-type world would seem to rule out such fripperies.

Effect   Not at all. As I said before, species can survive for all sorts of reasons.

Cause   Right, so one interesting thing comes out of this: while random mutation may provide a chemical explanation for the generation of new forms, your canonized 'natural selection' which is supposed in practice to weed them out in fact covers a multitude of sins. It is not just a matter of efficient food-gathering or fearsome weaponry or fecund reproduction, *this* species evolved because of a peahen's feather-fetish, a good healthy sexual perversion. Maybe the predominant driving-force in evolution has been boredom: one creature's urge to discover what lay over the mountain or beyond the sea; some renegade's desire to get away from it all or try something different...

Effect   A crocodile's dream.

Cause   This brings me to another general observation: the Darwinian world one usually hears described sounds like a pretty hellish sort of place: the individuals of a species competing with each other tooth-and-nail for the food supplies; the different species all locked in a continuous struggle for dominance; every creature preying and preyed upon in a round-the-clock rat-race; everyone battling against environment, climate and disease. Now I know that as an English middle-class homo sapiens I am a comparatively spoilt creature and heavily cushioned from many of Nature's harsh realities, but nevertheless this is not my general impression of the world. In fact, most animals seem to go about their daily business quite happily and easily and pleasantly thank you.

Effect   I quite agree Andrew, I quite agree. It is you who keeps flogging the 'survival of the fittest' motif, not I. I think it's very overworked.

Cause   Oh, there is danger, of course; there are predators; every so often someone gets eaten; once in a while the weather turns nasty. But on the whole, things aren't so bad. Maybe if I spent my time in the Amazonian jungle, or studying the habits of carnivorous spiders I would form a different view, but looking around here... the flowers, the butterflies, that girl's long golden hair. Why all this *beauty*?

Effect   This is very subjective though; beauty, remember, is in the eye of the... Ugh! How foul! No doubt to a fly, a dog-turd is a thing of beauty.

Cause   Quite so. It is the *sense* of beauty that has to be explained.

Effect   Hum... The Mammals. The Mammals are the most recently evolved class of vertebrates. They are warm-blooded, hairy and suckle their young. In all but a few primitive species their offspring grow in a placental womb and are born alive. Their brains are larger than those of the preceding classes. Our own order, the Primates, have elongated limbs and digits, forward-looking eyes and highly developed brains.

Cause   Ah, the Chimpanzees! Hey, what horrid little cages! No Sun, nothing much to climb, overcrowded.

Effect   Mm. I must say, they don't seem too happy.

Cause   This is a disgrace! A scandal!

Effect   And finally, of course, Homo Sapiens: powerful hind-limbs, arched feet, upright posture, a further-enlarged brain and free fore-limbs with grasping hands. Zoologically, man is a manipulator.

Cause   Too bloody true.

Effect   Man's ability to manipulate tools and his general versatility have allowed him to spread successfully to all parts of the globe. His intelligence, his capacities for problem-solving, language and the passing-on of information have led him to make numerous technological discoveries and to live together in vast, highly-organized communities.

Cause   Hooray.

Effect   In the last two hundred years or so, rapid scientific, industrial and medical progress have enabled him to gain uprecedented control over his environment, and even to explore nearby Space. In fact we have become so successful that we now pose certain threats to the Earth's whole ecosystem. Apart from our widespread destruction of wildlife habitats for intensive agriculture, our chopping-down of the tropical rain forests and our burning of fossil fuels are making significant changes to the composition of the atmosphere which if unchecked, could have disastrous effects on climatic conditions. We must think globally now, we have responsibilities. The Earth has become... our garden.

Cause   Amen. Or our graveyard perhaps? For none of this is to mention our prospect of nuclear war. Wasn't it Einstein who said that in 1945 everything changed except the way men think?

Effect   That's right. With man's harnessing of nuclear power has come another quantum-leap: for the first time ever a life-form has the ability to release enough energy actually to mutilate the planet and all life on it.

Cause   Congratulations. You speak of man's intelligence Malcolm, but what is intelligence? Surely, as a good Rylean, you can only judge a man to be intelligent from the ways in which he behaves, and one can only conclude that man as a species is intelligent from observations of how he, as a species, carries on? The fact that men built Nagasaki Public Library and wrote the learned books that filled it might suggest that men are intelligent. The fact that men then dropped an atomic bomb on it seems to prove that they are not.

Effect   But the fact that men could *build* an atomic bomb proves that they're intelligent.

Cause   Does it? Are you sure? Intelligence! Manipulation! I've had enough of your intelligence and manipulation! Too much intelligence and manipulation if you ask me, too much for our own and for everyone else's good. Too much language, too much ratiocination, too much addling of the mind! What other species goes around slaughtering its own kind just because they use a set of different names? What other species is happy to kill and die and torture for a few tuppenny-hapenny slogans? What other species lives by rules written in thousand-year-old books? What other species keeps fellow creatures locked in tiny stinking cells, for fun?

Effect   Okay Andrew, okay, but don't forget that *we* are products of this evolution too. We are all Mother Nature's children.

Cause   That's not good enough though is it? And you know it.

Effect   One thing I should make clear: the fact that my account ended with the development of Homo Sapiens must not mislead us into thinking that man is in some way the goal or purpose of the whole evolutionary process, or in some sense its highest or finest creation. An oak tree has no one particularly significant summit or direction, but has branches growing off in all sorts of different ways.

Cause   Oh spare us the mock zoological modesty! Of course we believe that we're the highest of the animals, our every action declares it: for a start we regard our own survival as being more important than any other's. I imagine that from its own point of view, every life-form seems to be the highest, and that to every life-form, everything that happens counts as 'Nature'.

Effect   The purpose of the disclaimer Andrew, is to remind us that the peculiar adaptations which have enabled man to become so successful so rapidly may prove no guarantee of his prolonged survival and may, as you suggest, be the causes of his equally rapid demise. We could be just a flash in the evolutionary pan. Some climatic catastrophe, of Nature's making or our own, could easily do for us and our fragile eco-dependencies what the Ice Age did for the dinosaurs.

Cause   Surely *we* are the climatic catastrophe now, with our unstoppable swarming, our insatiable appetites, our perpetual warmongering.

Effect   One thing we can say about man's place in Nature is that he is a very *recent* development. If you scale down the history of life on Earth to a period of twelve hours, it goes something like this. Midnight: appearance in the seas of the first primitive organisms – bacteria, algae, protozoans et cetera. It is then almost *ten hours* before the arrival of the early marine invertebrates, the ancestors of the molluscs and starfish. At about ten-thirty in the morning, the first green plants appear on land and the fish begin to evolve. At about ten to eleven, insects and primitive amphibians start adapting to life on land. Twenty past eleven and the mammals begin to develop, together with the forerunners of most modern trees and flowering plants. The apes do not emerge until a quarter to twelve and Homo Sapiens finally arrives in only *the last minute* of the twelve hours. Man's recorded history would account for a mere few seconds, while our recent period of technological revolution would scarcely register as a tick of the clock... My goodness, is that the time?

Cause   One minute to eleven Malcolm.

Effect   Damn! Now I'm going to be late! Come on, please, I've got to get back.

Cause   Okay, hold on, I just want to do the chimps a little favour...

Effect What *are* you up to?

Cause I always carry a bit of hacksaw blade with me; I once read a book about political prisoners... Here boy, here...

Effect Don't be stupid, he won't know what to... Stop! Look, he's putting it in his mouth! Now see what you've done!

Cause He's dropped it, down the grating. Phew! Thank God for that!

Effect Okay, now back to the car, please.

Cause I'm coming... This business about Darwinian evolution not having purpose though; it seems odd to say of an oak tree that it has no purpose. Come to that, it seems odd to say of a stone that it has no purpose.

Effect The point is that in the Darwinian explanation we do not have to invoke notions of a divine hand at work or of any grand scheme or overall plan.

Cause So you keep saying, yet even in your briefest of brief accounts, you yourself spoke of the Earth being *blessed* with the right conditions, you suggested that genetic mutation was *all that was needed* to get the process going, you added that natural selection *ensures that* the best adaptations prosper, and you even described us as being all *Mother Nature's children*. For the life of me, I can't see the difference between God the Father, capital G and F and Mother Nature, capital M and N.

Effect Forgive me Andrew. At times I may have expressed myself a little carelessly. There is a lot of loose talk in popularized natural history, I agree. This is a tendency that should be resisted.

Cause Interesting: it is a tendency, is to be resisted... Just as one has to apologize, I notice, for ending an account of evolution with Homo Sapiens.

Effect I suppose it's hard not to attribute purpose to a process that has resulted in one's own existence.

Cause Indeed Malcolm, indeed. No apology is needed I assure you.

Effect Objectively though, our branch of evolution, our direction of adaptation is only one amongst many.

Cause But surely, for a behaviourist, having a direction *is* having a purpose? 'Direction', there's another interesting word.

Trying, Flying, Multiplying

Effect   Well, yes... There are advances in adaptation, there are improvements in designs, there are directions, but no-one is designing the adaptations, no-one is doing any directing. Of course, we now, piecing together the story with hindsight, are assuming the role of designers, or rather, the role of design analysts, design historians, but the point is that the original occurrence of the designs can be explained solely by the operation at the individual level of ordinary natural laws of chemistry and ecology, without any reference to grand purposes or ends.

Cause   But not without reference to individual purposes and ends. At the individual level, individual ends. Purposes, desires, appetites, stratagems, plans, ends – at the individual level these were the very life-blood of your account. According to you, molecules *consumed* ingredients, *competed* with one another, *organized* protein chains; genes determined designs, issued instructions, transmitted information; cells used resources, performed functions, formed communities; organisms developed successfully, exploited conditions, improved their efficiency.

Effect   I wondered what you were writing.

Cause   Your whole story was fuelled by the assumption that at every stage creatures are all competing with one another, battling against conditions, fighting off predators, are all, in short, struggling to survive.

Effect   So?

Cause   So *purpose*, in the sense that it is every individual organism's purpose at the very least to survive, is at the heart of the Darwinian explanation. The notion of purpose is actually built into it, it is ingrained at an atomic level.

Effect   Well, yes, I suppose it is, if you want to see it that way. Of course mere survival is not enough. Every organism must also...

Cause   Must also improve, must also evolve, of course. But no organism can improve that does not *try* to improve, that does not *try out* any new adaptations. The reptiles had to try to fly.

Effect   What I was in fact going to say was that every organism must also *reproduce* successfully if it is to survive.

Cause   Ah, now explain this: why is it that creatures which are supposed to be hell-bent on winning the rat-race go in for such a manifestly handicapping activity as the bearing and rearing of young?

Effect   Simple: they have an instinct to procreate, it's part of their genetic inheritance. Obviously, for any genetic strain which didn't transmit such an instinct would automatically die out.

Cause   But if this instinct is transmitted in every creature's genes, why don't *I* feel it? I assure you that I don't... No, please, let's not get involved in any futile argument about subconscious repressions, just take my word that I can find no trace in myself of any desire or instinct to have children. Sex drive, desire for women, plenty of that, but that is something different.

Effect   Hm, interesting. I won't argue with you, but the subject does seem to be on your mind.

Cause   I accept that if I did have children I might discover my paternal instinct, but that again is something different.

Effect   Why don't we just say that in Nature, where there is no contraception, the sex drive comes to the same thing. Besides, if you genuinely *don't* have a procreative instinct and as a result you don't have children, your genetic strain *will* naturally die out. Q.E.D.

Cause   What about altruism then, the phenomenon of individual members of a species who are not immediately related co-operating together for the good of the herd? Ants, wolves, humans occasionally.

Effect   Again, if some sort of herd instinct or altruism promotes the survival of the species, which it may do for all sorts of reasons, then again, the gene carrying this instinct will naturally tend to become the dominant strain.

Cause   And what about altruism towards other species? Your membership of A.P.E.S., my abortive hacksaw mission? And I've seen chimps happily grooming dogs, and dogs happily suckling lion-cubs, on telly anyway.

Effect   I admit, we do have a problem with genuine altruism...

Cause   No kidding.

Effect   I suppose it might in principle be possible to argue that such behaviour-traits are in the long term interests of the species' combined surv...

Cause   Pshaw, pshaw, pshaw! Tell me straight: do you honestly believe in all this 'genes' business?

Andrew Cause's Genes

Effect Of course I do. What do you mean, *believe* in it?

Cause So according to you, each of the millions of cells in my body contains...

Effect Trillions Andrew, your body is made up of millions *of millions* of cells.

Cause Trillions, zillions, quillions, whatever; each and every one containing identical copies of a single molecule which somehow carries *my design*, carries all the characteristics of Professor Andrew Cause.

Effect Of Andrew Cause maybe, not of the Professor.

Cause So each of my quillion cells contains within it the design of all of them?

Effect Well, your DNA carries the general design of your body and of all your different cell-*types*, your skin cells, liver cells, brain cells and the rest, so when a skin cell dies or is damaged it is replaced by another skin cell, not by a brain cell, and vice versa. Your DNA thus dictates your general biochemical architecture, but obviously it does not carry details about your every single cell.

Cause But I thought the whole point of the DNA story is that my genes are supposed to determine all my physical characteristics, down to the finest details of my unique bone-structure, colourings and what-have-you?

Effect Yes but...

Cause So aren't these all matters of cell-by-cell arrangement? Take my liver for example, what's left of it: presumably it has a finite shape and size and is made up of a finite number of cells. Each cell must therefore be slightly different from the next, if only by virtue of having its own unique position in my liver.

Effect Ye-es...

Cause So given that each liver cell contains my own particular DNA molecule and also somehow knows exactly where it is in my liver, this must surely mean that each of my quillion cells is unique and that each is coded slightly differently? Doesn't the problem of cell-coding thus regress indefinitely?

Effect   There are many unsolved mysteries Andrew, and I am no expert in this field, but I sense that perhaps you are taking things too literally here... Try to think of DNA more as being a design *model* or a coded *formula*...

Cause   Haven't you just ended up removing the mysteries of character- istic-inheritance to a new and more problematic level, to a level where they are out of sight? This genetic mechanism was postulated to explain the mystery of why parents can and cannot pass various characteristics on to their children. What we have now is the even less tractable problem of explaining how sub-microscopic molecules can and cannot pass various characteristics on to other sub-microscopic molecules.

Effect   Yes, but...

Cause   I must say I find this idea of molecular models of Andrew Cause multiplying throughout my body wildly fantastical and faintly loony... The whole genes business seems systematically to put the cart, or rather the foal, before the horse: it is not my genes that carry around my character- istics, if anything, it is I who carry around my genes' characteristics – an all-important difference of *voice*.

Effect   The DNA explanation may seem wildly fantastical Andrew, but then the phenomenon of procreation *is* wildly fantastical: a single human ovum no bigger than a pinpoint and a single human sperm yet tinier still carry between them all the information necessary to grow into this most miraculous of machines, a human being. *Of course* the workings of such a process are going to be mysterious and extraordinary!

Cause   Phoof! Nothing *less* mysterious than that human beings should beget more human beings; nothing more predictable, nothing more dull.

Effect   What!? The miracle of childbirth!? You've no idea! You've no idea what's involved! The biochemistry, the physiology! The growth of bone- structures, muscle tissues, blood-circulation, respiratory system, digestive system, nerves, sense organs, brain, reproductive system and so on and so on. The human body is a zoological marvel, a wonder of the world!... Slow down a bit Andrew, you do waik fast.

Cause   I thought you were in a hurry.

Effect   For a start, the human skeleton is a quite extraordinary structure, each of its two hundred or so bones finely-honed and perfectly interlock- ing. Then the musculature, which consists of hundreds of interlaced and counter-balancing muscles, some joined to the bones by tendons, others supporting the body's various internal organs. Day in, day out, roughly once every second, the heart muscle pumps blood round the body through the network of arteries and veins and blood-vessels which...

Cause Yes, yes, I'm sure.

Effect The lungs absorb oxygen from the air and pass it into the blood-stream. The gastric juices in the stomach and intestines break down and digest food stage-by-stage, extracting from it all the nutrients the body needs for cell-regeneration and energy. The waste products are passed on down through the...

Cause Yup, yup, okay, okay.

Effect Then there's the immune system, with which the body fights off invading organisms and neutralizes harmful cells. There's the lymphatic system which transports fats around the... Hey, you're embarrassed aren't you? You don't like hearing all this, it's making you uncomfortable. Yes, that's it, you suffer from a sort of squeamishness, an inability to stomach the truth of what you really are. You'd prefer to forget about all this sordid animal physiology wouldn't you?

Cause I just don't find it interesting.

Effect That's because you're a vigorous young man with other things on your mind, but you wait until something goes wrong... It's all there Andrew, it's all there: your pancreas, your liver, your kidneys, your gall-bladder, your spleen...

Cause Yes yes, I've got the picture thank you.

Effect Your prostate gland, your adrenal glands, your thyroids, your pituitary gland... Ah, that's it isn't it? You hate to be reminded of your *mortality*.

Cause Yes, who doesn't?

Effect Your nervous system, your spinal cord, your motor neurons, your tongue, your taste buds, your ears, your eyes, your cerebellum – your brain's muscular control-centre, your olfactory system which detects smells, your optic lobe which processes the information from your eyes, your cerebrum or front part of your brain, responsible for the faculties of memory, language, learning and ratiocination, your cerebral cortex – your brain's outer layer which is generally regarded as the seat of consciousness, your...

Cause Ahh! My *consciousness*! At last! Now, hold on, tell me more about my consciousness Malcolm, tell me what *that* is made of.

Effect I... I... Er...

Cause Tricky isn't it? I have a friend who's a neurologist, an expert, quite a big name actually. Do you know what he said to me once: "For years I have been studying the intricate mechanisms of neurochemistry. I constantly wonder at the miraculous complexity of the human brain; at its awesome ability to receive signals, make calculations, issue commands, millions every second. It would take me a thousand lifetimes to begin to fathom it out; the more I learn, the more mysteries I uncover. Then, on top of everything, there is this *consciousness*. But that is something else, that is something different. You're the philosopher, that is your department." That's what a neurologist said to me, word for word. I'll never forget that.

Effect So what do you want *me* to say, what can *I* add?

Cause Well one thing you can add: you can tell me when and where in Darwinian evolution this elusive consciousness first put in an appearance. After all, you originally billed your account as science's explanation of how mentality came about, yet up to now I haven't heard a single mention of it.

Effect I suppose it all depends what you mean by 'mentality'.

Cause Ah no, it depends what *you* mean by it. This is *your* story remember. Presumably, at the very least mentality implies consciousness, so let's start with that shall we: when and where?

Effect Hmm... Er... Well, er...

Cause Come on Malcolm. You could doubtless put a rough date or era on the first appearance in the world of photosynthesis or of blood-circulation or of feathered flight, so what's the problem with consciousness?

Effect Perhaps one should say that consciousness evolved, gradually, that it came into existence bit-by-bit, that it developed as the animal species developed.

Cause Oh no, either a creature is conscious or it is not. Consciousness admits of no half-measures.

Effect   But that's simply not true: one can be drowsy, half-awake, semi-conscious as we say; we sometimes talk too of people attaining higher states of consciousness or heightened levels of awareness. Besides, you seem to be assuming that other forms of animal consciousness must necessarily be more or less like ours.

Cause   And you seem to be assuming that they must necessarily be in some way weaker than or inferior to ours. Especially odd in view of the fact that if alertness, keenness of perception and speed of reaction are anything to go by, most animals make most humans look *permanently* semi-conscious.

Effect   I wouldn't want to suggest that animal consciousness is inferior to ours Andrew, just that it is different, that's all.

Cause   So perhaps everthing is conscious, *in its own way*? Bats, bees, barnacles, bacteria...

Effect   Oh dear... Look, I'm not clear what it would *mean* to say that barnacles are conscious. Since I could never verify or falsify such an assertion, I don't...

Cause   Ah, I'm afraid it's too late for *that* particular positivist ploy. We've been through all that over other human minds. Besides, just a moment ago you happily used the phrase "other forms of animal consciousness".

Effect   Hm. Yes.

Cause   So where would you draw the line, and on what grounds?

Effect   I... I don't think I would want to draw a line exactly.

Cause   Oh come, you must be able to say *something*... Okay, let's start from the other end: give me an example of something which definitely is *not* conscious in your book.

Effect   Well... Stones. Obviously stones are not conscious.

Cause   Uhuh? And how do you know that? What makes it so, so *obvious*?

Effect   But... Surely... You're not seriously asking me to...

Cause   No need to get all het up Malcolm, just tell me how you know that stones aren't conscious.

Effect They're inanimate objects! They don't do anything, they can't behave in any way, they just sit there!

Cause I see, so behaviour is the criterion. And what if I were to point out that stones *can* behave? After all, they can roll down hills, they can beat against cliffs, they can crush skulls. And they can just sit there.

Effect But a stone can't feed and grow and die, it can't protect itself, it can't reproduce.

Cause No? Don't rocks feed on the sediment washed down by rivers or on the lava thrown up by volcanoes? Don't boulders gradually dissolve and wear and crumble into sand? Doesn't a flint protect itself with its hardness? Cannot a slate split into two?

Effect This is silly, you're just misusing words.

Cause Why, did you not yourself talk of organic molecules consuming one another? Did you not assert that the Earth's atmosphere shields it from harmful radiation? Did you not claim that proteins can replicate themselves? Which words did I misuse?

Effect But stones are, are just lumps of inorganic material!

Cause Oh, so the criterion is not an object's behaviour but its chemistry? You accuse me of foul play in the game yet you are concocting the rules as you go along. Think of, of an erupting volcano or a burning magnesium flare, or the sea, or an electric motor, or a flooding river, or the Sun, or an exploding bomb, or a boiling kettle: would you call all these inanimate objects, for none of them involves the chemistry of carbon compounds?

Effect Ah, well, yes, there is a sense in which...

Cause It seems to me grotesque that good, healthy, fertile English words like 'living', 'animate' and 'organic' should have got so arbitrarily mired in your obscure, impoverished scientific qualifications like 'carbon-compounded' rather than, say, 'hydrated' and 'cellular' rather than, say, 'granular' and 'oxygen-respiring' rather than, say, 'electrical' and 'vertebrate' rather than, say, 'spherical' and 'humanoid' rather than, say, 'lapideous'.

Effect Talk about the arbitrary use of words! What *are* you saying?

Cause I am wondering whether the ascription and non-ascription to objects of consciousness or animation have anything at all to do with these analytical, scientific distinctions of yours, however interesting and important they may be in their own particular ways.

Effect   But these scientific qualifications are not arbitrary or obscure, they are the necessary conditions, the actual connections that are found to exist in Nature. Their importance can be demonstrated!

Cause   How can you *demonstrate* a stone's lack of consciousness?

Effect   But what possible evidence could there be for ascribing consciousness to a stone!?

Cause   I repeat: one does not have evidence for ascribing consciousness to others, one has motives. As you said yourself, ascribing and not ascribing consciousness to others is exercising and failing to exercise one's imagination.

Effect   In which case, all I can say is that I cannot imagine a stone being conscious. Mnnnn... No, it won't come!

Cause   And does this tell us something about the stone or something about you?

Effect   I don't know, maybe it tells us something about both, about the relationship between human beings and stones, and about language too. Again, all I can say is that as far as I am concerned, only objects composed of biological, cellular material can count as living things.

Cause   Sticks then, what about sticks? They are composed of biological, cellular material are they not?

Effect   Yes, when they are attached to living trees, but...

Cause   Ah, now here's something I've been meaning to ask: what is the relationship between the life of an organism, this fir tree say, and the lives of its individual cells, the ones, for example, in... this twig?

Effect   I'm not sure that I've mentioned this so far, but it's a remarkable fact that in any complex living organism, like a tree, or Andrew Cause, the millions of individual cells which make up the organism are themselves continually growing, reproducing and dying throughout its life.

Cause   How about them then, the individual cells, they seem to fulfil your criteria. Could each of my cells have its own consciousness?

Effect   Don't be daft, the cells can only function as the constituents of the organism. And when their regeneration-processes start to slow down, that is when the organism as a whole begins to die.

Cause   Or vice versa. But there is some independence? This dying twig still contains living cells?

Effect   Ye-es, but...

Cause   So what about the tree then, the complex organism? The conscious conifer?

Effect   Do plants have feelings, all that? You'd better go and ask the para-science mob down in Arts Block.

Cause   Who, that loony Mister Eyewash with his lie-detectors and his lupins!? Leave it out! You don't believe that stuff do you?

Effect   Oh no, I wouldn't say I believed it, no, but...

Cause   But you think there's a genuine question?

Effect   Don't get me wrong, I'm, I'm ninety-nine percent sceptical about the whole para-science industry, but nevertheless I do think one should keep an open mind.

Cause   Really? You surprise me Malcolm.

Effect   No, my view is that one cannot sensibly talk of an organism's having feelings, pains or whatever, unless one can clearly demonstrate that it has *nerves*.

Cause   The jellyfish then? Didn't you say that the jellyfish has a simple nervous system?

Effect   Oh but that's little more than just a muscular reaction-mechanism. A jellyfish has no brain as such. Consciousness must have a seat.

Cause   Must it? Why a seat? Why not a dance-floor? Okay, worms then. So consciousness first *wriggled* into the world did it? How appropriate! I am right aren't I? Worms were the first creatures you credited with a brain?

Effect   We-ell, a brain in inverted commas I suppose, but...

81

A Defence of Privilege

Cause   It wasn't in inverted commas earlier on.

Effect   In reality though, we're talking about little more than a concentration of nerves.

Cause   "A concentration of nerves", that's a nice one! Are you listening, worms?

Effect   It's not really until one gets to the higher animals, the vertebrates, that the brain becomes a sizeable lump of tissue, capable of co-ordinating large quantities of muscular and sensory information. The cerebrum of a fish-brain, for instance, is still very, very tiny.

Cause   What does size matter? Every brain must have an outer layer.

Effect   The capacity of the cerebrum increases steadily through the amphibians, the reptiles and the birds, until in the mammals the cerebral hemispheres have become greatly enlarged, providing facilities for learning, recognizing, remembering...

Cause   Repeating...? I have heard all this before Malcolm, but what about *consciousness*? Where does *consciousness* first appear? In the Canadian catfish? The Tasmanian tree-frog? The great green iguana? The short-toed eagle? The anteater? The elk?

Effect   Hmm... Well... If by consciousness one means the ability to detect food, to react to danger, to respond to surroundings, to choose a mate, then yes, I suppose these creatures...

Cause   But feelings, do they have feelings? Do they feel desires, fears, pleasures, pains?

Effect   Obviously they have fears and pains, feelings of a sort, yes, but... Look Andrew, I don't want to deny it, animals are the genuine borderline cases, they stand half-way between...

Cause   Borderline cases!? What's the slightest bit borderline about, about a grazing deer, or a barking dog, or a courting pigeon? Why so begrudging in your ascriptions of mentality? Once again it's like trying to get blood out of a stone! As though this 'consciousness' were some priceless magic privilege of Nature which you are desperately trying to guard on Man's jealous, insecure, guilty little behalf.

Effect   But we *are* special Andrew: only the human brain has the enor-

82

mously enlarged cerebrum necessary for genuine intellectual faculties: the ability to wield the concepts of language, to make mathematical calculations, to analyze and store prodigious quantities of information...

Cause And so the behaviourist caterpillar turns into a butterfly!

Effect To apply and manipulate abstract theories, to discuss and evaluate moral principles, to formulate and implement social ideologies...

Cause All the things that foul us up.

Effect To contemplate, to imagine, to hypothesize. To investigate questions of logic and linguistics and psychology. To indulge in just the sort of speculative activities that we are indulging in: scientific research, philosophical argument and, indeed, evolutionary explanation...

Cause Careful, or hardly any *humans* will qualify!

Effect To create and appreciate great art, to identify and solve complex cosmological mysteries, to experience and communicate deep spiritual insights, to...

Cause To look where we are going? You got so carried away you walked straight past the car!

Effect Oh, so I have.

Cause And you have gone right round in a circle. Your story of evolution is most interesting, but as you have so clearly demonstrated, it seems to provide no convincing answers to questions like "What does mentality consist of?", "Which other objects in the world have minds?" and "How do I know that other people have feelings?", the sort of questions that are of concern to me.

Effect Okay, okay, so *you* answer them! They're your damnfool questions! All I've heard from you in response to everything I've said has been scepticism; scepticism and dismissiveness and derision. You say something for a change, something positive.

Cause I may be sceptical Malcolm, but I don't mean to be negative. Though our investigation has not yet come up with any clear answer, I myself have found it most illuminating. We have stalked our quarry, other minds, from three directions now: through Mill's commonsense argument, via Ryle's positivist behaviourism and now by way of your Darwinian account of evolution. Each time the quarry has in some way or other remained elusive, has continually evaded our detection, has refused to be pinned down, and each time we seem to have ended up staring one another in the face. The road always leads back to ourselves.

Effect   I'm sorry, I don't follow you.

Cause   Remember our conversation in Market Square. The very first philosophical question I asked was "How do you know that other human beings have minds?" Implicit in the very phrasing of my challenge were the assumptions (a) that human beings *do* have minds and (b) that other things do not. The question was loaded. The general philosophical conundrum "How do I know that there are other minds in the world?" automatically translates in the human ear into the question "How do I know that other *human beings* have minds?" When we gazed around Market Square, it was only the other *human* bodies we saw which counted as our *candidates* for mentality-ascription.

Effect   True, now I think of it.

Cause   Again, in our discussion of behaviourism, when you found that your positivist analyses entitled me to use M-verbs to describe the behaviour of non-human objects like litmus paper or computers or the sea, you accused me of being metaphorical and anthropomorphic and finally you simply laid down a law: M-verbs, you insisted, properly apply only to *human* behaviour.

Effect   I did, yes. I remember that.

Cause   And just now, your account of evolution, which was supposed to have explained "how mentality came about", instead just offered on the one hand an ancestral history of the human body and on the other a bald reassertion of the unevidenced claim that the only true mentality in the world is human. Yes, you *half*-granted a *half*-mentality to *some* animals, the 'borderline cases', but of course this is only because, being our near relatives, animals look and work and behave something like us.

Effect   I guess that's right.

Cause   But we have already concluded that the existence or non-existence of other minds is not something that I, that we, can prove or demonstrate. We have suggested that our belief in others has more to do with psychological needs or motives than with any rational assessments of which objects in the Universe are conscious and which are not. In fact of course, all we are doing is identifying with our own zoological kind, evincing our intellectual herd-instinct.

Effect   But that's natural enough isn't it? With whom would you expect us to identify?

Cause   It may be 'natural' in the sense of 'common'. It may be that all other animals identify only with members of their own species, I don't know, I haven't asked them. But it certainly doesn't have anything to do with the objective recognition of other minds. Hop in, we'd better go.

Effect   So what do you conclude?

Cause   I can think of no better expression to characterize these tendencies of ours than 'philosophical racism'.

Effect   Racism?

Cause   Yes, you must have heard of it Malcolm: people calling one another funny names on account of some trivial, perhaps even imaginary, physical characteristic: Jew and Arab, Xhosa and Shona, Greek and Turk, Nigger and Whitey, you know the sort of thing... As often as not it ends in blood and at the very least the contestants regard one another as inferior, sub-human. In a comparable way, attributing or denying mentality to other objects simply on the basis of the similarity or dissimilarity to ours of their bodily characteristics – form, physiology and behaviour-patterns – is by nature the airing of a racial prejudice. Our 'special' prejudice we could call it. Hold tight.

Effect   Slow down Andrew, please. I'm in a hurry, but I would prefer to arrive in one piece.

Cause   What a day! What a view! It's strange. When I look over this landscape I see the sky, the rolling hills, the fields and the woodlands; I see some grazing cows, a flock of crows, a moving tractor, a group of hikers; I look down and see the dashboard, I see my arms and my legs, I see you sitting beside me. My vision takes all this in quite evenly and smoothly, it betrays no sense of any... identification problems, it skates over the surface of things, it registers no sudden jags or jolts.

Mining the Landscape

Effect I detected a distinct jolt when we passed that hiker girl, the one in the blue denim shorts; you almost crashed the car!

Cause And then we speak. I learn how to use the words 'I', 'you', 'we', 'he', 'she', 'it' and I hear you using them, other people using them... The world goes into the third person, whilst I... I.... I am reminded of a remark of Wittgenstein's in which he compared the 'I' of consciousness with the 'eye' of my visual field. Just as one's eye does not itself appear in one's visual field, so the subject 'I' does not belong to the world, but is rather a limit of the world.

Effect What about mirrors Andrew? Are you sure you're not just being tricked by language, by the coincidence of an English pun?

Cause Oh our language is tricking us alright, it is tricking us in all kinds of ways. 'Consciousness' has become a common noun like 'cow'; so has 'woodland', 'sky', 'sunshine', 'life'. The phrase 'other minds' functions grammatically like 'those hills over there' or 'the products of my imagination'. Our language has mined the landscape with smoke-bombs and booby-traps of every sort.

Effect Language has enabled us to understand a great deal about the landscape though. It has enabled us, for a start, to learn how the landscape and the many life-forms that adorn it have come about.

Cause And it has tricked you into trying to deliver a third-person description of mentality. It has tricked you into trying to describe a person-less world, a world where there can be no-one either to offer or accept such a description.

Effect What are you saying, that the world did not exist before there were humans around to witness it? Are you trying to do a Berkeley?

Cause By no means. What I am trying to do is remind you that no world existed for humans, that there were no human perceptions or descriptions of any world before there were humans around. A simple example: when the first birds first flew, the world changed; not just in becoming inhabited by flying animals, but in becoming visible from the air; *that's* when the Earth became round. Berkeley was right in his way: what did or could an all-thing, no-person world exist *as*? For whom? To whom? In whose vocabulary could phrases like 'this inanimate stone' or 'the age of the Earth' or 'the origins of life' feature? I am not saying that the Earth did not exist then, I am pointing out that all that exists for us now are our assertions, descriptions and images of an uninhabited planet, our theories, explanations and text-books of the species' evolution.

Effect   So you are suggesting that the Darwinian account of evolution is untrue, or in some way subjective on our part?

Cause   I've no doubt that many of the events and phenomena that you've been describing *did* happen, but I regard your attempt to explain them in purely impersonal, b-verb language as being systematically inadequate, incoherent and misleading. As to your account's subjectivity, obviously it is subjective in so far as it is delivered by human beings in human language; for all your apologies and your zoological modesty, it was no coincidence that the climax of your story was the arrival of Homo Sapiens. No, in the end, my verdict on your account is: interesting, but so what?

Effect   How do you mean "so what?", so you and me.

Cause   Exactly. It is *our* evolutionary history, so naturally and rightly it is of especial interest and importance to us, but to accord it any greater or more general significance is merely to be anthropocentric. Every object in the world has an evolutionary history of some sort or other: molecules, stones, cells, cars, planets. Objectively, as you yourself have admitted, our story, our branch of evolution, our direction of adaptation is just one amongst many.

Effect   Maybe we can't help being anthropocentric though?

Cause   Again, take the case of computers, robots, machine-evolution: already we have computers which can calculate, remember, solve problems, identify faults, use and respond to language; we have robots which can propel themselves around on wheels or legs, can avoid obstacles, can recognize and manipulate objects. Already people are talking of machine-intelligence. Do you not think that someday we may credit computers with consciousness, ascribe machines mentality?

Effect   Oh I can't really imagine so. Computers run off electricity, they are not self-sustaining.

Cause   Who is? We each have our own particular ecological dependencies, everything has.

Effect   But you can only get out of a computer what you put in. These machines are all designed and built and programmed *by us*.

What a Nerve?

Cause We are all the children of our parents, we are all the products of our education.

Effect But these machines are metallic, they are not flesh-and-blood. They can't have feelings, desires, pleasures, pains.

Cause Can't they? Who says? And aren't they building, even now, machines which incorporate animal brain-tissue for its powerful memory capacity?

Effect I don't know. Sounds like science-fiction to me. Maybe. So?

Cause So, what with modern surgical advances in mechanical and electronic body-implants, the gap between human beings and robots is narrowing rapidly. And it's early days Malcolm, it's still early days. Who can say that we won't soon be confronted by questions about machines' moral rights?

Effect Well let's cross our bridges as we come to them shall we? I imagine that in practice we will discuss thoroughly any questions that arise, case by case. At the moment I have no doubts at all: as far as I am concerned, men are men and robots are robots.

Cause Are they though, and will they always be? I'm thinking not just about robots changing, but about you changing, your concerns changing... A while back you insisted that a brain and a nervous system are prerequisites of consciousness, but of course then arise the questions "What constitutes a brain?", "What counts as a nerve?" Is not a dashboard a car's brain, its wiring loom a nervous system?

Effect It looks as though this car's had its brains dashed out!

Cause Are not robots co-ordinated by computer brains of silicon? Are not their movements controlled by motor nerves of hydraulic hose? Perhaps the DNA molecule is a cell's brain, for according to you it has to store prodigious quantities of information. And what about the nucleus of the carbon atom, supposedly the inspiration for all of this?

Effect Oh come on Andrew, you are just misusing language again.

Cause Am I, or are you just re-displaying your prejudice? The issue is always pre-judged with you: you are *determined* to define mentality in such a way that only Man can qualify. It is not enough to behave, it has to be *human* behaviour; it is not enough to be brain and nerve and flesh-and-

88

blood, it must be *human* brain and *human* nerve and *human* flesh-and-blood. Animals are borderline only because they are something like us; robots will become candidates only when they become humanoid. There is anthropocentric prejudice wherever you look. It seems you can conceive of *no* non-human mind.

Effect   Ah no, not true. There is a form of non-human mentality of which I can conceive, and which I can conceive as being higher than ours.

Cause   Uhuh, and whose is that, God's?

Effect   I can conceive of there being intelligent life in Outer Space. Happy?

Cause   Over the Moon. Now who's been watching cheap movies?

Effect   No, not movies, astronomical facts. The statistics indicate that there must be quite a number of planets in our galaxy which have a composition and conditions similar to those of Earth and which are therefore likely to have generated some form of organic life. Given that on Earth the evolutionary process has produced a species capable of space-exploration and radio-transmission, there is a good chance that other technologically advanced life-forms, with similar capabilities, exist elsewhere in the galaxy. At this moment therefore, radio astronomers are carefully combing the radio sky for intelligent signals and we are sending out deep space 'messenger' probes and our own 'beacon' transmitters.

Cause   It's funny isn't it, all these scientists desperately searching for evidence of life in Space with huge radio telescopes and batteries of satellites, when all I have to do is to look up on a clear night and open my eyes.

Effect   Oh you're a UFO-spotter are you, I should have guessed.

Cause   No no, the stars Malcolm, the stars. There you are, once again you are not searching Space for life or intelligence per se, you are searching it *for things that resemble Homo Sapiens.* You are searching for creatures that look and behave and function something like us, that build machines something like ours, that transmit the sort of radio signals that we transmit. Our kind of so-called intelligent life is the only kind you will deign to recognize.

Effect   Yes, well... Anyway Andrew, you will be relieved to learn that as yet nothing definite has been detected. As a matter of fact, this failure presents us with something of a mystery.

An Ominous Silence

Cause   Oh splendid, why?

Effect   Well, if, as the statistics predict, intelligent life-forms do exist elsewhere in the galaxy, it is highly likely that some of them will have been around for longer than we have. So given the current rapid rate of our own technological progress, they would need to have been around for only a few moments longer than us, in terms of cosmological time, for them to have been able to colonize whole areas, if not *the* whole area of the galaxy; at the very least, they should by now have been able to identify the other habitable planets. In other words, if there are other advanced life-forms that are the slightest bit older than us, we would expect evidence of their existence to be everywhere. Indeed, we would expect them to be here. The question is: why aren't they?

Cause   That's easy: any life-form which gets smart-assed enough to master all this technology immediately blows itself to bits and burns itself out, exactly as we are poised to do. Either that, or the aliens have been here, taken one look and said *no thanks!*

Effect   Hm. I prefer to believe that we've greatly underestimated the complexity and delicacy of the conditions needed to initiate the whole organic process. I suspect that planets like Earth may in fact be a lot rarer than we presently assume.

Cause   It seems to me that you are making far too many assumptions all round. Who knows what alternative evolutionary histories are possible? Who can say what would have happened here if the Earth had been slightly hotter or if there had been less ammonia in its early atmosphere or if some other sort of proteins had won out in the molecular soup? What would have happened if the first creature to crawl successfully from sea to land had been a starfish or a sea-snail? What would have happened if the first vertebrates had had a different bone-structure or if the dinosaurs had survived the ice-age? What would have happened if pigs had grown the first feathers, or early man had chosen to become a swimmer?

Effect   Also, there have been many fortuitous but crucial circumstances in the course of human history: the balance of ethnological and geographical forces that generated the great Mediterranean civilizations; the coincidence of English chemistry and coal and capitalism that sparked off the industrial revolution; the geological gifts of oil and uranium that have fuelled our recent rapid advances in mass-production and high technology.

Cause   Athens might have been hit by an earthquake. Newton might have been born a dunce. Hitler might have got the bomb. Again, one wants to say: a hell of a lot of happy accidents. The curious ring of this remark should tell us something.

Effect   I know people have often said this in times past, but with all due detachment and objectivity it does seem as though we have now entered a particularly critical period in our and the Earth's history.

Cause   Of course another grand assumption made in your postulation of other galactic travellers is that that is the way in which *we* are going to develop. The idea that Outer Space is the next big Frontier; a kind of repeat-performance of the Europeans' great voyages of discovery and empire-building; ever-mightier machines to carry us to ever-farther new colonies in search of ever-richer sources of raw materials. But perhaps evolutionary advance *doesn't* consist in heaving great lumps of metal around the galaxy. Perhaps it consists in learning how to live properly here at home, how to live within one's adaptations, how to live together.

Effect   I thought you were the one who wanted us to fly?

Cause   Not before we can walk Malcolm, all of us. You are taking me too literally. I tell you one thing: if any intelligent aliens *do* exist on other Earth-like planets, one can hardly imagine that they will be exactly like us; at the very least they'll have pointy ears and green skin. So if our own, sordid, racist little history is anything to go by, when we do make contact with their expanding empire, with the best will in the world and all the philosophical insight in the galaxy, there will be a fight. You say that if they've been around for a cosmological moment longer than we have they should be here by now. I suggest that if they have been around for *five minutes* longer than we have, they will have worked this out for themselves and will have realized how foolish it would be to send out probes and radio transmissions. The last thing they would want to do is to give away their position; no wonder the *intelligent* radio sky is dark.

Effect   One hopes of course that any civilization that was that advanced would have got over any racist past.

Cause   Not so in our case evidently. Indeed it is the motive of military advantage that, above all, is driving us up there. Already the place seems to be infested with spy-satellites, laser-satellites, anti-satellite-satellites, anti-anti-satellite-satellites and so on.

Effect   There is another technology on the horizon which could also make a nonsense of our assumptions: genetic engineering. The pace of evolutionary change is itself taking a quantum-leap forward. We can now actively interfere in the process of random mutation, can speed it up, can contrive new genetic formations. Already we are seeing the artificial synthesis of novel proteins. This research could lead to all sorts of exciting developments in immunology and the fighting of decay and disease. We may even learn how to limit the effects of the ageing process.

Cause   So you said. Immortality, the biochemists' El Dorado! The Promised Land where the only growth-industry is moral philosophy! Ah well, if you come up with anything, put me on the waiting list Malcolm. I'll settle up with you later.

Effect   One day it may be possible to select precise characteristics in one's offspring, perhaps even to weed out the genes that carry our violent, racist and warmongering instincts.

Cause   Yuergh! Who would do the selecting and the weeding out, and why? It would only become another weapon in some war-effort.

Effect   You seem to be a compulsive pessimist.

Cause   Ah, perhaps they'll be able to weed that one out too. Of course, of course, it's all in the genes. It's all worked out, it's all programmed so that the top-dog species, the one with no more natural enemies, automatically turns upon itself to keep the whole show on the road, a sort of autumn wind that blows from within. Our racisms are in the genes, our theory of genes is in the genes, our philosophical attitudes are in the genes, perhaps even this conversation is in the genes!

Effect   Steady on Andrew, slow down.

Cause   Tell me this Malcolm: forget the tinkering, suppose that we, you, had complete control over genetic structure, could design and synthesize genes, DNA, chromosomes et cetera at will, what would you come up with? How do you see the ultimate life-form, the perfect organism?

Effect   Oh really, what a ridiculous question!

Cause   You think so? Okay then, how do you see man winding up? What is your image of the ideal human condition?

Effect   Well I for one am pretty happy with my condition as it is.

Cause   Oh come on, you can do better than that.

Effect I've never thought about it. Why, what's your little dream then, I presume you have one?

Cause It's more of a nightmare I'm afraid: I see an adult human brain in a sterile, evacuated jar, its arteries connected to an artificial blood-supply, its neural cortex connected to computers, all self-controlled; no more bodily aches or pains, no more sickness, no more ageing; no more anger, no more worries, no more work; just pleasures, beautiful sights, sweet sounds. every desire perpetually enjoyed and satisfied; a perfect equilibrium... I see this set-up getting miniaturized and miniaturized: a micro-chip, a micro-brain, a micro-cell, a micro-molecule, a being so endlessly evolved, so ideally adapted to its surroundings, in a state of such consummate... **(BANG!)**

Effect Christ! What was that?

Cause Bloody hell, the silencer's dropped off again! Damn!

Effect God, it sounds like an aeroplane! We'll have to stop.

Cause I know, I know... There's a lay-by on the left here somewhere...

Effect Oh Lord, I'm half-an-hour late already.

Cause Don't worry Malcolm, don't worry, it won't take a moment... Right... Now, I'll crawl underneath and you pass me the tools, okay? They're in the boot... Shit! Everything's red hot! Ouch! There should be a pair of old gloves somewhere... Ta... Now... Ugh... Aghh... Bugger... Ah... Ugh... Ah... That's better... I need a hammer.

Effect Ermm... No, sorry, no hammer.

Cause No hammer? Are you sure? Nothing else that would do?

Effect Oh dear... Er... Er... No, I don't think so, er...

Cause I know, look, see where my left foot is... just beyond there, in the grass, that large round stone... Yes, yes, that one... Great, thanks... Now then... **(BANG! BANG!)** Oww! **(BANG!)** That's got it... **(BANG!)** Splendid! Right Malcolm, can you find me some wire and a pair of pliers, should be in the left corner... Lovely, ta... Nearly done... There, how's that?

Effect Very good. Hadn't you better start her up though?

Cause You don't trust me do you?... There... Quiet as a ghost!

The Germ of an Idea

Effect   A pretty tormented ghost I'd say... Well, as long as it gets us back to town...

Cause   Insh' Allah!

✳   ✳   ✳   ✳   ✳   ✳   ✳   ✳   ✳   ✳   ✳

Effect   Ah, I know where we are now.

Cause   I told you it wasn't far. You're only half-an-hour late.

Effect   Forty minutes... Tell me one more thing Andrew, before I go: what does all this add up to? You have persuaded me that there is much that I don't understand about the problems of mind and body, and I can see that in a strict sense I cannot *prove* that other people have feelings...

Cause   Or that other things do not.

Effect   But what is your conclusion? You have dropped lots of dark hints about possibilities of non-human mentality, but what have you in mind? What is it to be, good old-fashioned animism? Spirits in the rivers, the hills, the trees? Consciousness in sticks and stones and steering wheels? Perhaps you were serious about the sea?.

Cause   I don't know, I'm not sure yet, early days... One or two ideas do occur to me. Try this: the Earth has feelings.

Effect   The Earth!?

Cause   Yes. Not soil earth, but the Earth, capital E, the planet Earth. Perhaps the Earth has perceptions, feelings, thoughts, memories, purposes, dreams. Perhaps the Earth has a mind. Perhaps its climates are its dispositions, its weathers its moods. Perhaps its terrains are its characters, its fauna and flora its expressions. If you demand proof of brain-processes, think of the events that lead up to those great displays of emotion, earthquakes and eruptions: the complex interplay of stresses and strains throughout the Earth's crust which sometimes seethe up into violent, tension-relieving outbursts... Yes, maybe... Maybe the Earth is a person. Why not?

✳   ✳   ✳   ✳   ✳   ✳   ✳   ✳   ✳   ✳   ✳

3

CAUSES
and
EFFECTS

Effect But Andrew, I don't see what could be *the point* of calling the Earth a person.

Cause Ah, well, now....

Effect Oh look, there's no need to take me to the door, you'll only get caught up in the one-way system. Just drop me off at the corner here, that's fine.

Cause No trouble... In fact I was rather hoping you'd invite me in. I'd like to see what you guys get up to in these 'labs' of yours. Would you mind?

Effect Oh... Er...

Cause I guarantee I won't get in your way.

Effect Well, I...

Cause Please Malcolm, just a quick look.

Effect Oh dear, I suppose so, but...

Cause I'll be good, I promise... Ah, "Parking for Authorised Laboratory Staff Only". You will vouch for me won't you?

Just an Impression

Effect   Heigh-ho... Okay, follow me...

Cause   Is there anywhere I can wash my hands? I'm afraid they're a bit grubby.

Effect   There's a sink in my room.

Cause   I say, what an amazing place! So many passageways, so many doors!

Effect   It used to be a school, once upon a time. We're all due to move soon, to a new complex being built out of town. Personally, I quite like these old rooms, they are ideal for small-scale experiments: the thick walls, the high windows, the quiet.

Cause   It's funny seeing them filled with all this modern equipment though, all this electronics... Do you know what this place reminds me of? Walking down these old corridors, catching glimpses through half-opened doors of white-faced boffins staring into screens and scribbling away at desks, it's just how I imagine a medieval monastery might have been, with all the monks in meditation.

Effect   They are not meditating Andrew, they are experimenting, that is the difference.

Cause   Oh I'm sure, I'm sure. It's just an impression.

Effect   I'm afraid you are going to find my experiment rather disappointing after some of these, it will probably seem a bit, er, banal. Anyway, here we are. Hold on a moment, the lock's sticky, I always have trouble with it... Ah, there we go.

Cause   Hey, what's that? Christ, what a thick piece of glass!

Effect   Nice isn't it? We call it the Billiard Table.

Cause   You play billiards on it?

Effect   In a way. I'll explain. Oh, you can wash in the corner there; you'll find some hand-cleaner in the cupboard... My particular field of study is hydrogen-fusion, the fusing of heavy hydrogen nuclei to form helium, the reaction that takes place in the Sun.

Cause   And in H-bombs.

Effect   Yes. In the H-bomb it is uncontrolled, but for years now physicists have been trying to confine and harness this process in a reactor. If we are successful, we will at last have a source of virtually unlimited energy.

Cause   Uh-oh.

Effect   No, you're wrong. This time it will be quite safe. No radioactive waste, no bomb-making applications, just a limitless supply of energy with which we will be able to, to, well, solve virtually all the problems of...

Cause   You don't really believe that do you?

Effect   I believe we will do it, one day. When, I don't know. It is proving a very hard technology to master. The temperature has to be extraordinarily high for fusion to occur, and the super-hot gas, or plasma, can only be contained by a magnetic field. The trick is to hold plasma of sufficient density at a sufficiently high temperature for a sufficient length of time for a chain-reaction to get going. Various very expensive research projects around the world are getting there slowly, inching towards the high levels that are required, but so far no-one has managed to achieve all the necessary conditions in a single machine.

Cause   I thought some blokes recently claimed to have discovered a way of producing this fusion at room temperature? Something about heavy hydrogen being absorbed by the metal palladium.

Effect   Yes, well, their act did produce a lot of publicity, but other experiments around the world have since discredited their claims. I was always sceptical myself, it all sounded rather... too easy.

Cause   Uhuh? I heard the jury is still out.

Effect   Well I'm afraid the verdict here is: back to work on the plasma.

Cause   I don't know why you bother, we've got the real thing out there. If only we organized ourselves, we could get all we need from the Sun.

Effect   Yes Andrew, you'd look good in a solar-powered sports car. *That* would slow you down a bit.

Cause   So where does the Billiard Table fit in?

Effect   Well, during the course of all this research, there have been a number of surprising setbacks. Many of the predicted effects have not occurred and many quite unexpected factors have come into the reckoning. The traditional models of nuclear interaction have failed us in a number of

A Model Plasma

respects and there is still much mystery about what exactly goes on in a high-temperature plasma. One recent surprise is that nuclear polarity, the orientation of the particles' spins, turns out to be a far more important factor than predicted. It seems that the collision-rate can be greatly speeded up if the ionized...

Cause   Yes, yes, but the Billiard Table, what about the Billiard Table?

Effect   So, what we are doing here is trying to come up with some new model of heavy hydrogen collision which will explain why this polarity-factor has so much effect. If we succeed we may be able to suggest some way of short-cutting to the ideal chain-reaction conditions. At present I am still at the stage of calibrating the apparatus, testing the accuracy of the measuring-instruments and working out the margins of error. So far, we have been studying the collision-characteristics just of ordinary billiard-balls of differing masses and sizes. Later, we will be using balls with magnetic polarities, non-symmetrical mass-distributions, biased centres of gravity and so on. Also we are building electromagnets to fit round the table so that we can see how magnetic fields affect the balls' spins, polarities, trajectories and impacts. It's all pretty speculative, but something useful may come out of it.

Cause   Uhuh? You're getting paid for this are you?

Effect   Yes, well, now you come to mention it Andrew, *I* have work to do, so if you'd like to...

Cause   It's alright, I'll just sit and watch. You carry on.

Effect   Hm... Red ball stationary at x zero, y zero; white ball in AC1 at x minus 8, y minus 5, spin zero; impulse set at...

Cause   What's that box Malcolm? Why have you put the white ball in a box?

Effect   It's what we call an auto-cue. It imparts a certain momentum and spin to the ball; it's triggered electrically... Impulse set at 3.3... Instruments ready, fire! White ball collides with red, moving off to x plus 5, y minus 1.3; red ball comes to rest at x plus... (**RING-RING, RING-RING, RING-RING**) Oh damn! That bloody phone! Always the way isn't it, just when you're starting something!

Cause   Yes, usually your supper. Leave it Malcolm, don't answer it.

Effect   You're right, I'm not here. It's probably for someone else anyway... Now, where was I? Ah yes, red ball comes to rest at *x* plus...

Cause   Excuse me interrupting, but tell me something: why, in your opinion, did the red ball move off just then?

Effect   I beg your pardon?

Cause   Why did the red ball move?

Effect   Because of the impact of the white ball of course!

Cause   The impact of the white ball caused the red ball to move?

Effect   Obviously!

Cause   And you saw that, you perceived that?

Effect   Of course I did!

Cause   You perceived the causing?

Effect   How do you mean?

Cause   Well I assume that you and I saw the same thing, yet all I saw was: red ball stationary; white ball moving; collision; both balls moving; both balls stationary. I had no perception of anything that could be called 'a causing', I saw just a series of events. Tell me more about this 'causing' you witnessed.

Effect   Well, I heard a sound, the 'click' they made on impact, if that's what you mean.

Cause   Presumably though, this too was *caused* by the collision?

Effect   Yes, true.

Cause   And of course, *whatever* had happened on their impact would have been caused by it, according to you. Even if every time the balls collided they gave off sparks, or we heard the Afghan national anthem being played on the sopranino saxophone, these would only be more events caused, as you would say, by the collision. The point is: a causal relationship is not something that is itself perceivable. So the question is: what sort of a relationship is it?

To Hume it May Concern

Effect   Humm.

Cause   That reminds me: I always carry a little book of quotes with me, 'To Hume it May Concern'. It's often useful.

Effect   David Hume? He's your mentor is he?

Cause   My mentor, my tormentor, which you will. I like his writing, certainly... Here we are:

> Let us therefore cast our eye on any two objects which we call cause and effect, and turn them on all sides, in order to find that impression which produces an idea - the idea of causation - of such prodigious consequence. At first sight I perceive that I must not search for it in any of the particular qualities of the objects; since whichever of these qualities I pitch on, I find some object that is not possessed of it, and yet falls under the denomination of cause or effect. And indeed there is nothing existent, either externally or internally, which is not to be considered either as a cause and effect, though it is plain that there is no one quality which universally belongs to all beings and gives them a title to that denomination.

Effect   Right, so in asserting that *A* caused *B*, we are asserting that there is a *relationship* between *A*-events and *B*-events.

Cause   Exactly. Hume realized that we only affirm the existence of a causal relationship between *A* and *B* when previously we have observed a number of *A*-events being each time followed by a *B*-event. From an isolated observation of an *A* being followed by a *B*, we can conclude nothing about *A* causing *B*; for that, we need to have built up a history of observations of *A*s always being followed by *B*s. This relationship of *always being followed by* Hume calls 'constant conjunction'. His conclusion is that an assertion that *A* causes *B* can rest only upon observations confirming a constant conjunction of *A*s and *B*s.

Effect   Fair enough, so what's the problem?

Cause   Ah, well, now: compare the following statements. Hold on, I'll just write them up on the blackboard:

1. Whenever in the past *A* has happened, *B* has happened.

2. Whenever *A* happens, *B* happens.

3. *A* causes *B*.

4. If *A* happens, *B* will happen.

1 is a summary of our past observations of the constant conjunction of *A*s and *B*s. On the grounds of 1, we formulate the general rule 2, and we can justify inductively predictions about the future, 4. But where does 3 fit in?

Effect   4 is true only if 3 is true.

Cause   Yes, but we don't need 3 to be able to assert 4. The grounds for both 3 and 4 are 1 and 2. 3 does not add anything. Of course, as we mentioned earlier, nothing we have observed in the past *proves*, in the deductive, mathematical sense, what will happen in the future; the certainty of 2, 3 or 4 is only as strong as the evidence that supports 1.

Effect   But surely 3 means a great deal more than 2? If 3 is true, then there is a sense in which if *A* happens, then *B* somehow *must* happen.

Cause   Exactly! In asserting that *A* causes *B* you are implying that if *A* happens, then *B*, in a special sense *has* to happen; you are implying that a relationship of necessity binds the two events, a relationship much stronger than that of simple constant conjunction, a relationship that turns 4 into *a law* of *A-B* occurrence. This extra relationship which is implied by 3 but not by 2 was christened by Hume 'necessary connexion', with an 'x'.

Effect   The 'x' is significant is it?

Cause   Maybe it is, in a way. At any rate, I will continue to use it to mark the Humean sense. There is something else in Hume's jargon that I'd better mention too. He distinguishes between two different sorts of mental event: 'impressions' which are, roughly speaking, equivalent to our immediate perceptions; and 'ideas' which are altogether weaker experiences and include our memories, reasonings, imaginings and so on. The necessary connexions of causal relationships, not being perceivable, Hume classifies as ideas. The big question is: where do these ideas come from? Could it be, Hume asks, that we get our ideas of necessary connexion from our personal experiences of being able to *do* things? The suggestion is swiftly rejected:

> ... to convince us how fallacious this reasoning is, we need only consider that the will being here considered as a cause has no more a discoverable connexion with its effects than any material cause... In short, the actions of the mind are, in this respect, the same with those of matter. We perceive only their constant conjunction.

Effect   Yes, I see the problem. So what does Hume conclude?

Cause   He concludes that our idea of a necessary connexion existing, for example, between *A*-events and *B*-events derives purely from our repeated experiences of perceiving *A*s being followed by *B*s. The mind, he suggests, develops a habit of moving from *A* to *B*, of expecting a *B* on seeing an *A*, and it is this habitual mental transition or expectation which gives rise to our idea of a necessary connexion between *A*s and *B*s:

> It appears then, that this idea of a necessary connexion among events arises from a number of similar instances which occur of the constant conjunction of these events... that after a repetition of similar instances, the mind is carried by habit, upon the appearance of one event, to expect its usual attendant and to believe that it will exist. This connexion therefore, which we feel in the mind, this customary transition of the imagination from one object to its usual attendant, is the sentiment or impression from which we form the idea of power or necessary connexion. Nothing farther is in the case.

Effect That's final is it? Well, it does seem a fairly plausible explanation, I admit.

Cause Yes, but an explanation of what? The trouble is that Hume's account is basically a psychological one. He has proposed an explanation of how it is that we come to have certain ideas in our minds and in our thinking, but so far he has said nothing at all about the existence or otherwise of any necessary connexions in the world. We are left with the question: do our ideas of causal necessity come from 'inside our heads', are they just the results of certain mental determinations or instincts or habits, or do they have as their source and justification the existence of any objective connections between events themselves? Positivism aside, this appears to be a genuine and important psycho/philosophical problem.

Effect And how did Hume get out of that one?

Cause I'm not sure that he ever did really. He struggled with it all his life, and his writing shows a significant change over the years. In his early work, *A Treatise of Human Nature*, he is adamant:

> Our idea of necessary connexion is... nothing but an internal impression of the mind, or a determination to carry our thoughts from one object to another... something that exists in the mind, not in objects... Nor is it possible for us to form the most distant idea of necessity considered as a quality in bodies.

His early conclusion is that our ideas of necessary connexion are entirely subjective.

Effect   But surely he cannot simply *deny* the existence of objective causal connections?

Cause   No, for apart from anything else, his own account is itself a causal one. His whole theory rests upon the assumption that our ideas are *caused* by our impressions; that, for example, our ideas of necessary connexion are caused by the customary transitions of our minds from events to events. By the time Hume wrote the final version of *An Enquiry concerning the Human Understanding*, some forty years after the *Treatise*, he had become acutely aware of the awkwardness of his position, and ended up suggesting that our ideas of necessary connexion somehow *run parallel* to the causal connections that exist in the world.

Effect   But that is ridiculous! That makes it just a, a *coincidence* that our ideas of necessary connexion match the objective connections between events.

Cause   Worse I'm afraid, it also renders us systematically *ignorant* of any such objective connections:

> Here then is a kind of pre-established harmony between the course of nature and the succession of our ideas; and though the powers and forces by which the former is governed be wholly unknown to us, yet our thoughts and conceptions have still, we find, gone on in the same train with the other works of nature.

Effect   Mad!

Cause   Again:

> As nature has taught us the use of our limbs without giving us the knowledge of the muscles and nerves by which they are actuated, so she has implanted in us an instinct which carries forward the thought in a correspondent course to that which she has established among external objects; though we are ignorant of those powers and forces on which this regular course and succession of objects totally depends.

Effect   Crazy!

Cause   And:

> The scenes of the universe are continually shifting, and the one object follows another in an uninterrupted succession, but the power of force which actuates the whole machine is entirely concealed from us.

Mystery, What Mystery?

Effect Quite preposterous!

Cause Quite so.

Effect And you have time for this sort of nonsense do you?

Cause But Malcolm, is not this nonsense precisely *your own* position? Is it not precisely the position assigned to us by the assumptions of your science?

Effect What?

Cause Is it not your scientific conclusion that the real, objective causal connections between physical phenomena are systematically out of our reach, are forever hidden from us behind the veil of perception?

Effect The Vale of where?

Cause The veil of perception. Is it not a consequence of both your and Hume's conception of a causally-connected world that it is not directly knowable? Since all our information about the external world comes to us only through our perceptions, and our perceptions are themselves *caused* by things, the conclusion must be that the real world, the things which do the causing, cannot directly be known. The causal processes involved in perception systematically place a veil between the objective, external world and our knowledge of it.

Effect But what can possibly be hidden from us here!? Red ball stationary, white ball moving, collision, both balls moving! Where is the mystery?

Cause Where indeed? And where is the causing? No causing, no mystery.

Effect Oh dear, look... look... All I know is that, that... that if I don't get these results in by one o'clock, I'll have missed the computer, so *please* let me get on and do some work!

Cause Of course. Sorry.

Effect Now, where was I? Right: red ball stationary at x zero, y zero; white ball in AC1 at x minus 8, y minus 5...

$$* \quad * \quad * \quad * \quad * \quad * \quad * \quad * \quad * \quad * \quad *$$

Cause Malcolm.

Effect Yes?

Cause Why do you keep repeating the same collision over and over again?

Effect In order to reduce the margin of error. For every set of collision-conditions, I do twenty tests and then average the readings.

Cause So the readings aren't exactly the same each time?

Effect Not exactly no. There are always bound to be minute, uncontrollable variations.

Cause So strictly speaking, the same thing can never happen twice? You can never actually *repeat* an experiment?

Effect I can, within specifiable margins of error. I've got the accuracy here down to plus or minus about two percent, which is good enough.

Cause Uhuh? And every twenty goes you are changing the characteristics of the collision in some way are you?

Effect That's right, yes.

Cause Ah, I see. I can't tell from here. And how many collisions have you logged so far?

Effect Well for this particular pair, I have worked out a programme-target of 100 different sets of conditions and at present I am about one third of the way through the series.

Cause So you have witnessed so far about 600 different, I mean individual, collisions?

Effect 640 in fact.

Cause And every time the white ball has hit the red, the red has started moving?

Effect What do you think?

Cause So on the basis of this evidence you would assent, presumably, to a causal law of the form: the impact of the white ball causes the red ball to move?

Effect Presumably.

Wha'appen?

Cause Uhuh, just checking... And you've got roughly another 1,400 collisions to go have you?

Effect Indeed I have.

Cause Heigh-ho. Okay, wake me up when you've finished, I think I'll take a little nap. I didn't get a great deal of sleep last night.

*   *   *   *   *   *   *   *   *   *   *

Effect Good God! Good Heavens! What on Earth!?

Cause Ergh... Eh... Rip-cord, where's the rip-cord? Wha'appen?

Effect Well I never! I wonder what caused that?

Cause What's the matter Malcolm?

Effect The ball broke! The bloody ball broke! I was on the 52nd set of tests: high impact, just off-centre, high spin-factor, everything normal; red ball on the spot, as normal; white ball ejected, as normal; collides with red ball, as normal; then crack! The red ball splits clean in two!

Cause And I missed it! Typical!

Effect I don't understand... The auto-cue seems to be alright...

Cause Funny isn't it: there's nothing quite so redundant as half a billiard-ball. You could use them as paperweights I suppose, it looks like you could do with a couple. What are billiard-balls made of incidentally?

Effect Glass. They're just large marbles really... No, nothing wrong with the white ball...

Cause Is that so? I would never have guessed that.

Effect Nothing wrong with the table... I don't know, it's most odd.

Cause Ah well, at least it has let you off doing any more of these awfully boring tests.

Effect Don't you worry, I've got plenty of spares. I must complete the series.

Cause But that's cheating! You can't just go on as though nothing has happened! Surely, this is an event like all the others? You must either accommodate this surprise in your proposed model or scrub the whole thing.

Effect But obviously this anomaly is quite irrelevant as far as nuclear fusion is concerned. I'm sorry if it's going to spoil your morning Andrew, but I'm afraid I must carry on with my...

Cause But Malcolm, Malcolm, here we have a real mystery! You can't just ignore such a turn-up! Look, forget all the nuclear fusion bit for a minute and let me inaugurate an entirely new area of research: billiard-ball disintegration.

Effect But what's the point? I'm not interested in billiard-balls!

Cause Ah, but I am, now. So tell me: how many collisions had that ball undergone, from new?

Effect Oh, er... It broke on the... 1,033rd go, to be precise.

Cause Plus the first one, the bosh-shot.

Effect Oh yes, the 1,034th go then.

Cause Right, so suppose I now make the general assertion that billiard-balls like this, undergoing tests like these last for only 1,033 collisions. What will you say?

Effect Well obviously one would need more evidence before coming to any conclusion like that. Besides, the white ball has already lasted for 1,03<u>4</u> collisions.

Cause Okay, so let's run through some more tests, you said you've got plenty of spares.

Effect Oh really! It would take weeks to...

Cause Only joking Malcolm, only joking... No, we can *imagine* all the possible results, that will be enough. Come on, put down your toys for a while and let's talk.

Effect But my tests! The computer! I've got to get the results in by one!

Cause You'll never be finished by one, it's gone half-twelve already.

Effect   So it has. Damn!

Cause   Don't worry, the billiard-balls can wait. I guarantee that a good chat will be far more valuable.

Effect   Well, I certainly won't get them done in time now, you're right there.

Cause   Is there anywhere we can go that's a bit more... comfortable?

Effect   We could try the common room I suppose. It'll probably be empty on a day like this. There's a coffee machine too.

Cause   Fine.

Effect   It's just down the corridor...

* * * * * * * * * * *

Cause   Ah, dexion and haircord, very tasteful!

Effect   The chairs are more comfortable though, that's what you wanted wasn't it?

Cause   So what, in your opinion, could have caused that ball to break?

Effect   Well obviously, its internal structure must have become weakened in some way. Perhaps shock-waves from the repeated impacts focussed on flaws, causing the molecular bonds to rupture and stress-fractures to spread throughout the...

Cause   That's funny, I had assumed it was the series of collisions which caused it to break.

Effect   Presumably it was, yes, but...

Cause   So why all this 'molecular bond' bit? Even before we've guessed at any possible test results, here you are diving into stuff about shock-waves and stress-fractures and flaws in the crystalline structure of the...

Effect   The structure's not crystalline Andrew, glass is not a crystalline substance.

Cause   Glass not crystalline?

Effect Nope. It is what we call an 'amorphous' material. Strictly speaking, it's a liquid, it flows.

Cause Glass a liquid!? I've heard it all now! You scientists come out with some real beauties don't you?

Effect No honestly, glass flows. Very slowly at ordinary temperatures, but it does flow. If you take an old pane of window-glass and measure its thickness at the top and its thickness at the bottom, you'll find that...

Cause Well well, so glass is a liquid. I'll try to remember that next time I'm having a drink; or putting my head though a windscreen... Look, let's forget this internal structure stuff for the moment can we, and stick to the facts, to what we can observe. Suppose we were to test all of your spare billiard-balls to destruction: the first possibility is that every ball disintegrates on its 1,034th go.

Effect Ridiculous! Impossible!

Cause Not *impossible*, surely?

Effect Absurdly unlikely though, and certainly not worth discussing. Things aren't like that, as you know. Of course there would be variations.

Cause Okay then, second possibility: the balls last for 986, 1,023, 1,004, 994, 1,041 and so on collisions, all within a reasonable range of one another and averaging out at, say, 1,012.

Effect A bit more plausible I suppose.

Cause In this case, my original assertions about billiard-ball disintegration would have been proved roughly correct, and could be revised to include an "*about* 1,033 collisions" or an "*average* of 1,012 collisions". The behaviour of the original ball would have been shown to be unexceptional; it would have 'fitted in with' the observed behaviour of these balls. We would have amassed a certain amount of evidence upon which we could base predictions about the life-spans of similar balls subjected to similar testing in the future.

Effect Okay, but we would not have *explained* the phenomenon of billiard-ball disintegration.

Cause How do you mean, 'explained'?

Effect Well... Suppose, for example, that it is only the *red* balls which break so easily, and that the white balls last for five or five hundred times as long, or last indefinitely. What will you say then?

Cause That the white balls last longer, what else?

Effect But wouldn't you want an explanation of the differences in life-spans? Wouldn't it occur to you that the red colouring-agent in the glass might perhaps be weakening the red balls' molecular bonds and might thus be the cause of their untimely disintegrations?

Cause It might well occur to me to test balls of other colours, or indeed, to test red balls that had been coloured with a different agent, or made in a different way, or in a different factory; but I don't see that I would want, or need, to start speculating about any 'molecular bonds'.

Effect So if you found significant variations, you would seek no explanation of them?

Cause Tell me this Malcolm: what explanation would you give for the variation you have assumed we would discover in the life-spans of the red balls? You only found it plausible, remember, that they would last for *about* 1,012 collisions.

Effect Well obviously, there are bound to be slight variations in the balls' internal make-up: impurities, flaws, differences due to changed cooling-conditions during manufacture and so on.

Cause Suppose that to the best of your ability you eliminated all of these factors and yet still found variation, as you doubtless would; what would you say then?

Effect One thing I could say is that the machines which make the balls are not precisely controlled enough, their measuring instruments not accurate enough.

Cause But isn't this the same problem? Will you not claim that measuring instruments and ball-making machines are governed by the same sorts of causal laws that govern the balls? Machines are no more identical than any other objects; just as we cannot conceive of two billiard-balls' being exhaustively identical, so we cannot conceive of two thermometers' being exhaustively identical.

Effect In which case we would concede that the more precise detail of each ball's composition is simply outside our control.

Cause   Just as in your original collision-testing you conceded that there are always minute uncontrollable variations, happily resigning yourself to repeating each test twenty times and averaging the readings. Minute, uncontrollable variations seem to be in-built.

Effect   Exactly, at this level, we would have to assume that differences in molecular structure were causing the variations.

Cause   Would we? Hm. It's funny how the molecular hypotheses always come in at exactly the points where the ordinary testable ones run out... Anyway, consider now a third possible outcome of our imaginary stamina tests: suppose my original assertion that these balls last for about 1,033 collisions is *not* so clearly confirmed; suppose that we have to test a fair number, a hundred say, before any sort of pattern emerges at all, and that the average life-span works out at around not *one* thousand collisions but *five* thousand, with perhaps ten percent disintegrating in the 500-1,500 range and others surviving over 10,000. In other words the life-span of our original ball was well below the average but was not unusually so; it still fits in with the general behaviour-pattern of these balls. In this case, we would be unable to formulate any precise or useful law of billiard-ball longevity.

Effect   No, but the results could be analyzed statistically, and would be best expressed in the form of a graph which showed the relative probabilities of finding balls of particular life-spans.

Cause   Suppose that you again tried tightening up the balls' manufacturing process but still discovered this enormously wide variation, what then?

Effect   We would have to conclude that our ball-making technique is very hit-and-miss and that the balls' structure-formation is a highly sensitive process, susceptible to the least changes in manufacturing conditions. Indeed, we would probably try to discover a new, more reliable method of producing balls of a high, uniform quality. But just because the balls' individual life-spans cannot in this case be predicted with any accuracy, this does not imply that the laws of physics, and in particular, the laws of inter-molecular bonding, cease to hold.

Cause   How do you mean? What is the point of claiming that the supposed laws of physics still hold if you cannot use them to predict, even roughly, how long a billiard-ball is going to last? Surely, if ball-longevity can be expressed only in the form of a graph of statistical probabilities, then that is that; there is, as Hume would say, nothing farther in the case.

Always Description

Effect   Hm... Look, take an example of completely random behaviour, such as the tossing of dice. The chance of a die landing on any particular side is one in six. We cannot predict on which side it will land next, but only that if we continue throwing it for ever, one sixth of the throws will land on each of its six sides. Now the fact that the die obeys the laws of mathematical probability in this way does not imply that it does not also obey the laws of physics, for of course its behaviour throughout is subject to the laws of gravity, motion, friction and so on. It obeys the laws of probability precisely *because* there is no factor causing it to fall on one face more than on another. Indeed, if the throws of the die did *not* conform to the mathematical odds, this would prove not that random motion is non-mathematical, but that this die's behaviour is in fact not random, that something – a biased centre of gravity perhaps, or a magnet – is causing it to fall on a particular face more frequently than one throw in six. Going back to the billiard-balls' wide range of life-spans, we might summarize thus: individually, each ball obeys the causal laws of physics; collectively, their behaviour conforms to a statistical pattern.

Cause   Ah, this is where a clear distinction begins, if you'll permit the expression, to crystallize. When you assert that a phenomenon conforms to a statistical pattern, all you are doing is describing, in a condensed way, what has in the past been found to happen. Strictly speaking, the billiard-balls' behaviour does not *conform* to the statistical pattern, it *gives rise* to it, it *generates* it. If, later on, we discover a ball that falls outside the pattern, that disintegrates, say, after only fifty-two collisions, the pattern is redefined, the graph is redrawn. Nothing is broken. Causal relationships, by contrast, imply necessity. Each ball *obeys* the *laws* of motion, is *governed* by gravity, is *subject* to friction; everything that happens, *has* to happen. In asserting a causal relationship you are doing a great deal more than simply describing a previously observed constant conjunction or statistical pattern.

Effect   Indeed, we are trying to explain things' behaviour in terms of *general* laws. Laws which govern the behaviour of *all* moving bodies.

Cause   So you scientists always say, but the trouble is you never *do* provide explanations Malcolm, you never *can*. All we ever get from you are further descriptions that are disguised as something else, but essentially descriptions nonetheless.

Effect   How do you mean, 'disguised'?

Cause   Go back to the second possible result of our imaginary tests: the assertion that the balls last for about 1,033 collisions is confirmed, we agreed, if the tests yield figures like 923, 1,102, 980, 1,092, 906 and so on, averaging out at 1,012. The question now arises: do we have here a law of ball-longevity or just an observed pattern? The fact that the balls' behaviour is fairly uniform may fool you into concluding that it is governed in some way and that each ball has to disintegrate within that life-span range. But of course the difference between this second possiblity of narrow range with reasonable predictability and the third possibility of wide range with little predictability is only a matter of the shape of the graph. Both possibilities are confirmed statistically. Both are essentially descriptions of what is in fact found to happen. Both support predictions that are most accurately expressed in terms of probabilities. Even in the case of the first possibility, where every red ball breaks after *exactly* 1,033 collisions, any 'law' you might want to establish to that effect would again come down to a condensed description of what in the past had been observed to happen.

Effect If they did all break on exactly their 1,034th goes, that really would be something odd, something worth investigating. But I thought we had both accepted that this suggestion is utterly implausible?

Cause Is it any more implausible than the suggestion that your original ball was about to break would have sounded half-an-hour ago? As I recall, just before that unexpected event, you had canonized the law "The impact of the white ball causes the red ball to move". So you see, even a supposed 'law' as banal as this was in substance only a condensed description of what at that time had always been observed to happen; the balls didn't seem to take much notice of it. All that we can ever get, all along, are descriptions of observed constant and not-so-constant conjunctions of events, of observed patterns of behaviour. Always descriptions, never explanations. Hume was right: in the end, all our sciences can discover is *how* things happen, never why.

Effect But I have told you: if it is the why-questions you want answered, like "Why do the balls disintegrate after about 1,033 collisions?" then we will have to investigate the balls' internal composition: the effects of the cooling conditions during manufacture; the effects of flaws and impurities in the glass; the effects of colouring-agents on the molecular bonding between...

Cause Yes, yes, I know, I know. But any so-called explanation along these lines is again going to consist just of descriptions of behaviour, descriptions of constant and not-so-constant conjunctions, albeit more detailed and more generalized ones. We will again end up with a load of

A Fundamental Mistake

"Whenever this, that" assertions: whenever there is a sudden drop in temperature..., whenever shock-waves focus on a flaw..., whenever molecules of colouring-agent K are present... and so on.

Effect   Well, if you want an even more detailed explanation, I could always go into atomic theory with you, and teach you about the electrical and nuclear forces that govern the interactions of the particles which make up the...

Cause   No thanks, not now. I can see that all I am ever going to get from you is more of the same. Even if you end up intoning the supposed fundamental law "Like charges repel, unlike charges attract", what is this but just another description of what is supposed to happen, formally another constant conjunction: whenever like charges..., whenever unlike charges... I can still ask the question: yes, but *why* is it that like charges repel? The difference is that the entities and events which feature in the constant conjunctions have by now become so obscure and problematic, the so-called 'explanations' so axiom-like that the asking of further why-questions at this stage starts to echo with pointlessness.

Effect   Obviously, in principle one can go on asking why-questions for ever, but to do so can become merely perverse and childish.

Cause   You misunderstand me Malcolm. I am not simply indicating the potential endlessness of asking why-questions, I am trying to explain why it is that you scientists cannot, in the sense you seem to require, answer why-questions *at all*. You can give us facts, descriptions of phenomena, recordings of constant and not-so-constant conjunctions of events and so on, but none of these can ever elucidate the causal connections which you assume to be their source.

Effect   What then, are you a latter-day Humean? Is it your conclusion that the causal relations, the necessary connexions between events in the world are forever out of our reach, that we can never, so to speak, get at them?

Cause   By no means. No, it strikes me that the manifest awkwardness and absurdity of Hume's conclusion should point us in another direction altogether.

Effect   Oh, and what is that?

Cause   Simply to deny the existence of necessary connexions, in either our thought or the external world.

Effect   What!?

Cause   Well, why make this inference of objective causal connections in the first place? We get nothing but trouble from the assumption, so why not try doing without it? This *does* seem to me to be an interesting experiment, and so far I have discovered nothing that refutes such an hypothesis.

Effect   What hypothesis, that causal connections do not exist?

Cause   In a nutshell, yes. Why don't we just stick with our observations of constant and not-so-constant conjunctions and leave it at that? Why make this further peculiar and problematic move of inferring the existence of unknowable necessary connexions? So long as we avoid a causal epistemology like Hume's ideas-and-impressions scheme, we will have no problems at all; at a stroke, the veil of perception problem dissolves, the free will problem dissolves, the...

Effect   You must be mad!

Cause   Mad? What have I said that's mad?

Effect   If there were no cause-and-effect in the world, if there were no connections between events, everything would be chaos, disorder, anarchy, it, it would be... impossible, impossible!

Cause   But of course there would be order! There *is* order! And there is disorder too. Remember: some events always follow each other, are constantly conjoined, like your original series of collisions; some events come out of the blue, are unexpected one-in-a-thousand occurrences, like the first disintegration; some phenomena, like our imagined billiard-ball longevity results, show wide or not-so-wide statistical variations; while in the extreme example of this, the die-tossing, behaviour can be perfectly random. In other words, there are constant conjunctions of events in the world, there are surprises, exceptions, there are patterns and there is randomness. This is all just as true for me as it is for you.

Effect   But if events occur in patterns and in constant conjunctions, certain things must be causing them to do so, and surely it is worth our while trying to find out what those things are?

Cause   No, no, no! By continually dragging causality into your thinking, you are neither guaranteeing nor illuminating the order and sequence in worldly phenomena, any more than you are banishing or explaining the disorder and randomness in them; all you are doing is investing your ideas about the whole shooting-match with this dreadful *necessity*. Think: when the same thing happened over 1,000 times and the movement of the red ball followed the impact of the white one, this constant conjunction, you said, proved the existence of a causal connection between the two events; then, when the red ball quite unexpectedly disintegrated on the 1,034th go, your immediate reaction was to ask for the cause of that event; next, whatever the result of our imaginary stamina tests, the life-span of each ball, and even their variations, would, you claimed, be causally explicable in terms of their molecular structures; finally, even random behaviour, like the falling of a die, is, you asserted, subject to the causal laws of gravity, motion, friction and the rest. In short, according to you, everything that happens is caused to happen.

Effect   Well obviously, every event has a cause, yes.

Cause   So what does it mean to say of any event that it is caused? If it is axiomatic that every event in the world has a cause, what is the point in asserting this of any particular event? You are not marking any distinction or drawing attention to any special circumstance.

Effect   Erm...

Cause   It seems to me that you are going to fall foul of the Verification Principle here. If your "every event has a cause" slogan is axiomatic, then no empirical evidence is going to be relevant to proving it true or false, so as a good logical positivist you must concede that it is therefore literally meaningless.

Effect   But it is not, not *axiomatic* exactly... Empirical evidence *is* relevant, *does* prove it to be true. All around us, all the time, we observe things being caused to happen, we observe...

Cause   No we do *not*! All we observe are things happening! We never observe any causation, any necessity; what we observe are regularities, sequences, patterns; and *ir*regularities too. We have been through all that.

Effect   Oh but surely Andrew, if there is no objective relationship between events that are constantly conjoined, then...

Cause   But there *is* an objective relationship between such events, the relationship of their constant conjunction; that is it and that is all. There is no need further to postulate the operation of any mysterious causation or necessity.

Effect So according to you, constant conjunctions of events are mere coincidences, just matters of luck?

Cause No *no* ! Quite the reverse! Coincidences are conjunctions of events that are surprising, remarkable, one-off, they are the exact opposites of regularly concomitant events. It was not a coincidence that during the original collision experiments the same thing happened every time for over 1,000 goes. It was not a coincidence, though it was very surprising, that the original ball disintegrated on its 1,034th go. It would not be a coincidence, though it would be even more surprising, if it turned out that all the red balls lasted for exactly 1,033 goes before disintegrating. It would, however, be a coincidence if the balls displayed a wide variation of life-spans which averaged out at exactly 1,000.

Effect But why? 1,000 is just a number like any other, it has no special mathematical significance. It is only our peculiar decimal counting system that makes it look important.

Cause Yes, but it would constitute a coincidence because the result we had arrived at in our billiard-ball stamina tests would have turned out to be one and the same as an important-looking number in our counting system. It is not every unpredicted concomitance that is worth remarking. If, as we suggested, our tests showed the average billiard-ball life-span to be 1,012 collisions, we would probably not regard this as being a coincidence merely because it also happened to be the population, six years ago, of a Tibetan village fifty-seven kilometres from Lhasa, whereas we might well think it so if it happened to be the number on the door of your experiment-room.

Effect Aha! So *that's* why you suggested 1,012 as the balls' average life-span!

Cause How do you mean?

Effect Why, 1,012 *is* the number on the door of my experiment-room: lab 12, first floor.

Cause Good heavens! What a coincidence!

Effect Oh come off it, don't tell me you hadn't noticed?

Cause No, honestly, I hadn't. It must have registered subconsciously I suppose.

What a Coincidence

Effect   Anyway, surely the point is that we call a concomitance of events a coincidence when although they occur together, we know that there can be no connection between them. So if, as you seem to be suggesting, there is no connection between events which are constantly conjoined, this presumably implies that all regularities are just series of repeated coincidences?

Cause   No, for if a coincidence is repeated, it ceases to be a coincidence. If we find that one event is always or often concomitant with another, we *do* infer a relationship between them, namely the relation of their constant or not-so-constant conjunction... Ah, now, there are times when the word 'coincidence' is used ironically, quizzically, as if with a raised eyebrow, when someone wants to suggest that there is perhaps more to a phenomenon than meets the eye, that perhaps after all there *is* some relationship between the events which has not yet been duly acknowledged. If, for example, the average billiard-ball life-span actually *did* turn out to be 1,012, the number on your door, you would doubtless regard this, dismiss it, as being a *pure* coincidence, while our ever-imaginative Mr. Eyewash would probably insist that this is *too much* of a coincidence to ignore and might well want to repeat the tests in the next room to see if the result there came out at 1,01<u>3</u>.

Effect   But that's ridiculous! How could there possibly be a connection between the number on a door and, and...

Cause   I didn't say there could be Malcolm. I don't suppose there can. That is why such a result would constitute a coincidence. It's funny how the mere mention of Mr. Eyewash irritates you so.

Effect   Well anyway, he'd have a job: room 1,013 is the broom-cupboard. I suppose he could have a chat to the mops about their aches and pains.

Cause   And explain to the hoover about necessary connexions.

Effect   I know! An example of a constant conjunction of events where we do not say that the one causes the other: every morning at eight o'clock, the alarm clock on my bedside table starts ringing...

Cause   Uhuh? I'd imagined you to have one of those automatic radio things, I can just see you waking up to the eight o'clock news.

Effect   Well yes, I do actually. Anyway, also, every morning at nine o'clock, the staff at the labs here arrive for work. So there's a constant conjunction of my...

Cause What time do you get in?

Effect Ah, well that varies, it depends whether I'm...

Cause Lucky for some eh?

Effect The point is there's a constant conjunction of my, my radio's going on and the staff's arrival at the labs, yet we do not say that my radio causes them to arrive on time, for obviously, none of them even hears it.

Cause Not much mileage in this one I'm afraid. Firstly, in choosing a phenomenon which involves human action, you have dragged in the free-will problem. I doubt if you would say that the lab staff are *caused* to arrive on time, even by their own alarm clocks; caused to wake up maybe, but perhaps free to choose what to do from then on. Secondly, to the extent that there is an apparent constant conjunction of events here, there is, in your terms, a causal connection between them anyway: a shared time-frame and synchronized clocks. Thirdly, there must be many occasions when the conjunction simply does not hold: Sundays, strikes, 'flu epidemics, power cuts, alarm clock breakdowns. And of course all we have to do to disprove it completely is to set your radio for the nine-thirty news.

Effect There isn't a nine-thirty news, but I see what you mean. Hm... I'm sure there must be an example...

Cause I'm afraid there ain't. The fact is that in moving from "*B* always follows *A*" to "*A* causes *B*" you add nothing whatsoever in the way of substantive meaning; you neither need nor imply any extra observations or evidence, you merely endow the observed conjunction with a mysterious, imaginary necessity. Remember that a "*B* has always followed *A*" statement provides just as strong grounds for predicting future events, it is just as useful as an "*A* causes *B*" statement.

Effect But surely, when you assert that there is a causal relationship between two events, you are implying that there is some sort of mechanism which accounts for their conjunction. In the alarm-clock example, you talked of a causal relationship between my radio's going on and the lab-staff's arrival for work, namely our shared time-frame and synchronized clocks. Similarly, what is implied by "*A* causes *B*" but not by "*B* follows *A*" is the existence of some kind of network of connections that can be traced from *A* to *B*, that if pressed for details, one could explain *why* it is that *B* follows *A*.

Cause "The white ball hits the red ball and the red ball moves". What could be or needs to be explained here? Why does a 'Why?' come into it? Certainly a scientist may want to highlight the detailed sequences, subtle patterns and unobvious conjunctions through which phenomena are related, but however minute his examinations, all he can ever derive from them will be more generalized and specialized conjunctions of events, more comprehensive and accurate descriptions of what is observed to happen. Our different sciences may be able to go on amassing more detailed data about the world indefinitely, may be able to discover ever wider, ever more complex, ever more subtle patterns amongst phenomena, and no doubt many of these discoveries will prove very useful to us, but always, and all along the line, the name of the game will be description, never explanation. Science is systematically unable to answer why-questions, constitutionally it cannot.

Effect   Oh don't be daft, of course it can! Look... I flick the switch and the light goes on. You ask: why does the light go on? I explain that the light goes on because there are electricity-conducting wires leading from the bulb via the switch to the mains and, ultimately, to the power stations of the national electricity grid which generate an alternating potential difference across the bulb's tungsten filament, causing it to incandesce and...

Cause   They're strip lights Malcolm, not tungsten bulbs.

Effect   Oh yes, of course, silly me... Well, which generate an alternating potential difference across the, er... ends of the tube, causing the neon gas in it to, er...

Cause   I'm sorry, you're wrong. These are mercury vapour fluorescent tubes, nothing to do with neon at all, quite a different sort of process. I believe they contain an inert gas of some sort, but it is the mercury vapour's ultra-violet radiation hitting the fluorescent coating on the inside of the tube which produces the visible light.

Effect   Really? I'd always thought these were neon... Anyway, whatever sort of lamps they are, in providing some such electrical account, surely we are giving a useful answer to the question "Why does the light go on?", an answer which helps us to understand the phenomenon? Presumably you will not deny that all these things, the power stations, the cables, the wires from the switch to the lamp, the processes that take place in the tube and so on have something to do with the light's going on?

Cause   Hm, how casually you toss in "the processes that take place in the tube"... But of course these things have something to do with the light's going on. What they have to do with it, and all they have to do with it, is that so long as, and whenever, all of these conditions are fulfilled, the light goes on; or, more strictly, whenever in the past they have been fulfilled, the light has gone on.

Effect   And that's all? No explanation? No answer to the why-question?

Cause   That is all Malcolm. A b-language account of phenomena, which is what science, at any level, attempts to be, is not in the business of answering why-questions, it is in the business of amassing information, of describing how the world works.

Effect   But surely, knowing how something works means knowing about the interactions that cause it to work?

Cause   Ah, "knowing how things work", a nice ambiguity. Ryle, remember, analyzed 'knowing how' as a capacity to *do* things, not as a capacity to understand them, not as some mysterious apprehension of occult necessary connex...

Effect   Yes, yes, but forget Ryle, I *do* want to understand things! I want to learn how things work, I want to discover the causal connections between phenomena!

Cause   Imagine: you arrive at the scene of a motor accident; a pedestrian has been knocked down and killed; you ask...

Effect   You weren't the driver by any chance?

Cause   No, but I did witness this, a couple of months ago. He died instantly. A cracked skull. You could see his brain.

Effect   Yeurreughhh!

Cause   Yes. You ask: how did it happen? The answer you both require and receive will be in the form of a description, a description of the events that preceded the man's death: he stepped out into the road without looking; the road was wet; the car went into a skid; he tripped on the kerb; the bumper caught him on the...

Effect   Had the driver been drinking? Was he driving too fast?

Cause   No, I don't think so. The police took statements, but I don't think they were going to prosecute... Anyway, this description is enough. It

121

adequately explains everything that happened, except perhaps for the pedestrian's carelessness. It works as an explanation by describing a series of events which *fit in with* our past experiences of wet roads, skidding cars, stumbling human bodies and so on.

Effect   I suppose you were there taking notes were you Andrew, gathering material?

Cause   Again, someone asks: how does the neon light work? Depending upon the context, it might be appropriate to reply: first the three outer red rings strike, one at a time, then the white wavy lines and stars start flashing and finally the word 'Coca-Cola' lights up in red and the whole display is held for five seconds before the sequence is repeated. Or: you push this button here, like this. Or again: the DC potentials applied across the ends of the tubes cause the low-pressure gases in them to conduct; migrating electrons collide with the electrons in the neon atoms' outer orbital shells, exciting them into higher energy-states and causing them to emit quanta of visible light of reddish wavelengths – or so the story goes. Neon lamps, incidentally, thus involve a quite different sort of process from the one that occurs in these fluorescent tubes: the neon gas itself conducts the current and gives off the light.

Effect   I see. How come you know about all this?

Cause   Ah, it's a hobby of mine actually; I used to dabble a bit in optical sculpture. I haven't done anything for a while now, but I do get the odd sign-making commission: names of restaurants, clubs, that sort of thing... Anyway Malcolm, does anything strike you about these three different answers to the "Why does the light go on?" question?

Effect   Well the first answer would be informative, I suppose, to someone who had not seen the light working before, though clearly this is merely a description of an observed sequence of events. The second answer would presumably be an instruction to someone being taught how to operate the display. Only the third answer, it seems to me, provides any sort of genuine explanation of the phenomenon, elucidates the physics behind it.

Cause   So it may initially appear, but on examination isn't this third answer in fact exactly like the first, isn't it just a description of a sequence of events, events such as electron-migrations, electron/neon atom collisions, light-quanta emissions and so on? Are not the two answers in precisely the same, formally descriptive, boat?

Effect   Maybe, but surely the third answer is an explanation as well as a description because, as in the car-accident case, this account fits the neon's behaviour in with our past experiences of other kinds of electronic, inert-gas and photo-emission phenomena. Yes, that's it, that's it! One could say that the whole purpose of scientific explanation, atomic theory, particle theory and the rest, is to fit all physical phenomena in with one another.

Cause But what sort of a fitting-in exercise can this be? Will not such attempts at fitting things in always formally consist of the cataloguing of constant and not-so-constant conjunctions, the describing of patterns and sequences of events which resemble patterns and sequences we have known before?

Effect Okay then, what about this... You ask: why does night always follow day, why does summer always follow spring? I tell you of the near-spherical Earth's rotation about an axis and of its elliptical orbit around the Sun. Does not my account *explain* the daily and yearly cycles which you experience, does it not genuinely answer your why-questions?

Cause It does, yes. It does so by fitting my knowledge of the daily and yearly cycles in with a certain picture of the Earth and the Sun in Space, in with my past experience of the behaviour, in models perhaps, of rotating spheres, elliptical orbits, light sources and so on. Again, this so-called explanation consists only of a description of events which fit in with various observed constant conjunctions. You have elucidated no necessary connections, you have answered no why-questions.

Effect Ah, but if you want to know *why* The Earth orbits the Sun ellipti-cally, I can go on to teach you about how the force of Gravity, which endows the objects here on Earth with weight also causes the movements of the...

Cause But this is not answering why-questions Malcolm, this is just giv-ing a phenomenon a name! And a pretty banal name at that, for 'Gravity' is simply the Latin word for 'weightiness'. Where does that get us?

Effect Oh, debunking Newton now are we?

Cause Of course I'm not debunking Newton, I'm merely trying to clarify exactly what it was he did.

Effect Well he did a lot more than give a phenomenon a name. For a start he demonstrated that the same inverse-square law of gravitational attraction governs the motions of both an Earth-bound apple and the Sun-orbiting Earth. He didn't just give a phenomenon a name, he gave a huge variety of apparently very different phenomena *the same* name.

Cause   Exactly. What Newton recognized was the existence of a constant conjunction which occurs in an extraordinarily wide range of observable phenomena. Bravo, but he has got us no closer to understanding *why* there is a gravitational attraction between objects. Anyway, that's only the Earth's orbit, what about its spin? Why night and day?

Effect   Ah, now that's a bit more difficult actually. It probably goes back to the formation of the Solar System; there are a number of theories, but...

Cause   Oh let's face it Malcolm: the only way in which science can explain the world is by describing what happens in it. All it can do is list the facts and try to identify the sequences and patterns amongst them.

Effect   Okay, okay, maybe you are right in a sense, maybe scientific explanations *are* of the nature of descriptions, but they are none the less useful or enlightening for that. They are descriptions, as you say, with extraordinarily wide ranges of application, they are descriptions in terms of which we can relate an enormous variety of physical phenomena.

Cause   Aha, this is the crux. If, as you now seem ready to admit, descriptions of events and their conjunctions are all that we can ever get from a b-language science, then the conclusion must be that there was no point in looking to such a science for *explanations* of phenomena in the first place. We have been expecting of our science something which it could never have provided. Descriptions of phenomena, atomic and otherwise, can never constitute elucidations of the causal connections that you assume actually to relate them. It is interesting that in the modified outline which you have just sketched of the nature and purpose of scientific explanation, there was neither mention nor implication of any idea of cause-and-effect.

Effect   But surely we do need the idea of cause-and-effect to provide a sort of, er, conceptual framework upon which to hang our physical observations?

Cause   An interpretational strait-jacket in which to confine them, more like. And a dangerous strait-jacket too.

Effect   Why dangerous? What difference does it make? You can interpret causal relationships as consisting simply of conjunctions of events, and I can see them in the scientific way as dependent upon the existence of certain objective connections, what's the odds? Presumably we both agree on the facts, and that is what matters.

Cause Ah, the facts, yes, the facts... I'm afraid that whatever you mean by 'the facts' in this context, the sort of interpretation we put upon them most certainly *is* going to make a difference, all the difference in the world. For a start, the belief in objective causal connections generates, as we have seen, a systematically mistaken theory of knowledge: it inspires this endless and perpetually futile demand for answers to unanswerable why-questions instead of simply recommending a search for more detailed descriptive information. A causalist is never happy, when all useful research into some phenomenon has come to an end, to say: well, that is the way things are and that's that.

Effect I should hope not! Such an attitude would have been a prescription for remaining in total ignorance.

Cause By no means; rather it is a redefinition of what can constitute genuine knowledge. You see the trouble, one trouble with this futile trek of yours towards the mirage of causal explanation is that in no time at all it sucks you into the epistemological quicksand of an atomic sub-world. Notice how, in each of the scientific stories we have heard so far, – the litmus-reddening explanation, the origin of organic life, the genetic mechanism of species-evolution, the account of a billiard-ball's disintegration and the tales of electric light-emission – your causal assumptions have inevitably, and almost immediately, led us into speculations concerning a whole host of molecular and atomic and electronic causes and effects.

Effect Naturally. What is wrong with that?

Cause A lot of things Malcolm, a lot of things. This atomic talk of yours is full of dangerous traps; already it has tricked you in a number of ways. The account of the neon light was a good example. The first answer was a report of an observed sequence of coloured lights, the third a description of a series of events like electron-migrations, neon-atom collisions, light-quanta emissions, remember?

Effect Yes.

Cause Although these answers were, we agreed, formally alike in being descriptions, yet you dismissed the first as being *merely* a description and hailed the third as providing a genuine causal explanation. Does this seem epistemologically sound to you?

Atomic Distraction

Effect I'm not sure, I...

Cause The reason why the third answer was able successfully to masquerade as an explanation was that it described events and phenomena *that cannot be observed*. This was a description from Hume's hidden world, the world beyond the veil of perception; this was an elucidation, as you tellingly put it, of the physics *behind* the observed phenomenon. You suggested that the account fitted the neon's behaviour in with our past experiences of electronic, inert-gas and photo-emission phenomena in the same way in which the motor accident description fitted that event in with our past experiences of skidding cars, wet roads and stumbling bodies. But of course the trouble is that we *don't have* past experiences of electron-migrations, neon-atom collisions, light-quanta emissions and the rest; these events are all outside the range of sense-perception and therefore do not feature in our experiences at all. What your atomic descriptions fit phenomena in with, if anything, is not our past experience of the physical world, but our scientific education, our inherited atomic jargons and pictures.

Effect But... But Andrew, when you say these are not within the range of sense-perception, you...

Cause You see: even now this atomic world of yours is threatening to divert our attention away from the subject under scrutiny, the idea of cause-and-effect. Let us try to keep atoms and the rest out of our discussion for the moment, we can come back to them later. For now, suffice it to say that your descent into an atomic causal sub-world predisposes you to expect that the connections between observable events will be only of certain particular kinds, kinds which are readily explicable in terms of whatever atomic theory it is that you have adopted.

Effect How do you mean?

Cause Go back to the billiard-balls: the original ball disintegrated quite out of the blue on its 1,034th go. We quickly started speculating about the various possibilities which might arise if we were to conduct experiments on ball-stamina. We wanted to fit that surprise event in with the behaviour of billiard-balls in general, right?

Effect I suppose you could say that, yes.

Cause And we found that this 'fitting in' could occur in a number of ways did we not?

126

Effect True.

Cause But now, there is another quite different possibility that we have not yet considered.

Effect Oh, I thought we had covered them all.

Cause No. Suppose that the behaviour of that original ball simply *cannot be fitted in*. Suppose that all the balls we subsequently test last for well over ten thousand collisions, or over ten million, so that the original turns out to be truly a rogue ball. What would you say then?

Effect Oh dear... I'd be pretty baffled I guess.

Cause Could this count as being an uncaused event?

Effect No of course not. Something must have caused that ball's rogue behaviour, even if we've no idea what. Perhaps it came from a different factory or a different batch. Maybe it went astray in the cooling machine.

Cause Suppose further investigations rule out any of these possibilities?

Effect Well perhaps... Oh, I don't know. More bafflement. I suppose if every hypothesis drew a blank, our final conclusion would be: something odd must have happened in this ball's history, but we don't yet know what.

Cause So a number of special features that attached to the original series of collisions would not even be considered by you as perhaps being of relevance. Certain hypotheses would not even get tested.

Effect I'm sorry, what special features, what hypotheses?

Cause Well for a start, couldn't one suggest that that original series of tests may have gone wrong because I wanted it to go wrong? Was that just a coincidence?

Effect What!? You mean...!? Of course! You sabotaged it! You had a go at the red ball while I wasn't looking! You cheat!

Cause Calm down Malcolm, calm down. Of course I didn't sabotage it. I didn't even touch it. I was asleep, remember?

Effect Oh yes.

Casting Aspersions

Cause Anyway, I wasn't thinking of sabotage. Couldn't simply *the fact of my wanting the experiment to go wrong*, my hope, have caused that ball to disintegrate?

Effect Your hope!? What, mind over matter? More Eyewash stuff? Are you seriously suggesting that the state of mind of the experimenter or of his audience can affect what happens in his experiment?

Cause Why not? If it's a causal law you want, I'm sure a law relating experimenters' mental states and their experiments' irregularities could easily be expressed in perfectly causal form.

Effect How preposterous!

Cause How interesting. How interesting that your scepticism of such an hypothesis should be so *vehement*. As though there were more at stake here than just the discovery, or non-discovery, of a new causal relationship.

Effect But of course there is more at stake! Such an hypothesis goes quite against all our past experience, it is completely counter-intuitive!

Cause Make your mind up.

Effect But we know things aren't like that! We know that things happen the way they do whether we want them to or not.

Cause Don't we also know that experiments always seem to go wrong when an audience is watching, when a demonstration is required? And after all, there is nothing counter-intuitive, apparently, about praying.

Effect Mm, I know what you mean about audiences putting a jinx on things, but that is just psychological, it has nothing to do with...

Cause Goodness, when I think back to my chemistry lessons at school, I can hardly remember a demonstration going *right*. It was a laugh a minute!

Effect Another thing about these sort of hypotheses: they are systematically uncheckable. Whatever happens, the believer can always claim to have been wanting it to happen.

Cause But one has to take the experimenter's word for the truth of his results in any kind of research, you said so yourself. Indeed I seem to remember you casually casting some aspersions about the integrity of...

Effect   Besides, such a relationship would be completely at odds with all our, our...

Cause   Our established ideas about atomic interactions? This is the crunch isn't it? This is why your scepticism of such a suggestion is so fervent. Not because such an hypothesis would not express a *causal* relationship, for it could; nor because such an hypothesis is quite contrary to experience, a claim with which some people might want to argue; nor yet because it carries certain problems of verifiability; nor even because it could not be 'explained' in some purely physicalist, b-language way, for after all, people's mental states according to your own account consist of neurochemical conditions in their brains; but above all because the confirmation of such an hypothesis would upset the applecart of your present atoms-and-particles picture too thoroughly and too irretrievably to contemplate.

Effect   Anyway, as you pointed out, you were asleep at the time.

Cause   So what? Are there not *subconscious* hopes and desires? The brain keeps working, you said so yourself.

Effect   Ah, now we really are in uncheckability-land!

Cause   Or, of course, I may have been pretending to be asleep...

Effect   You see: with such an hypothesis, there is no end to the let-out clauses available.

Cause   Exactly! And is not your atomic theory the biggest explanatory let-out clause of all time? Believing claims about what is happening in the subatomic world, or, as you say, in the subconscious, is not even a matter of trusting an experimenter's word, for these are claims which are *in principle* uncheckable, claims about events which are *by definition* beyond the range of sense-perception. Whenever an anomaly is observed, whenever the physical world springs a surprise, the atomic theorist can always change his tune, fudge his account or produce some let-out clause in order to preserve his central hypothesis. The main difference between the atomic scientist's let-out clauses and the para-scientist's is that the former can at present still be delivered without any obvious *blushing*.

Effect   So what are you suggesting then, that perhaps there *is* a connection between an experimenter's or his audience's hopes and his results?

Cause   What I am trying to demonstrate are the ways in which the explanations of the para-scientist are like those of the atomic scientist in being (a) expressible in typically causal form and (b) rendered virtually immune to disproof by their ability to generate more and more distant and obscure 'relevant antecedent conditions' which regress, in one way and another, into unverifiability.

Effect But are you seriously claiming that that billiard-ball shattered because you wanted it to shatter?

Cause Good heavens no! Of course not! Don't get me wrong Malcolm, I've got less time for Eyewash than you have, I don't even believe in his wincing wallflowers! I am simply trying to demonstrate how your atomic theory predisposes you to expect causal relations between observed phenomena to be of certain particular kinds. You tend to look only for relationships which will readily fit in with your preconceptions. You regard only certain sorts of hypothesis as being admissible, as worth testing. Thus, I suggest, your atomic theory may actually turn out to be a *stumbling-block* to your discovery of new relationships. After all, I don't find the suggestion that an experimenter's hopes, his brain-processes if you prefer, may affect his experiments' results intrinsically any odder than your account of, say, the electromagnetic transmission of television pictures or the genetic inheritance of animal characteristics or the explosive chain-emission of nuclear particles.

Effect Well you may not find it any odder, but I certainly do.

Cause That's because you've become set in your ways. I suggest that this whole causal view of the world, with its inevitable generation of an atomic, causal sub-world and its fatally limited b-language description of things is mistaken and misleading and unnecessary: mistaken in assuming that phenomena are governed absolutely by causal laws and are subject to an infinity of necessary connexions, be these laws and connexions known to us or not; misleading in that this assumption automatically invites a stunted, barren atomic theory which is incapable of accommodating any concept of mentality, freedom or value; and unnecessary in that we and our sciences could get along perfectly well, and probably better, without it.

Effect Humph! I think it's time for that cup of coffee.

Cause Yes, good idea.

Effect The machine's on the next landing...

✳   ✳   ✳   ✳   ✳   ✳   ✳   ✳   ✳   ✳   ✳

Cause Tea, coffee, cocoa, oxtail soup, cola, lemonade: there's a good choice.

Effect Hm, yes, but nothing I can really recommend I'm afraid. What would you like?

Cause Erm... Coffee please, white, one sugar.

Effect Okay, two coffees coming up...

Cause Thanks... Christ, it's disgusting!

Effect I know. I did warn you.

Cause It's absolutely revolting! I'll bet this has got as much to do with coffee beans as, as....

Effect As the soup has to do with oxtails. That's foul too.

Cause What's the point of giving you such a choice when it all tastes like puke? What a liberty! Who do they think they are? Another twenty pence down another bloody slot! Here, drink this, bastards...

Effect Oh don't Andrew, don't. You'll only gum up the machine.

Cause Good job too! About time! This is the only language that they understand.

Effect Some people do use it though. It's better than nothing. Each to his own eh?

Cause I know, let's go to the canteen in the English library. It's just round the corner from here, and they serve a *real* cup of coffee.

Effect Okay, we can leave by the side door. This way...

Cause I reckon after a while I'd be pretty glad to be moving out of this dump; all these gloomy corridors and gloss-painted walls. It all seems a bit like a prison somehow...

Effect Yes, well... So what is your conclusion about this cause-and-effect business? Are you recommending that we simply abandon all talk of causation, that we cease to use words like 'cause' and 'effect' altogether?

Cause In the end maybe, yes... But then again, no, perhaps not, perhaps that would be a bit, a bit... impractical. It's more a matter of investing, or rather, of *dis*investing, or *di*vesting these words of certain ideas and associations, of abandoning, for example, the belief in the existence of necessary connections.

Effect   Uhuh? This smells to me of the same insidious bet-hedging of which you were earlier accusing Ryle.

Cause   I don't think it does. Firstly, I am being quite open and honest about my intentions. Secondly, I am not asking you to deny or ignore any obvious or valuable truth; on the contrary, it seems to me that it is this utterly unjustifiable belief in necessary connections which is so insidious and dangerous... Besides, the verb 'to cause' does provide us with a very handy way of distinguishing between events which just happen to follow one another and events which are constantly conjoined.

Effect   Eh? But I thought you were claiming all along that these are one and the same?

Cause   No, no, *no*! Why are you being so perverse about this? Look, earlier on, right after the first billiard-ball collision of the morning, the telephone rang, remember? One event followed another, happened to follow another. You did not say that the collision caused the ringing because you know that such collisions are not regularly followed by the phone-bell. However you did say that the collision caused the motion of the red ball, for you knew that it had always done so. Saying that *A* caused *B* was just a convenient way of saying that *A* was followed by *B* and that *A*s are always followed by *B*s. The mistake I am trying to eliminate is the mistake of then assuming that because there is this constant *A*-*B* conjunction, there must therefore also be some further underlying relationship of necessity between *A*s and *B*s, some mysterious Humean 'necessary connexion' operating in every *A*-*B* occurrence.

Effect   So there's nothing actually wrong in talking about causation, so long as we think of it in the right way?

Cause   Yes, I suppose so. It's a matter of the way in which we see things. Don't worry Malcolm, I'm not the least bit sceptical about our vast body of scientific knowledge concerning the workings of the physical world, concerning its myriads of complex patterns and persuasions, not at all. Nor, if it comes to that, does my conclusion in itself directly affect how we ought and ought not to use that knowledge.

Effect   Well if that is the case, if this radical philosophical proposal of yours has no effect on what we do, then what on Earth is the purpose of propounding it? Why all this arguing?

Cause No *direct* effect on what we do, but plenty of indirect effect. Plenty of effect on what we say, for a start. If, for example, my conclusions about the status of the atomic theory were taken seriously, then...

Effect Yes, yes, I'm sure, but I and millions of other scientists find that theory indispensible. You'll just have to take my word for that.

Cause Uhuh?

Effect So realistically, practically, what possible advantage could there be in people's 'seeing things' in this crazy new way of yours?

Cause Well, one immediate advantage event-conjunctions have over causal laws is that they are never broken or confounded. A discovered exception to a physical law proves the falsehood of that law, period. At the very least the old law has to be rewritten. By contrast, irregular events for a non-causalist are merely odd statistics to be noted down as data, they don't indicate that he had been making a mistake about the world, or had been saying things that were untrue. When, on its 1,034th go, the red billiard-ball shatters... When night finally stops following day...

Effect When *what*?

Cause When night stops following day. Didn't you say that one day it won't? Are there not places on Earth now where the nights and the days last for six months? Is not the spin-less planet Mercury a place of perpetual night and perpetual day? I gather that places have been discovered in the Universe where even the so-called laws of Gravity cease to hold.

Effect Well all I can say is: I wonder just how much your non-causalist scientist would have discovered about the world. I can imagine him clearly: sailing serenely around with a smug, enigmatic smile on his face, filling up notebook after notebook with a mass of superfluous data but never actually *revealing* anything. No shocks, no surprises, just a lazy philosophical *che sera sera*.

Cause You really do *refuse* to understand don't you? The non-causalist would be just as keen to spot relationships as you are. He would be just as inquisitive, just as mathematical, just as shockable, just as surprisable. I know what your trouble is: you are confusing your own psychological responses as an observer with the objective states of affairs in the world which you are observing. You must not be misled by your feeling of certainty that night will fall in a few hours into thinking that it somehow *must* do so. What we witness when night follows day is not an extremely necessary sequence, but an extremely regular one.

Effect   So from where, in your opinion, do they come, my beliefs in the existence of objective connections?

Cause   Ah, this, of course, was Hume's question: what is the origin of our ideas of necessary connexion? His answer, remember, was a psychological one:

> This customary transition of the imagination from one object to its usual attendant is the sentiment or impression from which we form the idea of power or necessary connexion.

Effect   And you agree with that?

Cause   No way, for his answer is itself a causal one. According to Hume, one's mind is *caused* to make its customary transitions, and one therefore cannot help believing in necessary connexions. I, on the other hand, am suggesting that our ideas of natural necessity spring from a certain philosophical upbringing, a certain philosophical point-of-view.

Effect   And how does that help? What is the difference between Hume's customary mental transitions and your philosophical point-of-view?

Cause   Well, an important feature of a philosophical point-of- view is that it can *change*. Just as there is no necessity attaching to the constant and not-so-constant conjunctions of events in the physical world, so there is no necessity attaching to the transitions of the human mind. Your ideas of necessary connexion, according to Hume, are *customary*. But the word 'customary' is beautifully ambiguous: customs can come and go; we can choose to change them. Scientists don't *have* to believe in causation any more than night has to follow day. Perpetual daylight *is* a possibility!

❋   ❋   ❋   ❋   ❋   ❋   ❋   ❋   ❋   ❋   ❋

4

FREEDOMS
and
LAWS

Effect Hold on Andrew, I think we should cross the road by the lights.

Cause Oh sod that, it's quicker here.

Effect I'll, I'll catch you up then, if you don't mind.

Cause The new English block's just around the corner.

Effect I know... Hey! Look out! Behind you!

Cause Wow! The bastard! There, no problem...

           *   *   *   *   *   *   *   *   *   *   *

Effect Hi.

Cause What kept you?

Effect I told you it was safer by the lights.

Cause I was perfectly safe thank you, despite that performance by the pig in the Porsche. You know, there are some drivers who will actually aim at you to prove they have the right of way. The canteen's on the top floor: stairs or lift?

Choosing Things

Effect Lift... Is this what they call the Buttery?

Cause That's right. It's the *in* place at the moment. Where all the debs and politicos come to plan their careers, and everyone else's. Still, it shouldn't be so crowded during the vacation, thank God. We can sit out on the terrace... Et voilà! You grab a table. Two coffees?

Effect Yup.

Cause Anything else?

Effect Nope.

Cause Two white coffees please... Ta... There, now that's more like it...

Effect Yes, good.

Cause Right. Now Malcolm, let's approach this whole causation question from the opposite direction: are you a free agent?

Effect What do you mean?

Cause All these recent choices of yours: tea/coffee, drinks machine/ English canteen, traffic hopping/lights crossing, stairs/lift; were they, in your estimation, all made entirely freely? Could you have chosen differently in each case?

Effect Of course I could, yes.

Cause And yet you made these choices in a world where every event has a cause?

Effect I, I don't follow....

Cause To put it simply, you scientists seem to present us with a very baffling pre-philosophical picture of things. On the one hand you claim that all physical events and states of affairs in the Universe are irrevocably linked together in infinite chains, or webs, of causal connection: -cause-effect-cause-effect-cause-effect- endlessly interwoven backwards into the past and forwards into the future. While on the other hand we know from our own experiences of acting freely that we ourselves can actually *do* things, can initiate physical processes, can bring events about, things and processes and events which have absolutely no causal antecedents prior to our own free choice-makings. The trouble is that the two ingredients in this simple picture of the world are mutually incompatible, inconsistent. Sooner or later, one or other of them has got to go.

Effect Oh come on, this is a totally naïve presentation of the scientific view, this is childish. Surely we are both agreed that things are not that simple?

Cause Ye-es... But maybe there's a contradiction here that *is* naïve and childish. However you put it, I think you are going to have a problem: if you say that everything that happens in the world happens according to some law of nature or is subject to some sort of physical necessity; if you say that everything in the world, including human beings, consists entirely of atomic particles whose interactions are governed by fundamental forces; or if you say simply that every event has a cause, whichever way you present your assumption, it seems to me that you are going to rule out any possibility of genuine human freedom.

Effect Why? It is beginning to strike me that you are the one who is obsessed by the idea of laws and necessities, not I. Obviously you are taking things far too literally. I don't think many scientists nowadays would want to characterize their assumptions as being like that at all.

Cause No doubt they wouldn't, when confronted by the problem of free will, but I'm afraid that these are the inescapable implications of the scientific view. Presumably, at the very least, you would go along with the general assumption that in any physical process, given a set of conditions A, B, C and so on at time t_1, then events or states of affairs X, Y, Z will occur or prevail at later time t_2?

Effect Generally speaking, I suppose so, yes.

Cause In other words, you nail your flag, naturally enough, to the mast of Determinism, the belief that everything that happens is determined by its pre-conditions. The trouble is, it doesn't matter how high up the mast you choose to do the nailing, any sort of determinist flag is going to be enough to take all the wind out of human freedom's sails.

Effect But... But I don't mean that...

Cause Don't worry Malcolm, you are in good company on this one. The Christian theologians have virtually the same problem when they insist upon the omnipotence of their God. And God doesn't have to be all-powerful either, his all-knowingness will do the trick. The point is that so long as at the time t_1 there is in the Universe a fact – God's knowledge, the state of my brain-cells or whatever – in virtue of which X rather than Y will happen at time t_2, then however it may seem to me, when t_2 comes, I will not in fact be free to choose Y rather than X.

No Consolation

Effect   But this is ridiculous! The human brain is extraordinarily complex, as your neurologist friend admitted. There is no way we could forecast people's choices from data about their brains. Even if our neurology were a hundred, a thousand times more advanced than it is today, I doubt if we could use it accurately to predict people's behaviour.

Cause   So it is just a matter of the present inadequacy of our knowledge? Complete predictability is theoretically possible?

Effect   We-ell, theoretically perhaps... But in practice there is no need for the idea to worry us one jot. Since we are nowhere near attaining, and will probably never attain, such knowledge, I don't see that it need affect us.

Cause   But Malcolm, this suggestion does affect me, it worries me greatly. It is totally at odds with my knowledge of what it is to be a free agent. All it leaves me with is the consolation that whenever one of my predetermined so-called choices occurs, it *seems* to me that I have a free hand in it. And of course that is not enough.

Effect   Well, if you insist on putting it that way, maybe that's all you are going to get.

Cause   But isn't it rather odd to suggest that our apparent freedom of choice depends upon our ignorance of all the complexities of human behaviour, when in common practice our ability to choose freely is so crashingly obvious and simple: tea or coffee, white or black, with sugar or without?

Effect   Actually, I prefer real coffee black, now you come to mention it.

Cause   Oh, I'm sorry Malcolm, I thought you...

Effect   It doesn't matter, it doesn't matter.

Cause   Also, in this case, I knew perfectly well beforehand what I was going to choose, without this knowledge in any way jeopardizing the freedom of my choice when I came to make it. Indeed, I always choose the coffee when I come here, I find it exceptionally good.

Effect   Exactly, so if I knew *everything* about your background, habits, tastes, states of mind and so on, I could, in any given set of circumstances, predict what you will choose.

Cause   You reckon?

Effect   In theory perhaps, yes.

Cause   Hm... One thing: you must not confuse predictability with pre-determination. Some people behave fairly predictably, but...

Effect   Most people behave very predictably I'd say.

Cause   Fairly predictably, very predictably, we are back with the argument over Mill's constant and regular sequences. It doesn't matter. People's predictability, however we estimate it and whether we consider it at an individual level or en masse, has nothing to do with their personal or collective *freedoms*. I was not caused to drink coffee, I chose to drink it.

Effect   Caffein can be addictive Andrew, did you know that?

Cause   Oh tosh! It's your belief in necessary connections that is addictive, that is dependency-inducing. You have become so hooked on causality that not only do you now regard *human* behaviour as being predetermined, which is bad enough, but you even go on to imagine a whole *atomic* world that is entirely law-governed and freedom-less too.

Effect   Not so, as it happens. There is indeterminacy built into particle physics, by virtue of the fact that at the subatomic level the very business of detecting particles – of measuring their locations, velocities, energies and so on – itself affects the quantities being measured. Heisenberg's Uncertainty Principle introduces a systematic margin of error, ignorance, or...

Cause   A necessary indeterminism, I know. But still the assumption is that at any given time every particle *does have* a location, velocity and energy. As in the case of human choices, you are trying to use your ignorance of the facts to fudge over the implications of your assumptions. This is not what I mean by freedom. My freedom does not reside in the indeterminacy of subatomic particles any more that it resides in your present ignorance of the state of my brain-cells.

Effect   Okay, okay, forget the biochemistry, forget the physics; can't I claim simply that your predilection for coffee, your desire for coffee *caused* you to choose as you did? There can be psychological causes of behaviour as well as physical ones.

Cause   Ah, so if the physics doesn't get you, the psychology will! Determinism rules of course! Hmm... Psyche, psyche, psychology, such interesting words; from the Greek, needless to say. In Greek mythology Ψυχή was a young goddess, Eros' own beloved, a beautiful girl with butterfly wings, while the common noun 'ψυχή' one finds translated as 'breath' or 'life' or 'spirit'. Then our English words 'psyche', catalogued as 'soul', 'mind', 'consciousness' and 'psychology', defined as the scientific study of the nature and functions of human mentality; *human* mentality, note that.

Effect   I know a couple who send their dog to a pyschotherapist vet.

Cause   And now we even have 'behaviourist psychology', Ryle's example of which we analyzed earlier, wherein immortal Psyche dies and is condemned to an eternity of empty bodily sleep-walking. What strange and terrible things philosophy can do to our understanding and our language! It can even trick men into trying to draw up a pseudo-scientific, determinist account of human psychology, into attempting an atomic, third-person, small-m-language description of mentality: the Freudian subconscious with its ids, egos, libidos, superegos and all that crew.

Effect   Oh, I know that fashion has turned against Freudian psychology and that people are now aware of its limitations, we now realize that there is a lot more to human motivation than the brute sexuality Freud was so fond of invoking, but still there are many aspects of our behaviour which can be explained in terms of the operation of subconsc...

Cause   Nonsense Malcolm, nonsense! They don't exist, it doesn't exist! *We* exist, we, with our bad memories and our fertile imaginations, with our hypocrisies and our laziness, with our self-deceptions, our lusts, our greeds and our cruelties. We exist, not they.

Effect   So will you now deny that psycho-analysis can be a valuable and successful medical technique?

Cause   Oh I'm sure it can be, sometimes. Confronting half-forgotten fears and memories, reawakening long-repressed desires and angers, re-examining deeply-buried beliefs and images, nothing wrong with any of that, sometimes. In a way that's what a philosopher is doing, public psycho-analysis. No, what I distrust is this proposal of another causal sub-world, this sketching of another imaginary landscape.

Effect   I think once again you are taking the account too literally, but still...

Cause   While we are on the subject, another thing I distrust is people saying "Oh we realize now that there's more to human motivation than sexuality"; not because it's not true, for it obviously is, but because it smells of a special sort of modern prudery, a superior "We're above all that unfortunate business now". 'Brute' sexuality you called it, tellingly, as though good honest desire for another is something base and shameful.

Effect Oh no, I didn't mean that, I...

Cause It is worth noting that Freud's subconscious world and its mythological inhabitants fulfil exactly the same explanatory role for the determinist psychologist as the subatomic world does for the determinist physicist. Both are invoked in their respective causal explanatons precisely at the points where ordinary phenomena run out or fail; both depend for their apparent explanatory success upon a dive into an unwitnessed sub-world, concerning which all claims are empirically uncheckable; both can be revealed to us only through the jargon of their respective self-appointed experts.

Effect But this is bound to be so. No-one would expect the causes of human behaviour to be anything other than extraordinarily complicated.

Cause What could be simpler than my wanting a cup of coffee? Unless, of course, you are suggesting that I suffer from a coffee-*complex*?

Effect I am beginning to wonder. But surely Andrew, you will not deny that people's behaviour is affected by their childhood experiences, by their psychological make-ups, by their parental influences, by their education, by their families' socio-economic circumstances and so on.

Cause What is this Malcolm, one single theory of human behaviour or a host of different ones?

Effect This is not one theory, but nor... nor are they different theories. They are not theories at all, they are... are different accounts that are appropriate in different contexts.

Cause How gracious of you to grant us such a choice! See: your search for the causes of human behaviour has become neurotic! What have we now? Our genetic structure, our evolutionary past, our neurochemistry, our subconscious mentality, our childhood experiences, our psychological make-up, our family background, our education, our socio-economic circumstances, our bla and our bla and our bla-bla-bla! Everything but our own free will! Some of the items you mention are of doubtful existence; some may have relevance in certain medical researches; some may be reasons for treating people in marginally different ways, but none of them is *a* *cause of human behaviour.* It seems to me that you are here displaying all the classic symptoms of a deep and powerful subconscious fear.

Effect   Don't be ridiculous!

Cause   The fear of your own humanity. The dread of responsibility. The reluctance to face the fact that it is *you* who causes your actions, not your brain or your subconscious or your background. Rather, it is you who acts. You chose coffee. You chose it freely. You could just have easily have chosen tea. A series of events took place then which had absolutely no other causal antecedents.

Effect   Heigh ho, I suppose so. They were only very very trivial events though.

Cause   They may have seemed trivial to you mate, but they meant life or death to some poor tannic acid molecule! The point is: *any* free action is enough to break and ruin the endless web of causal connections which you try to weave around the world.

Effect   Okay then, I'll tell you what *your* trouble is Andrew: you think that by exercising these trivial little choices of yours, you can somehow demonstrate or prove that you are acting freely. Freedom has become a sort of hang-up with you. You seem actually to work at being your own man, to cultivate unpredictability. I bet if someone were to forecast, on the basis of knowledge of your background, tastes, past choices and so on how you were going to act in some particular circumstances, and you knew of their forecast, you are the type of person who would deliberately confound their expectations if you could, whatever the consequences, just to prove yourself a free man. Your worshipping of freedom is a sophisticated sort of *virility-complex*. You are suffering from a subconscious fear of your own normality.

Cause   Oh quite probably; nothing subconscious about it. There is, as you say, a perverse tendency of human beings to *defy* the well-meant rules and predictions so carefully laid down for them by the determinist philosophers and their friends, rather like those particles of Heisenberg's that are impossible to pin down. And of course this perversity, God bless it, is just as much a fact of human behaviour as its general predictability.

Effect   Sure, but this tendency, in turn, is perfectly predictable and explicable; it proves nothing.

Cause   So you are bound to claim. Of course nothing can be proved either way. You, in your own perverse fashion, can go on claiming to be able to predict, or rather, you can go on claiming to be able to explain, with the benefit of hindsight, why people behave as they do ad infinitum and you can perhaps even incorporate predictions of how your psychological 'discoveries' will themselves change people's behaviour-patterns. But now, who will predict what your predictions are going to predict?

Effect   This is silly. Anyway, I thought we had agreed that predictability has nothing to do with freedom?

Cause   Right. Human beings, like billiard-balls, can behave individually and en masse, in all sorts of different ways. They can behave randomly, like tossed dice. They can behave perfectly regularly: the first 1,000 collisions, my regular choice here of coffee. Some of their behaviour is best expressed statistically: 30 percent of the customers choose coffee, 40 percent choose tea. And they can act completely out-of-the-blue, can behave out of character, can be the one-in-a-million, can do something unique.

Effect   Ah, that's why you chose to be a philosopher isn't it? That fits.

Cause   Not necessarily. All one has to do is be oneself. The point is: just as you asserted that however a billiard-ball behaves, its behaviour is caused, so I can assert that whatever human beings do, their actions are free. The statistics, however they come out, are quite neutral with respect to questions about *why* billiard-balls or human beings behave as they do.

Effect   I thought you said that why-questions were bogus?

Cause   Ah, well, now, there *is* a kind of why-question, or rather a kind of why-answer that is not at all bogus, namely one that seeks or provides an answer in terms of the desires, motives and purposes of a mind. Earlier on, in your lab, you flicked the switch and asked: why did the light go on? We then examined various descriptions of events, none of which actually answered the why-question. One answer however, that *could* have done so would have been because you decided to turn it on.

Effect   But you could still have gone on to ask why I decided to do so. This kind of why-questioning is potentially just as endless as the other.

Cause   No. If your further reply had been "because I wanted to see better" or, in that particular case, "because I wanted to use the light's going on as an example", this really would have brought explanation-seeking to an end.

143

Acting Rationally

Effect   But...

Cause   Oh I know that it is possible to utter further interrogatives like "why did you want to see better?", but to carry on doing so is perverse and pointless in a way that asking "yes, but why do like charges repel?" is not. Asking why things happen is asking for the reasons for their happening, and of course it is only persons who can have reasons.

Effect   So the answer "because I wanted to see better" works, according to you, as a genuine explanation, because you yourself know what it is like to want to see better?

Cause   Something like that I suppose. Remember: people are not caused to behave in these or those ways, but have motives, reasons and purposes for doing what they do, whereas things, purely physical events, just happen. It is people who ask for and who offer explanations of phenomena; it is to minds that explanations must explain. It seems obvious therefore that any explanations of phenomena which are going to provide more than mere descriptions of events or catalogues of their patterns of conjunction, are going to have to involve the motives, reasons and purposes of persons.

Effect   So, by crossing Berkeley with Hume, causal necessity might, after all, turn out to be an idea in the mind of God?

Cause   Minds of *persons* I said, not minds of ghosts or gods. I use the word 'persons' quite deliberately, precisely because I want to avoid any nonsense about disembodied mentalities or vital spirits or any of that stuff. The last thing I want to do is to swap your world-view, infused as it is by your mysterious, occult, causal necessities, for some equally abstract baloney about the world being sustained by the Will of God. I am simply talking about people having reasons for acting as they do, about people acting freely and rationally.

Effect   But I don't get it. However freely and rationally people may appear to behave, they cannot escape the laws of Nature. However hard one grits one's teeth, one cannot defy gravity and fall upwards. Obviously you are endowed with a wonderful imagination Andrew, but you are still a human being, still a physical object of mass M, subject to the forces of...

Cause   Yes, yes, I know. You really love rubbing it in don't you? Of course my freedoms are not boundless, of course I am not free to do anything I want, but...

Effect   Not boundless!? Oh do be realistic: on a cosmic scale there is hardly anything we can control. The seasons, the weather, the tides, even the processes of our own biochemistry are ninety-nine percent outside our powers. Don't forget that human bodies, and indeed whole human cities, can be crushed like leaves by earthquakes, can be tossed like confetti by tornadoes, can be burnt like kindling by, by...

Cause   Nuclear blasts?

Effect   Take the experience of being buffeted by the wind. You say, in view of our own experiences of having reasons and purposes for acting, that only accounts in terms of the reasons and purposes of others will explain phenomena to us. But can't I equally well claim, in the light of my own experience of being a physical object, of being caused, for instance, to stagger by a high wind, that only accounts in terms of causal necessity will explain physical phenomena to me?

Cause   Hm, interesting, "My experience of being a physical object": a suitable title for a scientist's autobiography perhaps? But no, this is the point: is there anything in this physical-object-experience of yours that implies the operation of any sort of *necessity* between phenomena? Are you not perhaps being misled by your experience of, for example, being unable to help staggering in a high wind? Your mistake is to move from the knowledge that winds *can* buffet, that nuclear radiation *can* burn, that earthquakes *can* flatten cities to the assumption that they therefore *must* do these things. After all, here we are caressed by a deliciously balmy breeze in gloriously comfortable sunshine on the top of a perfectly solid building.

Effect   I must say, it is very pleasant up here.

Cause   Besides, it is by no means just a trick-reply to point out that in any case we *can* do quite a bit to control these cataclysmic phenomena: we can construct our cities of brick and stone to withstand tornadoes, we can build them on quake-resistant foundations or on quake-free sites, and we don't then *have* to drop nuclear bombs on them.

Effect   Oh well, yes, all that's obvious. We can ameliorate the effects of natural disasters and we can guard against them to some extent, but we cannot truly control the natural forces that drive them.

Cause   That *drive* them, there's a new one; 'cause', 'move', 'drive', sometime we must go into the histories of these words... Meanwhile, I must say I find all this defeatism remarkable, coming as it does from someone whose whole career is presumably founded upon the assumption that we *can* control the forces of Nature if we try.

Own Goals

Effect   I am only putting things in perspective.

Cause   For my part, as a free agent, it is only the things which I *can* do that concern me, they are the only things worth discussing. Things that just happen, just happen. They are there to be coped with, they are the weather, to me they are not important.

Effect   Not important!? Your bodily processes!? Can you consciously control you food-digestion, your blood-circulation, your thermotactic system? Are these of no importance to you?

Cause   My *what* system?

Effect   Your thermotactic system, the highly complex, finely balanced mechanism by means of which your body maintains the constant temperature crucial for its survival.

Cause   Ah, now this is an example of what philosophers call a teleological process, a process that is goal-directed. The question is: how can such a process be goal-directed if there are no footballers around, or at least no footballers awake, to kick the ball?

Effect   Sounds like our home team.

Cause   Seriously though Malcolm, doesn't the existence of such a mechanism demonstrate the existence of some non-human purpose at work in the world?

Effect   It implies the existence of some non-conscious regulation at work in your brain, that is all. It must not be forgotten that in the chain of bio-chemical phenomena by which body-temperature is controlled, the normal laws of organic chemistry are obeyed throughout.

Cause   But isn't it platitudinous, or even circular, to keep reminding us of this? Like "every event has a cause", it adds nothing. It is the biochemical phenomena that come first, not your so-called laws of them. Don't such processes again demonstrate the hopeless inadequacy of your b-language explanation? Look, you yourself have used words like 'system', 'maintains', 'crucial', 'regulation', 'controlled', 'obeyed'. Your account is bursting at the seams with purpose.

Effect   Yes, but isn't this because in this case we know that the net result of the process, its goal if you like, is our own survival? Surely, one can only judge a chain of events to be teleological if one can identify a person for whom its effects are recognizably beneficial?

146

Cause   Exactly. Since every process happens, as you would say, entirely according to natural laws, one cannot judge, simply from an inspection of a given chain of events, whether or not it is purposive; *that* depends upon one's recognition or otherwise of other persons and their goals. As in the case of the species' evolution, the oddness of asking whether the human thermotactic system is purposive arises because, to anyone who understands the question, the desirability of their own survival is too axiomatic to require mention.

Effect   But surely, by this argument, every organism, indeed every object in the world, would in theory be able to look at the natural processes that have brought it about and sustain it and say: wow, yes, there *is* purpose in the Universe, *I* am its purpose!

Cause   Congratulations Malcolm! Bravo! And now, may I suggest a small celebration: the conscious initiation of a chain of events by means of which we will do the impossible and in some measure assume control of our rumbling stomachs our thinning blood-circulations and our rising body-temperatures. I propose that we get the hell out of here, nip back to my car, drive to one of the riverside pubs, grab ourselves a pie and a pint and keep out of this Sun for a while: sunstroke no thanks!

Effect   Yes, good idea. But we'll have to hurry if we're going to be there by two-thirty.

Cause   They open later now, in the afternoon.

Effect   Do they really, are you sure?

Cause   Yes, they've changed the law, didn't you know? The trouble is it's now up to the publican, so you can never be sure... And they usually stop serving food at two-thirty, so we may be able to get a drink, but... but anyway, we should easily get there by then.

Effect   So before we go, just tell me this: is it your conclusion that *everything* in the world is a free agent, planets, billiard-balls, atoms, the lot?

Cause   Okay, why not?

Effect   So the Earth chooses where to have its quakes?

Cause   Maybe. It is always true of an earthquake that it could have happened somewhere else, or at a different time.

Exercising Freedoms

Effect And that billiard-ball chose to do the same thing over a thousand times?

Cause Perhaps it was following the line of least resistance, as we usually do. That would seem to be pretty reasonable policy.

Effect But what sort of freedoms can a billiard-ball exercise? What can a billiard-ball *do*?

Cause Who knows? Remember that a freedom is not discovered until it is demonstrated. Perhaps a billiard-ball is capable of growing arms and legs and turning into a man. Perhaps it is capable of bursting into sunshine or of annihilating a city. Perhaps it is capable of generating an entire Universe.

Effect How preposterous!

Cause Maybe, but not unlike some of the stories you expect me to believe.

Effect But... But they are different, they...

Cause Why? Because the billiard-balls they feature are beyond the range of sense-perception? Because we are free to imagine about them what we will?

Effect So, so you'll say then that there are no laws of billiard-ball behaviour, only their habits and tastes?

Cause I don't know, maybe they just follow a rule. It does seem to be a characteristic of free agents to make little rules for themselves. It is their rule, you might say.

Effect Oh really, this is too fanciful for words! If you can say that, you can say anyth...

Cause Malcolm, come here, look: see those traffic-lights, down there beyond the trees... Now watch: every time a light goes red, the cars before it slow down and stop. Here we have an absolutely constant conjunction of events, a conjunction so predictable, so reliable, that we literally stake our lives upon it. Yet we know that in fact each driver is perfectly free to ignore the red light if he chooses and drive on.

Effect Not perfectly free Andrew. He must obey the law. There is a law about stopping at red lights, in case you hadn't heard.

Cause Uhuh? And how is this law different from the laws of physics which you claim billiards-balls must obey?

Effect Ah, well, they... they involve a quite different sort of necessity, a quite different sense of 'must'.

Cause How can you tell though, just from observation? Suppose that some of the cars down there were fitted with a device which stopped them automatically at red lights, would we necessarily be able to tell from up here which cars were fitted with the device and which were not? Come to that, doesn't an experienced driver in fact behave rather like such a device, doesn't he simply respond to the red light out of unthinking habit rather than conscious fear of law-breaking, braking, as he himself might say, *automatically*?

Effect I don't know Andrew, I don't drive.

Cause You don't drive!?

Effect No, I prefer to use public transport.

Cause You can drive though, you have a license?

Effect Nope. I've never really needed one. My wife drives me around sometimes, she has a small runabout.

Cause Uhuh? Well, well, you do surprise me... Anyway, again, suppose that instead of us standing here gazing down, it was one of your elusive galactic life-forms on a flying visit, trying to discover whether any of the phenomena he can observe involve mentality and intelligence and freedom, trying to decide which events are governed by which sort of necessity and which just happen.

Effect One point about these two sorts of necessity is that it is always *physically* possible to break a *legal* law. Of course, for if it were not, legal laws would not be, be... necessary.

Cause Yes, but how does our visitor know that? Suppose, unrealistically, that ET had no bodily axe to grind with respect to other-mind recognition, suppose that he himself physically resembled a... a... ugh, a piece of chewing-gum: how would he distinguish the persons down there from the things? What lines would he draw between billiard-balls and cars and drivers? Yes, the most interesting question about computers and robots is not "When do we start granting them mentality?" but "How do we programme them to recognize it?"

Effect Well obviously, if ET were to observe us in any detail, he would soon discover that it is we who build and drive the motor cars, we who design and install the traffic-lights, we who programme and use the computers. And if he were really patient and observant, he would perhaps come to recognize and understand our designing and manufacturing practices, our law-making and law-enforcing institutions and procedures, even our intricate systems of government too.

Cause I wonder... But in any case, whatever ET observed, if he were armed with your causal interpretation of the world, he would assert irrefutably, as you do, that everything that happens here happens according to natural laws. Human behaviour could appear to him just as predictable, and as unpredictable, as the behaviour of machines.

Effect Well, one difference he ought to be able to spot is the contrast between the ways in which we respond to a driver who jumps a red light and to a car which has a brake failure or a traffic-light which has a breakdown.

Cause Exactly. Men, we say, *do* wrong, whereas machines *go* wrong; and when they do so, we blame, rebuke and sometimes punish the men, whereas we examine, repair and sometime redesign the machines.

Effect But then, perhaps in a sense men *are* machines, they are just very very very complicated ones. Perhaps blaming and rebuking and punishing people *are* our ways of repairing and redesigning them.

Cause Perhaps, like behaviourist analysis, such a remark only carries its apparent plausibility because it is expressed in the third person. Perhaps, at this very moment, somewhere in the depths of Space, one of our foolish little probes is being tortured by a squad of imperial chewing-gums. Perhaps, if he gazed down at this road junction, with its ceaseless to-ings and fro-ings of inanimate particles, ET would fall in love, with the traffic-light.

Effect And perhaps it's time for that drink. Come on Andrew.

Cause Okay, hold on, first I must go to the loo.

$$* \quad * \quad * \quad * \quad * \quad * \quad * \quad * \quad * \quad * \quad *$$

Effect Uhoh, it looks like you've got another parking ticket.

Cause No!? Ah, it's alright, it's only a duplicated note: "Warning. Cars parked on these premises without authorisation may be..." Well you know what they can do with that! Come on Malcolm, hop in... (**WHRRRRR**) Oh *no*!

Effect What's the matter, won't it start?

Cause Just a second and I'll try again...

Effect What does that red light mean? (**WHRRRRRRRRRRRR**)

Cause Nothing! Not a peep! What a bastard!

Effect You couldn't have run out of petrol?

Cause Hold on... Concentrate... Now, please be a good girl, please... (**WHRRRRRRR**) How bloody odd, no spark at all. Damn, I'm going to start running the battery down if I'm not careful, and the engine's probably flooded. Blast!

Effect It couldn't be anything to do with the silencer could it?

Cause Excuse me, I'm just going to take a shufti under the bonnet.

Effect Look why don't we walk, we could still do it if we hurry.

Cause I can't leave the car here, they'll tow it away or something. Don't worry, this won't take a minute.

Effect Ho-hum.

Cause Yes, as I thought, the spark plugs are soaking; I'll have to let them dry off in the sun. Still, at least that means the petrol's getting through. It must be the ignition... Contact breaker looks okay... Rotor arm... Distributor cap... Plug leads seem clean enough...

Effect Aren't those connections a bit loose?

Cause That's normal, it doesn't matter on the H.T. Could you turn on the ignition please... (**WHRRR**) Ouch! The ignition I said, not the starter!... Ta... Now let's see: good contact, strong spark from the coil... I dunno, it all seems to be okay to me, I don't understand it... I'll put the plugs back and try again...

Effect All done?

The Joys of Motoring

Cause Touch wood... Okay, here goes... **(WHRRRRRRRRRR)** **(WHRRRRRRRRRRRRRR)** Damn and blast!! Absolutely bugger all!! You pig!!

Effect Calm down Andrew, calm down... Don't start smashing things...

Cause You bastard! Ouch! Damn you! We'll probably be late for the pub now and I'm starving! Thanks a lot! Oh now where's the bastard spanner gone?... Christ, the plug's soaking wet again, it's too bad!

Effect Just leave it Andrew, forget it.

Cause Okay, okay, one last time... Right... Choke, ignition, starter... **(WHRRRPLPLPLBRRRRRMMMMMMM)** Banzai! Brilliant! Great! Good girl, good girl!

Effect Thank God for that!

Cause Well how peculiar, just when I'd given up. A mystery, a complete mystery.

Effect Maybe there was water in the petrol.

Cause In this weather?

Effect Right then, what about this pub of yours? Which one did you have in mind?

Cause The Volunteer, down by the river. Okay?

Effect Fine.

Cause Good... Now... Back to the lights... Right into the High Street... Left down... Hey! They've made King Street one-way! How bloody mean! We'll have to go down Monks' Passage... What!? "Pedestrian access only"? How useless!

Effect They changed all this last week, didn't you know?

Cause I'd only just got used to the last bloody system! What are they try-ing to do? The town was dead enough already!

Effect I quite like the new pedestrian zone actually.

Cause This means we'll have to go all the way down to the roundabout

152

and double back. Ten miles to go twenty yards! Great, that'll do wonders for the nation's oil bill!

Effect   Careful... Slow down... Hey! Didn't you see that? You just went through a red light! There was a pedestrian crossing back there!

Cause   No pedestrians crossing though were there? Kids playing games probably. I hate those Pelican things... Uhoh, that does it, a traffic jam!... Oh Christ!... Inch by inch. There must have been an accident or something...

Effect   No, I think it's the new traffic-lights.

Cause   Traffic-lights!? There used to be a roundabout here, a perfectly good roundabout, never any problem! Now look: queues in all directions! How stupid! How typical! Hell, it's twenty-past. I know, right down River Lane and cut through the back way... Oh now what? "No Right Turn". Why ever not? Don't say they've made River Lane one-way too?

Effect   I don't think so. It must be to stop people crossing the oncoming traffic.

Cause   Well sod that for a game of soldiers! Brace yourself!

Effect   Jesus! You're completely lethal!

Cause   Damn! There was a copper on that corner, he must have seen me.

Effect   He will have got your number too.

Cause   I doubt it, not at that speed. And the plates are well muddied.

Effect   He'll certainly have radioed ahead. What are we going to do?

Cause   Don't panic. We'll make a detour, ditch the car somewhere, quick...

Effect   There, the gateway on the left!

Cause   Good thinking Malcolm, perfect! They'll never look in here. What is this place?

Effect   I think it's the Institute of Criminology.

Cause   Brilliant! Like it! What a great little car-park: central, half-empty, I must remember this. I'll bung her out of sight over in the far corner...

Splendid! Well, it's still a bit of a walk, but if we hurry we might just make it...

Effect   Let's not rush if you don't mind. If we do we do, if we don't we don't.

Cause   Okay, as you wish... Now, where were we?

Effect   Natural laws and legal laws.

Cause   Ah yes: ET and the Thought Police.

Effect   Another difference between these two kinds of law, a difference which ET should be able to observe if he is painstaking enough, is that over time our legal laws *change*.

Cause   And our scientific laws don't?

Effect   Well, yes, of course they do, but... but our scientific laws change as our knowledge and understanding of the physical world steadily widen and develop.

Cause   But cannot our moral knowledge and understanding of the world widen and develop too?

Effect   Yes, I suppose in a way it can, but with scientific knowledge the assumption is that the behaviour of the physical world, of atoms, particles and so on is objectively, unchangingly *there*, waiting, as it were, to be revealed.

Cause   And moral knowledge is not objective?

Effect   We-ell, no, I don't think so, not in the same way. It is sort of... sort of defined by us, created by us as we go along. It is we who draw up our legal laws.

Cause   Uhuh. Yet there is such a thing as moral development? Our laws and our judicial procedures can improve?

Effect   Oh undoubtedly. I think they have improved.

Cause   Really? For example?

Effect   Well, I think our whole attitude towards criminality and punishment is a lot more enlightened than it used to be. Increasingly, we are coming to realize that criminal behaviour is the product of factors like poverty, social deprivation and broken family life, and often we are finding it more appropriate to rectify these causes of crime than to punish the criminals.

Cause Oh are we? How nice for us. Hmm. 'Enlightened', 'appropriate', 'rectify', such fashionable, modern words, so discreetly patronizing. Tell me Malcolm, do you believe that people are actually born as criminal and law-abiding types?

Effect People are certainly born into very different social and family situations, if that's what you mean.

Cause No, not that, I was wondering whether your account of the causes of criminality could also include innate biochemical or psychological characteristics. An American scientist claims, for example, to have proved the existence of a causal link between people's chromosome deficiencies, so-called, and their displaying certain criminal tendencies.

Effect So?

Cause You believe that you do?

Effect I don't know. One would have to study the facts.

Cause But such a suggestion makes sense?

Effect Why shouldn't it?

Cause Supposing you believed it to be true, what would you conclude?

Effect For a start, I imagine I might well conclude that it would be more, er, appropriate to treat such people for their chromosome deficiences than to punish them for their law-breaking.

Cause To treat them as machines in fact?

Effect Well, to treat them as people who are sick.

Cause Sick rather than different? Suppose this condition, this 'deficiency', proved untreatable?

Effect Then, er...

Threatening Criminality

Cause Also, if criminal behaviour is caused by a certain pattern of chromosomes, it follows that being law-abiding must be caused by a different pattern. Suppose a scientist were to claim that being a law-enforcer and being a law-maker are associated with distinct chromosome patterns too, what would you say then? How would you feel when you discovered that you had been one of the unlucky ones in the chromosome-lottery? How would you feel if you turned out to be one of the privileged?

Effect I... I... Look, surely it is better to eradicate the causes of criminal behaviour than merely to carry on punishing criminals?

Cause Ah, 'better', that's better. Hm, I'm not sure that it is better though Malcolm, if it means regarding criminality as a *medical* problem. I find the idea that criminal behaviour can be *caused* by this or by that highly suspect; not just because it can lure us into the hazardous game of trying to pin down slippery concepts like 'mental illness' and 'social deprivation'; nor yet because of all the alarming confusions that can arise between treatment and punishment, as when people are sentenced to psychotherapy or admitted to hospitals with bars at the windows; but above all because it commits a basic self-contradition in its interpretation of human action.

Effect A self-contradiction, how?

Cause Simple: if a person's criminal behaviour is caused, he cannot help it, and if he cannot help it, it is not criminal behaviour. Congenital criminality is a contradiction in terms.

Effect But if it were proved that there *is* a link between certain types of human behaviour and chromosome make-up, this would result in our re-classifying such behaviour as *non*-criminal. Our definition of criminality would have to change.

Cause No, it wouldn't have to change, we would decide to change it; or not. That is the point. We must be clear about what we are doing, about the implications of how we are thinking... I am reminded of another, rather strange way in which our notion of criminality is under threat, from the development of modern policing techniques.

Effect What, the spectre of everyone eaves-dropped, phone-tapped, radio-monitored, that old bogey?

Cause It's no bogey Malcolm, for some people it's already everyday life; tagging is being tried, boardroom bugging is routine, and just you wait till your research comes up with something... But no, I wasn't thinking of all that. Who knows what might be achieved just with better burglar alarms, faster patrol cars and more policemen? Suppose that, by one means and another, our police steadily improve their ratios of crime-solution and suspect-conviction. Say they managed to achieve a success-rate of seventy-five percent, what would happen to the notion of crime in such circumstances, assuming that this figure became common knowledge?

Effect   I imagine that a lot of would-be criminals would be deterred from law-breaking.

Cause   No, worse than that: whenever anyone was caught trying to break the law, attempting, for example, to rob the unrobbable bank, the very fact of the attempt could itself be cited as evidence that this person was of diminished responsibility and therefore not a genuine criminal. In a true police state crime becomes not only practically difficult but also conceptually problematic.

Effect   Surely what will happen in fact is that as the police's methods become more sophisticated, so will the criminals'. Already, I gather, the single most lucrative category of crime is computer-fraud. Criminality always changes in form, will always emerge in new areas.

Cause   In the police forces themselves, most likely. Incidentally, when did you last meet a socially deprived computer-fraudster? It is funny though, this way in which the police seem to have an interest, and not just the obvious one, vested in ensuring that crime continues, by-and-large, to pay. Paradoxically, the existence of successful law-breaking can be seen as morally valuable.

Effect   Ah, that suits you down to the ground doesn't it? So that's your excuse! The Anarchist Philosopher's Self-Justification! Well it won't stand up in court Andrew, I'm glad to say.

Cause   I doubt if it will, yet it is a better excuse than many that do seem to work these days. This is it you see: every time you determinists propose a new *cause* of human behaviour, you provide us ordinary folk with a new *excuse* for our wrong-doings. Have you ever read any Aristotle?

Effect   Erm, I seem to remember being made to read Aristotle at school: voluntary action, the drunken sea-captain, all that?

Cause   Yes. The principle is: we hold people responsible for their actions, and in particular we punish them for their law-breakings, insofar as we find their excuses "I could not help it because..." inadmissible.

Third-Person Alibis

Effect   Right.

Cause   What's interesting is how the admissible excuses have changed over the years. In Aristotle's day, the captain who had lost his ship would have found his plea "I couldn't help it" accepted when there had been a typhoon but rejected when he had been found pissed at the helm. One wonders what an Athenian court would have made of "he couldn't help it, he's an alcoholic", or "he couldn't help murdering his father and shafting his mother, he came from a broken home", or "he can't help mugging pensioners, he suffers from a chromosome-deficiency", or "he couldn't help raping her, he watched a porn video".

Effect   He couldn't help nicking the book, he's a kleptomaniac. He can't help driving dangerously, he suffers from a virility-complex.

Cause   I'm *not* a kleptomaniac Malcolm, and I'm *not* suffering from a virility-complex!

Effect   These excuses don't sound so good in the first person do they?

Cause   Indeed they don't. Many of them are actually difficult to utter. But of course nowadays an accused has lawyers to speak for him; he is referred to in the *third* person; his psychology, his personality, his behaviour are, as it were, laid on the slab, are poked and peered at by 'experts'.

Effect   Surely though, it is the court's duty to be as objective as possible?

Cause   Not if this means treating a man as an object. The lesson is: the more we accept causes of and excuses for human behaviour, the less we preserve in the way of human responsibility, dignity and self-respect. I remember reading a case reported a few years ago in which the warden of an old people's home was charged with the manslaughter and sundry other mistreatments of a number of his inmates. He actually pleaded, or rather his defence counsel actually pleaded, that he could not help his behaviour because, quote, "he had a rigid and inflexible personality".

Effect   Are you serious?

Cause   Honestly, it was in *The Guardian*. One wonders how long it will be before a defending counsel stands up in court and says: "he could not help it your Honour, he is a sadist", or: "he had to do it m'Lud, he is a criminal". Blaming one's personality for one's actions or indeed, blaming society for the ways in which people behave en masse, really *is* making a category-mistake. A man's personality is not something over-and-above or,

158

for that matter, under-and-beneath his various actions. Individual actions are logically prior to the notion of personality. Personality is only discerned over a period of time, as the pattern of a man's actions. Each time a man acts, he so-to-speak *defines* his personality and each time he is free to define it differently. A man can, after all, *change* his personality, and can do so consciously and deliberately.

Effect   To an extent perhaps.

Cause   To an existentialist for certain.

Effect   Anyway Andrew, I don't think these 'personality' excuses in fact cut much ice with the courts; they are only put forward in mitigation, as pleas for leniency of sentence. One needs to know the full facts in each case.

Cause   The interesting thing is that they should be thought worth offering at all.

Effect   By the way, what was the verdict on the warden?

Cause   Guilty of manslaughter, several times. He got eighteen months.

Effect   Only eighteen months!?

Cause   Yup, a year with remission... Tell me Malcolm, *why* do you think we punish law-breakers?

Effect   To deter others, to reform criminals, to protect society from dangerous men.

Cause   How predictable! How prudish! What a nice, modern, enlightened, utilitarian, deterministic answer! Deterrence, reform, protection. Not even the teeniest hint of revenge?

Effect   I hope not.

Cause   Okay then, what about frontal lobotomies for drivers who speed and life-imprisonment for drivers who drink? Capital punishment perhaps for jay-walkers? Plenty of deterrence-and-protection value there!

Effect   Oh come on Andrew, you're just twisting things again.

Cause   Am I? On what grounds? Heaven forbid that the punishment should fit the crime! Did you know that in Sweden the police are empowered secretly to take photographs of speeding motorists and to book them by post? You're innocently eating your breakfast one morning when bingo, in drops a letter saying "two weeks ago, da-de-da-de-da, you're nicked!"

Effect   They do that in some parts of the States.

Cause   Uhuh? So much for the Land of the Free.

Effect   Yes, they carry guns in the name of freedom there too.

Cause   So I hear. Just imagine the paranoia!

Effect   The drivers do stick to the speed limits though, most of the time.

Cause   Maybe, but is that the sort of driving we want? Is that the sort of *living* we want? We for our part seem to be neurotically obsessed by *safety*. Look at all the millions of petty rules and regulations that now govern car-ownership: how many millimetres of rubber are there on the tyres? How perished are the wiper-blades? Is the number-plate bulb working? Are the screen-washer jets unblocked? And when you do finally get the thing on the road, it's a one-way street here, no right-turn there, minimum speed limit, maximum speed limit, no stopping, no parking, no feeding the meter, no loading this side on alternate hours every third Tuesday. It's a total nightmare!

Effect   But Andrew, this is a perfectly reasonable price to pay for the privilege of owning such a complex and dangerous machine. In a small and overcrowded country like ours, where there is such a high level of car-ownership, private motoring is bound to be hedged around with all sorts of restrictions. You should regard having a car, even yours, as a luxury.

Cause   Oh come on, everyone has a car nowadays. Our whole economy depends upon car-ownership. A car has become a basic necessity.

Effect   I manage perfectly well without one. There are trains, buses, taxis...

Cause   Wives with cars. But don't you sometimes long for the freedom a car would give you? The freedom just to hop in and go wherever you want, to go to... to...

Effect   There you are: can't you see it's inevitable that the privilege of this great freedom will come with certain strings attached? The rules and regulations are all for your own protection.

Cause But that's it, everything's so *protective*! The function of the law and its officers is now becoming not only the deterrence and prosecution of criminal behaviour, but also the prevention of accidents. Police cars lie in wait in lay-bys, they hide behind hedges. Drivers are convicted *just* of exceeding a limit, *just* of drinking beer, not of injuring anyone, nor even of driving dangerously. I was under the impression that the law and the police were there to be appealed to in cases of dispute, not that the law is something which the police are supposed to go around *enforcing*.

Effect But in a modern, complex, affluent society like ours, where we are surrounded by potentially dangerous activities and technologies, you know that's just not good enough any more.

Cause They're bribed you realize. Every time a policeman successfully makes an arrest, every time he spots a rule-infringement, it counts towards a bonus in his pay-packet. Is *that* good enough in your opinion? Is it fair on the police? I appreciate that there have to be regulations, but it does seem to me that we are going too far down the order-and-safety-at-all-costs road. Why can't we ever stop and simply accept that beyond a certain point, life is dangerous, driving is dangerous? For of course they always will be. Perhaps beyond certain points there is a greater moral danger in further denial of personal responsibility, this trend whereby individually we avoid making decisions, just in case someone makes a wrong one, and collectively we make rules instead. Another example we have recently encountered: they are installing more and more traffic-lights on our roads, not only at every junction, but also at every pedestrian crossing too. Gone are the good old belisha beacons and leaving it to the drivers' discretion, now it's all flashing lights and following instructions.

Effect The drivers never used to stop! Honestly Andrew, the old Zebras were hopeless, and they were always causing accidents. I far prefer the Pelicans.

Cause And do you know how much traffic-lights cost to install? Over ten thousand pounds for each...

Effect Maybe, but they are better. Surely, if the introduction of these crossings saves only one life a year, it will have been worth it?

Cause No, no, no! This is the most dangerous nonsense! If life-saving is the sole object of the exercise, then perhaps we should ban motor cars altogether, and certainly we should ban motor *cycles*. No doubt a few lives a year would be saved if the ghastly railings they now erect at city road junctions were extended along *all* pavements and walkways, or if they actually made it an offence for pedestrians to cross roads other than at lights, or...

Effect   They already have, in Germany.

Cause   Maybe even the owning of *model* cars should be licensed, or their manufacture outlawed, on the grounds that every year one or two children put them in their mouths and choke on them. Or might do so.

Effect   Now you're being silly again. Apart from anything else, that would be quite impractical.

Cause   On the contrary. It is far easier to control the manufacture of things than to control their use.

Effect   I must say, one thing I can't understand for the life me is why we manufacture, or allow to be manufactured, cars which happily do more than 120 miles-per-hour or less than 20 miles-per-gallon and *then* get all steamed up about road-safety or fuel-economy and pass a law restricting drivers to 50 or 60.

Cause   Rather like the way in which the Superpowers spend their energy designing and building and stockpiling ever-deadlier new weapons and *then* go through all this posturing over disarmament.

Effect   Mm. But surely, when we *can* quite easily do something, when we *can* introduce some practical new law or procedure which will make life safer, it would be equally mad for us *not* to do so? As far as I am concerned, the introduction of Pelican crossings is just a perfectly sensible and comparatively easy way of making crossing the road a bit less hazardous. You're so paranoid. You talk as though our freedoms were constantly under attack.

Cause   They are Malcolm, they are. The jungle is always waiting to take over. From our freedom of speech to our freedom to cross the road, we must patrol the frontiers with vigilance.

Effect   Well I agree, but I do believe that our best defence against the jungle, against anarchy, is the Rule of Law.

Cause   Unless the Law itself becomes the jungle. I fear the legislators far more than I fear the hooligans.

Effect   Uhuh? You seem to see conspiracy in everything.

Cause   There is conspiracy though. For a start, there is the conspiracy of the traffic-light manufacturers.

Effect   Oh phooey!

Cause   Of course there is, at ten grand a go! And there is the conspiracy too of those *philosophical* traffic-light manufacturers, the determinists and their friends. I have a vision of a world where people have finally lost their will to make decisions, where people don't think for themselves at all, but merely follow rules and regulations. A society of sleep-walking zombies.

Effect   Then what? The heroic philosopher-knight hurtles by in a shiny white sports car and wakes everyone up?

Cause   You may laugh, but already we can witness the sight of lines of cars stopped at red lights when it's quite safe to drive on, and of crowds of pedestrians waiting at the kerbside when the road is perfectly clear. And people have been killed obeying little green lights.

Effect   So I suppose you would actively seek to increase the dangers in life, would go around spilling oil on the roads, and tin-tacks, just to give your ego its vicarious little freedom-thrills?

Cause   Calm down Malcolm, calm down. Look: I agree that saving life is in general a desirable end, but it is not the end to end all ends. We must always have in mind what sort of a life it is we are striving so anxiously to save. Take another example: the law which makes it compulsory to wear seat-belts, even for back-seat passengers now. Here we are passing laws to protect ourselves from ourselves. I am not even to be allowed to endanger *my own* life any more.

Effect   But if that's the only way to make people wear their seat-belts, and if the wearing of seat-belts saves lives...

Cause   We're not children Malcolm! How paternalistic is the State going to be allowed to get? It's not even as though this was done out of genuine humanitarianism, it was simply a matter of saving government money: help the Health Service, make your accidents fatal!

Living with Statistics

Effect   And what about all the human misery? What about all the bereaved families? Who clears up the mess after the New Year's Eve booze-up? You should hear my eldest daughter on the subject. She's a casualty nurse at the Accident and General.

Cause   Well there you are, she is hardly in the best position to form a balanced view. Don't get me wrong Malcolm, the N.H.S. nurses are saints, I know that, but we should not forget that *they* are providing the service, not we. When we start passing laws on the grounds that they'll save work for the hospitals or start justifying punishments on the grounds that they'll save money for the prisons, that day we really will be in trouble.

Effect   And how bad do the accident statistics have to get before you'll admit that we're in trouble there?

Cause   Statistics can be used to prove anything. In societies where populations are measured in millions, there are bound to be horrific-sounding facts and figures. The trick is to leave them as facts and figures, to regard them as social phenomena rather than social problems.

Effect   Uhuh? Did you know that before the seat-belt law was introduced, over six thousand people died every year in road accidents in this country.

Cause   Did you know that the figures were higher in the 1920s?

Effect   Were they really? Are you sure?

Cause   And what effect did the belt law have?

Effect   The figures dropped significantly. They reckon 200 lives were saved in its first year.

Cause   Only three percent, even with the novelty-value. Three percent is significant is it?

Effect   It is to the 200. I gather there is one rather worrying new statistic though: the number of *pedestrians* being injured has risen. It is suggested that seat-belted motorists feel safer and therefore take greater risks.

Cause   Oh wonderful! Splendid! Human perversity strikes again! The genie of freedom refuses to be strapped in!

Effect   Yes, the pig in the Porsche, remember? Anyway Andrew, all these arguments about the infringement of liberty were thoroughly discussed when the law was passed. The issue's now been settled. You'll be questioning motorcyclists' compulsory crash helmets next.

Cause   And why not? They aren't compulsory in Greece. Nothing is *settled* Malcolm, nothing is ever *settled*! Why this assumption that once a law is in the statute-book it must stay there for good? As though progress will inevitably bind us ever tighter in a great determinist ratchet. After all, it is far easier to repeal laws than it is to draw them up.

Effect   Obviously a balance has to be struck, a number of balances have to be struck, but I do think you are exaggerating the burden of rules and regulations that weigh upon us. As usual, you are getting things out of all proportion.

Cause   Getting things out of proportion? Me? Christ, here we are arguing about seat-belts and Pelican crossings while the whole oil-thirsty civilization in which we are travelling is speeding steadily towards the pile-up to end all pile-ups! Bloody hell, what's the point of these countless footling little rules when all roads lead to the nuclear abyss? We are behaving like a man checking his tyre-pressures and polishing his hub-caps before driving his family saloon off a cliff.

Effect   This is why our programme of fusion-research is so important. It is my belief that if we can secure this potentially limitless source of energy, we will at last have eliminated the likeliest single cause of war, the competition for fuel-supplies.

Cause   It is we who are the causes of war Malcolm, there are no others. We, with our dreary little tribalisms, our thoughtless little appetites, our stumbling, stammering ideologies, our foolish, stunted philosophies. It is a philosophical problem in the end. Logical positivism has provided the attitude. Science has provided the means. Determinism, naturally, provides all the excuses – our genetic make-up, our evolutionary ancestry, our tide of history. Yet in fact of course, what we have here are perfectly simple free choices: go on building the bombs or stop building the bombs; press the buttons or don't press the buttons.

Effect   But Andrew, if we genuinely *are* free agents, as you keep claiming, how can you consistently go on to suggest that certain of our beliefs can *endanger* our freedom?

Cause   Such beliefs can be dangerous because they can endanger our *sense* of freedom. Unfortunately, determinism can achieve a curious sort of self-verifying plausibility by appealing to man's awful capacities for laziness, self-deception and abasement. It is easy to follow rules, comfortable to conform, tempting to offer excuses, convenient to deny responsibility. Worse still, the more we think of our behaviour as being causally determined and the more we organize our society accordingly, the more traffic-lights we install, the less we will be in the habit of thinking rationally and choosing responsibly, the more sheep-like we will actually *become*. This is why philosophy is so important, for it is in philosophy that we decide how to see ourselves. Philosophy is the most important of all our freedoms, for it is our freedom to choose how free to be... Oh damn! It's three o'clock! We've blown it!

Effect   Oh dear.

Cause   England, bloody England!

Effect   But we can't turn back now, having come all this way. It's only a little further... Come on, let's try...

Cause   There's no point Malcolm, we won't get food this late, forget it... This country's barbaric! It's uncivilized! It's...

Effect   It's open! We're in luck! And there are people still eating!

Cause   Why, so there are... Great! Phew!

Effect   Okay, what do you want?

Cause   Ermm... Steak and kidney pie, beans, chips and a pint of Farmers please. Ta. I'll try and bag a table.

*   *   *   *   *   *   *   *   *   *   *

5

UNIVERSALS
and
FAMILIES

Effect Pie okay?

Cause Soya chunks with just a dash of whalemeat, lovely.

Effect Well if you will choose that sort of rubbish...

Cause Honestly, I've had better tuck than this in the Calcutta slums!

Effect I suppose we were lucky to get anything. My quiche is quite passable actually.

Cause The ale is real enough. I like this Farmers.

Effect Oh, er, it's something else I'm afraid, the Farmers was off.

Cause Really? Well anyway, it doesn't matter what it's called, it tastes good.

Effect Andrew...

Cause Yes?

Effect Something worries me about all this philosophy of yours.

Cause Good. What?

What is a Table?

Effect Isn't this all just a game we are playing, a game of words? I find your arguments interesting, clever, seductive even, and I admit that I seem curiously unable to fault them, yet... yet if you conclude by asserting that the Earth may have a mind and that stones may be conscious and that billiard-balls may have purposes, then surely all you are doing in the end is misusing language? If you can say things like this, you can say anything, which is to suggest, of course, that you are saying nothing. Words do have meanings, you cannot bandy them about willy-nilly. For all your precious freedoms, you cannot choose to use language in any way you please. Even words as evidently problematic as 'mentality' and 'consciousness' and 'purpose' must have meanings, so shouldn't we establish and agree exactly what mentality *is* and what consciousness *is* and what purpose *is* before we start ascribing them to all and sundry?

Cause Uhuh? Okay, I'll tell you what mentality and consciousness and purpose are if you'll tell me what planets and stones and billiard-balls are.

Effect I'm sorry?

Cause Well, why start with words which you have characterized as 'evidently problematic'? Presumably we must learn to walk before we can run, so let us begin with something evidently simple. What is... What is... (RAP-RAP) What is a *table*?

Effect A table?

Cause Yes, a table. Nothing problematic or obscure about a good solid oak table one would suppose. You tell me: what is a table? What is the definition of tableness? What are the criteria of tablehood?... Hold on, I'll just clear away the plates...

Effect Ermm... Well, a table has four legs, for a start.

Cause Not so, there's one over there with only three. And the table in the corner's got a single central... Christ! Look at those legs! The bird in the black hat. I do think legs are very underrated as an...

Effect They all have flat tops. All these tables have flat surfaces, on which people can put their drinks, their food.

Cause I'm afraid not. The pin-table in the other bar has a sloping glass top, and one is not *allowed* to put drinks on the billiard-table. Hey, it's free, do you fancy a game? Come on, a penny a point.

Effect Oh, er, no thanks.

Cause   A fiver a game then?

Effect   No, really, I'm useless, I don't play. And if I did, I wouldn't play for money.

Cause   Spoil-sport.

Effect   Ah, one thing they do have in common: all tables stand on the floor.

Cause   Erm... There, what about the bird table hanging outside on that apple tree?

Effect   Oh yes, oh dear... Maybe the common factor is that they're all designed for the same sort of purpose.

Cause   I don't think so. Look at the tables in the garden, they are made from old sewing-machine treadles.

Effect   Well at least they are all man-made.

Cause   Nope. I can see some picnickers on the bank using a tree-stump as a table.

Effect   So perhaps it is how an object is used that counts?

Cause   I'm afraid that's irrelevant. I could chop up this table and use it for firewood. I could turn it upside down and float down the river on it. I can even use it as an example in a philosophical argument.

Effect   Oh this is stupid! For every suggestion I put forward, you come up with a counter-instance. Once more you are just playing a game!

Cause   True, and a game that you're not going to be able to win.

Effect   So what's the answer? There must be *something* common to all tables.

Cause   I'm afraid there isn't Malcolm. I promise you that whatever definition of tableness or criteria of tablehood you propose, I will be able to point out an example of a table which does not conform to your definition or fulfil your criteria. Remember too that to be of any use, your definition must not only include all tables, it must also distinguish tables from all other objects with which they might be confused, such as stools, shelves, the bar and so on. Furthermore, there is a whole host of tables which we haven't mentioned yet: there is the table of charges pinned up by the cash-register, the somewhat disgusting table they serve here for lunch, the railway timetable over there on the wall, the geological table on which the city is built, the...

Effect   Oh but these are not true tables, they're...

Cause   Truth-tables, there's another one.

Effect   Truth-tables?

Cause   Yes, they're used in logic, to check the validity of inferences.

Effect   What, sort of philosophical ouija boards? Look Andrew, these are all *trick* examples.

Cause   On what grounds? Besides, a trick example is still an example. A trick table is still a table.

Effect   This is a waste of time! You are just being perverse!

Cause   No Malcolm, it is you who is being perverse, with your blind assumption that there must be some feature common to all tables, your relentless search for non-existent criteria, your futile demand for neat definitions. Language is not like that. There are no definitions of words or concepts, even apparently simple ones. There is no criterion of tablehood, or of anything-else-hood.

Effect   Hmm. Well, it seems we have a bit of a problem then.

Cause   Indeed. It's called the Problem of Universals and it's as old as the philosophical hills. The problem is this: each of the common nouns in our language applies to a number of individual objects; that is how nouns work, that is why they are useful. There are many tables, many planets, many stones, many men, many brains, many minds, many purposes and so on. In each case, the numerous objects are said in the old jargon to be the instances of a universal, and in the newer jargon to be the members of a class. The traditional question has always been: in virtue of what property or properties are the numerous individual objects all instances of the same universal or members of the same class? Or, in our present example: what makes all tables tables? As we have already demonstrated, even in an apparently simple case like this, no definition works.

Effect   *Some* terms can be defined though, surely? In my scientific studies I am constantly using words that are the subjects of definitions, of absolutely rigorous, black-and-white definitions. A body's inertial mass, for instance, is *defined* as being the fixed ratio between the net force acting upon it and the acceleration produced in it: m equals P over a.

Cause This is an interesting subject, the two-way traffic between ordinary-language uses of words like 'mass' and their borrowed, scientifically-defined uses. Also there can be interesting relationships when different scientific definitions are proposed for the same word. These different, specialized uses are often explicitly recognized. I notice you qualified the noun 'mass' with the adjective 'inertial'; you were taking no chances.

Effect Some scientific words are not borrowed from ordinary language, but exist only in their technically-defined usage: the thermodynamic term 'entropy' for instance.

Cause Ah yes, entropy, I never could quite understand what that was. Something to do with the degree of muddle in one's thinking, I seem to remember.

Effect Mathematical and geometrical terms are defined too. A square *is* an equilateral rectangle.

Cause Isn't a square also a number raised to the power two? Or a place in a town where there might be an open market? Or anyone who doesn't dig jazz music? But yes Malcolm, I agree, many scientific and mathematical terms are special cases and are susceptible of precise definition. If we had more time, these matters would merit further investigation, but for the moment please let us begin at the beginning, with ordinary objects and ordinary language, whose nouns are not bound by the disciplines of definition. In real life, objects and words are not subjected to formal examinations or written tests. Unlike someone who wants to join the IQ club Mensa, *this* fellow... (RAP-RAP) did not qualify as a member of the class 'tables' by filling in a form or answering a questionnaire.

Effect Funny you should mention that, I'm a member of Mensa.

Cause Are you really? Well you could have fooled me! And you fell for the old table-routine? Real life Malcolm, real life! In real life, one teaches a child how to use the noun 'table' not by issuing him with complex sets of instructions or lists of criteria but by pointing to tables whilst uttering the word. In ordinary language, words are thus defined, as we say, *ostensively*.

Effect But if, as you claim, there are no criteria applicable to the words of ordinary language, what makes all tables tables and all chairs chairs?

Realism and Nominalism

How can we ever be sure that the ostensive definitions we are giving are the right ones? How can we talk of incorrect usage? Even if it cannot be pointed out or described in language, there must be *something* peculiar to all tables which enables us to recognize them as such.

Cause   That was Plato's conclusion, roughly speaking.

Effect   The theory of Forms and all that? Another distant, school-days memory: some weird doctrine about the physical objects on Earth being mere shadows or images of these abstract, ideal *Forms* which dwell in a superior, heavenly intellectual realm beyond that of ordinary experience. I seem to recall that the use of capital letters was supposed to be of especial significance. Very strange.

Cause   Indeed. Who taught you Plato Malcolm, your physics teacher? Obviously you have taken the theory far too literally. Plato has suffered much caricaturing at the hands of his detractors. He is cast as the archetypal Realist, a philosopher who, despite the absence of an identifiable property common to the instances of any universal, nevertheless asserts that there must in fact *be* such defining properties. For Plato, this defining property of every object is its displaying of or its conforming to its absolute Ἰδέα, while for us, his Greek word ''Ἰδέα' *can* be translated as 'Ideal' or 'Form'.

Effect   Exactly, which is not what I mean at all. His 'Forms' theory is hopelessly mysterious and far-fetched. No-one nowadays could believe in objects' having non-perceivable properties or would assent to the existence of a realm of abstract ideals. Surely, one thing is obvious: the instances come first, not the universals.

Cause   The instances of what?

Effect   Of... of... Look, Andrew, isn't this all just a linguistic problem, a matter of how we use words? Perhaps the search for definitions and criteria was a red herring. Tables are tables by convention. Tables are tables because we call them tables. That's it! The property all tables have in common is simply the property of being named 'tables', by English-speakers at least.

Cause   And *this* theory Malcolm, has the property of being known as 'Nominalism.' Nominalism is the philosophical belief that the only feature shared by the instances of a universal is their common name.

Effect   Of course! Why didn't I think of it earlier?

Cause   Because earlier it would have sounded platitudinous; true but plat-itudinous. Within this suggestion the original question still remains, or rather is now rephrased as "Yes, but *why* do we call all tables tables?" or "Yes, but how do we know what to call things?" Obviously there is a sense in which naming-practices, and indeed all language-use is a matter of observing conventions, but as you pointed out, word-usage can be correct or incorrect. The conventions are not arbitrary. This object remains unquestionably a table however many times I call it a chair, and all sorts of thoroughly non-linguistic evidence would be relevant to proof of the fact.

Effect   Okay, okay, so the Realist's position is either simply false or unac-ceptably mysterious, and the Nominalist's position is perfectly true but unhelpfully platitudinous. Where do we go from here?

Cause   To Wittgenstein, so the story has it.

Effect   Ah, Wittgenstein.

Cause   You've read him? The *Philosophical Investigations*?

Effect   Well, er... No. But I've heard some of the quotes. One of the girls gave me a copy for Christmas. I confess that I haven't yet got round to...

Cause   Your daughter's a philosopher is she?

Effect   Ella, yes. She's just completed her second year.

Cause   Really? Is she enjoying it?

Effect   I think so. Look, why don't we adjourn to my rooms in College, it's just round the corner from here. We could go through the Wittgenstein together. I'd like that.

Cause   Fine. Why not? The pub's about to close anyway. How much do I owe you for the grub?

Effect   Oh, forget it, forget it...

＊ ＊ ＊ ＊ ＊ ＊ ＊ ＊ ＊ ＊ ＊

Cause   Wow, what a great room! What beautiful furniture! It's like an antiques shop! That desk is amazing! How much does this lot set you back?

Naming Games

Effect It comes with the job Andrew. To tell you the truth, it's not quite to my taste, but never mind. The Persian carpets are mine... Now, sit yourself down... Ah, here we are: *Philosophical Investigations*.

Cause Okay, let me find the place... I guess I should explain first that Wittgenstein's main interest here was in the different ways in which we use *language*, ways which he christened 'language-games'. He therefore found it apt to take as his example the common noun 'game':

> Instead of producing something common to all that we call language, I am saying that these phenomena (the different language-games) have no one thing in common which makes us use the same word for all, – but that they are *related* to one another in many different ways. And it is because of this relationship, or these relationships, that we call them all 'language'. I will try to explain this. Consider for example the proceedings we call 'games'. I mean board-games, card-games, ball-games...

Effect Word-games, computer-games, table-games...

Cause Come to think of it, isn't *Tables* a game? Isn't that the old name for Backgammon? Back-gaming, that is.

Effect Olympic games, and so on. What is common to them all? – Don't say: "there *must* be something common, or they would not be called 'games'" – but *look and see* whether there is anything common to all. – For if you look at them you will not see something that is common to *all*, but similarities, relationships, and a whole series of them at that. To repeat: don't think, but look! – Look for example at board-games, with their multifarious relationships. Now pass to card-games; here you find many correspondences with the first group, but many common features drop out, and others appear...

Cause Then there is 'game' as in wild game, fair game, endgame..

Effect When we pass next to ball-games, much that is common is retained, but much is lost. – Are they all 'amusing'? Compare chess with noughts and crosses. Or is there always winning and losing, or competition between players? Think of patience. In ball games there is winning and losing; but when a child throws his ball at the wall and catches it again, this feature has disappeared. Look at the parts played by skill and luck; and at the difference between skill in chess and skill in tennis. Think now of games like ring-a-ring-a-roses; here is the element of amusement, but how many other characteristic features have disappeared!

Cause   Would you call ring-a-ring-a-roses a game?

Effect   And we can go through the many, many other groups of games in the same way; we can see how similarities crop up and disappear. And the result of this examination is: we see a complicated network of similarities overlapping and criss-crossing: sometimes overall similarities, sometimes similarities of detail. I can think of no better expression to characterize these similarities than "family resemblances"; for the various resemblances between members of a family: build, features, colour of eyes, gait, temperament, etc. etc. overlap and criss-cross in the same way. – And I shall say: 'games' form a family.

This, I take it, is what they call the 'Family-resemblances Analogy'?

Cause   Well spotted! The suggestion is that the instances of a universal do not share a common feature or set of features, but rather display a network of similarities and relationships in the same way that the members of a human family display a pattern of criss-crossing resemblances rather than a single common trait or set of traits. Games form a family, tables form a family, the uses of language form a family and so on.

Effect   How obvious! How elegant! That is why it's pointless and mistaken to ask questions like "What is a table?" or "What is a game?" or "What is language?"

Cause   Or "What is mentality?" or "What is freedom?" or "What is purpose?" It is mistaken if by asking such questions one expects to get answers in the form of definitions, criteria and instant explanations, but by no means pointless if one thereby generates discussion and investigation. We began with the question "What is a table?" and although we found that we could not come up with any common feature or pat definition, yet our conversation did not consist merely of a listing of examples. Our procedure, of your proposing criteria and my indicating tables which do not fulfil them, frustrating though it may have seemed at the time, did lead us to some sort of understanding of the, the *concept* of tableness. In studying the various examples and remarking upon their criss-crossing characteristics – four-leggedness very common, flat-toppedness another strong trait, frequently used in eating and so on – we were registering the family resemblances to be observed amongst tables. Noting the resemblances between the members of a human family is not just a matter of pointing to each one in turn, but also involves saying things like "Look, she has her mother's eyes".

Effect   Tell me though: if the solution to the Problem of Universals turns out to be so simple, why on earth did it take so long for philosophers to twig on?

Cause Well personally, I am not so sure that Plato, for one, *hadn't* twigged on. Even at a superficial level, Wittgenstein's analogy and Plato's theory bear, shall we say, a remarkable family resemblance. If one were forced to distil from Wittgenstein's writing a single-phrase answer to the question "What do all the instances of a universal have in common?", it might well be: a pattern of similarities. So let us look for a moment at our uses of the word 'pattern'. One can think of a pattern as being a configuration of objects or a sequence of events. The stars form patterns in the night-sky, billiard-balls form patterns on a billiard-table. There are patterns in human history, patterns of philosophical reasoning.

Effect One can think also of pattern in the sense of design or plan, as in dress-patterns, knitting-patterns. In metal-working a pattern can be a template or a mould, from which thousands of copies are cut or cast.

Cause And in *this* sense, you see, 'pattern' can become synonymous with 'model' or 'archetype' or *'form'*. This is where we hit translation problems, and not just Platonic ones: Wittgenstein wrote his *Investigations* in German.

Effect Oh, I didn't realize that.

Cause The other thing to say is that Plato's "Ἰδέα" can of course be translated in different ways. According to the lexicon, 'ἰδέα' can also mean the appearance or look of a thing, its re-semblance, we might say; compare the latin word 'species'. It can also mean 'kind' or 'sort' or 'class', words which have a far less archaic and mysterious ring than 'Form'. Finally, and most obviously, it is our English word 'idea' and if 'idea' sounds a bit prosaic now, howabout 'concept'? In suitable translation, Plato's theory can sound not strange and old-fashioned, but bang up-to-the-minute.

Effect What tables have in common is that they conform to or feature in *our concept* of table.

Cause That sounds pretty post-war to me. We are poking around here at the very nub of the relationship, the interface as some would call it, between sense-perception and physical objectivity, between intelligent observer and external world, between thought and language and things. Everything depends upon the translations. Although Plato had no micro-computer, he had the same optic lobe that we have and he spoke virtually the same language. This is why genuine philosophical problems and insights are, if you'll forgive me, universal: unlike figures of speech, they do not age. Of course neither we nor Plato nor Wittgenstein are primarily interested in universals like 'table' and 'game'. As Wittegenstein's central concern in the *Investigations* was our use of language, so Plato's central concern in *The Republic*, the work in which he most clearly outlined his theory of, of Ideas, was our notion of Justice. As usual, Plato begins his dialogue with a 'What is...?' question. Socrates asks "What is Justice?" Then, when various definitions of Justice are submitted by his protagonists, Socrates systematically shoots them all down with counter-examples. Although no apparent progress is made and no clear conclusion is agreed, yet in the course of the dialogue the reader arrives at a steadily greater understanding of the nature of Justice and of its criss-crossing similarities and relationships to other moral concepts.

Effect   The journey, not the arrival. Well, as long as we're not going round in circles.

Cause   Thus when you ask me, as you did early this morning, "What is philosophy?", do not be disappointed, nor accuse me of evasion, when I fail to come back with a quick or simple answer. Although Socrates and Plato and Aristotle and Descartes and Berkeley and Hume and Mill and Ayer and Ryle and Wittgenstein were certainly all philosophers, there is no one thing that they were all doing. It is hard to think of any feature that they have in common, apart from their obvious humanity and their sex.

Effect   Oh one thing, surely: they all wrote on problems of a rather abstract...

Cause   Not so. Socrates never wrote a word. Or if he did, he certainly never found a publisher.

Effect   What?

Cause   True. Socrates, both as a philosopher and as a man, exists for us only through the writings of others, principally those of his pupil and disciple Plato. Socrates himself never put, put scribe to tablet. And Wittgenstein, after his *Tractatus*, was reluctant to be published too, openly doubting the quality of his *Investigations*.

Effect   Is that so? Tell me Andrew, have *you* written anything?

Cause   Er, no... no, not really. I once wrote an essay on the concept of weather, but I never had it accepted.

Effect   Whether with an 'h'?

177

Beyond Lexicography

Cause Oh no, with an 'ea'. "The Concept of Weather and How to Live with It", very English. I am working on a book at the moment actually, something of a magnum opus.

Effect Uhuh? Have you a publisher?

Cause No, not yet. I have tried to interest one or two, but... well... I think one has to have a name to get anything published these days, or family connections.

Effect What is it, a layman's introduction?

Cause Ye-es, but, but more than that, I hope.

Effect Have you thought of a title?

Cause No I haven't really bothered. At first I had the idea of calling it "All at Sea", but on second thoughts I decided this sounded a bit, a bit...

Effect Wet?

Cause Yes... As far as I am concerned philosophy must have some purpose. The philosopher's job is not *just* to chart the networks of criss-crossing similarities between the instances of universals, not *just* to trace the complex patterns of family resemblance and relationship amongst our various intellectual and moral concepts. This is work for cartographers and lexicographers and genealogists, the sort of people one tends to find around this place.

Effect Yes, I know the types. Biographers too, there's another.

Cause By the way Malcolm, I have a pet argument which proves that universities, paradoxically, are the last places in the world in which to discover philosophy. Since philosophers are necessarily people reacting against prevailing ways of thinking and philosophy is necessarily their intellectual revolt, a university which is in every sense an intellectual establishment, is going by definition to be the last place in which to find either.

Effect In which case what are you doing here? Are philosophers also necessarily inconsistent?

Cause Cartography and lexicography and genealogy may be very interesting, but by themselves they can change nothing. The true philosopher proceeds from such understandings of how things presently are to the indication of long-neglected or even hitherto unnoticed *new* similarities and relationships.

Effect   And you think that this is what you are doing when you suggest, for instance, that the planet Earth can be regarded as a person?

Cause   Maybe, yes, at least issuing a re-minder. Why not?

Effect   Well it seems to me you've got a pretty odd idea of what constitutes a family resemblance, that's all I can say. For my money I'd prefer us to stick with the Wittgenstein.

Cause   I thought you might. It has so much more authority, doesn't it, when it's down there bound in hardback.

Effect   Now what? You're not going to start attacking the family-resemblances analogy are you?

Cause   Well, it seems plausible, as far as it goes. But then it doesn't go very far. I've got a strange feeling that it can tell us more about our notion of family than it can about our Problem of Universals. Think: when Wittgenstein talks of family resemblances, one imagines a family photograph. One imagines a group of...

Effect   Hold on, I should have some family snaps somewhere, I'll just try to find...

Cause   Not to worry Malcolm, not to worry. Don't look, imagine! It's so much quicker. Imagine a family group of, say, a father, mother and four children. Six people give a reasonable number of possible person-to-person comparisons. Think of the sort of similarities we might recognize: she has her brother's eyes, he has his father's nose, the girls have their mother's hair colouring – assuming the photo was in colour, she has her father's air of gravity and so on. What now if someone said: look, she has her husband's mouth?

Effect   Well obviously, that would be a mistake. If there were a resemblance, it would be a sheer coincidence.

Cause   Uhuh? Why?

Effect   Obviously, because... because...

Cause   You see: when our imaginary photograph was set up, it was not people's resemblances, or the lack of them, that decided who was to pose in front of the camera. It was not the existence of any network of criss-crossing similarities between the six people which conferred upon each his membership of the family. Individuals are members of particular families by virtue not of any patterns of resemblance which they may display, but of certain historical facts: in the years bla, bla, bla and bla, A and B begat W, X, Y and Z.

Effect That goes without saying, so what?

Cause So right from the start the family-resemblances analogy suffers from a fatal weakness: in the case of a conventional human family, unlike that of a universal or class, there *is* a set of criteria definitive of family-membership. Family-memberships are matters of historical fact.

Effect Surely though, there can be disputes over family-membership just as there can over class-membership? Indeed, when there is doubt concerning a person's parentage, physical resemblances, or a lack of them, can often help in settling the case.

Cause Maybe. Maybe not. Such evidence *can* be terribly misleading. The point is that physical resemblances are never *definitive* of family-membership; this is defined, and only defined, by the person's progenital history. We have the problem with universals precisely because they are not blessed with any such set of other, definitive criteria. The question is: how do we decide, and how does this analogy help us to decide, what things are to pose in our various universal family photographs?

Effect Perhaps Wittgenstein is concerned simply to say something about classes as he finds them rather than to answer questions about how we in practice recognize class-members or resolve classification disputes.

Cause Can these issues usefully be dissociated? Suppose that our imaginary photographer were to start playing with us a game of spot-the-family. Suppose he got our family of six to pose against a background of, say, a hundred people selected randomly from the street. Do you think you'd be able to pick out the right six?

Effect I should think so, if the photograph was reasonably good.

Cause Even if the six were scattered throughout the crowd?

Effect Er... well...

Cause Suppose you did not know either the size or the composition of the family you were looking for?

Effect   Ah, that might be more difficult.

Cause   Remember that there are some families *all* of whose members, including husband and wife, seem to share a common feature, while there are others whose members bear no obvious criss-crossing similarities to one another at all... Again, suppose that a black-skinned man, a black-skinned woman and four black-skinned children were scattered amongst a hundred white and Asian and mixed-race subjects and you were told that the father of the mystery family was an African, or was a black African, would your obvious choices necessarily prove to be the correct ones? Think of the differences between playing spot-the-family in a Welsh or an African village and playing it in cosmopolitan central London... There are a hundred-and-one ways in which an artful photographer could trick us. There are a thousand-and-one ways in which that most artful of all camera men, real life, can confound our repertoire of easy assumptions and predictable prejudices.

Effect   But isn't this what Wittgenstein was saying, that the resemblances between the members of a class, like those between the members of a family, are not clear-cut but criss-cross and overlap? That they can, as you suggest, be very complex and very subtle?

Cause   Of course, but quite apart from the fatal weakness presented by the existence of the other, historical family-criterion, his analogy fails *even as a picture* unless one imagines a very idealized family set against a very unrealistic, racially pure background. The picture works only if the pattern of resemblances between the members of each family are much more marked than any patterns of *inter*-family resemblance. In a truly multi-racial society where mixed marriages are commonplace, or even the rule, this may simply cease to be the case. I repeat: don't think of families, look at them!

Effect   So what are you saying, that there are no such things as family resemblances?

Cause   One thing I would certainly say: they are very overrated. Remember, it is not a pattern of resemblances that decides who is to pose before the camera. Once it has been taken, people seem to find in a photograph, just as they seem to read into an analogy, more or less what they want. People *look for* family resemblances; they expect and hope to find them; proud grandparents search for similarities between their children and grandchildren. As often as not, it strikes me, people are clutching at straws, are imagining likenesses where none exist, are *believing in* their resemblances. My sister's got three kids, and as far as I'm concerned they're like chalk, cheese and chamber-music. Some people say I look just like my brother, others are amazed that we're even related. In short, family resemblances are in the eyes of their beholders.

Effect   So you don't believe in inherited characteristics? You don't believe in genetics? You don't believe that traits are transmitted from parents to offspring by the genes?

Cause   Ah, them again. I don't believe in genes, no. I thought I'd made that clear.

Effect   I assumed you were joking. So seriously you don't believe in the existence of genes?

Cause   Nope, sorry. Genies maybe, but not genes. I don't like the way they've been neutered.

Effect   Look, I know funny things happen, I know there are throwbacks and quirks, but when did you last hear of white parents conceiving a black child, or black parents a white? And *please* don't start telling me about albino negroes or celts with skin diseases!

Cause   Inherited characteristics Malcolm, inherited characteristics. Of course children inherit characteristics from their parents! Of course there are patterns of genetic inheritance, all sorts of patterns: there are strong patterns, broken patterns, sometimes no pattern at all. What I said was: I don't believe in *genes*. I don't believe in chains of invisible billiard-balls determining everything for us. Genetics, the study of observable patterns of inheritance, is presumably as old as life itself, and is certainly as old as the Book of Genesis, but the gene is only a very recent invention, 'genes' is a comparatively modern word, a fiction that goes back only a generation or two. It was genetics that generated the mythology of genes, not vice versa.

Effect   But without a theory of genes, how can we possibly explain the patterns of inherited charac...

Cause   We can't. All we can do is observe and describe them. A theory of genes can explain nothing, all it does is removes questions about characteristic-transmission to a fictional, molecular level. It is just another symptom of your obsession with causal connections, another demonstration of how your endless cause-and-effect search forces you to resort again to a fantasy sub-world. We have been through all this.

Effect   So family resemblances are just coincidences?

Cause   No, no, *no*! Again you *refuse* to see don't you!? There are patterns: patterns of conjunction, patterns of resemblance, patterns of inheritance, observed patterns, that is all.

Effect   But there are bound to be biochemical links between parents and their children Andrew, it's obvious!

Cause   As a matter of interest, how much can they accurately predict at the moment about people's offspring?

Effect   Oh, er, certain things about blood-groups, tissue-types, the likelihoods of various inheritable defects and diseases, that sort of stuff. As far as detailed characteristics go they can't predict very much, but with the advent of sperm and ova banks, there is talk of being able to punch in desired sets of rough physical and psychological traits and match them up by computer.

Cause   Uhuh? More work for the moral philosophers!

Effect   I imagine that one day it may be possible to give everybody a detailed, computerized, personal genetic read-out.

Cause   Ah, so I *am* a number! It's queer, you actually *want* to believe in these biochemical links of yours, you look for them. Like the proud grandparent, you seem to *need* the idea that your children share some special, unique, occult family resemblance with you. In a similar way, many whites do not just regard blacks as people who happen to have a different skin-colour, but tend to infer from this obvious superficial characteristic the existence of some more fundamental, unseen, mythological difference, a *racial* difference. Nature, of course, knows no such prejudice: black men and white men *are* the same under the skin, biochemically and otherwise. Genes are just the modern version of 'blood-relations', a web of psychological cords tying each of us to some abstract, imaginary biochemical motherland.

Effect   Not entirely imaginary though Andrew. I'm afraid there *are* such things as racial characteristics.

Cause   Of course there are Malcolm! I'm not blind! The point is that the obvious differences are the *only* differences. They are not symptoms of some other, hidden set of dissimilarities. If we came to realize this, we might realize further that, even as far as physical characteristics go, skin-colour is not a particularly interesting family resemblance anyway.

Effect   However, it is an immediately recognizable characteristic that is passed on directly and without exception from parents to children, a characteristic which must therefore be caused by the transmission of certain genes.

Cause   But why this last clause? What does it add? How does it help? Why aren't you happy with the constant conjunction? Like Wittgenstein I urge: don't say this regularity *must* be caused by some mechanism called 'genes', but look and see what relationships there *are* and leave it at that. See how your causal view of the world already threatens to divide humanity from humanity... Look Malcolm, if you insist upon a causal explanation, why don't I suggest simply that people's *living together* causes them to resemble one another? People do say that husbands and wives often grow alike over the years. Maybe that remark "she has her husband's mouth" was not a mistake after all.

Effect   Oh but that's simply foolish: a black child brought up by white parents will remain black however long they live together. I am talking about the characteristics conferred by a mother upon her own child, the fruit of her own womb.

Cause   Of course, but then perhaps pregnancy is just a particularly extreme example of two people living together.

Effect   And what of the characteristics inherited from the father?

Cause   Conception too: a particularly extreme example of *three* people living together.

Effect   Oh come off it! Remember, women can be inseminated artificially these days.

Cause   People have some odd ways of living together, who am I to comment? Seriously though Malcolm, I've no wish to deny the obvious about inherited characteristics, I've just no wish to move from the obvious to the unobvious, to the highly unobvious postulation of these problematic genes of yours. Remember, none of this is evident from a simple photograph: what we see when we play spot-the-family is not a photo of a hundred different gene-patterns, but a photo of a gathering of human beings...

Effect   That is the starting-point, I agree.

Cause   Okay, so let's move on now and imagine that our photographer were to increase the number of his subjects from a hundred to a thousand... Suppose that he used wider and wider angled lenses to include a huger and huger crowd...

Effect   No, the best way to photograph a large gathering is to use a camera that pans horizontally. This avoids wide-angle distortion. That's how they used to take our College photo. Look, there, over the mantlepiece.

Cause   Oh let's see... When was this?

Effect   Umm... Twenty-five years ago... More... I shudder to think.

Cause   Look at that! Not a girl to be seen! You'd think they didn't exist! From this you'd guess that human beings popped out of giant eggs, all aged about eighteen and all wearing suits and ties!

Effect   Bet you can't spot me.

Cause   Er... There! Easy! You haven't changed a bit... Oh look, how funny, the same bloke's got in twice, at either end... Unless they're twin brothers.

Effect   Good heavens, so he has!

Cause   He must have tricked the photographer and sprinted round the back.

Effect   Well, well, I've never noticed that before. I remember that guy, he always fancied himself as a bit of a joker.

Cause   Okay, now imagine a photograph a hundred times bigger than this... Imagine everyone in the city stood before the camera...

Effect   Hold on, hold on...

Cause   Picture the population of England... Of Europe...

Effect   This is silly...

Cause   Picture all the people in the world... Now... What have we but all the living instances of the universal 'Human Being'? Humans, Wittgenstein would be obliged to say, form a family.

Effect   The brotherhood, I'm sorry, the siblinghood, of man.

Class Consciousness

Cause   The question is: can we, on the basis of patterns of resemblance, usefully *sub-classify* this great gathering into races, tribes and families? And if so, why and how?

Effect   Well obviously some racial distinctions like skin-colour would be immediately apparent.

Cause   Would they though? If all the people posed in the photograph were thoroughly mixed up, who knows what networks of criss-crossing similarities would strike us most forcibly. Everything would depend upon what we were looking for... Suppose our visitor ET were to scan the picture... You have mentioned the black/white distinction, but what about male/female, young/old, fat/thin, short/tall, smiling/frowning? The photograph could be mapped in many different ways.

Effect   Most of which would be of aboslutely no use or relevance to anyone. This all goes to show how little an inert, two-dimensional photograph has to do with real human beings or real human life. By itself, a simple group portrait tells us nothing about its subjects' geographical origins, nationalities, languages, religious beliefs, political persuasions, economic circumstances, lifestyles, customs, tastes... Come to that, a still photograph doesn't indicate that people are capable of *behaviour* at all. That college photo could have been posed by a bunch of dummies.

Cause   No doubt Malcolm, no doubt... You are right of course: in all important respects a photograph of a man is quite unlike a man, for a photograph is just a piece of flimsy paper. But then so far we have not been looking for important respects, we've been looking for family resemblances, for similarities in facial features, eye-colour, build and so on.

Effect   Wittgenstein also mentions gait and temperament.

Cause   So perhaps we should be thinking of a movie of our family group, or of a video.

Effect   But then there will be questions about how people are to be filmed, who is to direct the movie, who is to do the editing. And in the end again, all we are left with is a fixed sequence of two-dimensional images which can have nothing much in common with real people and their real lives. Forget photography! I don't know why you mentioned it, Wittgenstein didn't. You keep quoting him, so don't imagine, read! Don't think, look! And don't look at photographs, look at families!

Cause   Okay, but the more one looks at families, at real families in real

186

action, the less important, or even noticeable, become the supposed family resemblances upon which Wittgenstein's analogy depends. He mentions gait and temperament, but will you confidently assert that *these* characteristics are transmitted in the genes? Surely gait and temperament are more likely candidates for the 'living together' hypothesis? We are in an area of uncertainty here. Theorists differ over the extents to which characteristics like these are inherited and acquired. In the end, given the fact that no two babies are born identical and that it is impossible to reproduce absolutely...

Effect   There is some research which seems to indicate that certain psychological characteristics can be inherited. Interestingly, identical twins that are reared together tend to display psychological differences while identical twins that are reared apart tend to show psychological similarities.

Cause   Ha! The perverse little genie strikes again! We are coming down to the point where no two people can be identical simply by virtue of the fact that no two people can simultaneously occupy the same space, physical *or* psychological. In any case, I assume you would agree that as far as learning behaviour is concerned, the parental and social and evironmental influences on a child are far more obvious and significant than any characteristics it may have inherited genetically.

Effect   Most child-behaviour comes from imitating parents, certainly.

Cause   And from reacting against parents. I can't imagine, for example, that anyone would suggest that the genes are responsible for the members of a family *getting on well together.*

Effect   Do I detect the smell of unhappy childhood?

Cause   Look at the list of 'relevant distinctions' you have just compiled: nationality, language, politics, religion and the rest: not one of these all-too-powerful acquired characteristics owes a single atom to the workings of your precious genes.

Effect   True enough.

Cause   Take your own children Malcolm, your two girls...

Effect   Three girls.

Cause   Three, gosh! What characteristics can you honestly say they have inherited from you?

Effect   Well, skin-colour for a start, roughly speaking, though I suppose

Umbilical Cords

Chrissie, the youngest, is a bit darker... People do say that Ella, our second looks facially rather like me...

Cause   You sound as though you don't agree.

Effect   It's not for me to judge is it?

Cause   Is that all? Nothing else? Sex, obviously not. What about gait, temperament, personality?

Effect   Er... I'm not sure... I suppose Jean, the eldest, has a side to her which is a bit like me in some ways, but...

Cause   Don't we all?

Effect   I think the experience of having children teaches one that in the end, or I should say in the beginning, children are born with pretty well-defined personalities of their own.

Cause   No? I don't believe it! Born with their own personalities?

Effect   But of course the fact that children's personality-traits cannot always clearly be traced back to their forebears' does not mean that they are not determined genetically. Innate psychological characteristics must be transmitted by the genes along with physical features.

Cause   Isn't it marvellous! Even before the poor little bugger has opened his eyes and started learning the bad news, you've got him shackled down by his blood-lines, by his ancestral roots, by his family DNA-chains. Why can't you let birth be what it is, a fresh start, someone new? Why all these mythic umbilical cords? Why can't you accept that the only important relationships between you and your children are the obvious ones?

Effect   What do you mean, the obvious ones?

Cause   Well, that your daughters were conceived when they were conceived by you and your wife, that they grew for nine months or so in *her* womb, that they were born when they were born, that they grew up where they grew up, and that, er... well, that's all.

Effect   That's all!?

Cause   Yes, these are the only *real* relationships between parents and children, and they are the only relationships that matter. Everything else, all this stuff about 'blood lines' and 'genes' is nonsense, a dangerous mythology. The only real connection between a mother and her new-born child is the obvious one, the physical one. And once that is cut... it is cut. Cut!

Effect   What!? This is outrageous!! You obviously have no idea whatsoever about motherhood, about the bonds between a mother and her children. You talk of the "nine months or so in her womb" as though her baby were temporarily renting a room there! Don't you think that such an intimate tenancy is bound to generate an immense bond of love between mother and child, that strongest, most precious of all human bonds?

Cause   It doesn't always seem to do so though does it?

Effect   Oh, nearly always.

Cause   Uhuh? But anyway, so what? A bond of love is not a genetic relationship.

Effect   And what happens when baby is born? You say that when his cord is cut, that's it, he's on his own; but baby's going to die on his own unless someone does something, and smartly too. I mean who, in your scheme, is going to look after this one-hour-old, fully independent free agent that you've dreamt up?

Cause   I don't know, that's another question, nothing to do with genetics.

Effect   What? Don't you think that it is the people who bring the children into the world who should be responsible for bringing them up?

Cause   Ermm... No, not necessarily... I'd rather put it the other way round: I don't believe that it is necessarily the *right* of the natural parents to bring up the child.

Effect   Are you serious!?

Cause   Perfectly.

Effect   Oh, well in that case, I... I don't think there's much point in us continuing with this conversation. Obviously you've got some huge chip on your shoulder about parenthood or something. I can see we are just going to end up losing our tempers.

Cause   Speak for yourself Malcolm. You're the parent around here, surely you should be able to discuss these questions calmly and rationally?

Effect   Look, er... Excuse me Andrew, but I'm going to make a cup of tea now, if you don't mind...

Cause   Go ahead. Excellent idea.

※ ※ ※ ※ ※ ※ ※ ※ ※ ※ ※

Effect   What a beautiful afternoon, not a cloud in the sky!

Cause   Please Malcolm, let me try to explain. At least hear me out.

Effect   Milk?

Cause   Oh, er, yes, thanks... Earlier on we agreed, did we not, that in general we hold people responsible for their actions insofar as we find their excuses "I could not help it because..." inadmissible.

Effect   Sugar?

Cause   No, ta... Well it seems to me that a very good example of an excuse that is no longer morally admissible is: I could not help having a baby.

Effect   Here... I'm afraid I've slopped it a bit, sorry.

Cause   Our recent discoveries of various more or less acceptable methods of birth control mean that this excuse would not now, er, stand up.

Effect   Fruitcake? Biscuit?

Cause   No thanks. In short, it is now open to us, indeed it is our duty, to regard child-bearing as a moral act.

Effect   And don't we so regard it?

Cause   Not really, not in a full sense, no. As an activity, child-bearing has never been the subject of legislation, the subject of formal, judicial censure. Of course there have been ideas about the proper and improper circumstances in which to have children, and the having of children out of wedlock used to be, and to some extent still is, frowned upon and stigmatized, but it has never been regarded as meriting... as meriting any officially-administered punishment for example.

Effect   And you think that it should be?

Cause   No, of course not, but... but...

Effect   But what?

Cause   Look, go back to square one: giving birth is giving someone life wouldn't you say?

Effect   You could put it like that I suppose.

Cause   And the opposite of giving someone life is taking someone's life?

Effect   Ye-es.

Cause   And taking someone's life, deliberately, is murdering them, is it not?

Effect   So?

Cause   Well, there's presumably no doubt that the act of murder has moral status, indeed it is generally regarded as being the most *im*moral of all actions; it is most definitely the subject of legislation and its perpetrators are most certainly deserving of official punishment. So on the face of it, is it not very odd that child-bearing, the precise opposite of murder, its complement if you like, is not accorded correspondingly high importance? Is it not strange that child-bearing is not the subject of any institutionalized sanction or honour?

Effect   That's silly: nearly every woman is fertile, nearly every man potent.

Cause   Nearly everyone is capable of murder.

Effect   Besides, I don't think you're right anyway. Surely there is a sense in which we do publicly regard childbirth as being a good, a happy, a praiseworthy event?

Cause   Oh yes, but only in a vague, generally thanksgiving sort of way, as one might respond to the good weather or to a lucky escape. I am wondering why child-bearing is not within the province of legislature, is not officially regulated or rewarded in some way.

Effect   Surely it is though, through the tax system, the child benefit scheme and so on?

Cause   Crumbs of financial comfort maybe, but not exactly a demonstration that the State regards child-bearing as being a particularly virtuous activity, or as having any special *moral* status. Similar crumbs are dished out to people who have the misfortune to be disabled or blind. This is it you see: as a society we still treat childbirth as though it were a matter of luck, something outside our control, something which just happens. But of course this is not true any more: we can now *choose* whether to have children, and when.

Effect But this is nothing new. We have always been able to control our procreation, simply by controlling when and with whom we have sex.

Cause Yes, but sexual behaviour, and as some would say *mis*behaviour, has always been legitimate, admissible, has never really been regarded as an appropriate area for the operation of law.

Effect Oh yes? What about rape, and child-molesting?

Cause Certain extremes of personal abuse become criminal, obviously, but apart from these, as far as the law goes, it's a nudge, a wink and a blind eye. In the past it seems to have been generally accepted (a) that men and women cannot help having their sexual appetites, (b) that within certain fairly wide limits they have the right to satisfy them...

Effect The *man* has the right to satisfy *his*. In the past, women's sexual rights have been largely denied or ignored.

Cause And (c) that the child-bearing consequences of this general sexual freedom, being rather unpredictable, are matters of luck. But this assumption (c) is simply not true any more. In the past, child-bearing has not been regarded as a moral act because there has been no point in so regarding it. The mother's excuse "I could not help it" would always, for different reasons and to different extents, have stood up in imaginary court. She could perhaps have helped, or at least controlled, her sexual desires, but then sexual indulgences in themselves are minor, pardonable transgressions and not properly the concern of the law.

Effect This has not always been the case though, and in some parts of the world women are still publicly punished in the most barbarous ways for what we would consider to be peccadillos, or just pleasures.

Cause I know. Hideous. But no doubt the barbarisms arose as attempts to avoid the social chaos of unwanted and uncared-for children. Now, thanks to our ability to control conception, such deterrents to sexual freedom are no longer necessary. What we have not yet fully grasped is that the quid pro quo for this new freedom is our procreative *responsibility*. Because a mother's excuse "I could not help it" doesn't now automatically stand up, it has become *practicable* to treat child-bearing as a moral act.

Effect   This is blatant sexism! You pass all the responsibility for childbirth onto the mother! A typical male cut-and-run attitude! No wonder you have no success with women.

Cause   Not at all. It's not my fault if it's the woman who gets pregnant! It's not me who's the sexist, it's Nature, Mother Nature!

Effect   Really Andrew, I applaud everything you say about racism, but when it comes to sex...

Cause   Look: regarding and treating people differently on account of some trivial physical characteristic like skin-colour is evil. Regarding and treating people differently on account of their sexual denomination is not only life's most joyous instinct and most powerful driving force, it is also, I would venture to suggest, our cardinal moral duty.

Effect   Dearodearodear!

Cause   Have I said something controversial? It's sex that makes the world go round! At least it's sex that makes the world go on going round.

Effect   Okay, there's no need to shout.

Cause   Oh, I know that a lot of things don't necessarily follow from the fact that women can have children and men can't, but an awful lot of things *do* follow from it. And given that questions about child bearing and rearing might well be thought amongst the most important moral questions we face, surely it follows that sexual discrimination in such matters should be morally paramount, or rather, is morally axiomatic?

Effect   If I may say so, I think you will have to revise some of your attitudes drastically if you're going to stand any chance of having your book published.

Cause   Has it come to this? One can't call a spade a spade for fear of some foolish, faddish censorship? I hope I'll always be able to revise my attitudes Malcolm, but for sure I'll never pretend to rewrite the facts of life.

Effect   Well I will: women can now be inseminated artificially; offspring can be cloned asexually; a fertilized ovum has even been implanted and grown successfully in a *man's* gut.

Finger Printing

Cause All this is going to be compulsory is it?

Effect Don't be silly. The point is that it's possible. It's already helping many infertile couples.

Cause All sorts of things may be possible. Perhaps it will be possible for babies to be conceived and born... anonymously, outside the human body altogether. Would that beget true sexual equality? Would that deliver women's liberation?

Effect I don't know. Maybe it would.

Cause Is that what women want? Is that what children would allow? Perhaps you'll find a genetic way of engineering out the whole dirty, old-fashioned, troublesome business. Perhaps you would have people buy their relationships from social supermarkets where all one's needs and desires are specified precisely like the vitamins and minerals on a cereal packet.

Effect Of course not, that's ridiculous, no-one wants that.

Cause Exactly. That would be brain-in-dish time. We'd all be cutting and running then. Which returns us to the point from which we must start: that by and large women get pregnant and men do not.

Effect Yes, well, I'm happy to inform you that your carefree, laissez-faire virility-romp has recently been dealt a bit of a blow, if not by the feminists, by forensic science. There is now a method of genetic fingerprinting whereby a child's father can be identified with ninety-nine percent certainty.

Cause Christ, is there really!? How is it done? I thought genes were invisible; how can they leave fingerprints?

Effect Oh it's nothing to do with actual fingerprints. It's a highly complex process in which the DNA from a sample of a person's blood or semen is isolated and analyzed. It has been found that a short mini-satellite DNA sequence in an intron of the myoglobin gene, when extracted and subjected to electrophoresis in an agarose gel...

Cause Yes, yes, but what do they come out with, what can they see?

Effect Oh, a sort of blurred pattern of lines on a photographic plate, rather like a line spectrum.

Cause Phew! So that's all!

Effect   The pattern is specific to each individual and can be recognized in the pattern of his or her offspring.

Cause   I'm surprised it's taken them so long.

Effect   Well they've got it now and it's admissible evidence, so watch it!

Cause   What are you implying Malcolm? I've got nothing to hide! Hm, well that's going to put a few cats amongst the pigeons. It looks like gloves on all round... But this only *strengthens* my argument. I'm in favour of *increasing* parental accountability. It should now be practicable to put *both* parents in the dock. She won't automatically get away with "I couldn't help it" and he won't automatically get away with "You cannot prove it".

Effect   What's all this about putting parents *in the dock*? You are talking about child-bearing as though it were *a crime*.

Cause   And don't you think it is, sometimes? Surely, we all know of cases when we have wanted to say, and indeed may have said that so-and-so's having of a child was criminally irresponsible: the haemophiliac parents who quite predictably go ahead and have haemophiliac children; the middle-aged woman who ignores all the advice and gives birth to a mental defective; the AIDS sufferer who knows the score but doesn't warn his girlfriend. Now at last we can give our assertions about responsibility some muscle.

Effect   Very dangerous ground. Any moment you'll be talking about weeding out weaknesses, genetic selection, the breeding of a better species, all that superman stuff. First goose-steps in fascism.

Cause   Evolution I thought you called it.

Effect   So did Hitler and his death-camp surgeons.

Cause   Look Malcolm, I'm not advocating any death-camp surgery, I'm merely suggesting that it's wrong of haemophiliac couples to have children. I know of a case where it seems that the mother actually *wanted* to have her handicapped child so she could be certain that someone would always be dependent on her.

Effect   That's a terrible thing to suggest!

Cause   No, it's a terrible thing to *do*. And what about the girl of sixteen with no husband and no money who has a baby for what she thinks is the fun of it? She soon finds herself unable to cope, another toddler goes into care, another childhood's ruined. Does *that* sound like responsible behaviour?

Effect   Okay, okay, I agree with you, people should be more careful about having children, but I wouldn't want to lay down any laws about it. I see no point in treating such irresponsibility as criminal. At least we seem to agree that the child's welfare is the main concern, so how is punishing its parents going to improve that? Surely a single mother is going to have enough problems anyway, bringing up a kid on her own?

Cause   As though the child itself were her punishment?

Effect   Well, no, but... but if anything she needs helping, not penalizing.

Cause   But Malcolm, you are confusing two evidently different activities: child-*bearing* and child-*rearing*. You have assumed that the responsibility for rearing a child necessarily falls to its natural parents or parent. In a world where conception just happens, this may be the most practicable general rule, but now that it's at last under our control, questions about child-*rearing* responsibilities can be considered quite separately.

Effect   Oh nonsense, of course they can't, they're bound together hand and foot!

Cause   Once the cord between mother and baby has been cut, that's it: no hidden, occult genetic connections, no absolute, God-given moral responsibilities, nothing!

Effect   Monstrous! So what would you do in practice? Forcibly sterilize haemophiliacs? Lock up HIV carriers? Sentence broke sixteen-year-olds to abortions? What about the careless mother who refused? Prison?

Cause   Oh, er, I don't know, a fine maybe.

Effect   Ah, "a fine maybe". Good God, how can you toss off such grotesque suggestions so casually!? How will a fine help her bring up the child?

Cause   I am not assuming that she would necessarily bring up the child. As I say, I am trying to *separate* child-bearing and child-rearing, I am questioning *the whole genetic family system*.

Effect   So what, your 'offending' mother is not only imprisoned or fined, but also has her baby *forcibly snatched*!?

Cause Er, well, I wouldn't put it like that... I think perhaps we are concentrating too much on the criminality aspect. In saying that child-bearing should now be regarded as a moral act, my more general purpose is to suggest that it is now a proper subject for laws and rules and regulations.

Effect What do you mean, licenses to have children!?

Cause That's one possibility, certainly.

Effect But I thought you were *against* the spread of laws and rules and regulations, I thought you were the great *champion* of personal liberties?

Cause I'm not against laws per se, I'm against the multiplication of trivial laws, unnecessary laws, laws without sound justifications, laws which infringe basic human rights.

Effect And isn't it a basic human right to have children? Haven't I the right to raise a family if I wish? And what gives *you* the right to say otherwise?

Cause Okay, keep your hair on! You react, interestingly, as though I were impugning your virility. I don't see that it is at all outrageous to question this so-called human right. Do you really think that it should be the right of everyone who can to just have children, as many children as they like?

Effect How do you mean, *just* have children?

Cause Has everyone the right to have a child merely because they *want* one, for whatever reason? Perhaps on a whim or for self-gratification, perhaps to improve their confidence or image, perhaps to rescue a relationship or to entrap a partner... Surely to assent to such a proposition is to confer upon a person or a couple far too much power over another's life? Surely such vital decisions simply cannot be left to individuals?

Effect But who *does* have the right to decide? Who is going to say who can have children and who can't, and on what grounds?

Cause Come come, this problem is common to *all* law-enforcement. Who gives Parliament the right to pass laws? Who gives the police the right to make arrests? Who gives the jury the right to reach a verdict? Who gives the judge the right to pass sentence? It is crazy that in a society where on all sides human rights and freedoms are being ever more tightly circumscribed by petty rules and regulations, where individuals are ascribed ever less moral intelligence and personal responsibility, this quite extraordinary and apparently indefensible right still goes quite unchallenged. A man who is not deemed responsible to choose when to wear a seat-belt or where to cross the road, is, apparently, perfectly responsible to decide, if he fancies, to bring half-a-dozen people into the world. Or half a gross.

Effect You'll be pleased to learn that in China they have acted upon your advice and have introduced a law limiting every couple to just one child.

Cause Yes I know. You see, it can be done. I guess that Wittgenstein's analogy is not going to mean much to the young Chinese is it? Still, they've got a different sort of language anyway, a different sort of problem.

Effect Yes, overpopulation. They have been forced to limit the size of families by the threat of famine.

Cause Exactly. An admirably pragmatic and civilized move, if they can pull it off, but somehow made for all the wrong reasons. I am arguing that child-bearing is now a proper subject for legislation *whatever* the facts about populations and resources, simply on the grounds (a) that since it concerns the giving of life it should be treated as a moral act if it is practicable to do so, and (b) that thanks to birth-control it *is* now practicable to do so.

Effect But laws are introduced not to complete the neat theorems of moral philosophers, but to solve or control pressing problems.

Cause Taking a global view, there aren't many of the Earth's problems that wouldn't be solved, or at least greatly alleviated, by reducing its human population. Whichever way you look at it, the world is getting mighty overcrowded, explosively hungry. And it is an explosion not just of populations, but of *aspirations* too, the global demand for...

Effect Sports cars?

Cause It'll come Malcolm, it's bound to come. It would be a shame if it came for the wrong reasons, or in the wrong way.

Effect Okay, but forget the apocalypse. Here, now, in England, where there is no population explosion and no threat of famine, I don't see why we need even to contemplate such a controversial and troublesome piece of legislation.

Cause In England we don't call it overpopulation, we call it unemployment. Here, the famine is of jobs, the pressing problems are those other close relatives of overcrowding: city poverty, racial tension, police hostility, youthful boredom, family breakdown, child abuse, baby battering... Again, it is not just that we regard indiscriminate procreation as a basic human right, but that our present family system confers upon the genetic parents all sorts of extraordinary rights over a child once it has been born: the right to indoctrinate it religiously, politically and artistically; the right to inflict upon it, deliberately or otherwise, bizarre psycho/sexual attitudes; the right to decide what it will eat, how it will dress, what it will read, where it will be educated and so on.

Effect But Andrew, children are not fully developed, they are not fully responsible. They are simply not capable of making such decisions for themselves.

Cause Aren't they? Any of them? Children's rights and responsibilities are becoming a matter for public debate, albeit usually rather muddled. What about physical violence? At school the point is moot, but at home...? A child's genetic parents apparently have the right to beat it at will, to crack its skull against walls, to use its face as an ashtray, to lock it in drawers, you know the sort of thing. Often the law intervenes only when the kid is dead.

Effect Some of the extreme cases are terrible, it's true...

Cause Remember, I have no extra right to hit someone who is mentally sub-normal, quite the reverse. If you hit someone in the street and especially if you hit a child, you are most provocatively breaking the law. But if you hit *your own* child, no problem, no-one bats an eyelid.

Effect Don't get me wrong Andrew, I hate physical violence and I used to smack the girls only as a last resort, but in the end I do think that this ultimate sanction is part of the powers necessary to parents for their children's proper upbringing. I believe that if you had children of your own you would soon realize this.

Cause All too soon I fear.

Effect In Sweden, where it's against the law for parents to hit their children, I hear it's snooper-city.

Cause And the kids are bored witless, take to drink in their teens, all that. One thing I notice Malcolm: you mentioned "the powers necessary to parents for their children's proper upbringing"; 'proper' as opposed to 'improper'. This implies that you could list certain objective criteria to determine (a) whether or not a particular family situation is suitable, materially, psychologically or whatever and (b) whether or not the adults possess the necessary natural aptitudes and acquired skills for a child's 'proper' upbringing. In other words, there are good or bad parents, in good or bad family situations, bringing up children well or badly.

Effect   Er... yes, I suppose there are certain minimal criteria, though again I would hesitate to lay down the law about such things. On balance though, I do believe that a conventional, monogamous marriage of love, even a poor one, does provide the most caring relationship, the best chance for children to grow up in happy harmonious, stable surr...

Cause   Stable!? With the rate at which marriages break up these days? I don't know about you, but when I think of the friends of mine who've married... All those post-honeymoon disillusionments, all that frustration, staleness and boredom, all those sordid wranglings over money and bitter love-tuggings over the kids, all that wasted emotional energy... No Malcolm, love is a notoriously fickle forecaster of family stability. When they see the dreadful messes we make with our fanciful freedoms, it is small wonder that the old-guard Indians prefer to *arrange* their marriages.

Effect   Oh yes? I can see you getting on famously under *that* regime!

Cause   Well, at least I wouldn't have to choose, to choose and be chosen. You never know, I might get lucky... Why just *two* adults anyway? I should have thought one could argue that this creates the worst possible psychological environment for a child: the whole Oedipus/Electra syndrome, where the wife's love naturally transfers from husband to son and the husband's from wife to daughter, generating all those familiar jealousies and conflicts... Again, what is the *proper* number of children? Is the two-parent relationship as good for a ten-child family as it is for a two-child family? And think of all the *one*-child families there are: what a terrible waste of human resources *that* constitutes. I have a vision of millions of intelligent, active young women each trapped in her own separate little house or flat all day looking after a single toddler.

Effect   But there are playschools, neighbourhood crèches, community centres; not enough maybe, but...

Cause   Exactly, there are better family systems. Again, why should the parental responsibilities fall to these two adults rather than to those two? A couple who were good parents for children A, B and C might, for any number of reasons, prove to be bad parents for children D, E and F. Is there any guarantee under our present, 'natural' system that children are going to end up with the parents who are right for them? Presumably, as we said earlier, no-one will claim that your postulated genes cause their subjects to get on with one another, yet surely this is the characteristic above all which we desire in our families? What a crackpot system it is which foists cohabitation upon people who simply do not like each other! What a recipe for psychosocial disorder!

Effect You regard yourself as one of the system's casualities I take it?

Cause No, I think I've been very lucky really, considering... Home was a bit grim sometimes, but I guess that's par for the course.

Effect What does your father do?

Cause He was a surveyor. A professional man, you know: worry, over-work, exhaustion, protracted bad moods; Ryle please note.

Effect Brothers? Sisters?

Cause One of each. We hardly met in childhood, we were all sent off to board at public schools, so-called: in loco, as they say, parentis.

Effect Did you have a bad time?

Cause No I didn't actually, though I know plenty who did. I enjoyed it. Rule-breaking 'S' Level, great fun!

Effect It must have been terribly expensive for him.

Cause Yes, when I think... all those fees, all that struggle, all that penny-pinching sacrifice to support a family he hardly ever saw and never really seemed to enjoy. Funny old game isn't it?

Effect I don't suppose you've ever thanked him for any of that?

Cause And now this place.

Effect Did he want you to follow in his footsteps, to become a surveyor?

Cause Of course. It was a black day when I chose philosophy... Strange really, for in a way I suppose I have followed in them...Things are fine now.

Reproduction

Effect So there you are you see: it all works out in the end... I accept that our family system isn't perfect, but as usual you do exaggerate its defects. Children are not *that* fragile, not *that* precious, they are pretty hardy, independent creatures, most of them. I think one can overestimate the psychological damage that children can suffer, at the hands of even the nuttiest parents. Most children turn out alright.

Cause No they *don't* Malcolm! No they *don't*! They turn out repeating the same old prejudices, the same old bigotries, the same old clichés. They end up behaving in the same old ways, making the same old mistakes, fighting the same old wars. Look where all this is leading! "It all works out in the end." *What* all works out? Poverty, disease, starvation, violence, war – that's what works out for most people. Of course it works out in the end, it has to! And always despite the system! I don't know, maybe a happy childhood *should* be a matter of luck, maybe home *should* be a poor or troubled or violent place, maybe children *should* want to leave their families as soon as possible, to stand on their own two feet, to cut off from their roots, to strike out in new directions. What good is all this mamby-pamby "caring loving stable relationship" crap? What sort of training is that for the real world outside? How is that going to generate invention and ambition and rebellion? Maybe we should actually throw tin-tacks in the family road, maybe education should actively encourage rule-breaking. I don't know, I don't know...

Effect Oh no, no, I don't mean that.

Cause Of course not! Of course not! Look, if all this upbringing, all this education and all this talk means anything, it must mean that we should try to *improve* our family system, to *improve* the ways in which we educate children, to *improve* the world we hope them to inherit.

Effect Right.

Cause So don't take everything so personally. What's it all about if we don't learn from our mistakes, if we can't talk things through, work things out, if the discussion always degenerates into self-justification? Don't think back, look ahead! Earlier on you asked: don't you think that it's the people who bring the children into the world who should be responsible for bringing them up?

Effect Yes, and your reply was: not necessarily.

Cause Ah, but now, if by "the people who bring the children into the world" one means child-bearers, that is adults in general, then of course

202

the answer is an unequivocal 'yes'. *We* are responsible for bringing up the next generation, *we* institute the family systems and the educational arrangements.

Effect   So what would you actually do, what are you proposing?

Cause   Okay then: one nice, surprisingly easy little proposal would be the scrapping of inherited surnames.

Effect   What!?

Cause   Why not? Now's the time. Feminist wives are understandably disgruntled about surrendering their maiden names, so why not let's choose children's second names from a list, like we choose their first? Or we could go back to Doomsday Book times, when people's second names were what they did or how they looked. Dispute settled!

Effect   But... You couldn't just... It would cause untold confusion. What would be the point?

Cause   Apart from anything else, it might be a first step towards breaking down all the old barriers of clan and tribe and race.

Effect   Uhuh? And then what? What is the philosopher's great new family system? Babes wrenched from their mothers' arms at birth? Toddlers farmed out to State nurseries? Children forced through vast mass-education factories?

Cause   Isn't this more or less what happens now, minus the emotive language? A moment ago you were all in favour of neighbourhood crèches, while presumably your mass-education factories are in fact our comprehensive schools. And when it comes to motherhood, don't modern economic pressures drive most young mums straight back to work anyway?

Effect   But actually depriving a mother of her natural child, that is something else. I tell you Andrew, the bond between a mother and her baby is the most intimate, most...

Cause   *Her* baby, there you go! Babies are personal property, they are owned, like slaves used to be. In divorce the custody of the children may be fought over, along with the family income, house or car.

Effect   You would be tampering with the most powerful, most fundamental bond of human love we know. Forget the genes if you wish, but surely the baby's nine months in its mother's womb must count for everything? When I think of what Connie went through to have Ella... It's absurd to dismiss the feelings that pregnancy generates as mere possessiveness.

Cause Is it? One wants to ask a lot of questions here. To what extent is this pregnancy-generated bond a natural, instinctive one as you suggest, and how much is it the product of social conditioning? Is a similar bond felt by the natural father?

Effect Sometimes it is, certainly. A terrible thing happened just last month: one of my research colleagues lost his little boy. He was only eight, a lovely lad. The father's absolutely broken up.

Cause I'm sorry Malcolm, I'm sorry, but it proves nothing. A child can go to pieces when it loses its bunny-rabbit or its teddy-bear. And I'd murder anyone who tried to nick my car... Eight. Sad. How did he die?

Effect Leukemia.

Cause Really? Anything to do with the father's research? It is a bit unusual isn't it? A chance contamination perhaps?

Effect No, no, of course not, out of the question.

Cause Uh? Next, of course, one has to ask if this supposed pregnancy-generated bond is felt by the baby; experiments seem to indicate that any mother will do. Then there is this new 'surrogate' motherhood, which seems to demonstrate that your allegedly all-powerful bond is often perfectly breakable.

Effect Ah, well, personally I'm not sure about the morality of this surrogacy business...

Cause We're not considering the morality of the business, we're just trying to establish the facts... In any case one can also go on to ask if this bond is necessarily a force for good in the child-rearing process. When you spoke of what your wife went through to have Ella, it almost sounded as though her pregnancy was something for which Ella would be required to *pay*. Sometimes a mother's perhaps unwanted pregnancy and subsequent sacrifice seem to be used as blackmail weapons against the child's moral rights. Indeed the whole child bearing-and-rearing enterprise is often portrayed as though it were some great burden or affliction: a woman's lot in life.

Effect   But child bearing and rearing *is* hard work and *does* require great self-sacrifice, take it from me.

Cause   Oh I'm sure it does, of course it does. But this is no excuse for those parents one knows who make their children *suffer for* the obligations that parenthood places upon them. Again remember: having children is now a matter of choice.

Effect   You keep emphasizing the responsibilities Andrew, but there are great rewards too: the first time they smile, and walk, and speak; watching them grow and learn and develop.

Cause   Yes, yes, I'm sure, I'm sure.

Effect   And in a way, the greatest reward of all *is* the responsibility. For the first time in my life, someone really depended upon me, someone else mattered more than I did. We lived *for* them. It was a great lesson. I reckon it's a lesson that would do you a bit of good.

Cause   Oh, yes, very probably. Why is it that people who have had children always try to *proselytize* people who haven't? As though we are missing out on some great religious experience.

Effect   Perhaps you are.

Cause   You seem to want everyone to be a parent. Why can't you accept that it may simply be the case that some people are best suited to some tasks or lifestyles, and others to others? More self-justification perhaps?

Effect   Okay, if that's the way you feel about it, why don't you stick to philosophy and leave parenting to the parents?

Cause   Another thing I hate is what children do to adults. Most of the couples I know have gone brain-dead the moment they had a kid: you can't hold a sensible conversation with them; you can't keep their attention for more than ten seconds; sometimes you can't even get a word in.

Effect   Oh, that must hurt...

Cause   I suppose in truth my book is my baby, and until that is born...

Effect   But you can't carry on with this futile lechering all your life.

Cause   Why not...? Don't worry Malcolm, I have had steady relationships, I have lived with girls, but marriage has, has somehow never seemed... right. The one time I did propose, virtually on sight, the girl turned out to be a lesbian.

Effect   Oh yes?

Cause   It's true! Hmm... I wonder what an impartial observer, ET for example, would make of it all; if he viewed human affairs through a blurring, low-resolution telescope, I wonder what he would deduce about our relationships. I imagine he would spot the sexual distinction easily enough and would notice that adults generally go around in male-female pairs... I guess he would notice some male-male and female-female pairings too, and people who are AC/DC...

Effect   You do realize, Andrew, that each of us is a mixture, sexually speaking. The chromosomes which determine our sexual denominations come in two types which...

Cause   Yes, yes, so I gather. Be clear though: in reminding us of this you are not blurring the sexual distinction, you are canonizing it at the molecular level... Presumably ET would identify the male-female union as being the source of human regeneration and might therefore invoke Sexuality, under some name or other, as the most important drive governing human interactions, but beyond that, what in practice could he predict? What could he say about human affairs at an atomic level? What forecasts could he make about our choices of partner or of which pairings will issue in children, the things that for us are all-important? What could he say about the subtleties of our sexual attractions and liaisons? The mannerisms, the quirks, the inexplicable fascinations that make them work; the trick of a smile which clinches a deal, the careless remark that ends it all; the chance meetings, the dropped handkerchiefs. One thing we know for sure: there is nothing *simple* about sexual relationships. Yet although Love is an infinitely mysterious chemistry, objectively it is the most important of all, for it is the one that determines who is to be.

Effect   Do you really have no desire for children?

Cause   Not so far. I don't think I like them very much, from what I've seen. Not everybody does you know. I can't stand their naked, unfettered little appetites with their demand, demand, demand; their crying, their tantrums, their wilful stupidity; the ugly cunning with which, even at an early age, they play one parent off against the other. I'm just not interested.

Effect   It sounds like it runs in the family.

Cause   I'm sure I'd be impatient, irritable, just like he was... Yes, perhaps that's it: I'm afraid of repeating those mistakes, I dread discovering that, that...

Effect   Oh but surely, if you can talk about it...? As you say, what's the point of all this philosophy if it doesn't help you to learn from the past? I thought you were all for escaping from family patterns, all for breaking the mould?

Cause   Can one though, in the end?

Effect   Of course one can! You're just afraid of responsibility. You're all talk, no action.

Cause   The strangest thing of all is that he's *terribly* supportive of my book and my battle to be published. Perhaps a dedication...

Effect   You sit there with your pen and your paper and your clever-dick arguments, but when it comes actually to doing anything... That's what philosophy's about isn't it, trying to rearrange the world on paper! You think that with just a few strokes of a biro you can reorganize whole societies, can abolish time-honoured family systems, can introduce wonderful rational schemes for planned breeding and parenting... Well all I can say is that I live in the real world, the real world of mothers and fathers, of strong feelings, of working compromises.

Cause   I live in that world too, unfortunately.

Effect   And in the end, change of this kind is always going to be limited, thank goodness, to what ordinary people are prepared to accept. Think of the terrible anguish if the State were to start parting mothers from their newborn. Imagine the outcry! Again, think of some bureaucracy trying to assign parental rights, subjecting couples to tests for suitability, assessing who is fit to rear children and who is not. People would never stand for such things!

Cause   Ah, but that's where you're wrong. People do. These practices are already quite common: here, now, in England. I am thinking not only of the all-too-frequent cases when the State, in the form of the social services, intervenes, sometimes forcibly, to remove a child from the ill-treatment of its natural parents, but also of *adoption*, whereby natural mothers for one reason or another give up their infants for other couples to raise. People do not find it the slightest bit unacceptable that prospective adoptants should be subjected to rigorous vetting-procedures, means tests and so on. Indeed, there would doubtless be considerable public outcry if such procedures were *not* compulsory.

Effect   Hmm, yes, true enough. I should know, we had to go through all that to get Jean.

Cause   You what!?

Effect   Yes, our eldest girl Jean, she was adopted. I don't know why I didn't mention it earlier. I guess I'd forgotten. Two years after we got married Connie was told she'd never have children, and since we both wanted one very much, we decided to adopt. Strange, it was almost as though her experience with Jean cured her of whatever it was, for less than a year later she was pregnant. The doctors couldn't believe it when she had Ella.

Cause   Really? How extraordinary! Jean knows she's adopted does she?

Effect   Oh yes, we told her when she was eight; it didn't seem to worry her in the slightest. I don't think it matters to any of them; it certainly doesn't matter to us. As far as we are concerned, she *is* our real daughter. She's happily married herself now. She's expecting their first in December. Hold on, let me find that photo I was looking for... Ah, here we are...

Cause   I say, what gorgeous creatures! And your wife too... You are a lucky man Malcolm, you must be very proud.

Effect   Hey, hands off! This is my best print! See if you can spot Jean, the odd one out.

Cause   Er... There, bottom left.

Effect   No, that's Chrissie, the youngest. Ella's on the right, the philosopher. Jean's the one standing at the back, behind Connie.

Cause   Uhuh? Well I never would have guessed. There you are you see: it matters not one whit!

Effect   Okay, but I still say that in the vast majority of cases the natural family is the best possible child-rearing situation. I don't believe that will ever change.

Cause   Maybe you're right Malcolm. Maybe in general it is the best system, I don't know. I don't much care.

Effect   What!? After all that!? You don't much care!?

Cause   Maybe it is, maybe it isn't. In the end I am concerned not to canvas one family system rather than another, but to demonstrate merely that our ideas about families are not fixed or laid down. The point is that there is not one family system, there are many. Family systems change and evolve. Family systems can be discussed, planned, chosen. Laws and practices concerning family life are constantly under review. The family, in short, is something we are free constantly to redefine.

Effect   I think you have proved your point, so what?

Cause   So, if we refer these conclusions back to Wittgenstein's analogy and the Problem of Universals, we may come to see that what goes for the human family goes for all other universals too. Universals like 'Table' and 'Game' and 'Philosophy' are no more fixed or pre-defined than 'Family'. Ditto 'Mind', ditto 'Purpose', ditto 'Freedom'.

Effect   We are the masters of our language, in other words?

Cause   If you wish... I say, look! A cricket match! There, on the green beyond those trees, to the right of the river... Cricket, now *there's* a game for you!

Effect   You like cricket?

Cause   Of course. Why don't we go over and watch for a while? It has cooled down a bit. It looks beautiful out there...

＊　＊　＊　＊　＊　＊　＊　＊　＊　＊　＊

6

GOODS
and
MORALS

Effect   Ah, look, a bench, over there beyond the tree.

Cause   Splendid... What a scene! What a setting! Ah cricket, the greatest game of all!

Effect   Do you play Andrew?

Cause   Me? Oh, no... Squash is my game. I do love to watch cricket though. Howabout you?

Effect   I play for the Occasionals, in the Sunday League. Passable off-spin bowling, a few runs sometimes.

Cause   Really? It looks like being a great summer doesn't it, with the West Indians coming. They're amazing, brilliant in all departments: Richards, Greenidge, Marshall, Ambrose, they are supermen.

Effect   I don't know, our lot don't look too bad this year... Botham can be a superman too. And Gooch, Smith, Gower...

Cause   But where are our fast bowlers? We've got no-one to match theirs.

Effect   Ah, but we've got the spin. I think there might be a few surprises. Personally, I find the endless parade of pure pace rather boring. I think

Moving the Wickets

there's something to be said for obliging sides to include at least one specialist spinner.

Cause Oh come off it! That's just changing the rules to give yourself a better chance of winning. You set the rules and then you stick by them. If fast bowling wins matches and they've got the best, so be it. The game's the game.

Effect Yes, but the game is changing, for the worse in my opinion. Games and their rules have always evolved as their circumstances have changed, as I'm sure you'd be the first to accept. It's commercial pressure and television that's causing the trouble: all this emphasis on sheer pace and physical confrontation is highly dangerous. Bowlers should aim at the stumps, otherwise it's only a matter of time before someone gets killed. I hate to see all this bouncing people out and batsmen wearing helmets.

Cause I'm of the school which maintains that the best defence against fast bowling is a good eye.

Effect Easily said, from the safety of the boundary.

Cause Good shot...! Oh, was that a four?

Effect Yes, I think there's a rope out there.

Cause Ah... Hmm... Boundaries... Rules... Circumscriptions... That's what we try to do in language isn't it, to trap things with words. And not content with that, we then try to draw lines round the words themselves, to *define* them... Again, in our diagrams, our models, our maps, nice neat lines... Tell me Malcolm, did you ever see the Berlin Wall, or the East/West German border?

Effect I never did, no.

Cause It was an extraordinary sight. The wall of course, cutting straight through the heart of the city, but the border too... I can see it now, sweeping a hundred-metre swathe through a great pine forest. A beautiful green, rolling landscape of rich, dense forest suddenly defaced by a rude, nude, neatly-shaven slash; mined no doubt, lined with high electric fences and precise parallels of barbed wire, dotted to the horizon by a monstrous column of watchtowers and machine-gun posts. From either side of this manicured scar the tall pine-trees brooded darkly, the crows flew back and forth across the divide, the wind and rain blew seeds and leaves this way and that while the night-time mice scurried deftly through the no-man's land.

Frontiers on land are always weird; everything changes and yet nothing does. But there it was especially strange: *not even the people* either side believed themselves to be of different nationalities.

Effect Yes, that must have felt very odd.

Cause Hmm... 'Drawing Lines', that might make a good title for my book.

Effect Ah yes, tell me more about this book of yours: when do you think it will be finished?

Cause Soon, soon, though I've been saying that for a long time. A publisher's the problem.

Effect Well I wish you luck. I'll look out for it. Andrew... Cause isn't it?

Cause I won't be using my real name, that's for sure. I want this to be controversial, and I can do without the loony mail.

Effect What, so you'll use an alias? That's intellectual cowardice!

Cause What do you mean? It's the book that counts. Besides, to be true to my own argument about families I ought to drop my surname anyway, for philosophical reasons.

Effect Phooh! Intellectual cowardice. That or tax evasion.

Cause Simple prudence.

Effect So what name will you use?

Cause I'm not sure, I haven't decided... I suppose I would keep my first name and then use... anything, it doesn't matter... your first name for instnce: Andrew Malcolm. There, that sounds okay, that sounds like a, a philosopher. In fact, yes, I remember, that was the name of the extreme behaviourist I was talking about, the one who claimed that having a dream means waking up and telling a story: Norman Malcolm. Norman Malcolm was the philosopher who never had a dream, I can be his brother Andy, the one who always dreamed of being a philosopher! Andrew Norman, Andrew Nomen, Andrew No-name, I don't know... Mind you, I don't think he was much of a philosopher, to tell you the truth.

Effect And howabout you? Andrew No-man if you have to hide behind a nom-de-plume.

What are Morals?

Cause It's strange Malcolm, for a scientist you have a remarkably developed sense of morals.

Effect How do you mean, "for a scientist"?

Cause You have been evincing moral convictions all day: you were affronted by my 'disabled' sticker; you disapprove of my driving; you have reprimanded me for my attitude towards women; you are a member of A.P.E.S.; you talked of man's responsibilities as a global gardener; you seem to have pretty firm ideas about laws and punishments; you regard it as an adult's right to have children; you have defended our genetic family system; and now you are even accusing me of cowardice for writing under a nom-de-plume!

Effect So? Surely it is extremely *important* for a scientist to have a developed moral sense?

Cause Of course it's important, the trouble is that it's inconsistent. Just as the scientific view of the world apparently rules out any possibility of genuine human freedom or choice or preference, so the scientists' philosophical godfather, logical positivism, seems to rule out any possibility of genuine significance for statements of value or responsibility or morality. In some ways I envy you your moral certainty, in others I find it rather disturbing... For my own part, the more I study moral philosophy, the less certain I become about the nature of moral goodness. Is it objective or subjective? Where does our moral sense come from? Are moral qualities natural qualities? Is there such a thing as *absolute* morality? There are so many questions, so many paradoxes, so many ways of approaching so many problems. I don't know, I guess morality's just not my strong point.

Effect I think you may be right there.

Cause So what *is* morality in your opinion? Or rather, to start with the particular, what are morals?

Effect Ah, you're not catching me out like that again! I thought we had just demonstrated the mistakenness of asking 'What is?' questions.

Cause No, no, there's nothing wrong with asking the questions. That exercise is always valuable. The mistake is to demand or expect particular sorts of answer. Come on Malcolm, what are morals? I'll give you a clue: Latin *mos, moris*: way, manner, custom, habit, fashion.

Effect   Our word 'moraes' in fact. There you are then: morals are ways of behaving.

Cause   Uhuh, so animals and machines and stones and billiard-balls, they all have morals?

Effect   Oh no, obviously only people can have morals... I suppose one does hear expressions like "Good dog!", "Naughty cat!" sometimes, but I don't think they imply the ascription to animals of *morals* exactly.

Cause   Why not? Cats and dogs have characteristic ways of behaving don't they? Animals have habits, customs, social rules even.

Effect   But animals behave by instinct, they have no sense of right and wrong, they have no conscience.

Cause   How can you possibly know that? Isn't this your philosophical race-prejudice again? Besides, what's with this 'sense of right and wrong' and this 'conscience'? I thought you said that morals are just ways of behaving?

Effect   Yes, but...

Cause   Remember: everything behaves in some way or other, even so-called inanimate objects.

Effect   Inanimate objects can't have morals! Objects have no moral status at all, they are morally neutral.

Cause   What about a nuclear bomb? A metal cannister specifically de-signed to destroy cities as totally, to kill human beings as copiously and to poison regions as thoroughly as possible – such an object is morally neutral is it?

Effect   Nuclear fission is nuclear fission. It is a natural process which we have discovered how to harness, for better or worse. It is what we do with it that is morally good or bad.

Cause   So nuclear bombs are not bad things after all?

Effect   Bombs are... are *objects*. Bombs are designed, passive; bombs are built, passive; bombs are dropped, passive.

Cause   Bombs explode, active intransitive; people burn, ditto; unborn children are maimed, passive. So what? What does language prove?

Effect   It reminds us that it is only people who can properly be said to have morals, not things. Any other usage of the word is simply cranky.

Cause   Is it? What about stories?

Effect   Stories?

Cause   Yes, stories, anecdotes, legends, myths – they sometimes have morals don't they? Films can have morals, plays can have morals, arguments can have morals too.

Effect   Oh really! Always a red herring!

Cause   Why, it's the same word isn't it?

Effect   Oh yes, but, but it's *people's* morals that we are talking about, it's *human* morals that are our concern!

Cause   Ah, I agree that *human* morals are the ones that concern us... Okay, so human morals are the ways in which humans behave. Now then, let's see... A motor mechanic behaves in certain ways when he repairs a car. Are these therefore his morals?

Effect   No of course not, these are just his skills and techniques. His morals are more general, more important, they concern the way he lives.

Cause   Surely his car-repairing techniques will be extremely important to him if he earns his living by them and spends his working day as a mechanic?

Effect   Yes... But his morals specifically concern the ways in which he behaves towards other people. They are his *social* behaviour.

Cause   Ahh.

Effect   Yes Andrew, some people behave well towards others, some behave badly.

Cause   I see... So in assessing a man's morals you are evaluating him in some way?

Effect   Of course. If, for example, your car mechanic repaired someone's brakes in a slipshod fashion, then I think that *would* count as morally bad behaviour, for it would be endangering someone else's life.

Cause Uhuh, so casually blowing up someone's engine wouldn't matter, morally speaking?

Effect Oh, well, yes, it would, but...

Cause Perhaps a man's morals consist of his social dispositions, his tendency to be introvert or extrovert, to be friendly or withdrawn?

Effect Oh no, morals are not natural characteristics; they are not like good looks or innate talents. Morally speaking, we are all born equal.

Cause Ah, so the chromosomes-cause-criminality theory has bitten the dust has it?

Effect Oh, er, yes, I think it probably has...

Cause But given that in fact people are all born different, with different gifts and different family backgrounds, what can it mean to say that they are born morally equal?

Effect It means that when we judge a person's morals, we take into account these inequalities, we make allowances for their circumstances, their misfortunes. Indeed I regard it as a moral duty to work wherever possible to *minimize* social inequalities.

Cause What's this about judging people? As I said Malcolm, for an impartial, scientific observer of the world, you do seem to have a remarkably developed moralistic streak, a surprisingly censorious side. Why can't you just leave people alone?

Effect Because there are a lot of weak and elderly and disadvantaged folk in society who need to be protected from thuggery and exploitation, intellectual and otherwise. In morality everyone has an equal chance and equal responsibility, no-one is underprivileged.

Cause Hm. This 'Morality' of yours is beginning to sound like some kind of escapist's dream-world. Are you suggesting that it is immoral to value people for their good looks or their innate talents? Surely this is against Nature?

Effect Perhaps Andrew, morality is our *compromise* with Nature. I think of morality as the *reining-in* of our natural instincts and appetites, as the *harnessing* of our competitive urges. Of course I'm not saying that we shouldn't value people's natural gifts, I am saying that these do not count in our *moral* estimations of them, they do not count as *moral* qualities. Moral qualities require effort, practice even.

Cause   Ah, so they are like social skills? The ability to charm, the art of entertaining, mastery of the make-up brush?

Effect   Certainly not, these are much too superficial, much too manipulative to be *moral* qualities. I am thinking of deeper, more general impulses.

Cause   Taking an interest in others then?

Effect   Ye-es, warm... But no, stronger, stronger than that...

Cause   Inquisitiveness? The desire and ability to discover and understand people's backgrounds and motives? A thorough knowledge of psychology and sociology?

Effect   No, it's not a matter of amassing information or of acquiring knowledge... Though morals can perhaps be *learnt* in a sense...

Cause   Well, I must say, these 'morals' of yours are proving to be very obscure and mysterious qualities indeed.

Effect   Not at all, they are commonplace. They are displayed in some measure in every kind of human interaction. A man's morals are simply the ways in which he lives in society.

Cause   Ah, they are his job, his work, his career? Behaving morally means being a politician or a priest or a policeman or a social worker?

Effect   No of course it doesn't! It's not so much what one does as the way in which one does it.

Cause   Uhuh? So the professional burglar's morals consist of the ways in which he leaves his victims' houses, how much mess he makes, whether he spares the items of sentimental value?

Effect   No, obviously not, but...

Cause   What about an SS Commandant? Or a nerve-gas chemist?

Effect   No, no, I...

Cause   Or a fusion-bomb researcher?

Effect   Hey! What are you implying? Look Andrew, I repeat: point one, I do *not* research into fusion-bomb technology. Point two, there is no such technology. Point three, the H-bomb already is a fusion bomb...

Cause   Point four, everyone's got to make a living. I know Malcolm, I know.

Effect   You don't! You know nothing! You know nothing about the physics. You know nothing about my work. I resent your accusation.

Cause   I didn't realize I'd made one.

Effect   Why... Why do you always try to pick a fight? Why are you so difficult?

Cause   Sorry Malcolm, it's my job... Seriously though, your fusion reactor could be used as a power source couldn't it, to power a beam of some kind?

Effect   Yes I suppose so.

Cause   Well there you are then: bombs, beams, they're all the same.

Effect   No they're *not* all the same! Beams are useful only as *defensive* weapons, they can be directed only against enemy miss...

Cause   Ahh! Ahh! So you *are* a weapons man? A star-warrior? I thought so! Horrifying isn't it, how diffuse the lines of responsibility have become. The weapons systems, the research programmes, the commercial interests, the political pressures, they are all so complex now, so fragmented, so elusive... Nobody actually gets their hands bloodied any more do they?

Effect   There's no blood on my conscience either. I am just a scientist, a seeker after knowledge; I cannot be held responsible for how politicians, or their constituents, use that knowledge.

Cause   So you're happy to be a tool of the Government? You are their employee, remember.

Effect   You are too. In the end I guess we all are, we're all guilty.

Cause   Guilty of a mighty category-mistake. You see: the word 'morals' has become so emasculated that now its reference is relegated merely to people's general considerateness or good manners.

Virtues and Values

Effect   Or to their bedroom-behaviour, I know.

Cause   Meanwhile, Athens burns.

Effect   I agree, I agree, the word ought not to be trivialized. I see a man's morals as being not particular details or aspects or areas of his behaviour, but the underlying values which guide the whole pattern of his actions, the fundamental principles according to which he lives his whole life.

Cause   Ah, so we were wrong, morals are not ways of behaving, they are values and principles?

Effect   Mind you, although qualities like generosity, consideration and tact may not be the most spectacular of moral virtues, yet they are good evidence of a man's general concern for others. And if I may say so, they do make a good start.

Cause   Well I say they are quite value*less* unless illuminated by understanding, perspective and clarity of thought.

Effect   No Andrew, moral goodness *must* spring from selflessness. All the cleverness in the world is worth nothing if it is not dedicated to helping one's fellows.

Cause   But *who are* one's fellows Malcolm, *who are* one's fellows?

Effect   Oh, well bowled...!

Cause   Hang on, hang on, what's happening here? Suddenly it's all 'duties' and 'virtues' and 'values' and 'oughts'. What began as a straightforward factual investigation into the meaning of the word 'morals' has turned into a discussion of how the word *ought* to be used. Your first suggestion was that morals are simply the ways in which people behave, yet now here we are arguing over how we think people *ought* to behave. Something has gone wrong.

Effect   Er... Yes... Strange....

Cause   Somewhere along the line we have stopped inquiring and started recommending. Let's try again: are morals the ways in which people in fact *do* behave or are they the principles according to which people *ought* to behave?

Effect   Er, well, it looks as though, strictly speaking, they are the principles according to which people *ought* to behave. After all, we do talk of
people behaving *im*morally and *a*morally... Yes, yes, that's it, morals are a
common code of conduct which the members of a society *ought* to follow.

Cause   Uhuh, so we were wrong again, it is not individuals who have
morals, but societies?

Effect   Properly speaking I suppose, yes. A society's morals are the set of
rules and principles...

Cause   And prohibitions no doubt.

Effect   ...in accordance with which its members ought to behave.

Cause   Ah, so they are rules and regulations, the laws of the land?

Effect   Well no, not exactly, although a society's morals are reflected in
its laws and its administration of justice. No, morals themselves are more
fundamental, more general, they are *the justification* of legislation.

Cause   Eh? These 'morals' of yours seem more and more like quicksilver.

Effect   For one thing, infringements of moral rules do not necessarily
entail formal punishment.

Cause   So how does any obligation attach to them? What does it mean to
say that people *ought* to behave morally?

Effect   It means that... that these are the ways in which people are
advised, encouraged, exhorted to behave.

Cause   Advised by whom? By you? By the Church? By the advertising
industry? By the CIA? This 'morality' of yours is beginning to sound like a
confidence-trick being pulled by the ruling élite, a spell being cast upon the
troublesome masses by the country-house-and-cocktails set.

Effect   No no, morals are above all that, they are more... more *universal*
principles. They apply at all levels of society. Indeed I would say that the
higher up the power-structure you go, the greater people's moral responsibilities become.

Cause   Ah, so people's moral responsibilities are not all equal as you
insisted earlier?

England Expects...

Effect   Oh, um... er no, no, I suppose not, but...

Cause   So if these obligations apply throughout the society, from top to bottom, where do they originate?

Effect   They, they are general expectations, they are the ways in which one is expected to behave.

Cause   Oh, one is *expected* is one!? Expected by whom? Her Majesty? The Royal Palm-reader? The Worshipful Company of Alternative Parapsychologists?

Effect   Okay, in your case, not expected, just hoped.

Cause   Hoped by whom? Optimists? Pessimists? Parents? Whence comes this vague, subjective, powerless hoping?

Effect   From one's fellow human beings Andrew, from one's fellow human beings, the people whose existence you so resolutely refuse to acknowledge; there's nothing the slightest bit subjective about them, I assure you. Morals are just the principles of behaviour to which the consensus expects us to adhere.

Cause   Uhuh? And where are these principles laid down?

Effect   They aren't actually laid down anywhere, they're not inscribed in tablets of holy stone or anything. They... they are expressed in our social behaviour patterns, in our juridical procedures, in our political...

Cause   I thought you said they are rules, principles, a code. This implies language. Surely they must be written down somewhere? If they're not written down, how do I know that you are interpreting the social behaviour patterns or the consensus of expectations correctly? How do *you* know that you are interpreting them correctly?

Effect   Well, one place where they *are* written down, in very complex and detailed form, is in our thousands of legal precedents, statute books, acts of parliament and so on. As I say, the laws of the land do reflect our morality, they are an expression of our moral values.

Cause   You don't expect everyone to read all that do you?

Effect   Secondly I suppose, our morals are set out in the writings of the legislators and commentators and moralists whom we generally regard as being authorities. Moral points are illustrated too in our literature, in our plays, films, television programmes and so on.

Cause   Ah, so my "stories have morals" remark was not so much a red herring as a bullseye.

Effect   Thirdly, there are the instant, condensed principles or maxims upon which all or most people agree. We have mentioned some already: we hold someone responsible for their actions insofar as we find their excuse "I could not help it" inadmissible. We have agreed, I think, that the punishment should always fit the crime, and that it is the people who bring a child into the world who are responsible for bringing it up. Most people would assent to the principle "Do as you would be done by" and so on.

Cause   So moral laws *can* just be laid down in books, like the Koran or the Bible? And the original Ten Commandments *were*, after all, inscribed in tablets of holy stone.

Effect   I suppose so, yes.

Cause   Compare the theocratic edict "Thou shalt not lie" with our secular "Honesty is the best policy". You suggest that these rules or maxims represent a kind of consensus, are "what most people would agree", but earlier you asserted that it was a moral duty to try to eradicate social inequality. Now I'm not at all sure that most people in this country would agree with that. In fact I don't believe that *you* believe that most people would agree with that. I think you were just recommending a state of affairs which you personally believe ought to exist.

Effect   I did qualify my remark by saying *I regard* this as a moral duty.

Cause   True, but how can you consistently go on to talk about morals as being the *consensus*? If morals are just how most people in fact behave or are a set of agreed rules or norms of social interaction or are a consensus of expectations, then one cannot argue on moral grounds that things should be any other way. Just as one weakness of Wittgenstein's family-resemblances analogy was that it fossilized word-usages, so a fatal weakness of any positivist interpretation of moral statements is that it fossilizes social behaviour-patterns. It becomes impossible coherently to argue for social change.

Effect   But of course it's possible to argue for social change. It's vitally important that we argue for social change, it's our moral duty!

Knowing Better

Cause Of course it is Malcolm, of course it is. What have we been doing for most of the afternoon if not arguing about how we think things *ought* to be, arguing for and against all kinds of current practices and principles? The point has been well demonstrated.

Effect Exactly!

Cause So the last thing that morals can be are principles which are defined by how and what a society as a matter of fact behaves and believes. In arguing for and against social changes we have been appealing to moral principles whose authority is quite independent of, and presumably over-and-above, those of current social practice.

Effect Hmm, yes, I see what you mean... Oh dear, it really is terribly confusing isn't it, this morals business...

Cause Bowled him! Middle stump! He looks fast, this guy. Perhaps they should sign him for England...

✳ ✳ ✳ ✳ ✳ ✳ ✳ ✳ ✳ ✳ ✳

Effect Couldn't it all be just a problem of ignorance?

Cause Sorry?

Effect All this confusion over moral goodness, over the right ways of behaving, over the right ways of living together. I'm sure if people understood what was in their own best interests...

Cause Hey, why have they brought a spinner on?

Effect I think the quickie pulled a muscle... Yes, I'm sure if people knew what was in their own interests, none of these disagreements would arise.

Cause What, so morality is a sort of tacit, social, you-scratch-my-back-and-I'll-scratch-yours deal?

Effect Maybe it is, yes.

Cause And an individual's motive for behaving morally is long-term self-interest?

Effect Perhaps that is so.

Cause   Yet only a moment ago you were insisting that moral goodness must spring from selflessness.

Effect   Oh, yes, I was...

Cause   I'm afraid that any attempt to reduce apparently selfless behaviour to some complex expression of self-interest will suffer not only from this obvious logical incoherence, but also from a perverse implausibility when confronted by many actual examples. Besides extreme cases of saintliness or heroism like the nameless European bourgeois who renounces everything to help with African famine-relief, or the unknown soldier who voluntarily dives onto a grenade to save his fellows, there are also the countless everyday kindnesses and charities which people perform, often with no possibility of reward. Again, your membership of A.P.E.S. is an interesting case... Or perhaps you will say that people do good because it makes them *feel* better?

Effect   No. Of course not. You are right, to try to reduce all moral behaviour to self-interest or self-gratification is absurdly jaundiced, if not downright self-contradictory. Genuine altruism does exist... But nevertheless I would suggest that many moral disputes are predominantly factual. Everyone would agree, for example, that the purpose of laws and social systems is to maximize human happiness.

Cause   Would they? Whose happiness?

Effect   Oh, I don't know... the greatest happiness for the greatest number, something like that.

Cause   Utilitarianism. And who is now going to define human happiness? Is it not the case that as soon as one tries to give this word 'happiness' any substance one discovers that different people can find their happiness in quite different things and ways? Who is going to decide which happiness is genuine and which fake? Who is going to do the measuring and the counting? How are all these questions to be decided?

Effect   People's happinesses, we could say, form a family; there will be patterns of resemblance. These matters could be, and are, decided by debate and discussion and compromise. They are decided by consensus.

Cause   It's funny, now here *is* a principle upon which everyone is agreed, even politicians: everyone claims to be a democrat, in public at any rate.

Effect   Yes, and everyone condemns hypocrisy.

Cause   Tell me this though: if it is simply a question of people coming to understand what is in their own best interests, why is it that people come up with such an extraordinary variety of answers? Not just within each society, but between different societies?

Effect   Well obviously, different societies have had different histories, have evolved in different circumstances. Naturally they will have developed different ways of living together, different moral codes. This proves my point precisely.

Cause   So one moral code is no better or worse than another? You would not claim, for example, that our morals, 'Christian' morals as they are still sometimes called, are better than Islamic ones?

Effect   Oh no, I don't think I'd want to say that... What's right for them is right for them and what's right for us is right for us.

Cause   And that's that?

Effect   I think so. We might hope for change I suppose, for more tolerance and understanding on both sides, but in the end, who are we to judge?

Cause   Who are they? Yet many of them show no such compunction.

Effect   But the Muslims have their own beliefs, their own traditions, their own culture which in many ways is as admirable as our own and in some ways may be better.

Cause   Better? Did I hear you say 'better'? That gives the game away doesn't it? The different codes *can* be rated morally.

Effect   Oh, er, yes, but, but it would only be an opinion, er...

Cause   So there's nothing wrong with the Muslims' treatment of women? The buying and selling of wives as though they were cattle? That's just their way?

Effect   At least they forbid the debasement of women by pornography.

Cause   Having all the girls go around in bin-bags, is that the best way of coming to terms with sexuality?

Effect   It was the women who chose the veil, as a matter of fact, as protection from the likes of you.

226

Cause   What about the chopping of pickpockets' hands and the flogging of careless drinkers?

Effect   Careless or carless? Look Andrew, I don't like a lot of the things that go on in Muslim countries, but then I don't like a lot of the things that go on here.

Cause   Sure, but you have no qualms about condemning what you don't like here. Why these double-standards, this mealy-mouthed liberalism, this back-to-front bigotry? Surely your overriding moral duty is to speak out for what you believe? You would find plenty of Muslims who would agree with you; they have moral debates too you know.

Effect   But I don't see that I have the right to...

Cause   The right to what? Where does 'a society' begin and end? Do we two, sitting here on this bench constitute 'a society'? Could we lay claim to our own morality? Is a gang of bank-robbers a society, is a cricket team? Do moral responsibilities lapse at Dover?

Effect   No, of course not, but...

Cause   I thought you said that moral principles are over-and-above the laws of the land, I thought you said that they are universal?

Effect   Yes, but...

Cause   So why the hedging? Why the "who are we to judge..." and the "what's right for them..."?

Effect   You are beginning to sound like some sort of imperialist moral *crusader* Andrew, you know where that can lead.

Cause   Perhaps the world is at a cross-roads.

Effect   But other societies are at different stages of development from our own. Culturally, materially, technologically, politically, they face quite different problems.

Cause   Of course, true, true, and as you say, one should make allowances for other people's circumstances, other people's history, but we all share the same world now, and it's not flat any more. We are all living in the age of birth control and nuclear weapons.

227

The Final Solution

Effect But in other societies people have quite different life-expectations, quite different religious beliefs, quite different ideas about man's purpose on Earth.

Cause That's funny, I thought you said earlier that people's aspirations are pretty much the same the world over.

Effect I think ordinary people's material aspirations probably are, but I am talking now of their religious beliefs and political ideals.

Cause I reckon that priests' and politicians' aspirations are pretty much the same the world over too.

Effect But the creeds can be quite different.

Cause Exactly, different societies can espouse quite different creeds proposing quite different definitions of human happiness. Bang goes our neat utilitarianism: useless I'm afraid.

Effect Yes... Oh dear...

Cause And what would you have said about Germany in the thirties? What was right for the Nazis was right for the Nazis? Genocide was just their way?

Effect No, of course not!

Cause Yet there was a society which was hardly different at all from ours, culturally, materially, technologically, politically.

Effect The bitterest conflicts are always between the closest relatives.

Cause And here we are, forty years on, with our bitterest foe now our staunchest ally and our staunchest ally now our bitterest foe. Paradoxically it is as though to the most macroscopic, cataclysmic human behaviour – international conflict – moral principles seem to be the least applicable.

Effect Yes, in warfare there is a more or less *total* suspension of moral constraint.

Cause All is fair in love too. It'll be the total suspension of everything, next time.

Effect A Third World War? I don't think there's going to be one. It's my belief that the extraordinary destructive potential of nuclear weapons may at last have brought man to his senses. The big powers know that an all-out, or even half-out, nuclear conflagration would now do such massive and such long-term damage to the planet that there could be no victory for either side. Both know that its initiation would be mad, suicidal.

Cause   Mutually-assured destruction has never been much of a deterrent before, in divorce proceedings, for example; and suicide is common enough.

Effect   But things are different now Andrew, war is different. A one-megaton nuclear weapon is *not* equivalent to a million tons of TNT, it represents a quantum leap in terms of energy-release. A single multi-warhead rocket can launch a whole campaign. The effects of nuclear weapons cannot be confined; radioactivity is carried on the wind, it is no respecter of barbed-wire barriers; fallout can spread from continent to continent. Already we have glimpsed the awful consequences if...

Cause   A Kiev crane-driver gets drunk and half the sheep in Scotland have to die.

Effect   There is now enough nuclear material stockpiled to irradiate the entire planet, to kill all higher life-forms several times over, perhaps to cause a new ice-age. The half-lives of the fission products can be hundreds, even thousands of years, many times a man's life-span. All this is new, it has changed everything.

Cause   Except the way men think.

Effect   Isn't this a perfect example of what you were saying earlier though: that new technologies and abilities confer upon us new moral responsibilities? Just as birth-control, you argued, perhaps obliges us to treat child-bearing as a moral act, so nuclear weaponry now obliges us to... well, not to use it. Is there not already evidence of this new sanity at last beginning to break out? Despite its huge arsenal, the Soviet Empire has collapsed almost bloodlessly.

Cause   So far. It looks fearfully touch-and-go to me. In any case, it's only a breathing-space, a lull. Personally, I cannot understand the Americans being so keen to foist the market system on them; surely the last thing they want is an economically *healthy* Russia emerging with all that firepower? Besides, while it's good to see the empire dying, it's not so good to see what's crawling from the rotting carcass: the teeming larvae of grubby racial rivalries; a horde of ill-formed chrysalid states all struggling to beat their angry nationalistic wings; and stirring from its uterus, a ravenous, despotic, renascent Mother Russia. Who knows what may lie in store?

229

Hunkering Down

Who knows who's in charge of business? I'm sorry Malcolm, but it doesn't fill me with much peace of mind. Keep hunkered down and keep manning the radar, that's what I say.

Effect   I disagree. I think there's a real opportunity here to make progress with arms reduction. Now's the time. We must respond, help them to re-adjust, show them we mean peace.

Cause   So Russia may have had a temporary setback, but what of all the other countries so busily refining their uranium? If in the end the bomb's unusable, why are so many nations around the world so keen to get hold of it? Will you suggest that they are thinking *illogically*?

Effect   Obviously there are still many problems, many trouble spots; the world is still a dangerous place; but I thought we were talking about a Third World War, a *global* confrontation? Surely you'll admit that the shadow of Armageddon has at least receded, that there has been some good news lately?

Cause   So what now? An enlightened America on international point-duty for the next hundred years? We can all sleep easy for a while?

Effect   Why not? As a socialist it's not my dream scenario, but I could imagine worse.

Cause   America is only a bloke's name, did you know that? The Latinized version of Amerigo Vespucci, an Italian explorer of the fifteenth century who claimed, erroneously or fraudulently, to have been the first European to set foot on the continent. America is thus in fact a bastardized christian name based on a mistake, or a lie. It's strange how such a bogus, stitched-together, traditionless country, such a racial, cultural and religious melting-pot can inspire such patriotism in its people. I wonder how enlightened they will be when the oil starts running out. Already, we have glimpsed...

Effect   You're *determined* to be gloomy, aren't you? You *need* your para-noia, you'd be lost without it.

Cause   I'll bet you were scare-mongering with the best of them, five years ago. I'll bet you were joining the peace marches, studying the blast effects, talking of survival-rates, warning of a holocaust.

Effect   I was, yes. I'm a member of CND as a matter of fact.

Cause   So you were campaigning to scrap the weapons that you now claim have brought world peace?

Effect   I still am.

Cause   Now *that's* thinking illogically if you like! Nothing has changed, Malcolm, nothing very important has changed, under the surface. It's just that we turned out to be on the winning side... for the moment. It's all still there, all the monstrous apparatus, and it wasn't built for nothing... Remember, even now, whey-faced college kids in Washington are working out the megadeaths on wristwatch calculators; giant submarines are still stalking the cold, dark, silent depths; plutonium production-lines are rumbling relentlessly, from Texas to Tashkent; deep in bunkers all over the world, well-fed military men continue to plan their aftermaths. They think they've got it all worked out, with their TV propaganda ploys and their computerized battle-plans; with their civil servants, their sperm-banks and their lead-lined incubators... But sooner or later they'll have to surface, and when they do, I'll be there, I'll be ready for them. I've got my catering packs and my geiger counter, my cyanide capsule and my sawn-off shotgun!

Effect   I'll bet you have, too.

Cause   I have a theory about the next war. There's one way in which those scare-films go wrong: thanks to your push-button technologies, most of the crucial gambles and decisive battles will be won or lost within the first few computerized minutes. Indeed, I imagine that the outcome will largely be settled after sixty seconds or so; eventually I guess, it will all come down to the infinitesimal calculation-times of the rival computer chips.

Effect   The latest development is optical computing, computers which make calculations at the speed of light.

Cause   So I hear. In such circumstances the element of surprise will obviously count for everything. It follows that the least likely scenario of all is the gradual build-up of tension in some traditional international trouble-spot. If either side ever believes itself to be in a position to win the initial race against micro-time, it must start its button-pushing when the enemy is least expecting it. Ergo, it could happen at any moment. It could happen today. It could have happened already... Christ! Where are the cricketers? Were they all out? Where's everyone gone?

Effect   They've gone in for tea I think. It looks like fifty overs a side. Oh damn! Damn, damn, damn!

✳   ✳   ✳   ✳   ✳   ✳   ✳   ✳   ✳   ✳   ✳

Who Cares?

Cause   Why so glum Malcolm? What's the use of worrying? Che sera sera. I would have thought that as a scientist, a determinist, you would regard war as being just another of the ways in which human beings behave, something they can no more help than digesting or ageing. As far as I'm concerned, any species which can even *contemplate* what we are contemplating deserves to perish. Sod society! Bugger my so-called fellow men, with their ghastly, greedy little power games, with their prodigious madnesses and crimes, good riddance to the lot of them, that's what I say! A shame about the animals I suppose, but, well, I won't be here to miss them so why should I care?

Effect   You're just saying all that, you don't mean it. You do care, you must care!

Cause   Must I? Why? Why should I care about *any*one else?

Effect   But you... you...

Cause   You see, here's the biggest problem of the lot: in a causal world, how can moral obligations arise *at all*? Where do moral feelings come from in the first place?

Effect   Well, as I said earlier, the existence of genuine altruism does present something of a problem for the Darwinian account of evo...

Cause   Yes, yes, but there is another problem that's more fundamental, more logical. On the one hand, since moral characteristics and feelings apparently occur naturally, they must have as their source some sort of natural instinct or faculty or biochemical cause. On the other hand, if immoral behaviour and responses to it are caused by genetic make-ups or brain-processes or psychological reflexes or whatever, how can it be right to blame people for behaving badly, or indeed to praise them for behaving well?

Effect   Forgive me, but I'm not sure I quite understand.

Cause   You're not the only one. Hume couldn't crack it either; once again, it seems to me, it was he who found the nub and once again a comparison of his earlier and later work reveals much. The jargon was different then of course; genes and neurological events and super-egos had not been invented. Hume talked instead of moral sentiments and affections, which he tried to explain in terms of his theory of ideas and impressions. In the *Treatise* Hume invoked the notion of *sympathy*. 'Sympathy' he used in something like the way in which we now use the word 'empathy', characterizing it as an involuntary psychological mechanism or reflex-action through which each of us becomes engaged by the feelings of others. Here:

> Sympathy is nothing but the conversion of an idea into an impression by the force of imagination... When any affection is infused by sympathy, it is at first known only by its effects and by those external signs in the countenance and conversation which convey an idea of it. This idea is presently converted into an impression and acquires such a degree of force and vivacity as to become the very passion itself, and to produce an equal emotion as any original affection...
>
> It is indeed evident that when we sympathize with the passions and sentiments of others, these movements appear at first in our minds as mere ideas and are conceived to belong to another person, as we conceive any other matter of fact. It is also evident that the ideas of the affections of others are converted into the very impressions they represent, and that the passions arise in conformity to the images we form of them. All this is an object of the plainest experience.

Effect Humph. So he is saying that when, for example, I see someone else in pain, my perception of their pain-behaviour becomes converted through this process of sympathizing into a sort of second-hand feeling of pain in me?

Cause Exactly. And of course this second-hand feeling of pain moves you to try to alleviate its cause, namely the other person's distress. Hume thus cites symapthy as being the source of all our moral affections: pity, compassion, benevolence and, for that matter, malice, envy, hatred and so on.

Effect Well, the explanation does carry a certain plausibility, in a quaint sort of way.

Cause Oh come off it Malcolm! It doesn't stand up to philosophical examination for a moment!

Effect No, I don't suppose it does. The detail sounds rather peculiar, the ideas-and-impressions bit, and there's something queer about the notion of second-hand pains, but the general *shape* of the explanation seems to be roughly right. Some process *like* sympathizing or empathizing must be at the heart of our involvements with one another.

Cause But the shape of the argument is hopeless! For a start it again puts the motive of moral actions down to selfishness, the desire to alleviate one's second-hand pains.

Causation the Culprit

Effect Mm, yes, but...

Cause The question is: how can a natural faculty or process like sympathy ever give rise to a moral virtue like benevolence? Sympathy is innate, involuntary, like sight or digestion; yet benevolence, its supposed moral offspring, is a duty, an obligation, a quality one *ought* to display. If everyone is born with this faculty of sympathy, why is it that some people are more benevolent than others?

Effect Maybe some people have a more developed faculty of sympathy than others. After all, people are born long-sighted and short-sighted.

Cause In which case it is wrong to blame and punish people for being thoughtless and cruel and pointless to encourage them to be benevolent. You do not castigate someone for being blind.

Effect Yes, yes, I see that. We seem to be back with the chromosomes-cause-criminality conundrum.

Cause Right. The language changes but the problem remains the same. The very word 'sympathy' illustrates the point: Hume used it to mean a natural instinct or reflex-action, but since his day it has itself evolved into a moral obligation. In modern parlance sympathy for others is a quality one *ought* to display while 'empathy' perhaps now fulfils the role of the supposed morally-neutral faculty.

Effect How did Hume resolve all this?

Cause I'm not sure that he ever did. The revealing thing is that in his later work, the *Enquiry*, he introduced and came to rely upon an even more slippery word, 'humanity'. In 'humanity', the dilemma is beautifully crystallized. Sometimes Hume interprets humanity as a natural faculty:

> It is needless to push our researches so far as to ask why we have humanity or a fellow-feeling with others. It is sufficient that this is experienced to be a principle in human nature...

> The notion of morals implies some sentiment common to all mankind which recommends the same object to general approbation, and also implies some sentiment so universal and comprehensive as to extend to all mankind... These two requisite circumstances belong alone to the sentiment of humanity here insisted on...

> This affection of humanity, being common to all men, can alone be the foundation of morals, or of any general system of blame or praise.

Sometimes he refers to it as a moral virtue:

> It appears that utility is inseparable from all the other social virtues, humanity, generosity, etc...

> And if the principles of humanity are capable in many instances of influencing our actions, they must at all times have *some* authority over our sentiments.

Sometimes he simply falls into confusion:

> The social virtues of humanity and benevolence exert their influence immediately by a direct tendency or instinct...

> Though there was no obligation to relieve the miserable, our humanity would lead us to it; and when we omit that duty, the immorality of the omission arises from its being a proof that we lack the natural sentiments of humanity.

Effect   He is going round in circles.

Cause   Yes. Or rather, he is trying to square the circle. Humanity, you see, is perfectly ambiguous: on the one hand it is, by definition one might say, the feature shared by all human beings, it is their common family-membership; on the other hand it is that universal human obligation which people so frequently fail to fulfil. All humans are human but all too few are humane.

Effect   Humans, however, are presumably under no obligation to be Humeans... It's strange: at one moment it seems as though the relationships between moral qualities and the natural faculties which generate them are inextricably intimate, residing in the subtlest of verbal ambiguities; at another they seem to be separated by an utterly uncrossable logical wall. However hard one tries to keep one's balance, one cannot help falling down on one side or the other. Even the words slip out of one's grasp like wriggling fish, shooting either this way or that. I am beginning to think that no amount of factual information about the world or about human behaviour can ever by itself generate any moral evaluation or recommendation.

Cause   Bravo, that's what Hume concluded in his celebrated 'is/ought' passage:

> In every system of morality which I have hitherto met with, I have always remarked that the author proceeds for some time in the ordinary way of reasoning and establishes the being of a God, or makes observations concerning human affairs, when of a sudden I am sur-

prised to find that instead of the usual copulations of propositions *is* and *is not*, I meet with no proposition that is not connected with an *ought* or an *ought not*. This change is imperceptible but is, however, of the last consequence. For as this *ought* or *ought not* expresses some new relation or affirmation, it is necessary that it should be observed and explained and at the same time that a reason should be given, for what seems altogether inconceivable, how this new relation can be a deduction from others which are entirely different from it.

Effect   That's right! That's right! That's where we went wrong earlier. We started by simply trying to discover how the word 'moral' is used and ended up arguing over what we thought to be desirable human qualities. We *must* be clear when we are describing matters of fact and when we are making judgements of value; these are two quite different activities.

Cause   But can we, and are they? How can we avoid evaluating things, recommending things? Do we not recommend things every time we speak, even if only certain word-usages? We have both been recommending things all day. Again, just now, you recommended something: "We *must* be clear" you said. Hume, even in his 'is/ought' passage, himself starts with an observation and ends with a recommendation: "it is necessary that it should be observed and explained..." He continues explicitly:

> But as authors do not commonly use this precaution, I shall presume to recommend it to the readers, and am persuaded that this small attention would subvert all the vulgar systems of morality and let us see that the distinction of vice and virtue is not founded merely on the relations of objects, nor is perceived by reason.

Effect   But if right and wrong do not reside in matters of fact and cannot be decided by reason, what are we to conclude? That Good and Evil are occult, universal forces into which we somehow tune with a mysterious sixth sense? Morality waves whizzing about in an imaginary ethical Ether? That's crazy! Oh, what a muddle! It's hopeless! And it all seemed so clear!

Cause   Ah, the cricketers...

Effect   Andrew, please, please, what is the way out of all this?

Cause   Well one way out is to stop building imaginary logical walls... It looks as though they've got to make two hundred and forty-three to win. Just under five an over...

＊　＊　＊　＊　＊　＊　＊　＊　＊　＊　＊

Effect   So where would you start?

Cause   Erm... With the forward defensive stroke I suppose.

Effect   No, no, where would you start in trying to find a way out of this dreadful moral mess? We seem to be further away than ever from any clear idea of what moral goodness is.

Cause   Oh, that. Well, as I say Malcolm, you're speaking to the wrong man on this one.

Effect   But you've obviously thought a lot about it, you must have some ideas.

Cause   Some ideas yes, some random jottings, but all very obvious, nothing profound; I'm not sure they add up to very much.

Effect   Okay, but anyway, go ahead.

Cause   Well, needless to say, I start from a point of view that is quite different from yours. You approach things with the assumption that the world and everything in it is subject to cause-and-effect, is governed by physical laws. As we have seen, for you, the existence of consciousness, mentality, freedoms and now, moral values presents serious problems and has to be 'explained' in terms of physics; but of course it cannot be. I, by contrast, begin in the knowledge that I am a conscious, thinking, free agent who can choose things, prefer things, value things. For me, just as freedom is a condition of mentality, so value is a dimension of freedom. The existence of neither freedoms nor values stands in need of any explanation at all. It makes as much sense to ask "How can people exercise freedoms?" or "Why do minds value things?" as it does to ask "How can bodies occupy space?" or "Why do objects persist?"

Effect   Yes, but why *moral* values, why *moral* goodness?

Cause   Hold your horses, hold your horses! First things first. Why *any* sort of goodness? We must begin by looking at how the word 'good' operates in ordinary, non-moral contexts, for after all it can be used to qualify *any* kind of noun... Right then Malcolm, what is a good car, in your opinion? What makes a car a good car?

Effect   No, no, let *me* ask *you* this time: what, in *your* opinion, is a good car?

Cause   Well, mine for a start.

A Good Vehicle

Effect What!? Your MG!? It's a wreck! It's rusty, it's falling to bits, it's dangerous, it's noisy, it's unreliable and I bet it's heavy on petrol.

Cause It is quite. But it was cheap, I got it from a scrap-yard and it's great fun to drive. It's fast, it's stylish, it's easy to work on, it's...

Effect Uhoh, this is just the 'What is a table?' game again.

Cause No. On that occasion we were not disagreeing over what is and is not a table, we just found that we could not arrive at a pat definition of tableness. This time we are actually in dispute over what qualities are desirable in a car. This is an argument about values, not facts.

Effect Facts are highly relevant though. As a matter of fact your car is rusty. As a matter of fact its silencer is broken. As a matter of fact it does x miles to the gallon. There are objective standards. Performance figures are performance figures.

Cause Are they though? Presumably what were good performance figures for cars of fifty years ago would be poor ones for cars of today. Standards can change drastically over the years.

Effect Exactly, designs are refined, technologies develop, car standards improve, improve according to certain objective, measurable criteria. In the present one can only judge things by the present.

Cause Well I like it, it does what I want, it's good for me. I hate new cars.

Effect You just like it because of the image; you're on an ego-trip.

Cause So, what's wrong with that? What's *your* image? What sort of car does your wife drive?

Effect One of the new, small hatchbacks. Nippy, economical, comfortable, roomy, adaptable. A very good design actually.

Cause Not much good if you've only got a hundred pounds to spend, not much good in the fast lane, not much good if you want the wind in your face.

Effect Round your feet more like.

Cause Not much good to a farmer who wants to get around his fields or to a builder who needs to pick up a ton of bricks or to a banger-racer who likes the odd roll-over.

Effect   No, obviously not. A car is good only insofar as it fulfils the particular function desired of it. And I suppose, given that a car has to fulfil a variety of functions, a single choice is always going to be something of a compromise.

Cause   Why? My MG suits me perfectly! It fulfils completely the function desired of it, it gives me pleasure. Why can't cars and driving be ends in themselves?

Effect   But if a car is dangerous, if it wastes precious fuel, maybe it should not be allowed on the road, maybe your ego should not be allowed its careless joyriding.

Cause   Uhuh? So who is going to decide the function of a car? Plato? General Motors? The Ministry of Purposes?

Effect   Why not? A moment ago you were questioning my right to have as many children as I wish, I don't see why I can't question your right to...

Cause   You just can't stop grinding that dreary old axe of yours can you? Everything becomes political. We can't even discuss a simple question about motor cars without getting embroiled in your high-minded morality.

Effect   Maybe we can't.

Cause   Anyway, one point is agreed between us, for what it's worth: a thing's goodness is dependent upon its fulfilling its *function*. This lesson is as true for us now as it was for Aristotle two-and-a-half millennia ago. In *The Ethics*, Aristotle began not only with physical objects but also with human activities and with 'good' the noun rather than 'good' the adjective. The common translation of his opening sentence reads: "It is thought that every activity, artistic or scientific, in fact every deliberate action or pursuit, has for its object the attainment of some good." Here 'good' is actually synonymous with 'function' and with words like 'purpose' and 'end' and 'use'. Aristotle quickly concedes that some activities, like the gratification of desire, the pursuit of pleasure, the enjoyment of beauty and the striving for artistic excellence can be ends-in-themselves, but otherwise it is always possible to ask: what is *the good* of doing so-and-so?

Effect   What is the good of studying philosophy if all it leads to is confusion and doubt?

Greater Goods

Cause   Indeed, a good question. What is the good of scientific research? What is the good of technological innovation? What is the good of a limitless energy-source? These are all genuine questions. Maybe a wise confusion is better than a foolish certainty. Maybe the good of confusion and doubt is to lead one to greater understanding. Anyway Aristotle, who for many years had been Plato's pupil and disciple, began by noting that goods automatically form a *hierarchy*. His first example was saddlery. The good of saddlery, he said, is horsemanship; the good of horsemanship, military expertise; the...

Effect   Well that's debatable for a start.

Cause   ...the good of military expertise, victory.

Effect   And that's no longer so obvious.

Cause   Okay, try car-making then: the good of car-making is to provide transport, is it not?

Effect   To provide *privately-owned* transport I suppose, yes.

Cause   And what is the purpose of privately-owned transport would you say?

Effect   Whose purpose? For the car manufacturers and the oil companies obviously the purpose is to make huge profits.

Cause   Not to satisfy public demand?

Effect   To keep transport out of union control more like.

Cause   Funny, I would have thought you'd be in favour of the motor industry because of all the employment it provides.

Effect   Maybe, but what about other priorities like energy-conservation, pollution-reduction, city-life improvement?

Cause   Voilà! Once again you see, our discussion of car-making has been overtaken by questions about higher social and political issues. It seems not only that our workaday activities like food-growing, house-building, car-making and so on furnish and support the achievement of higher, more important ends, but also that evaluations of our workaday activities can be made *only in the light of* the higher principles of politics and ethics, principles which again automatically vie with one another for priority. And if moral principles are characterized simply as being those which feature at the highest levels in this natural hierarchy of goods, then the question of why moral values are the most important no longer arises: that is what they are. Aristotle concluded from this, plausibly enough, that before we can make any sense of the mass of evaluations and decisions, moral and otherwise, which we have to make every day, we must try to determine what is at the apex of this pyramid of values, what is the principle which illuminates the whole hierarchy. This good of all goods, following Plato, he called *Absolute* Goodness.

Effect   Hold on. I can see, sort of, that goods are automatically hierarchical in nature, but why do they necessarily form a *single* hierarchy? Why a pyramid, why not a mountain range? Why *a* Good of all goods? Surely moral goodness resides in the art of *compromising* between conflicting priorities?

Cause   Maybe it does, maybe Compromise is the Supreme Principle. Don't worry Malcolm, Aristotle's answer to the question "What is Absolute Goodness?" was not a simple one-word affair. The *Nicomachean Ethics* is quite a long book. His problem of course, was to identify the good or function of human life.

Effect   Ah, tricky.

Cause   We've not even been able to agree on the function of the motor car, a human artefact, so how are we ever going to agree on the function of man?

Effect   Or of woman?

Cause   There are so many ways to be, so many things to live for, so many dreams to fulfil!

Effect   Again, one wants to ask: why should there be one function common to everyone? Different people have different tastes, different talents. Surely they can live, as you would say, for different goods?

Cause   That's unusually liberal of you Malcolm! Your Supreme Principle has suddenly turned from Compromise into Personal Freedom! In the end, the only sort of answer that a philosopher, or anyone else, can give to such a question is to propose a model, to describe an ideal. What else can one do, how else can one proceed? Thus, when all the analysis has been done and all the philosophical points have been put, Aristotle's answer to the question "What is a good man?" is to offer to his readers his detailed selection of human virtues, his model man. Similarly, Plato's final attempt in *The Republic* to answer the question "What is Justice?" is to have Socrates describe at length his ideal of a just state.

Effect   Isn't this very subjective though? Isn't it now possible for everyone to propose their own models of moral goodness and then live by them; in other words for people to do whatever they like? Worse still, the way becomes open for skillful manipulators to offer to the public a whole range of *bastard* moral models: gun-toting racists, fascist superheroes, renegade law-enforcers, all the sort of stuff that seems to be so fashionable in the States at the moment.

Cause   This is the danger of course, but then this is always the danger. The point is that some models are objectively better than others. In this sense, everyone is free to put forward their own explanation of why the Sun appears to orbit the Earth. The aim is to discover the right model. I know that moralizing in terms of models is unfashionable amongst intellectuals nowadays for the reasons you mention, but there is a greater danger, it seems to me, that this competition of values will be lost by default. Without ideals, humanity is rudderless, directionless, aimless, a prey to sudden storms. We are *drifting* towards catastrophe.

Effect   Okay then, give us a laugh, describe us *your* Moral Ideal! I can just imagine what Andrew Supercause is like.

Cause   Well, I... ermm... I don't really know, I... Oh nice stroke! They're doing well these two, they're scoring quickly. Hmm... eighty-two for one after fifteen overs, that means they need...

Effect   Hey, you're flunking it!

Cause   I'm not flunking it, I've, I've just got nothing much to say. I'm not going to start listing all the things I approve and disapprove of in people, that would take a week! Besides, who am I to judge, I...

Effect   Come on, you're the one who proposed this moral model idea, you must be able to say something.

Cause   Well... One thing I suppose: generally speaking, I do find myself far more in, in sympathy with the Greek virtues than with the Christian ones. All that stuff about piety and humility and self-denial and sin and sacrifice, I don't see that any of that's much good in the modern world; I imagine it had more to do with resigning downtrodden peasants to a miserable lot: a medieval poverty-trap. Of course Aristotle extolled virtues like goodwill to all men, consideration for others, liberality, modesty and so on, but he also recommended qualities like dignity, self-esteem, proper ambition and a healthy desire for pleasure.

Effect   Just up your street eh? I don't suppose he mentions social responsibility anywhere?

Cause   Oh don't start Malcolm. Aristotle is just far more in tune with modern thinking, that's all. Don't worry, he stresses from the outset that virtues consist in striking balances between extremes. Courage and generosity and good temper are laudable, but foolhardiness, profligacy and effeteness are to be condemned. He also mentions qualities like practicality, prudence and intellectual understanding. Plato even regarded physical fitness, artistic appreciation and the acquisition of knowledge as being moral duties, of a sort.

Effect   There's nothing new is there, nothing under the Sun.

Cause   Indeed, especially since it seems that the end of the world is as likely to come as a result of incompetence, stupidity or ignorance as it is of evil ambition. Finally, of course, Plato actually enthroned the study of philosophy as the highest of all moral duties.

Effect   He would do wouldn't he, he wanted to sell his books.

Cause   Plato argued that it is only through the study of philosophy that we can arrive at any understanding of Absolute Goodness, understanding which is vital if we are to administer our everyday political and moral affairs with wisdom and justice. His ideal Republic is ruled by philosopher-kings.

Effect   Well all I can say is: thank goodness it's only a model!

Cause   And what about the real world? Perhaps Plato was right. It's extraordinary isn't it, here we are at the dawn of the Space Age and men are still conducting international relations roughly as they did five hundred years ago, when European mariners in wooden ships were setting sail for the edge of the oceans, when every expedition meant a new World Map. Now it is the era of moon-travel and laser beams, yet in the military and the foreign office, people still fill posts that were created when war was handfuls of men firing arrows across fields. Young career-diplomats are proud of their traditions merely because it is the tradition to be so.

Effect   Well yes, I agree that the old models have got to go.

243

Statelessness

Cause   Domestically, politicians still deploy arguments and jargon that were first coined when starving children were slaving in English coal-mines and world wars were fought on horseback. Radioactivity had not been dreamt of in those days; the atom had no nucleus; the nearest thing to a space station was the Eiffel Tower! Oh, the old issues remain contentious, naturally, they always will, but the problem is different now, completely different. Our overriding priority, our Good above all goods is now the survival of the species, the preservation of the planet. This is the Supreme Principle which from today must illuminate all our moral and political decisions. As you said: we must think globally; nuclear weaponry has rendered the concept of the nation-state obsolete.

Effect   Logically, that appears to be true, but of course in reality it is only nation-states that can muster the technologies. We seem to be stuck with them. Thus we are confronted by a perfect paradox.

Cause   This is it: you may not like the sound of Plato's imaginary ideal Republic but at least he had the temerity to propose one, to try to envisage a better society. Today, when our need for new political model-making has never been greater, no-one dares seriously to think ahead or to map out a non-irradiated, a-national future world.

Effect   I don't reckon Plato or Aristotle would be going along with any of this though, it sounds as if military supremacy and patriotism were at the top of their list.

Cause   They were high on it certainly, but then things were different in their day: the world was flat and infinite, not an overcrowded sphere; war was cavalry-charging and archery, not tampering with the upper atmosphere. In the past perhaps the good of one's country *was* the Supreme Good. There's nothing to say that the Supreme Good cannot *change*.

Effect   So what happens to our present international frontiers, do they just fossilize?

Cause   Why not? Our city walls have. Let countries become football teams, development areas, customs controls, that's about all they're good for. If conflict really is an evolutionary necessity, if people actually want to die for some tribal rivalry or other, then perhaps we should start searching Space for the men with pointy ears, seriously, quietly. If we are going to end up fighting them, let us begin now, while the Earth is still a fit place from which to fight.

Effect   But you must know that's all nonsense-talk, pure science-fiction?

244

Cause   So much the better.

Effect   Okay okay, all very fine idealistic reasoning Andrew, but back here in the real world, where most people still believe in Queen and Country, what are you recommending that we actually *do*? Join CND? As I say, I already have.

Cause   I'm not sure. Paradoxically, perhaps disarming is the *last* thing we should do. It is the bombs that have brought about this new moral situation, you said so yourself. There are an awful lot of things to dismantle before we get to *those* detonators. There are the military governments, the arms industries, the bureaucracies, the nation-states themselves: a million miles of barbed wire and red tape. But first and foremost there are the ways of thinking which sustain these institutions: we have to dismantle a whole world-view... Oh good catch! There's a bit of a collapse going on here: three wickets in two overs... A hundred and eleven for four...

Effect   It's strange isn't it, this concern we have for future generations... Even if I were to accept all this, there is still, it seems to me, one great problem with your argument, the problem that you posed earlier and that Hume tried to solve with his faculty of sympathy: why should I care about others *at all*? How do I know that this Absolute Moral Goodness has anything to do with other people?

Cause   How do you mean, what is the good of living together?

Effect   No, that is obvious, but again gets us no further than self-interest. The question is: how can you prove to me that the Supreme Principle is not Selfishness?

Cause   Aha, this is where our morning's discussion of the 'other minds' problem comes in. I would like to suggest that recognition of the existence of other minds *is* the recognition of moral responsibilities towards them. It is not that there are two events, first the recognition of the existence of another mind and second the acceptance, or denial, of responsibilities towards that mind. Rather, there is a single action: recognizing another person is making a moral commitment to them.

Effect   Oh no, that cannot be right. It seems to be all too possible for people to recognize the existence of others and then be perfectly vile to them. Surely, that is the whole problem?

Cause   But perhaps we should say, in a behaviourist way, that when X mistreats Y, X's mis-behaviour demonstrates that X does *not* in fact recognize, or does not fully recognize, that Y is a person, whatever X may claim to the contrary. Perhaps we should say that recognizing others *means* behaving well towards them. After all, surely the oddness of the utterance "I realize that this object lying screaming in the road in a pool of blood is a person, but I don't see why I should be concerned about him" does not reside so much in its callousness as in its incoherence. It reveals not merely a moral but a *logical* misunderstanding, like that betrayed by the assertion "I know that benevolence is a moral obligation but I do not see why I should be benevolent".

Effect But if it is a matter of such obvious logic, why are some people so immoral?

Cause Because they have not come fully and consistently to recognize the existence of other minds. And this can be seen as a *philosophical* failure.

Effect In which case surely a wrongdoer could simply plead philosophical stupidity or ignorance, just as a Humean malefactor could have pleaded a natural lack of sympathy or a modern criminal can plead a chromosome deficiency?

Cause No, for everyone has *a duty* to recognize the existence of other minds, all other minds. In this sense, as Plato suggested, our highest moral duty is a philosophical one.

Effect Oh, again, that cannot be right. The most hospitable, most generous, most caring people in the world are the multitudes of uneducated poor, people who have never heard of Plato or Hume.

Cause Oh yeah? The generous multitudes are the first to herd into great tribal armies when suitably manipulated. In their shadows there are always the ambitious politicians with bankrupt careers waiting for the chance to exploit the ancient loyalties, to bewitch your 'caring poor' with stories of how things used to be. Beware of multitudes, Malcolm, with their brooding, bloodstained ghosts; they can be *possessed.*

Effect Mm, any new model will have to be extremely clear.

Cause Think of the Nazis' treatment of the Jews...

Effect Or the Zionists' of the Palestinians... You see, it's all very well asking us to renounce our nationhood, but there are many peoples in the world still struggling to achieve theirs.

Cause The question is: how can the cycles of racism ever be broken? Think of our own recent African slave-trade...

Effect *Our* slave trade? I thought you had just decided to renounce your nationality?

Cause It hardly seems adequate to say that the British shippers behaved immorally towards the Africans or that they failed to respect their moral rights, for as far as the British were concerned, the Africans *did not have* any moral rights, they were not regarded as being people at all. In the end the crime was a failure of other-mind-recognition, the mistake was philosophical.

Effect The Greeks went in for slavery too I understand.

Cause Racial atrocities are not merely examples of people mistreating or exploiting one another, they are demonstrations of the failure of people to recognize one another as people. And remember, just as there are degrees of recognition, so there are shades of racial prejudice and strengths of moral commitment.

Effect Are you saying that all immorality is ultimately racist in nature?

Cause I am saying that all immorality stems from failures of other-mind-recognition and that genocide provides a particularly clear and extreme example of such a failure. Genocide is the eclipse of *all* philosophical vision; it is *total* blindness.

Effect It is a sort of mass-hysteria, a communal madness.

Cause No, it is worse than that, for a madman is deemed to be of diminished responsibility. A genocide has to be calculated, constructed, sanctioned, institutionalized. The next great blindness is going to be mightily deliberate... And your big-hearted peasants, the billions who'll freeze to death silently or starve in unreported famines, will have no inkling. Still, why should we worry about people we have never seen?

Effect This is what troubles me about your theory Andrew. You have simply laid down a law that everyone is under a moral obligation to recognize the existence of other minds, all other minds, but isn't it still open to some rival moralist to propose an alternative Supreme Principle? Couldn't an ambitious dictator equally easily insist that the Good of all goods is Racial Supremacy, and base his moral-political decisions on that? Doesn't your theory finally end up drifting in the same rudderless boat as all the others?

Moral Objectivity

Cause   I don't think so, for in dropping our moral anchor here, at the very depths of philosophical and psychological imperative, we can hear any further questions echoing with banal illogicality. The existence of other minds is a fact about the world. The correct recognition of others and hence of one's obligations towards them is simply an element, by consensus the most important element, in one's apprehension of the truth. I suppose people can still utter the words "Why should I seek to discover the truth?" but what could they possibly mean by them, what could they be asking? The truth, after all, is what I should seek to discover.

Effect   You seem to be trying to make it a matter of *logic* that one should care for others. Surely this cannot be right?

Cause   Surely it cannot be wrong? If one accepts the primacy in the world of mentality and freedom and one ceases to regard them as phenomena which stand in need of causal explanation, then the concepts of preference, value and moral goodness *do* follow and inter-relate as a matter of logic.

Effect   Would you say then that moral feelings and values and obligations are objective?

Cause   Why not? It is certainly objectively better to be sitting as we are in this blissful place enjoying a conversation and a cricket match than it would be to be dying in agony of radiation-poisoning, gazing out over a blasted, arid, sterile crater... They're staging something of a recovery, by the way: a hundred and fifty-six for four with twenty-two overs left.

Effect   So you would accept that there is such a thing as moral progress, that there have been moral advances since Plato's time?

Cause   No, I don't think so really.

Effect   Oh surely! Of course there have! Your own example was the slave-trade, but that was banned, slavery has been abolished.

Cause   Uhuh? Nowadays we say we find the idea of slavery shocking, but we happily talk of 'The Third World'. Yet a Californian can fly to Ethiopia in a few hours while for Plato the journey would have taken weeks.

Effect   Wasn't the introduction of courts-of-law and trials-by-jury a moral advance? Wasn't the advent of parliamentary democracy a moral advance?

Cause   Hmm. I'm not at all sure about parliamentary democracy, or what presently passes for it here, and as for courts of law...

Effect   Wasn't the formation of the United Nations a moral advance? Wasn't the Declaration of Human Rights a moral advance?

Cause   Noble ideas, without doubt, but in practice...? Beneath the veneers of civilization, the beast marches on. No, I see no progress on the basic level of other-mind-recognition. The same old evils seem just to continue on ever bigger scales.

Effect   So in your view moral progress essentially would be a process of, of *de-racializing*?

Cause   I think so, yes... But I don't like the word 'process', again that's too passive. Perhaps we should think of human civilization as being like a child's growing up, gradually learning that there are others in the world, gradually learning to respect others' rights, gradually learning to treat people properly, maybe. And of course although a child's growing up is partly a biological process, it is also its moral duty. Humankind, like a child, has a duty to grow up in these respects, a duty to improve its understanding of the world and its behaviour towards others.

Effect   Do you conclude then that there are *absolute* moral responsibilities?

Cause   I conclude that moral responsibilities are absolute in the sense that there can be no end to their improvement, that always we can and should improve our understandings, our ways of treating one another, our ways of thinking and living.

Effect   But do you believe that we have higher, non-human obligations?

Cause   It's funny isn't it, as if we haven't already said enough... People don't seem to be satisfied with the idea that human beings' highest obligations are to one another, as though our decision to blast ourselves to pieces somehow doesn't matter very much, is our own business and so be it. I suppose they find abstract philosophical theorizing about Absolute Goodness rather hard to follow, rate Plato hard going, and so prefer to invoke some great non-human object or name onto which they can shackle all their moral guy-ropes... And *that*, in case you hadn't guessed, may be the purpose, a purpose, of suggesting that perhaps the Earth has feelings, that perhaps the Earth is a person.

A Close Finish

Effect   Ahhh... I see...

Cause   Bowled! A hundred and sixty-four for five with twenty-and-a-bit overs to go, this is going to be close! And the light's beginning to fail... I'd like to stay and see what happens if you don't mind.

Effect   Oh sure, sure...

Cause   Look Malcolm. Look towards the lowering Sun: see the soft, darkening silhouettes of the trees, the gentle curves of the hills beyond, the long shadows of the cricketers on the greenly-glowing grass, the tumbledown pavilion; hear the late afternoon blackbirds, the sweet clunk of bat on ball, an occasional shout or echo of laughter. When one takes in all this and quietly murmurs the word 'good', is one just passing an aesthetic judgement on the beauty of the scene... or something more?

※   ※   ※   ※   ※   ※   ※   ※   ※   ※   ※

7

GODS
and
MODELS

Effect Hey, I shall be late for Hall if I'm not careful. I like to dine in College on Wednesdays. I'm afraid I must go.

Cause Can I come?

Effect What, to Hall?

Cause Is there any chance of getting me in?

Effect Well, I, er... It's High Table, one has to give notice...

Cause No problem. I'll pretend to be one of the Fellows.

Effect The porters will spot you. Besides, you haven't got a gown.

Cause I'll nick one, borrow one, there are always some lying around.

Effect Oh dear, look I...

Cause Go on Malcolm, trust me, trust me.

Effect Honestly, I...

Cause Please.

A Christian Scientist

Effect Well, we can walk back together, but I'm not promising any-thing...

Cause Great! Thanks.

Effect Oh Gawd!

Cause Ah, that reminds me. There's something I've been wanting to ask you: do you believe in, in... *that* Fellow?

Effect Believe in God? Well, yes, as a matter of fact I do.

Cause You're a Christian?

Effect I, I've always considered myself a Christian, yes, though I'm not sure how big my 'C' is. Why?

Cause I've seen that your chosen moral virtues and values are, roughly speaking, Christian ones, but do you honestly believe in the Christians' God, in Christian theology?

Effect Certainly.

Cause An all-powerful, all-knowing, all-loving Creator?

Effect I think so, yes.

Cause And you believe in the divinity of Jesus Christ, Son-of-the-Father, who died that we may be forgiven our sins, all that?

Effect Ye-es, although...

Cause The Virgin-birth, the miracles, the Resurrection?

Effect Ah, well, erm, I'm not sure that one should take these things too literally, but...

Cause What about the Holy Ghost and the Devil, Satan, Lucifer, the Prince of Darkness?

Effect I, er, no, I don't think I'd want to...

Cause And the angels, the Cherubim and Seraphim?

Effect Ah, but belief in winged divinities goes back to pre-Christian mythologies, so...

Cause   So what?

Effect   Look Andrew, I'm not a religious historian and I'm no kind of theologian. All I can say is that I believe in an all-loving, all-sustaining Creator and in the teachings of Jesus Christ.

Cause   His teachings, but not his divinity?

Effect   Er, I believe his were the words of God, in, in...

Cause   In translation? In the sense that God has many messengers? In the sense that Mozart was, they say, touched by God, or Coltrane was His voice? In the sense that we are all His children?

Effect   I'm genuinely unsure about this question; I have taken your part in discussions with Dogma, but...

Cause   In which case, why do you call yourself a Christian rather than just a theist, why do you believe in God rather than in, say, Allah? Is this just a difference of language? Whatever we may think of some of the Moslems' ways, Mohammed was surely right in his theology: any Creator who could do all *this* surely wouldn't need to resort to a stunt like the New Testament? Incidentally Malcolm, do you know the Koran?

Effect   I did try once, but it read to me more like a revolutionary's military journal than a book of religious revelation.

Cause   Poetry and philosophy, the two hardest things to translate. People often forget that Jesus was a politico too, a troublemaker.

Effect   Oh, I admire the Moslems' idealism, their asceticism, their mistrust of imagery, but what is the result? Multitudes bowing obediently before inscribed stone texts.

Cause   Oh, I'd expect you to approve of that.

Effect   Well, whatever the success or failure of our puny attempts to identify Him, in imagery or in scripture, in lavishness or simplicity, in art or in science, all I can say is: I believe in a Creator.

Cause   And you don't find this religous faith to be in any way at odds with your other assumption that the World consists entirely of physical particles governed by causal laws?

253

Another Language

Effect   Not in the least, no.

Cause   Amazing!

Effect   Why so? Why should they be at odds? There are no scientific assumptions 'at odds' with the existence of a Loving Creator. Indeed, one can say that in the order, symmetry and beauty which the scientists have discovered to run through the Universe, one can see the hand of a Creator at work. You mustn't think of God as being some sort of ancient grey-bearded puppeteer, or as being a physical power in the Universe like the force of Gravity. God *transcends* the realm of three-dimensional space and time, He...

Cause   Oh come off it Malcolm, don't give me all that *Honest to God* stuff! I'm astonished that a scientist like yourself, who has such rigorous, no-nonsense, feet-on-the-physical-ground epistemological criteria with respect to your own field of study, can be so vague and woolly in your religious assertions. You suddenly start speaking another language! It's strange isn't it, it seems very fashionable nowadays for scientists, especially the eminent ones, to proclaim themselves men of religion after all. Specialists who have spent their lifetimes in highly disciplined research into the patterns of genetic mutation or X-ray crystallography or particle collision phenomena and who have risen to the top in their various fields, often get surprisingly mystical when finally faced with ontological questions about the 'objects' of the theories they have for so long been employing.

Effect   I know what you mean.

Cause   This crisis, together with the opportunity to publish, apparently, more or less whatever they wish, usually results in some unlikely religious affirmation or other; either a bizarre excursion into the revelatory scriptures of oriental mysticism or else the safer bet of obeisance to Christian theology and all the jargon that goes with it. Generally speaking, this seems to be little more than an exercise in intellectual guilt-assuagement: an attempt firstly to compensate themselves for the spiritual sterility of their real life's work, and secondly to achieve academic acceptability in the eyes of their non-scientist colleagues.

Effect   Oh nonsense! What a horrible cynic you are! I take it that *your* religion is to sneer at others'?

Cause   Maybe it is. Religions make me sick. I detest gods, all gods!

Effect   You what!?

Cause I detest gods. Gods are what religions are about aren't they?

Effect Well, all religions are theistic in some way or other I suppose, yes.

Cause Tell me then, what *is* a god, in your estimation?

Effect A god?

Cause Yes, a god: little g, little o, little d.

Effect What, as in Greek gods or Roman gods?

Cause For example, yes. What are they, what were they?

Effect Well, they were... anthropomorphisms, representations in human form of certain abstract ideas or natural forces: Venus the goddess of love, Mars the god of war, Neptune the god of the sea and so on...

Cause There's nothing abstract about love or war or the sea.

Effect No, but as general ideas, as *universals*... That's it, the gods existed as anthropomorphic representations of certain important universals, as beings endowed with superhuman powers to control Nature.

Cause That's funny, I thought Venus and Mars and company existed only as lumps of sculpted marble or wood or bronze. Or as paintings on vases or as characters in stories.

Effect Yes, yes, these were the *representations* of the gods...

Cause So what was the god itself, I'm not quite clear? Was it the abstract idea, the natural power, or was it the humanoid representation, the lump of marble?

Effect Well, er...

Cause And anyway, how can a twenty-foot-high ten-ton lump of stone chiselled into the shape of a human body possibly *represent* an abstract universal idea as you suggest? Presumably, to be any sort of a representation a thing must have some feature or features in common with that which it is supposed to be representing?

Effect But I have heard it asserted that the classical sculptures do manage to capture and express something sublime, something spiritual, something divine even.

Cause   Some of the best Greek ones maybe. But in any case, this is a judgement on their *artistic* quality rather than on any representational accuracy. There are sublime classical sculptures of young men and women, just as there are crass ones of gods and goddesses. The question is: how can any lump of stone, however beautiful or ugly, however well or badly chiselled, possibly be a representation of an abstract idea or a natural force?

Effect   Well not a representation then, but a symbol. I guess you could say the statues *symbolized* the deities.

Cause   So you insist that the gods themselves were somethings other than their recognized symbols or representations, were above and beyond these artefacts?

Effect   Yes surely. We must distinguish here between the gods themselves and their graven images.

Cause   Do you think we can?

Effect   Yes. The pictures, the carvings, the statues, these are the creations of men, they were just idols, icons. The gods themselves were, as we said, abstract ideas, superhuman forces and the like.

Cause   Ah, so the gods actually *are*, or *were*, the abstract ideas and not merely the representations or symbols of them, as you suggested earlier?

Effect   Er... yes, I suppose they were.

Cause   So they did not in fact exist?

Effect   Er, well, no, but... Look, can't we say that Venus and Mars and Neptune and the rest existed *for the Greeks*?

Cause   Well whatever else, *they* certainly didn't exist for the Greeks! Venus and Mars and Neptune were the Roman gods, not the Greek ones.

Effect   Oh yes. Hera and Ares and... Poseidon then, if you insist on the Greek words.

Cause   It's not just a matter of words Malcolm, by no means. Translating the Greek word 'τράπεζα' into the Latin 'mensa' into the English 'table' is in no way at all like recognizing the similarities between the Greek god Ἄρης and the Roman god Mavros. These latter are proper names, words that begin with capital letters; note that they have different English equivalents, Ares and Mars. To change a god's name is to change the god. All we can say is that Mars fulfilled roughly the same role for the Romans as Ares fulfilled for the Greeks.

Effect   'Τράπεζα', is that our word 'trapezium'?

Cause   It must be a relative. I believe it means 'four-sided' or 'four-legged'.

Effect   Hm. Anyway, point taken: so Hera and Ares and Poseidon existed for the Greeks, just as Venus and Mars and Neptune existed for the Romans, agreed?

Cause   Aphrodite.

Effect   What?

Cause   Aphrodite. The nearest Greek equivalent to Venus was Aphrodite, not Hera.

Effect   Oh Christ! Aphrodite then, so Aphrodite and Ares and Poseidon existed for the Greeks, do you accept *that*?

Cause   Existed as what, where? As the statues in their temples and the etchings on their vases?

Effect   No, no, no! More than that. They existed as symbolic images, as conceptions of supernatural powers, as abstract ideas, what you will.

Cause   But where, where?

Effect   In... in the minds of their believers.

Cause   'Their believers' being those people who were in the habit of kneeling down in front of the relevant lumps of stone, the relevant 'idols'?

Effect   Well, yes... but no, not necessarily...

Cause   In other words, the gods were just figments of the Greeks' duped imaginations? The Greeks were conned by their priests? Aphrodite and Ares and Poseidon and the rest didn't exist *objectively* at all?

Effect   Well obviously there weren't any real super-human beings wandering around ancient Greece, if that's what you mean. There wasn't in fact some divine warrior called Ares striding about Olympus dressed in armour and intervening in human wars every now and then, of course not.

257

Taking Things Literally

Cause   And you think the Greeks believed there was?

Effect   I don't know, I've never really thought about it. I guess that the average Greek-in-the-street probably believed what he was told. Perhaps he did take the myths literally, I don't know.

Cause   In which case wouldn't he have been in error? Wouldn't he have believed in the existence of something which in fact did not exist? Wouldn't he have been like the child who believes in Santa Claus or the tribe which believes that unicorns exist or the civilization that conceives of the Earth as flat?

Effect   Hmm. Perhaps in the end we cannot be sure exactly what the Greeks did believe. Maybe their gods acted as ideals of human perfection, as heroic images, as models.

Cause   But what of the Greek intellectuals? Surely one cannot imagine that *they* took their mythology literally?

Effect   Honestly Andrew, I've really no idea.

Cause   You see Malcolm, perhaps when in our modern, enlightened, patronizing way we remark that of course the gods of the Greeks and the Romans did not actually *exist*, it is *we* who are taking the old tales too literally. And not just taking the tales too literally, but taking the whole business of believing in gods too literally too.

Effect   Perhaps. I suppose it all depends what one means by this word 'exist'. It is clearly not enough simply to distinguish between things which exist and things which do not. Things can exist in different ways, in different ways for different people, in different ways at different times. As you have said, the question is: what do things exist *as*? Venus and Mars and Neptune existed as ideas or ideals or deities in the minds of the Romans; the Caesars existed in the flesh, as their emperors. While for us, the Roman gods exist as myths, fictions or pieces of sculpture and the Caesars exist as historical figures.

Cause   So you believe that you can draw a clear distinction between mythological figures and historical ones?

Effect   Of course! There are such things as facts Andrew, historical facts.

Cause   Okay, what about the Trojan War? Can you sort out the fact from the myth? Oh yes, there was a King of Mycenae by the name of

Agamemnon who led a Greek allied naval fleet against the Anatolian city of Troy in the year *x* BC, and...

Effect   Oh, there is a date is there?

Cause   Yes, I think about 1250 is the one presently in favour. Homer's battle, it seems, was only the final episode in a long, ten-year campaign of raids and skirmishes. Obviously there are facts, however vague and uncertain: something must have happened. Surely there was a king Priam of Troy, and there was a Clytemnestra, wife of Agamemnon. But what of the fabled interventions of the goddess Athene and the god Apollo? What of Hector and Achilles? Were these real people, local chieftains perhaps? Were they mythic heroes or demi-gods? Does it matter? After all, for us, the whole saga exists only as a story anyway.

Effect   No, not just a story, there is evidence, there are remains. One can go and visit the archaeological sites of Mycenae and Troy, one can go to Athens museum and see Agamemnon's mask.

Cause   So-called.

Effect   Certainly it matters Andrew, of course it matters. We must try to distinguish between historical fact and mere legend or myth, otherwise we wouldn't know *where* we were.

Cause   But where is the borderline? Where does myth end and history begin? Again, think of the Old Testament: Adam and Eve, Noah, Abraham, King David, Joseph and Mary. Who will sort out the fact from the fiction? And who cares? Who can *prove* whether Jesus was the son of man or God?

Effect   Look, Andrew, I will admit that there are grey areas, that things are not always clear-cut, that it is sometimes difficult, even impossible, to decide such matters. But the fact that the distinction has a blurred borderline does not make it any the less real or important. Apollo and Athene were Greek gods. Adolf Hitler and Karl Marx were men of history. You and I are real people.

Cause   Hmm. Anyway, let's get back to gods shall we, gods qua gods. Remember that there are countless other examples besides the familiar ones of the Greeks and the Romans. There are the gods of the Egyptians and the gods of the Celts; the gods of the Norsemen and the gods of the Africans; the gods of Indian mythology and of Chinese. Gods of a thousand different human cultures from around the world. Gods for whom we in the West don't even have names.

Effect   Okay, okay, and there are still people in the world who believe that there are spirits in the trees and rivers and hills, so what?

Cause   So what do all these different gods have in common? If you are going to insist upon the importance of these distinctions, you must presumably have a clear idea of the distinguishing features of god-hood. I will ask you again: what *is* a god exactly?

Effect   I thought we had agreed: a god is an anthropomorphic representation or symbol of certain...

Cause   Anthropomorphic? What about Ganesh, the Hindu elephant-god, or Horus, the Egyptian god with the head of a falcon? The early Aegeans, apparently, had bull-gods and snake-gods too, not to mention the countless weird creatures that roam around in Greek mythology: Pegasus, the winged horse; Cerberus, the many-headed dog; the Chimaera, part lion, part goat, part serpent.

Effect   Okay, okay, not anthropomorphisms necessarily, but... creature-images of some sort; and usually human, or at least human*oid* ones.

Cause   Is that so though? What about the ancient Egyptians' or the South American Incas' worship of the Sun and the Moon? It seems to be the case that the Incas worshipped the Sun which they called 'Inti' and the Moon 'Mama Quilla' as gods *simply as they are*. No representation going on, no symbolism, no creature-imagery, no abstract-ideas-mongering, just the good old Sun and the good old Moon, full stop.

Effect   Uhuh? But some sort of personification or at least personalization is involved, surely? Regarding something as a god does imply the attribution to it of personality, of mentality. Gods are seen as intelligent beings with desires, intentions, purposes, pleasures, memories and so on.

Cause   Ah, so it *is* possible, after all, to attribute mentality to what you have been calling inanimate objects: the Sun, the Sea, the planets?

Effect   People have in the past I suppose... Of course it's *possible* to believe in all sorts of things.

Cause   I'm glad to hear it. And what about money or power or success or progress?

An Unholy Family

Effect   Come again?

Cause   Well, don't we say of certain people that they seem to regard money or political power or career success or technological progress or other quite *im*personal things as gods? Money has no memory, I can vouch for that.

Effect   Oh, but these are special uses of the word 'god' surely? We don't mean that such people *literally* regard money as being a god, what we are pointing out is that in an unusually fervent way they *worship* money, they make its acquisition their main aim in life. There, incidentally, is another feature which all gods have in common: they are all objects of worship.

Cause   What about Kali, the Indian goddess of death and destruction? She is not so much worshipped by the Hindus as hated, feared, dreaded by them.

Effect   Okay, but obviously they... they are in awe of her; she is regarded as being a superhuman power, as someone or something higher and mightier than humanity itself. Yes, that's it: the gods are regarded as being *super*natural powers, *super*natural forces. They are part of Nature, are within Nature, yet they are also somehow *above* Nature, in control of Nature. The humanized deities of the Greeks were more than just legendary heroes and heroines, they were *super*human beings, they were endowed with certain specifically divine qualities.

Cause   Such as?

Effect   Immortality for a start. Wasn't their vital distinction between the mortals and the immortals?

Cause   Again the yearning for immortality, the desire to live for ever, to leave something behind, if only a name. That's why their art of sculpture was so important; 'sculpture' is Greek for 'creation of beauty'; sculpture was itself an activity half-way divine.

Effect   Obviously you can't have your gods being born and growing up and dying like ordinary human beings, your gods must live forever.

Cause   Must they? What about our description of film-actresses as 'screen goddesses' or pop singers as 'idols' or, interestingly, 'stars'? Here, the features of iconizing and hero-worship hold good, but certainly not the attribute of immortality.

Ye of Many Names

Effect   So perhaps these are people who, now in celluloid rather than marble, do 'live on' in a sense?

Cause   Sometimes maybe, if Time wills it, and future historians. There can be false gods too remember, the idols with feet of clay.

Effect   But isn't this a rather a special use of the word 'god'? I can see that you are trying to turn this into another of your futile 'hunt-the-feature' games. Any minute now you'll be asking me to spot the qualities shared by the Olympian deities and the gallery seats in a West-End theatre!

Cause   They are both high up; they both survey human drama; they...

Effect   Oh Lord!

Cause   And then of course there are the One-Gods, The Fathers Almighty, The Allahs, The Jehovahs and the rest of them. How many One-Gods are there in the world I wonder, and how many people have died in their various names?

Effect   Look, shouldn't we just conclude once again, that gods, like tables and games, are not all possessed of one defining feature or set of features, but rather display a network of overlapping and criss-crossing similarities. Gods, in short, form a family.

Cause   Fair enough, okay. And given that this family is going to have to include your own peculiarly characterless, evanescent, omnipresent-yet-one-and-only, beyond-above-and-without-the-world-yet-participating-active-and-within-it, immaterial-yet-all-material, all-powerful-and-all-knowing-yet-free-will-and-choice-allowing, all-loving-yet-pain-condoning, behaviour-judging-yet-sin-forgiving, Christian-yet-modern-style, Creator-type-capital-G-God, *that* Bloke, the network of overlapping and criss-crossing similarities between the family-members will have to be very very wide-ranging and be likely to involve the perception of some extremely subtle relationships and very hard-to-define characteristics.

Effect   I imagine it will.

Cause   Ah, is this your Hall? Perfect timing! Christ, I'm starving!

Effect   Please Andrew, I'm not sure about this...

Cause   Oh go on, be a sport! Hey look, there are some gowns on the rack there; I'll just borrow one...

Effect But High Table have all gone in, you'll stand out a mile!

Cause I'll pretend to be a big name in Polish linguistics, okay?

Effect Oh dear!

Cause Keep walking Malcolm, keep walking!

Effect Ssh! And don't sit down until Grace has been said...

* * * * * * * * * * *

Cause There you are Malcolm, no problem at all. Mmm. This pork's not bad. The vegetables are a bit Thalesian though.

Effect Thalesian?

Cause Thales, the first philosopher in recorded history; he thought the world was made of water.

Effect Ah.

Cause Have you ever studied the pre-Socratics?

Effect Studied what?

Cause The pre-Socratics; the early Greek philosophers, the ones who were around before Socrates.

Effect Oh, no, I haven't.

Cause Very rewarding. It's all there; they ran the whole gamut, more or less.

Effect What 'whole gamut'?

Cause Well, they seem, between them, to have invented, examined and rejected more or less every kind of cosmological theory that the human mind has managed to come up with, all before 400 BC.

Effect Oh yes?

Cause Yes. Every kind of theory about what this ever-changing multi-faceted world we inhabit is made of, about what is its ἀρχή, its archetype or principle, about its element or elements, about whether it is monistic or pluralistic, about whether it is continuous or atomic – 'quantized' as I guess you'd call it. Apple sauce please.

Effect   Uhuh? And what was their conclusion?

Cause   They arrived at no one conclusion, of course not... Mmm, nice wine. No expense spared up here eh?... No, there was no consensus, just a series of disputes.

Effect   But they thought the world was made of water?

Cause   Thales did. Not bad for a first try I'd have thought, given that ninety-five percent of the world *is* water according to you lot.

Effect   No. ninety-five percent of *you* is water, I imagine that's what you're thinking of.

Cause   Well anyway, the interesting thing is that Thales, in about 600 BC, not only assumed that there was *a* principle or element of the world, but also identified it as being a particular, perfectly ordinary physical substance; he gave a modern, chemical answer to the question. As a scientist you may not agree with Thales, but at least you're in dispute with him.

Effect   I wasn't aware of it.

Cause   You'd probably have a rather harder time with Anaximander, the first philosopher to write a book, who, in the face of all the weaknesses from which Thales' chemical theory suffered, proposed as his ἀρχή of the world 'τὸ ἄπειρον', which is usually translated as 'the indefinite' or 'the endless'.

Effect   That sounds a pretty safe bet. And it still seems to accord with your vegetable observation too.

Cause   Then came Anaximenes, who suggested that the prime candidate for τὸ ἀρχή was ' ἀήρ', from which comes our word 'air'. adding that there were certain other 'basic forms' or 'elements' which made up the world too, including Fire, Earth and Water. Then there was Xenophanes, who went off on a rather more religious tack and tried to unify the family of 'elements' that was already threatening to multiply by proposing that τὸ ἀρχή was "Εἰς Θεός', 'One God'. And it's still only 550 BC! Heraclitus of course conceived of the world as being sustained by Fire, as consisting of opposing forces or tendencies in perpetual conflict, as being in a state of constant change or flux. One cannot step into the same car twice. The river of rust flows endlessly from Earth to...

Effect Oh do hurry up and eat your dinner Andrew. They'll be bringing dessert soon.

Cause I'm sorry, too much talking. Say, don't you want your pork?

Effect No, help yourself.

Cause Great, thanks. You're not a vegetarian are you?

Effect I don't eat meat, no.

Cause Really? As a matter of principle?

Effect I don't know. I don't make a big issue of it, if that's what you mean. I don't particularly like meat, and I don't see why some poor pig should have to die simply to gratify a primitive fetish of ours. Meat's not especially good for you. You can get all you need from plants.

Cause That's funny, I had always understood that the arrival of the carnivores represented a great leap forward in evolution, that meat-eating is far more energy-efficient than grazing.

Effect Well, yes, for the animals, but we can now be efficient in other ways, much more efficient. Did you know that it takes over two-and-a-half acres of good grassland to feed one cow and that if that land were used to grow the right crops, it would yield...

Cause Yes yes, I'm sure, but I'm afraid I like my meat too much Malcolm. If I can afford it I will eat it. Bugger pigs. Mm, yum yum!

Effect Yuk!

Cause Anyway, then there were the famous mathematician and musical theorist Pythagoras, who saw *number* as being the principle behind all things; Parmenides the logician, who tried to arrive at an account of τὸ ἀρχή of the world through pure deductive reasoning; and Zeno, who in his celebrated paradoxes wrestled with the question of whether time and space are continuously divisible or are ultimately particular. Ugh, what funny mustard!

Effect Achilles and the tortoise?

Cause Right.

Effect Talking of which...

Cause Next came Empedocles, who to the mathematics of Pythagoras and the logic of Parmenides added scientific observations of the physical world and of Nature, concluding that the world is made up of a quartet of elements Fire, Air, Earth and Water, which are governed by two fundamental universal forces, Love or Attraction and Strife or Repulsion. Empedocles' cosmological system worked well enough for the best part of two thousand years.

Effect "Worked well enough"?

Cause Was generally accepted, was common knowledge, was used by chemists.

Effect By *al*chemists maybe.

Cause Then, if you add to all this the theories of Leucippus and Democritus that matter consists of minute indivisible particles or *atoms*, from 'ἀ-τόμos', 'that which cannot be cut', you have amassed all the ingredients of our modern scientific cosmology, and it's not yet 400 BC! We're still pre-Socrates! They even suggested that these atoms come in different shapes and sizes, move in an infinite void and combine and separate in a variety of arrangements – without so much as a magnifying-glass for help!

Effect All very impressive Andrew, but I honestly don't see that the methods and theories and aims of modern atomic theory owe anything whatsoever to the speculations of the early Greek philosophers. I'm sorry to disappoint you and all.

Cause That's alright Malcolm; it's no skin off my nose. We're all entitled to our opinions. There, finished! I must say, that was excellent.

Effect Anyone can sit around on a mountainside speculating about the nature of the Universe.

Cause Ah, cream caramel, my favourite!

Effect If only science were as easy as that...

Cause Any more plonk up there?

Effect I notice for example, that throughout your little 'history of Greek cosmology' you made not one single reference to any physical discovery, any chemical experiment or any attempt at measurement made by these guys.

266

Cause   But how could they, they had no apparatus, no measuring instruments to speak of. Their only experimental weapons were their senses and their intellects.

Effect   Exactly! No wonder cosmological theories were ten a penny!

Cause   Are you not having your caramel Malcolm?

Effect   Modern atomic theory by contrast, was not arrived at through idle speculation or day-dreaming, but arose as a result of certain specific experimental discoveries, was conceived in order to explain certain empirically confirmed chemical observations.

Cause   Ah, is that so? Perhaps you could tell me a bit more about this, it's a subject which interests me greatly.

Effect   Okay, if you wish, but I suggest that we get out of here first and try to find somewhere a bit quieter.

Cause   Have you anywhere in mind?

Effect   Well, there is the new Senior Common Room, but I'm not sure if we'll be able to use it; it's not been completed yet, the conversion. I suppose we can try. Have you finished?

Cause   Ready when you are.

Effect   Right then, follow me, it's across the Quad...

    *   *   *   *   *   *   *   *   *   *   *

Cause   Brrr! It's getting a bit nippy!

Effect   Mind the scaffolding Andrew, it's rather dangerous in the dark. Careful: cross by the planks to the left...

Cause   Modernization job going on is there? What was it? It looks like a church.

Effect   That's right, it was the original chapel. When the College grew to its present size at the turn of the century, they built the new chapel and this became the library, and now that the computerized library block over the river has been completed they are converting this into new Senior and Junior Common rooms and bars. They are even talking of having a discotheque in the Crypt.

The Future S.C.R.

Cause Tut tut!

Effect I don't know what state the new S.C.R. is in at the moment; I expect there will be a few paint-pots and things lying around, but at least we should get a bit of privacy. Most of the profs still use the old room over in the Cloister. Oops, mind that rope, the lighting on these stairs is a bit poor. Ah, here we are!

Cause Say, what a lovely room!

Effect It's going to be nice isn't it? The little arched windows make it rather cosy. Hold on, I'll see if I can find any heating...

Cause Brr, yes, this gown's not much use.

Effect Hey, you should have put that back!

Cause I will, I will, don't worry. Ah, there by the sink, a couple of stools... I know, let's sit over in the corner out of the draught; there's a power-point for the fan-heater too... No chance of a corkscrew I suppose, to get the vino going?

Effect Oh, now where did you get that?

Cause High Table of course. Hid it under the gown. I think that must be what they're for.

Effect Honestly, you're impossible!

Cause It's alright, no-one saw. Hm, I guess I'll have to use the thumb trick. Are there any glasses anywhere?

Effect No.

Cause Oh come on Malcolm, stop sulking. It's here now, you may as well help me drink it. Look, these tea-mugs will do, I'll give them a rinse.

Effect Seriously Andrew, I find your behaviour disgraceful, quite disgraceful. And after being invited in too.

Cause I know, I'm sorry, unforgiveable. Here, cheers!

Effect Cheers.

Cause Right, now come on: tell me about this atomic theory of yours.

Effect Well, as I am sure you already know, all matter is composed of Atoms, that is, consists of numbers of discrete particles which...

Cause Uh? Do I *know* that? I've been told it, and I know that it's an obvious way of... an obvious *assumption*, but I don't know it in the way I know there's a rubber plant in my room or in the way I know that two plus two make four.

Effect Well whether you know it or not, it's a matter of fact. It is also a matter of fact that atoms themselves are made up of yet smaller particles: heavy, positively-charged particles called 'Protons' and heavy, neutral particles called 'Neutrons' grouped together in a 'Nucleus', around which orbit lighter, negatively-charged particles called 'Electrons'.

Cause Ah, now, I certainly do not *know* any of this; these are by no means obvious assumptions. Oh, I've been *taught* about the structure and constituents of atoms, but I can't say that I myself have any direct knowledge of them.

Effect But surely you accept the findings of science Andrew, the common knowledge of these matters that has built up over the years, just as, for example, you accept the facts of history? One can claim to doubt almost anything but...

Cause Forgive me Malcolm, but now you mention history, I think I'd be more interested to hear a chronological account of how our present atomic theory has evolved than simply to sit through a statement of your current beliefs. You just leapt straight from an introduction of your atomic theory to claims about the existence of electrons and protons, yet I believe that this development in fact took over a hundred years.

Effect If you want the history, I suppose we have to begin with the English chemist John Dalton, whose theory of atoms emerged in the early nineteenth century as the most satisfactory explanation of how the chemical elements combine to form compounds. Dalton postulated that elements consisted of discrete, finitely-sized, ultimately indivisible particles called atoms, all the atoms of a particular element being similar to one another in size, shape, weight and properties, and the atoms of different elements being *dis*similar in these respects.

Cause Already it is clear that this atomic theory is going to be inextricably bound up with a distinction between elements and compounds.

Elementary Ideas

Effect   Obviously. You do understand the difference between elements and compounds I take it? And mixtures?

Cause   Remind me.

Effect   Elements of course, are substances which cannot chemically be broken down into other, simpler substances; compounds are substances which are formed by the combination of two or more different elements in certain fixed proportions by weight and which have constant, definite chemical properties; while mixtures, as the term implies, are just mixtures of different, chemically uncombined substances in no fixed proportions by weight and with no constant or definite chemical properties.

Cause   It is interesting, isn't it, how *drastically* the new chemistry was at odds with the cosmology that had preceded. According to the new theory, three of the four 'elements' of Empedocles and Aristotle – Fire, Air and Earth – were not even compounds, but were actually only *mixtures.*

Effect   So much for the merits of meditating on mountainsides... Anyway, the great contribution of Dalton was his postulation that when chemical elements combine to form compounds, their atoms bond together in simple whole number ratios: 1:1, 1:2, 2:3 and so on.

Cause   Isn't it the case though that in those days the accepted list of 'elements' was very different from the list we know today? The Daltonian selection still included a number of substances which we now regard as being compounds and omitted others which we now regard as being elements. Indeed there were still plenty of chemists around who believed in the Phlogiston theory, the theory that when a substance burnt it released an inflammable chemical called 'Phlogiston' into the air.

Effect   Well obviously a complete, accurate picture did not emerge all at once. There were bound to be mistakes and omissions. Progress depended upon the slow and painstaking gathering of experimental information. Unfortunately, Dalton was not a skillful enough experimenter to be able to prove the validity of his key 'multiple proportions' postulate himself, and it was left to later chemists like...

Cause   What? I thought you claimed that the atomic theory arose as a result of certain experimental discoveries! Now here you are saying that the theory came first and the observations which confirmed it came later.

Effect   Well... yes... but thinking was going that way. Fairly accurate, quantitative chemical analysis had begun around that time. People had come to accept that compounds were chemical combinations of elements in certain fixed proportions by weight; cases had been discovered of different compounds that could be formed by combinations of the same elements in different fixed proportions by weight. Dalton's atomic theory, with its law of multiple proportions, was a brilliant, natural, logical way of picturing what was going on in such cases. The fact that it was confirmed in experiment only later affects neither its validity nor the value of its insight.

Cause   Uhuh? So "thinking was going that way"...

Effect   Anyway, once the new atomic theory of chemical combination had been established, the next task was to compile data about the different elements' comparative Atomic Weights. This was a matter of measuring experimentally the elementary weight-to-weight proportions found in different chemical compounds and working out their molecular structures or 'formulae'.

Cause   Their what structures?

Effect   Molecular. A *Molecule*, from the Latin 'moles' meaning 'mass' or 'very small amount', is the smallest discrete particle of a chemical compound formed, as Dalton postulated, by simple whole-number combinations of elementary atoms. So, over a period of years, the pattern of the elements' atomic weights was discovered.

Cause   The pattern?

Effect   Well, the series. The elements could be placed in a series of ascending atomic weights.

Cause   Of course they could, although I gather that even this research was very far from being free from dispute and controversy; not only were there many contradictory experimental results and uncertainties about compounds' molecular formulae, but also there were fundamental disagreements over how such a scale was to be drawn up.

Effect   But none of these controversies affected the principle or the importance of the exercise. Since atomic weights were to be proportional, it was just a matter of which element to take as the standard, as unity; there were those who favoured Hydrogen and those who favoured Oxygen, that's all.

Cause   Oh yes, by the way Malcolm, tell me this: why are Hydrogen and Oxygen always referred to as 'H-two' and 'O-two'? Why the 'two'?

A Quirky Pattern

Effect Ah, now that's because in their normal gaseous state, these elements exist not as single atoms, but as molecules, in which pairs of atoms combine together as...

Cause But I thought that molecules were the smallest discrete particles of *compounds*?

Effect Normally, yes, that is so, but some of these gaseous elements exist in molecular forms too. Oxygen, for example, has another allotrope O-three, called 'Ozone'.

Cause An 'allotrope'?

Effect Allotropes are just different forms of the same element or compound. The element Carbon, for example, can exist as either diamond or charcoal or graphite or soot.

Cause Eh? And you call these the same substance?

Effect They are different allotropes of the same element, yes. The word comes from the Greek 'ἄλλος' meaning 'other' and 'τρόπος' meaning 'way'.

Cause But if Oxygen can exist as O, as O-two and as O-three, how can you ever be sure of its atomic weight?

Effect Oh Andrew, one can, one can. I would have to go into the molecular theory of gases, the work of the French and Italian chemists Gay-Lussac and Avogadro and all that. Just take it from me that one can measure relative atomic weights.

Cause Hmm. Okay, so the elementary atomic weights, based upon some arbitrary standard, can be placed in ascending order, so what?

Effect So if you study the list carefully, as the Russian chemist Mendeléef did in the 1860s, you can discover a pattern in them. Mendeléef noticed that if you place the elements out in series of increasing atomic weight, the members of certain clearly defined chemical families, the Alkali Metals, the Halogens, the Inert Gases, will occur at regular intervals, intervals which get longer and longer as the series progresses.

Cause But surely, if the intervals get longer each time, it can't be much of a pattern?

Effect   There certainly is a pattern. It can be seen most clearly when the elements are arranged in what is called The Periodic Table.

Cause   Ah, there's one we forgot at lunchtime, with a capital 'P' and 'T': a candidate for Plato's Table of Forms perhaps?

Effect   Mendeléef found that if the ascending atomic weight series was written out into a number of horizontal rows or 'Periods', certain of the chemical families would appear as vertical columns or 'Groups'.

Cause   I understand that he had to play some pretty arbitrary tricks on the series in order to get any sort of a pattern out of it. The periods all vary in length, there are the so-called 'transition elements', there are the rare earths, there are cases of apparently quite dissimilar elements occurring in the same group, there were many gaps in the table...

Effect   Ah now there you are! The gaps have all been filled in! There were gaps in the original table it is true, but new elements have since been discovered which fill them. The table actually predicted the existence of certain previously unknown substances; what more can you ask?

Cause   Well all I can say is that there are bound to be patterns in Nature; there are patterns in the random tumbling of dice. You will find patterns in anything if you are looking for them.

Effect   But you don't have to look for the patterns Andrew, they are there! There are clear, definite patterns in the chemistry, in the atomic weight measurements!

Cause   Well I never saw them! Even the series of the so-called elements' atomic numbers, the order in which they feature in the periodic classification, is by no means parallelled by the series of their atomic weights. In fact I seem to remember that there were even places where elements had to be entered 'out of order' just to preserve the supposed pattern of chemical families.

Effect   If you say so. Such apparent anomalies would have occurred where a variety of isotopes exist.

Cause   Ah, 'isotopes', now what are they?

Effect   'Isotope' comes from the Greek words 'ἴσος' meaning 'equal' and 'τόπος' meaning 'place' or 'position'. Isotopes are different forms of the same element.

More Strange Words

Cause   Oh now what? That is plainly a contradiction in terms, surely?

Effect   No, they have the same atomic number and the same chemical properties, but...

Cause   If they have the same properties, how can you tell them apart, how can you distinguish between them?

Effect   By their different atomic *weights*, that is how.

Cause   Fudge! Fudge!

Effect   Not at all Andrew, a fact, a fact! Most elements occur naturally as two or more different isotopes. This has been shown in experiments.

Cause   What experiments?

Effect   Experiments in mass spectroscopy, for a start.

Cause   First carried out when?

Effect   At about the turn of the century. In a mass spectroscope a beam of ions passes through an...

Cause   A beam of what?

Effect   Of 'Ions', from the participle of the Greek verb 'ἰέναι' 'to go', literally 'that which goes'. Ions are atoms or radicals which have gained or lost one or more electrons and which therefore carry a net negative or positive electric charge. A 'Radical', before you ask, from the Latin 'radix' a root, is a group of commonly associated atoms which often goes through chemical reactions internally unchanged.

Cause   What is the difference between a radical and a molecule, and what are electrons?

Effect   Oh come on Andrew, you must have heard of electrons!

Cause   I've heard of them, I've heard the name, but I've never been quite clear what sort of things electrons are. To begin with, why the name?

Effect   From 'ἤλεκτρον', the Greek for 'amber'.

Cause   Really? Amber, that's nice: neither red nor green.

Effect   I'm sorry?

Cause   Nothing. I once knew a girl called Amber.

Effect   Amber is a naturally-occurring substance, a fossillized tree-resin in fact, which when rubbed becomes charged with static er... electricity. Anyway, the Electron is a tiny particle of negative electric charge. It was first discovered definitively in 1893 by the English physicist Joseph Thomson in his experiments with cathode rays in which...

Cause   'Discovered'? In the book I read it was 'invented'.

Effect   The Electron is in fact the *unit* of negative electric charge.

Cause   It *is* the unit or it is *taken* as the unit?

Effect   It *is* the unit, and it has a mass of 1/1800th of the mass of a simple hydrogen ion, that is a Proton.

Cause   Eh?

Effect   A Proton. From the Greek again, meaning 'the first', as in 'proto-type'. This is where we came in: early this century a number of theories of atomic structure were being proposed and tested against the experimental observations. The theory of the New Zealand physicist Ernest Rutherford emerged successful: every atom consists of a nucleus of a number, the atomic number, of heavy positively-charged protons clustered together, around which orbit the lighter, negatively-charged electrons forming...

Cause   Hang on! I thought it was a law of electric force that like charges repel. How can these positive protons possibly be clustering together?

Effect   Ah, well, at short ranges these particles are subject to the far more strongly interactive *nuclear* forces which overcome...

Cause   One's childish notions of commonsense. Naïvely, one also wants to ask questions like: if all substances are made of atoms and all atoms contain electrons, why don't all substances conduct electricity?

Effect   In order to explain atoms' normal stability, the Danish physicist Niels Bohr postulated that the atomic electrons must fall into certain defined orbits or 'energy levels'. Then in the early 30s the theory was further modified by the discovery that besides the protons, an atomic nucleus also contains a roughly equal number of heavy, electrically-neutral particles called 'Neutrons'.

Cause   Ah, now guess where the words 'neuter' and 'neutral' come from?

Split Definitive

Effect Erm... I'm not sure.

Cause It's from the Latin *ne uter*, meaning literally 'not either'. Neither, neuter. Incidentally, I always find it interesting to think that only a few miles from here people speak a language of which every noun has a gender, in which there is no single synonym for 'it'.

Effect Yes, in French atomic physics, all the particles are masculine.

Cause Uhuh? How disappointing. So anyway, your atom is not atomic at all, but in fact is composed of yet smaller particles?

Effect It is not literally atomic, no. Since its heavy nucleus is orbited by the lighter electrons, an atom is in reality largely empty space.

Cause Isn't this a contradiction in terms? Doesn't all this make a complete nonsense of Dalton's original conception and the original notion of 'elements' as macroscopic substances?

Effect Well... yes, it does in a way. But we don't want to be hamstrung by words' literal meanings or by etymology do we? It soon became clear that Dalton's original picture of the elementary atoms as being discrete spherical solid lumps was inadequate; it could not explain their electromagnetic properties, their spectra, how they bonded together, their patterns in the Periodic Table and so on. The modified Bohr atom successfully achieved many of these objectives and also explained why...

Cause Wait a minute, you are leaping ahead too fast! You are telescoping years and years of research and controversy and argument between rival theories into a single paragraph. In barely a couple of minutes you have gone from the proposal of a list of 'elements', a controversial enough exercise in itself, to the postulation of elementary 'atoms', obviously another hornets' nest, now to highly problematic pronouncements about their detailed internal constitution. At the very least a premature advance, wouldn't you say?

Effect Well you did ask for a summary.

Cause True, I did, but I would have liked just a little more historical perspective, some sense that we are dealing here not with open-and-shut cases but with mysteries, speculations, hypotheses. You are presenting things as though all controversies have been settled, as though we are now possessed of a catalogue of facts. I'm still having a hard time with your Periodic Table, with your list of 'elements'; the pattern of family resemblances amongst them seems to be very hard to spot. Look, according to you there are now elements – Sodium, Potassium – which are so highly reactive that they do not occur in Nature uncombined; there are elements – Neon, Argon – which are so *un*reactive that they do not combine with anything; there are elements – Technetium, Prometheum and most of Period 7 – which can only be synthesized artificially for fractions of a second so that the sole reason for their claimed existence seems to be their ability to fill a gap in the Table or to immortalize the name of some dead scientist; some of your elements exist as solids, some as liquids, some as gases; apparently there are even elements like Radium which spontaneously break down into other elements. Now *there's* a contradiction for you!

Effect   But that is an example of radioactive decay, not a chemical process at all.

Cause   Ah, yes, *radioactive* decay. Am I right in thinking that radioactivity was first discovered by accident?

Effect   I'm not sure that it was by accident exactly; in the 1890s the French physicist Becquerel found that photographic plates left overnight in a drawer got fogged by a nearby lump of the naturally-occurring mineral pitchblende. The Curies later isolated the Radium in pitchblende as being the source of the mystery rays.

Cause   And what do you mean by saying that radioactive decay is not a *chemical* process?

Effect   It involves the break-up of the atomic *nucleus*, it is not a process caused by changes in inter-atomic bondings.

Cause   But aren't you here jumping the gun again, or putting the cart before the horse? You are using a later theory to try to explain an anomaly in an earlier one, in an earlier attempt to identify 'the elements'; later not only in the historical but also in the epistemological sense. To me now, with no atomic preconceptions, the suggestion that supposedly elementary Radium can turn spontaneously into supposedly elementary Lead is absurd, a feeble joke.

Effect   But that's why we have to go into atomic structure, to explain such phenomena.

Cause   Or why, for a start, we should abandon the idea that Radium is an element. This is it you see Malcolm: once a theory, a theory that at a certain time fitted some of the then-known facts reasonably well or fitted them better than the rival theories then on offer is accepted, it becomes sacrosanct, whatever new evidence or interpretation crops up afterwards and despite the fact that new discoveries may later make it a nonsense. New discoveries result not in a rejection or re-examination of the original assumptions, but in an ever-increasing complication and embellishment of them.

Effect   Of course the atomic theory has grown very complicated over the years, because our knowledge of the phenomena has become vastly more detailed. The theory is complex because the world is complex. At this point perhaps I should mention some other difficulties. Also around the turn of the century, in order to explain certain odd photo-emission results, the German physicist Max Planck suggested that light is not, as in the traditional view, an electromagnetic wave-motion, but is 'quantized', taking the form of discrete parcels or bundles of energy. A young Albert Einstein adopted this suggestion in his explanation of the photoelectric effect and later, in the 1930s, it was found that the application of wave-mechanics and this 'quantum' theory of energy explained beautifully Bohr's pattern of electronic energy-levels. This all suggests that an atomic electron is not a precisely defined particle tracing a clear-cut orbit, so much as a 'bundle' of charge within a, er, certain area of location probability. Each electron is thus identified by a set of four 'quantum numbers', including a property interpreted as *spin*. Add Heisenberg's uncertainty factor and Einstein's predicted relativistic effects and I'm afraid the whole thing becomes rather hard to visualize, but it does fit the...

Cause   So you're now admitting that the atomic account you were giving me *just five minutes ago* was in fact tosh?

Effect   Not tosh exactly, but... a simpler picture, an easier picture to grasp to start with, er...

Cause   I get it. But sidestepping, for the moment, the quantum quicksand, where does all this leave dear old Dalton's list of chemical elements? Shouldn't the Periodic Table have been dismantled long ago? Why the endless fudging? It should never have survived the isotope business.

Effect   What's the problem? The isotopes are perfectly explicable in terms of atomic structure, this is where the neutrons come into play. For each element, the number of neutrons in its atomic nucleus can vary, and although this variation does not affect its chemical properties it does affect certain other characteristics, notably its atomic weight as measured by a mass spectroscope.

Cause   Does the neutron actually exist, or is it perhaps just an explanatory device dreamt up to keep the theory going?

Effect   Of course it exists. Admittedly it began life, in about 1920, as an hypothesis of Rutherford's, but it was discovered definitively by the Englishman James Chadwick in his experiments on Beryllium in 1932.

Cause   Oh, as late as that?

Effect   Chadwick demonstrated that certain extremely penetrative high-energy emissions could be explained only in terms of heavy, proton-sized neutral particles. This discovery also solved a number of other problems, including the phenomenon of isotopy.

Cause   Uhuh. So the number of neutrons in an element's atomic nucleus can vary?

Effect   Within certain limits.

Cause   And within those limits the neutron-number, if I may call it that, is indeterminate?

Effect   No no, it can vary, but it can only take one of a number of fixed values. Some elements have only one known isotope, some have two, some have three and so on. Tin, if I remember rightly, has nine or ten.

Cause   That's odd. Is there any reason why some elements should have only one isotope while others have several, or why, in the latter cases, the neutron-numbers take some values but not others?

Effect   Er no, not that I know of, though I suppose there may be a reason.

Cause   And when an element does have more than one isotope, do the different varieties occur together in fixed proportions by weight?

Effect   Generally speaking yes, an element's isotopic distribution and hence its atomic weight is roughly constant whatever the source of the sample, although there are, I believe, a few instances in which this is not the case.

Cause   But the isotopic proportions are not fixed in the way that the constitution of a compound is fixed and they can be changed artificially without affecting the element's chemical properties? The different isotopes do not combine together in a molecular way for instance?

Effect   Oh no, nothing like that.

279

Instabilities

Cause So there is no chemical reason why the isotopes occur in the proportions in which they are found to occur naturally?

Effect No, I guess not; that is just the way things are.

Cause Hmm. So if one regarded each different isotopic form as being in the strict sense a different substance, then most of what we have up to now been calling elements are not really elementary at all, but are in fact *mixtures*, that is, they occur only as two or more substances mixed together in no fixed proportions by weight?

Effect Strictly speaking I suppose, yes. But it all depends how one defines the terms 'substance', 'element', 'compound', 'mixture' and so on.

Cause Quite.

Effect I would remind you though that none of this affects the fact that the different isotopes of a given element display exactly the same chemical properties.

Cause Only if one defines the phrase 'chemical properties' in a rather peculiar way too. Tell me Malcolm: if one does regard all the different isotopic forms as being distinct elementary substances, how many of them are there altogether?

Effect If one takes the first 86 elements, that is up to the end of Period Six after which everything starts to get a bit radioactive and unstable, I think there is a total of something like 270 different natural isotopes known to date.

Cause And has anyone managed yet to discern any pattern in all of this? In the series of ascending isotopic weights for example?

Effect Not to my knowledge, no. But then there is no reason why there should be such a pattern, for one can go on adding or subtracting, or rather, trying to add or subtract neutrons to or from atomic nuclei ad infinitum. Most such attempts result, of course, in the production of isotopes which are highly unstable and radioactive.

Cause Ah, tell me more.

Effect Besides the 270 stable isotopes there are also many more *un*stable varieties whose nuclei spontaneously decay and break up, emitting radioactivity in the form of particles or Gamma rays – very high frequency electromagnetic radiation. Some of these processes are extremely slow with half-lives of thousands of years, like the natural Radium example you mentioned earlier, while others take only minute fractions of a second.

Cause Uhuh? So where would you draw the line between 'stable' and 'unstable'?

Effect I... I don't think one can draw a line exactly.

Cause I thought you just did: your figure of 270.

Effect Ah, well...

Cause How many isotopes are there altogether then, stable and otherwise?

Effect I'm not sure, I expect there are over 1,000.

Cause And couldn't it be the case that in fact *all* atoms are always undergoing some form of nuclear decay and just that some of them are doing so at much much slower rates than others?

Effect I suppose it's true that any nucleus will break down under *some* circumstances, but...

Cause It strikes me Malcolm that what are decaying here are not so much your atomic nuclei as your ideas about elementality.

Effect There's nothing new about any of this Andrew, we have been studying decay phenomena for years now. In cyclotrons and synchrotrons, machines which accelerate atomic and subatomic particles to very high energies, we have amassed an enormous amount of data about the effects of nuclear bombardment, particle collisions, irradiation and so on. Hey, what's that noise!?

Cause It sounds like a bird... Yes, look, there, up in the rafters. Christ, it's a crow!

Effect It must have come in where they're mending the roof and got trapped... What a monster!

Cause It's going to damage itself flapping around like that... What can we do? Hang on, that fan-light up there... It looks as though this handle may do it... Yes! It's opening! Go on boy, off you go...

Effect Gone, phew!

Unclear Fission

Cause   Gone, minus a couple of feathers... So remind me then Malcolm, what's supposed to happen in an Atomic bomb?

Effect   Ah, well, that involves nuclear *fission,* a whole new ball-game, a more dramatic process altogether, in which an atomic nucleus under particle bombardment actually splits into two. Under some conditions this nuclear fission can result in the emission of further particles for further such collisions, thus introducing the possibility of a *chain* fission-reaction.

Cause   B-bmm!

Effect   In the Hydrogen bomb, Plutonium-fission is used as the detonator of an uncontrolled hydrogen fusion reaction, in which Deuterium nuclei combine together to form Helium.

Cause   *Deuterium* nuclei?

Effect   Yes, Deuterium, or Heavy Hydrogen, is the isotopic form which is found in minute quantities in water with a single neutron added to its proton nucleus, making it much more fusible than common Hydrogen.

Cause   So fusible Deuterium and non-fusible 'common' Hydrogen are the same element, in your book? Despite the former's H-bomb effect?

Effect   Yes. They have the same chemical properties. In nuclear power stations the energy-source is not Plutonium, but a controlled reaction of fissile Uranium.

Cause   Notice the names here.

Effect   Uranium occurs naturally as a mixture of three isotopes: U_{238} about ninety-nine percent, U_{235} about one percent and U_{238} in minute amounts. It is only the U_{235} isotope that can successfully sustain a chain-reaction, so to be of any use the U_{235} must be isolated and the natural Uranium 'enriched'.

Cause   So the U_{238} is harmless?

Effect   It will undergo fission, but it won't sustain a chain-reaction. It's harmless, yes.

Cause   Yet, again, you insist on calling these the same substance, the same element? You will say that U_{238}, a harmless powder, has the same chemical properties as U_{235}, the destroyer of worlds?

Effect Yes, they have the same atomic number.

Cause Indeed you have a strange chemistry Malcolm, a very strange chemistry!

Effect But this is nuclear physics Andrew, an entirely different area of investigation from that of ordinary chemistry. We are dealing with quite different types of reaction.

Cause Different types of reaction or different types of jargon?

Effect Both. Different types of reaction, certainly. For a start, the bond-energies of the nuclear particles are far far greater than the nucleus-electron bonds. In nuclear fission for example, the relativistic mass-loss or turning of matter into energy predicted by Einstein actually becomes a significant, measurable effect.

Cause So I hear. But why the 'whole new chemistry'? Even scientists talk of 'the Solar fire' or of a 'nuclear fireball'; will you suggest that they are making a mistake, or claim that they are not talking literally? Is not the modern discovery of relativistic mass-loss at least formally akin to Lavoisier's eighteenth-century demonstration that when a combustible substance burns in air, its initial weight is less than that of its residues? Isn't the problem in both cases one of atomic visualizability?

Effect I don't know what you're talking about, or rather, *you* don't! Oxygen combustion is a perfectly ordinary chemical reaction, it is a quite different sort of process from nuclear fission, or fusion. You simply don't know enough about it. Honestly Andrew, there is really no point in our discussing these things, given that you are so ignorant of the facts.

Cause Facts, what facts? Give me an example.

Effect Okay, fact one: the ionization potentials of the outer electrons of most elementary atoms fall within the range from one to one hundred electron-volts. Fact two: the bond-energy tied up in the two-proton helium nucleus is about twenty-eight *million* electron-volts. You see, a quite different order of magnitude, a factor of about ten to the power six!

Cause Just as I thought, throttled by your own theory, jailed in your own jargon! You cannot even express the new 'facts' to which you are appealing except in terms of your already-accepted atomic theory.

Effect Oh really!

Nuclear Proliferation

Cause Besides, so what? What does order of magnitude prove anyway? I'll bet the planet Earth is at least ten to the power six times the size of the average billiard-ball, but what of that? After all, at an intuitive level there is no obvious reason to distinguish between...

Effect At an intuitive level, exactly! What use is intuition in questions of nuclear physics? Please Andrew, let's not go on, this conversation is getting absurd, I am afraid you are out of your depth here.

Cause Oh certainly I am out of my depth here Malcolm, but you are too. In speculating about the atomic and subatomic we are all out of our depth, in more ways than one. The trouble is that since the inception of your atomic theory, that theory which at first seemed to be so helpful and so clear, every new discovery, of which there have been hundreds, and every new anomaly, of which there have been thousands, has required obscure and complex new fudge-factors and hypotheses. Every new order-of-magnitude jump has precipitated a plunge into yet darker subatomic depths. The story started with atoms and molecules and their order-of-magnitude relatives ions and radicals, yet in no time at all and without so much as a philosophical by-your-leave you were talking of this supposedly elementary world as being in fact made up of a triumvirate of far smaller particles called electrons, protons and neutrons. And no doubt there are plenty more where they came from.

Effect Oh yes. For a start of course, there is the Photon, the massless quantum of electromagnetic radiation, from 'φῶs, φωτόs', the Greek for 'light'. As I think I explained, both light and electrons have a curious double-nature: in some phenomena they behave like waves, in others like particles or quanta.

Cause Er, um... A light particle of zero mass that sometimes behaves like a wave, I see. Perhaps they should call them the 'Schizon'.

Effect Then there are the numerous particles that have been identified in the many cosmic ray and accelerator experiments that have been conducted since the 1930s. These objects can be grouped into a number of distinct particle families and sub-families. First there are the strongly interacting Hadrons, from the Greek 'ἁδρόs' meaning 'bulky', which include the Nucleons, protons and neutrons, the Mesons, from 'μέσos' meaning 'middle', a large sub-group of comparatively unstable intermediate particles, and the Hyperons, from 'ὑπέρ' 'above' which have masses greater than that of a proton. Second there are the Leptons, from 'λεπτόs' 'light', including the electron, the Neutrino, a virtually massless highly penetrative neutral particle, the Positron, the positively-charged anti-particle to the electron which...

Cause   *Anti*-particle?

Effect   From the Greek word 'ἀντί' meaning 'opposite'. Every particle has an Anti-particle, a sort of mirror-image which is of identical mass and electric charge but of opposite sign. When a particle collides with its anti-particle they annihilate one another giving off a burst of electromagnetic radiation.

Cause   Ah: politics.

Effect   Incidentally, *this*, you'll be pleased to learn, is where much of the new bomb-research is directed. A marble's worth of Anti-matter would make a one megaton explosion.

Cause   Uhuh? More wine?

Effect   Then there are the hypothetical massless force-carrying 'Gauge' particles which transmit the Weak Interactions. I should perhaps explain that besides the cosmic forces of Gravitation and Electromagnetism with which we are familiar and which act at a distance, hadrons are also acted upon by the binding nuclear or 'Strong' force and all particles are susceptible to other 'Weak' forces; these strong and weak forces operate only at close range.

Cause   Is that so?

Effect   New particles and effects are turning up all the time. In recent years we have had the discovery of the Omega-minus particle, of the Psi-particle, of new particles called 'Goldstone Bosons'...

Cause   Have they discovered the Phlogiston yet, or the Pinocchio Particle, or the little old lady who lives in a shoe?

Effect   No, but there is the 'Bootstrap' view. There is talk of neutral currents, of gravity-carrying particles called 'Gravitons' and of gravity waves. There is even speculation about *anti*-gravity, that is gravitational repulsion.

Cause   Ah, yes, I know about that one. You do believe all this do you Malcolm, you take it seriously?

Effect   Well I'm no great particle specialist myself. If you like I could introduce you to a colleague of mine, Professor Jargon, who's a bit of a whizz-kid in the new...

Cause   Oh, er, no thanks, no. I'm asking *you*. Do you believe in all these new particles and forces and whatnots? Do you honestly believe they exist?

Effect   Well yes, they, they exist, of course they exist. Most of these particles have been studied for years now. We have accumulated masses of detailed data about their behavioural characteristics and their interactions.

Cause   I'm sure you have. And I'm sure too that now that *this* elementary family of 'fundamental particles' has grown so vastly complex and absurdly unwieldy, it is only a matter of time before some scientist comes along and proposes yet another cosmological descent into yet another new scheme of *sub*-sub-atomic particles, of which these hadrons and leptons and the rest *are made*.

Effect   It's already been done. The new Quark theory has been advanced precisely in order to make some sense out of the...

Cause   The new *what* theory?

Effect   The Quark theory. The name 'Quark' was proposed by the American Physicist Murray Gell-Man, who borrowed it from James Joyce's *Finnegans Wake*: "Three Quarks for Muster Mark!"

Cause   That fits: Joyce too made up his meanings as he went along.

Effect   It was postulated that all the members of the hadron family could be accounted for in terms of different combinations of a set of three constituent Quark particles which carry fractional electric charges $+\frac{2}{3}$, $-\frac{1}{3}$, $-\frac{1}{3}$ and which are distinguished by three characteristics known arbitrarily as 'Upness'. 'Downness' and 'Strangeness'. Later it was found necessary to add to the list a fourth quark endowed with a fourth property called 'Charm'.

Cause   This gets more Joycean by the word: a stream of unconsciousness novel.

Effect   Of course each member of this quark family is mirrored by its anti-quark and the eight different varieties combine with one another in ways analogous to the mixing of the three primary colours; hence the coining of the new phrase 'Colour Force'. It is thought that the quark-bonding colour force is itself 'carried' by strings of intermediary 'coloured' particles called 'Gluons'. Unfortunately...

Cause   Stop, stop, stop! Look Malcolm, don't you think there's something a bit mad about all this? Isn't your so-called explanation now out of control? Aren't things now beyond a joke?

Effect   Well, I know that the theory seems to have got into a bit of a muddle, but they are hoping that they will soon be able to effect a grand synthesis of the different cosmic forces and come up with a single calculus which will reduce everything to...

Cause   Oh wise up Malcolm! Wise up! Don't you see that the muddle you are in is not just a temporary confusion of data or a present lack of a satisfactory quark theory but is rather the result, the inevitable result, of the whole systematically misguided enterprise.

Effect   What misguided enterprise?

Cause   The whole enterprise of trying to track down *the elements* of the world, of attempting to identify and describe *the atoms* of which all things are made, of expecting to find *some physical objects* which will explain the Universe. Do you know something, I have a theory about these 'atoms' of yours.

Effect   *You* have a theory?

Cause   Yes, and when I use the word 'atom', I am using it not in your strict, narrow denotation, but to cover *all* the objects that have, at one time or another, been put forward as candidates for the role: Dalton's atoms, Bohr's protons and electrons, Gell-Mann's quarks and all the rest of them; and all their relatives too. I would lump them all together.

Effect   You would? I see. So what's your theory then Andrew?

Cause   That they are all gods.

Effect   I beg your pardon?

Cause   They are gods.

Effect   Gods!?

Cause   Yes, they are all members of the god-family, with which we familiarized ourselves earlier. Together, they constitute *a mythology.*

Cause's Theory

Effect   And how do you make that out?

Cause   Well Malcolm, I would like to draw your attention to a number of striking family resemblances which I have noticed; it will then be up to you to judge for yourself. Obviously, you will at first find this a rather startling and outlandish claim, so I do not expect you to recognize it all at once. However, I do hope that you'll consider seriously the features I mention, and perhaps even go on to add some of your own.

Effect   Okay, anything for a laugh!

Cause   Hold on, I'll turn the heater up. Move in closer.

Effect   Yes, it's quite draughty in here.

Cause   Right. Now then, one peculiarly god-like feature of these atoms of yours is their uncomfortable dual nationality; they inhabit, or are supposed to inhabit, two very different sorts of world simultaneously. Atoms began life, at the hands of the pre-Socratics, as creatures of logic, whose nearest relatives were the abstract concepts of mathematics and geometry. Just as in pure geometry a line can be conceived as being made up of an infinitely large number of infinitely small *points*, so matter can be conceived as consisting of an infinitely large number of infinitely small point-masses or 'atoms', which, being infinitely small, are indivisible. The atom, like the point, can begin life as a conceptual device, as a logical fiction.

Effect   It doesn't *have* to begin life that way though.

Cause   Maybe not, but as soon as the point descends from the Platonic realms of pure geometry and becomes represented in the real world as a mark in the sand or as a pencilled dot on a sheet of paper or as a pixel on a screen, it at once abandons its claims to geometrical perfection or infinite smallness and it acquires instead all sorts of finite, physical, measurable characteristics. Similarly, as soon as one ascribes to atoms particular shapes and behaviour as Democritus did or allots them certain determinable sizes and masses as Dalton did, one is trying to drag them, kicking and screaming from their abstract birthplace of logic and geometry into our real world of physical objects and chemical change.

Effect   So much the better.

Cause   But of course as soon as atoms set foot in our difficult old physical world, various very important things happen: for a start, all our statements about them at once cease to have the certainty of logical deductions and become instead inductive generalizations, validated by empirical observation and experiment. They all become open to question.

Effect   Again, so much the better.

Cause   The trouble though, as with all theological attempts to explain how gods can both belong to another world outside space and time and yet also interfere in this one, is that this attempted metaphysical emigration, this 'transcendence', is in the end always unsuccessful. Atoms can never really manage either to tear themselves away from their ideal mathematical world or to set up shop in our real physical one. They live, if anywhere, in Limbo.

Effect   But I don't get you, what is 'unphysical' about an atom?

Cause   A number of things, a number of things. There are several characteristics which atomic entities have in common with one another which mark them out as belonging to a quite different ontological family from that of ordinary physical objects. It is my contention, as I say, that these characteristics fit them in most obviously with the pattern of criss-crossing resemblances we noticed earlier amongst the family of *gods*. Before I attempt to list these characteristics I ought to point out that each of them bears on all the others, to the extent that the headings in the list are inevitably somewhat rough and arbitrary.

Effect   I'm sure they are.

Cause   Right, here goes: firstly of course, there is their distinctly unusual property of being *indivisible*. Proposition One: No physical object is indivisible, or: every physical object is composite. Now we could argue about whether this proposition is an inductive generalization proved true by experience and/or a 'law of thought'; whether for example, it is the case that we cannot *conceive* of a physical object that is indivisible. But whichever way we take it, the proposition certainly seems to be true; true without doubt and without exception. Except for atoms.

Effect   But atoms, I thought we had agreed, *are* divisible, they *do* have a structure, we realize this now.

Cause   Oh we realize it now, but we didn't realize it back in the nineteenth century, when the existence of atoms was first suggested. Of course not, it wouldn't have made sense to concede their divisibility *then*, for the atom was being proposed as the fundamental particle, as the ultimate building block; that was the point. And that has been the point each time since: of protons, of electrons, now of quarks. Each time indivisibility is of the essence.

Effect   Hmm. I think you may be exaggerating the importance of indivisibility in all this. Each time we learn that what had previously been taken as a discrete particle in in fact a composite, this can be seen as a further step, a very important further step, in our ever-advancing knowledge of the structure of matter.

Cause   So why was indivisibility postulated in the first place? And why is it a stipulation each time? Why this repeated mistake?

Effect   Because... Because... we can only take things a step at a time, we must have some toe-hold.

Cause   Anyway, indivisible and otherwise, there is another feature which all these atomic 'objects' have in common which marks them out as being definitely not-of-this-world. Like all sensible gods, they inhabit a realm peculiar for being endowed with a certain sort of *perfection*. The Atomic world is not perfect in the way that the Christians' Heaven is perfect, in being without pain and suffering and loneliness though it *is* a world without pain and suffering and loneliness, but rather it is perfect in its bleakness. In contrast with the real, physical world, everything in the atomic realm is perfectly *mathematical.*

Effect   Ah, but...

Cause   Look: in the real world no physical quantity can ever be measured *exactly*, no two phenomena ever occur *precisely* similarly, no process ever obeys the laws of physics or chemistry *perfectly*. Now again we could discuss at great length whether these truths are statements about the world and its inexactness or are axioms in our conceptions of measurement and of physical knowledge, but either way a state of imperfection results. By contrast, because the atomic world you describe, like the notion of perfection itself, is entirely a product of our own imaginations, with atomic and subatomic measurements no such endemic inaccuracy problem is involved.

Effect   You are quite wrong Andrew! At this level of research it is *extremely* difficult to get accurate experimental results, to determine particle masses, velocities, energies. In fact there *are* systematic indeterminacies involved. As we mentioned earlier, Heisenberg proved that there are theoretical reasons why one cannot accurately determine at a certain time both a particle's position and its velocity or energy, since the very taking of the measurements itself affects the properties being measured.

Cause   Oh yes, but I'm not talking about that. I'm not talking about the accuracy of *our knowledge* of the mathematics of atomic interactions and of their constants, or about how we arrive at the figures which relate them to our macroscopic standards, what I am pointing out is that atomic objects are *conceived of* as behaving perfectly mathematically. Heisenberg himself conceived them so. Of course they are mathematical, for these, theoretically, are *the units*; of mass, of charge, of energy, of what-you-will; ideally, all one need do is *count* them.

Effect   Ideally perhaps, but as you say, we are not living in an ideal world. I don't see what you are getting at here. We interpret these objects' behaviour purely mathematically, I grant you, but this is all we can do.

Cause   Exactly!

Effect   But this is what physics does, this is what physics is about!

Cause   The trouble Malcolm, is that these atomic objects of yours are *only* mathematical. Ordinary objects and phenomena can of course be described in *non*-mathematical ways, but your sort of atomic objects can not. The obvious reason for this is that, Feature Three, atomic objects are not open to sense-perception; we cannot see or touch or hear them. And this is not because they happen to be out of sight and reach and earshot, like the other side of the Moon or a table in an unviewed room or a car-smash in the next town, but because they are actually *defined* as being beyond the range of sense-perception. Since atoms are invoked as being the causes, the constituents of everything perceivable, atoms themselves cannot be perceived; *logically* they cannot be perceived.

Effect   Ah, now...

Cause   This brings us straightaway to peculiarity number four: because atomic objects cannot be perceived or pointed out, the words we use to denote and classify them, unlike ordinary common nouns, cannot be defined ostensively. One cannot, for example, do what we did in the pub this morning in the case of 'table' and indicate various objects and say "this is a table, that is a table, over there is a table" and so on, thereby assembling some pattern of application for the word 'table'. By contrast, your word 'electron', denoting as it does a *non*-perceivable object, cannot be defined in this way at all, its application being strictly laid down in a verbal, technical definition which stipulates a certain set of precise physical properties.

Effect   You're not too keen on precision are you, of any kind?

Common Nouns and Proper Names

Cause I am being precise, in my own way. I am being precise, admittedly rather vaguely, about different classes of words and about the different classes of objects denoted by them. What I am indicating here is that the relationship between atomic language and atomic objects is importantly different from the relationship between ordinary language and ordinary objects. Not just in that its primary concern is to elucidate the mathematical relationships involved, but in the whole matter of word-object denotation. The techniques of recognition and classification of atomic particles and forces are quite different from those of ordinary life or ordinary macroscopic physics. In short, it seems to me that these words 'Proton', 'Electron', 'Quark' and the rest function more as *names* than as *nouns*. Since, as with the older gods, the beings which these words purport to denote are themselves outside the range of sense-perception, our choices of the words which are to stand for them are in a sense quite arbitrary; they are proper names merely.

Effect But they are not arbitrary Andrew. Particles are usually named according to their, their family traits as you would say. There is method in our nomenclature.

Cause I don't doubt that there is method in it, most of the time. After all, people have reasons for choosing the first names they choose for their children, usually. Even when a new particle is christened 'the Quark', a name which carries no associations at all, you will doubtless want to claim that this is the point. But nevertheless all names are in the end quite arbitrary in a way that common nouns are not. Re-naming the Quark 'the Quirk' or calling one of its properties 'strangeness' rather than 'sidewaysness' or, for that matter, choosing the nom-de-plume Andrew Malcolm in preference to Andrew Cause is an operation of no great linguistic importance or difficulty, whereas to propose that instead of, say, the English common noun 'stool' we use a new word 'charkin' would be absurd.

Effect But that's an unfair comparison, surely? A word like 'stool' has a long history; its meanings and its scope have evolved naturally over hundreds of years of everyday usage. It is bound to be more deeply rooted in the soil of the language than any of the comparatively young, tightly defined terms of science. Besides, the nouns and noun-phrases of ordinary language *can* be just as tightly defined and restricted in scope as those of physics; I've been thinking about this since lunchtime. Take the word, the phrase 'billiard-ball' for example. Not much scope there... I've no doubt that there are precise physical criteria laid down to which all true billiard-balls must conform. It may be that some of the balls we were calling billiard-balls this morning were not true billiard-balls at all.

Cause Would you say if such were true that we were therefore making *a mistake?* And if so, of what kind? This is interesting, for of course the extent to which the noun-phrase 'billiard-ball' does have this restricted scope is the extent to which (a) the word 'Billiards' is *a name,* the name of a particular game, (b) this game is strictly defined in terms of official, laid-down, man-made and thus arbitrary, rules and stipulations – that billiard-balls must measure *x* and weigh *y* and so on – and therefore (c) the phrase 'billiard-ball' is after all *not* a phrase of everyday language but of a peculiar technical sub-language or jargon, of a highly specialized language-game.

Effect But can one draw such clear lines between technical language and everyday language? I am suspicious of this 'everyday language' of yours. Plenty of terms that start off as purely scientific ones can and do pass easily into everyday use as scientific explanations come to be generally understood and accepted.

Cause The words get absorbed as the machines get used and the jargons get assimilated. Sure, atomic terms can percolate into everyday use, but they do so only insofar as they can find some sort of denotation in the real, perceivable, physical world. Please remember here that I am specifically concerned with *atomic* concepts, not with scientific explanation in general. *Nuclear* bombs for instance, and *electron*ics. It is interesting that it is this derivative word 'electronics' that is passing into everyday language, while the noun 'electron' still remains pretty much out in the cold. Obviously, this is because there are no objects around that can be defined ostensively *as* 'electrons'. The word is therefore not a common noun, but a proper one; it is a name.

Effect But that's ridiculous, a proper name is a label assigned to a single particular object. There are thousands upon millions upon billions of electrons in the world.

Cause Are there? Or is there just one? This brings us to a fifth feature that sets atomic objects irrevocably apart from physical ones: they are all identical. That is, all atomic objects of the same type are identical. Proposition Two: No two objects are qualitatively identical; by which I mean no two physical objects. No two grains of sand, no two billiard-balls, no two human beings, no two stars are ever *exactly* the same or would, if subjected to an exhaustive series of tests, ever behave in an exactly similar manner in exactly similar circumstances.

Effect Ah, now this is a Catch-22 proposition surely, for whenever two objects do behave exactly identically in a series of tests you will always be able to claim that the series has therefore not been exhaustive. Perfectly circular, this proves nothing.

Cause   It proves something, whether about the world or about our ways of thought; compare Proposition One. Maybe it's that we cannot *conceive* of two objects or sets of circumstances or patterns of behaviour ever being exactly identical. Incidentally, I think you will find that your own cause-and-effect metaphysics, if pursued to its logical conclusions, will itself render the phrases 'the same thing', 'the same behaviour', 'the same circumstances' literally meaningless anyway. But never mind, it doesn't matter, for in practice the problem never arises. In real life no two objects ever *are* exactly the same. Can you tell me of any two physical objects in the world, any two *non-atomic* physical objects that are identical, that are absolutely identical?

Effect   Er...

Cause   Whereas of course, all electrons are conceived, are defined, are necessarily qualitatively identical. Absolutely identical.

Effect   But they have to be! They would not function in our explanations if they were not so.

Cause   Exactly! An electron in circumstances *A*, *B*, *C must* behave in ways *X*, *Y*, *Z*, for if it did not do so, it would have to be something other than an electron.

Effect   This is not true Andrew, there are many areas in particle physics where there is a wide measure of indeterminacy, theoretical indeterminacy, where objects' behaviour can be expressed only in terms of probabilities.

Cause   The point remains the same. It doesn't matter how imprecise the stipulations *X*, *Y* and *Z* or whether they involve disjunctions or whether they are only limits or expressible only as probabilities, anything which does not conform to these stipulations *simply on that evidence alone* cannot be an electron, or at least cannot be an electron as it has hitherto been defined. Suppose a particle physicist is performing tests on a certain type of fundamental particle called the 'Silly particle'. Suppose that after years of obtaining uniform results for the behaviour of Silly particles, he creates some set of circumstances in which out of the blue, one of the Silly particles does something irregular: it disintegrates when the others accelerate or it veers to the left when the others go straight on. Suppose also that this effect is 'confirmed' in the sense that further tests prove that one in a hundred or one in a thousand or one in a million Silly particles behaves in this 'irregular' manner. What will he say? He might claim that his discovery proves that there are *two types* of Silly particle, the β-Silly particle and the α-Silly particle, each with its own newly-defined set of characteristics, in which case the phrase 'Silly particle' would now denote not a single particle type but a particle family. There might on the other hand, be good reasons for calling the new β-Silly particle a new kind of *meson*, a Silly meson perhaps, on account of its displaying certain mesonic family traits. Whatever happens, the one thing the physicist will *not* be able to say is "Some Silly particles do this and some do that" and leave it at that. The instances of one of your atomic universals cannot be distinguished, they can only be counted.

Effect   Okay, so what?

Cause   Sixthly and finally, atomic particles, unlike real physical objects, are eternal, are unchanging. Proposition Three: No physical object lasts for ever. Proposition Four: No physical object is immutable. These propositions, whatever their status, again appear to be absolutely true generalizations. Even the Sun and the Earth, you say, have finite life-spans. Everything we know is born, comes into existence, is synthesized, grows up, changes, evolves, decays, dies, is destroyed. The oldest rule in the book. Yet here we are, in the latter half of the twentieth century AD postulating the existence of atomic objects which are everlasting and unchanging. 'Stable' I think was your word. It is, as you remarked, a common family resemblance amongst gods to be *immortal*.

Effect   But Andrew, there are plenty of particles that are not stable at all. A free neutron has a half-life of about thirteen minutes and some particles decay in microseconds.

Cause   Which naturally leads you to conclude that such particles are not truly fundamental after all, but are made up of other particles which do *not* decay, ever.

Effect   Of course.

Cause   Of course, the same old mistake begetting the same old mistake. You talk of particle families, yet once again you labour under a very two-dimensional-snapshot idea of family resemblances. If it is the stability of matter you wish to explain, instead of this implausible postulation of a fixed number of eternal constituents, why not conceive of, say, roughly stable or even evolving populations of self-regenerating particles, particles

295

with procreative life-spans and changing characteristics? Your search for immutability does not seem to have proved very successful, the names of your 'elements' are now changing by the decade. I believe that of the 'older' particles only the electrons are still managing to cling on to their fundamentality, or am I out of date?

Effect   And the photons.

Cause   Ah yes, the photons too, thank goodness.

Effect   But Andrew, doesn't the fact that our ideas about these particles' status change as we discover more about them demonstrate that they are very far from being god-like?

Cause   Not at all. Religions and mythologies evolve like everything else. Gods and our beliefs in them come into being, grow up and pass away too. May it always be so. Some, of course, last longer than others. To Bacchus!

Effect   Oh, er, cheers!

✳ ✳ ✳ ✳ ✳ ✳ ✳ ✳ ✳ ✳ ✳

Cause   Something wrong Malcolm?

Effect   Yes, yes. I'd like to go back, if I may, to the third feature in your list, that atomic objects are not open to sense-perception. This is simply not true any more.

Cause   What? We can see atoms now? Where? Show me!

Effect   Now now, there's no need to be clever.

Cause   No? I should have thought there was every need to be clever, very clever indeed. Presumably just having twenty-twenty vision is not going to be enough.

Effect   Look, obviously we cannot see atoms and particles with the naked eye, but we can see them with the aid of instruments.

Cause   Ohh.

Effect   What's wrong with that?

Cause   I don't know, somehow one wants to say that seeing *is* a naked

296

experience. "Seeing with the aid of instruments" sounds like a disguise, a muffled contradiction in terms.

Effect   Oh nonsense! The eye itself is an optical instrument!

Cause   How much are yours worth?

Effect   The eye is only a lens. A miraculous lens maybe, but a lens nonetheless, a focussing mechanism, a colour detector.

Cause   And the optic lobe, the brain, are those only instruments too?

Effect   Yes, in a sense.

Cause   Uhuh. And who sees with the aid of those would you say?

Effect   I, er... I... We seem to be back with the riddle of consciousness... One odd aspect of the scientific account I'll grant you: we cannot actually *see* light. We see *by means of* it, we experience its effects, but we do not actually, er, see it.

Cause   It's funny, I had always thought of seeing as being a direct interaction with the world, as a simple one-to-one relationship with things, with visible things... Oh I know that to a scientist my seeing is just another third-person physical process requiring explanation, is just another law-governed chain of causes and effects – the passage of light rays from source to object to eyeball, electrical signals from retina via optic nerve to brain – and I know that, whatever else it is, my seeing *is* a physical process dependent upon all this, but somehow to me, a person who sees things, none of it is very important, or even very interesting. Once my eyelid is open, anything that comes before my eye is not an aid to seeing, but is an object to be seen.

Effect   But that's absurd! What about contact lenses, spectacles, magnifying glasses, binoculars?

Cause   Exactly, they are all objects I can see.

Effect   But are they not aids to seeing? Can they not help you to see things better?

Cause   Sometimes they can.

Effect   So where will you draw the line? With a microscope one can make out the structures of individual cells and the patterns of crystal formations.

Artificial Light

With a telescope one can discover that what to the naked eye appears to be a single star is in fact a cluster of stars. Surely you will not say, on account of our use of these devices, that we do not see these things or that these things are not real?

Cause   No, I will not.

Effect   So, with our more powerful, more advanced new scientific instruments we can see smaller and smaller objects: molecules, atoms, now even *inside* atoms.

Cause   But I thought there was a limit to the power of a microscope, a theoretical limit, something to do with the wavelength of light?

Effect   There is a limit to the magnifying power of the optical microscope, yes, but with an ultra-violet microscope, which uses non-visible light of a shorter wavelength, it becomes possible to see the shapes of some of the very long chain molecules of organic chemistry.

Cause   Forgive me, but 'non-visible light' sounds like yet another contradiction in terms.

Effect   The human eye is sensitive only to a comparatively narrow band of the whole electromagnetic spectrum. Low frequency infra-red radiation we can feel as heat, but ultra-violet and radio waves and X- and gamma-rays are beyond the range of our senses.

Cause   So how can we see anything with the aid of an ultra-violet microscope?

Effect   Ah, well, the ultra-violet light is focussed onto a photographic plate which *does* produce a visible image.

Cause   I don't like the sound of this. According to your own account, what we are seeing here is not an object but a visible image on a photographic plate. Already we are beginning to lose the beautiful, essential *directness* of perception. Already we are becoming dependent upon hypotheses, theories, postulated phenomena which we cannot directly sense and about which we therefore have to make deductions.

Effect   Dogs can hear high-pitched whistles which we can't hear. Bats are optically blind, but navigate by means of ultrasonic echo-location. Many creatures are far more sensitive than we are to low-frequency vibrations like earth tremors. The resolving-power of the eagle's eye is proverbial.

And of course the human sense of smell is one of the most underdeveloped in the animal kingdom. Surely Andrew, you will not assert that such sights and sounds and smells do no exist just because it so happens that human beings are unable to perceive them?

Cause   Not necessarily, although I may well ask you to be clear about exactly how claims like these are justified. However, one thing I will assert, until the cows come home, is that such sights and sounds and smells are not sensible *to us*. Another thing I will assert is that there is no sense at all in which molecules and atoms and particles can be said to be perceivable.

Effect   No, it is possible Andrew, with the right machines, with the right detectors. Following on from the ultra-violet microscope there is the X-ray microscope, which uses electromagnetic radiation of still shorter wavelength, and there is the electron microscope, which instead of light uses a beam of electrons which passes through the specimen and is focussed by...

Cause   But I thought electrons were already sub-microscopic, were themselves non-visible objects.

Effect   So?

Cause   So they are already problematic, are themselves fraught with difficulty and doubt. Any account of what is happening in such a 'microscope', in terms of which its 'results' will have to be interpreted, will necessarily involve a whole mass of theory and will therefore systematically be open to question. One is looking at things not only through a highly complex machine but also through a funnel of scientific preconception.

Effect   No more so than is the case with visible light. There is no shortage of theory involved in the workings of an ordinary optical microscope.

Cause   I don't doubt it Malcolm, I don't doubt it.

Effect   In an optical microscope light rays are reflected, refracted and focussed by lenses, while in an electron microscope the electron beam is controlled and focussed by electromagnetic coils, that is the only real difference.

Cause   But now you are talking not of light, nor even of non-visible light, but of a stream of non-visible particles!

Effect   Ah, but as I have explained, there is a sense in which light itself is a stream of non-visible photons. Like electrons it has this double nature: in phenomena such as interference and diffraction light behaves like a wave-motion, while in photo-emission it behaves like a stream of discrete parti-cles or 'quanta'. You must already know all this from your work in optical sculpture.

Cause   Must I?

Effect   Similarly, when electrons are emitted from a hot cathode, as in a television tube, they behave like waves and are called cathode rays, while in a scintillation counter, individual...

Cause   You see! As soon as you start involving theory, all is doubt, dis-pute and dual nationality! You are even arguing with yourself and neither of you is making any sense!

Effect   Honestly Andrew, if you want to understand these areas of physics better, I really think you should study quantum theory and wave mechanics, otherwise...

Cause   And now you try to blind me with science. I don't need to study the theory of anything to know what it is to *see*, that is the point. Anyway, what does one actually see with one of these electron microscope things, besides, I imagine, a great lump of hardware sitting in a laboratory?

Effect   The electron beam produces a visible image on a fluorescent screen, just as it does in a cathode ray tube.

Cause   So what one sees is something like a television picture?

Effect   In effect.

Cause   So we are now thoroughly removed from any sort of direct per-ception. Apart from all the hypothesis and theory involved in the workings of the machine, we in any case end up seeing a rather peculiar kind of thing.

Effect   What is peculiar about a television picture? It is just a visible image made up of hundreds of...

Cause   Exactly, it is merely an image, it is not a normal, fully-fledged physical object. Seeing a television picture of a man is a quite different sort of optical experience of a quite different sort of 'object' from seeing a man or indeed, from seeing a television tube. Worse than that, in the case of a man, since we can compare the image with the real thing, we are in a position to judge whether or not our televising process is successful and to what degree it is accurate. In the case of the electron microscope however, we have no other way of 'seeing' the objects supposedly being televised, so all claims about the genuineness or accuracy of the final image have to go fatally unsupported.

Effect Ah, but this is not true. The results obtained with electron microscopes tie in very closely with those obtained by other methods and in other fields.

Cause I'll bet they do. They have to. I notice incidentally, that one 'obtains results', one doesn't actually see things.

Effect But one can see things: cell-structures, chromosomes, even some individual macro-molecules.

Cause Ah, so we're still well above the particle level?

Effect Of course. When it comes to particles we need quite different machines and techniques altogether. Firstly, numbers of charged particles can be counted by means of geiger and scintillation counters, in which each particle triggers a pulse of current conducted by a tube of gas under a high potential difference or produces a scintillation in a phosphorescent material, which pulses or scintillations can be amplified into audible bleeps or visible flashes and counted electrically.

Cause So what are counted, the particles or the bleeps and flashes?

Effect Secondly, charged particles can actually be seen in cloud chambers and bubble chambers, in which tiny droplets of supersaturated vapour are caused to condense on charged ions produced by particle/gas-molecule collisions, leaving visible, photographable tracks along the paths of the particles. Then there are detectors which...

Cause Hold on, hold on! Surely Malcolm, even if I were to take all these claims of yours at face value, which I certainly do not, they would in no way imply that we can therefore *see* these postulated fundamental particles? Seeing the vapour trail left by an aeroplane is nothing at all like seeing an aeroplane.

Effect One can learn quite a lot from the trail though.

Cause Even if one has never seen or flown in an aeroplane?

Effect Certainly, if one knows a bit about the fuel it's burning. We have detectors consisting of three-dimensional lattices of charge-sensitive wires which can plot the courses of charged particles produced in collisions with great precision. The information from all the sensors can be synthesized by computer into a complete, three-dimensional picture of exactly what happens in each event.

Cause An image on a screen again?

Effect Yes, but this time an image that the computer can turn through 360 degrees.

Cause Ah yes, I've seen film of that on TV.

Effect In practice, different sorts of detector are used to detect different sorts of particle; it depends upon the particles' mass-energy, electric charge, collision characteristics, numerosity and so on what will prove the most effective method of detection.

Cause Hmm. It's marvellous how subtly 'accurate perception' has turned into 'effective detection', how gracefully even second-hand 'visible images' have now given way to 'received information' and 'computer-synthesized pictures'.

Effect There is a problem of course, with detection of the electrically neutral particles like neutrons and neutrinos, which cannot directly be picked up by any of these methods. The trick here is to get the particles to initiate some process, nuclear disintegration for example, which results in the emission of charged particles which *can* then be detected by one of these methods.

Cause Ah, you really have lost me now Malcolm, lost me completely. Everything has become so indirect, theoretical, problematic, third-hand, surely it no longer makes sense to talk of these 'objects' as being in any way *physical*, never mind visible or perceivable?

Effect Not so Andrew, particles can be photographed, photographed directly.

Cause Really? *Trick* photography presumably?

Effect No no, there are all sorts of photographic emulsions which are themselves sensitive to the passage of charged particles. In these emulsions the tracks and collisions of particles can be recorded directly, without the interpretation of any intermediate effect.

Cause   Hold on, you must be careful with this word 'photograph'. As in the case of 'televisual image' some important points should constantly be borne in mind. Firstly and most obviously, seeing an image of a three-dimensional physical object beamed onto a fluorescent screen or projected onto a surface or printed on photographic paper is nothing like seeing the object itself. Secondly, when we talk of a photograph we normally mean by that word a printed or projected image of some visible object or scene which has been produced directly by the action of light; 'directly' implying by some chemical process rather than via the eye and hand of an artist.

Effect   Exactly.

Cause   Right, so one thing one immediately wants to say is that if *light* is not involved, we have instantly lost the prefix 'photo-' from the word 'photograph'. One may be able to perform all kinds of experiments with chemical emulsions on plates and produce all sorts of patterns of marks and lines and you may be able to recognize a number of family resemblances between the chemistries of the various emulsions used, but I would have thought that if light is not involved, then by scientific definition, the process cannot correctly be called *photo*graphic.

Effect   Isn't this just a semantic point?

Cause   Thirdly, in ordinary photography we therefore have a criterion for deciding how truly and how accurately photographic any such process is: namely the test of how precisely the visible image of the object or scene so produced 'matches' the real thing. One exposes a certain sort of chemical film inside a certain sort of camera in front of a certain illuminated family group; one then decides how successful the photographic process is, the film, the camera, one's exposure-technique, by examining the printed or projected image to see how distinctly and how accurately it corresponds to the family group. If the subtle, detailed patterns of family resemblance turn out not to be discernible in the photograph, this will be because of a lack of photography, not because of a lack of family resemblance.

Effect   Okay okay, but one can extrapolate from one's knowledge of ordinary photograhy. What about the uses of X-rays? Isn't X-ray photography photography?

Cause   This again, is a useful technique because there exists a testable and proven correspondence between what is seen in the developed X-ray plates and what is found within the patient's body or inside the passenger's luggage, or whatever it is.

Effect   Again, one can extrapolate.

Cause   This point is important not only because it establishes a criterion of authenticity for these various techniques, but also because it reminds us how the techniques were and are still being discovered and perfected: years of hard work and trial-and-error aimed at improving photographic correspondence. However, with subatomic, non-visible objects *there cannot be such correspondence*, there never can be any criterion of authenticity.

Effect   Okay okay, I take your point that these nuclear emulsions and so on are not photographs in the ordinary sense; they are not photographs of the particles themselves, but they are photographs of the particles' *tracks*.

Cause   No Malcolm, they are not photographs *of* anything. Exposing a daylight film outside a camera and producing a totally blackened negative is not photographing daylight, any more than scratching a negative with a pin is taking a photograph of a pin-scratch or treating the film with a blow-lamp is taking a picture of heat.

Effect   But experiments with nuclear emulsions do not result in a chaos of blackened or scratched or melted plates, they reveal recognizable tracks of clearly-identifiable particles' paths through the emulsions. One can learn a lot about a car's behaviour and physical characteristics from a study of the tracks it leaves in a mud.

Cause   Even if one had never seen or driven a car?

Effect   Certainly, if one knows a bit about the mud.

Cause   But why this word 'tracks'? Aren't you already jumping to conclusions by using a word so loaded with implications? You do not call the furrows made by the wind in a sand dune or a cross-country route planned by a hiker or the marks left by a pen on a handwritten page *tracks*.

Effect   So what will you say that they are? Ghost writing?

Cause   I will say that they constitute evidence of what happens, or better that *they are the results*, when certain chemical emulsions are subjected to certain tests: when one does A, B and C, patterns X, Y and Z are produced on such-and-such plates. Beyond that, all is speculation, hypothesis and theory, plausible or otherwise. No *photography* is involved, that is the point.

Effect But this is ridiculous! You are going to end up saying that any-thing we cannot actually *see* is therefore not real!

Cause No, I am going to end up saying, or rather, I am going to *begin* by saying that anything which cannot be seen is no ordinary physical object.

Effect But Andrew, you are placing far too much importance on things' *being seen*. There are lots of things in the world that we cannot see: the table in the room next-door, billiard-balls in a cardboard box, the other side of the Moon, the...

Cause The pictures in other people's minds?

Effect The radio-galaxies that emit their light in the non-visible part of the spectrum. We don't conclude because we cannot see these things that they therefore do not exist. In science as in life, we continually have to infer the existence of objects and phenomena that we cannot see.

Cause Note however, that all the objects which you mention *could* be seen, if we were in the right place, if they were unpacked, if the right light were shining on them, and *could* be perceived in other ways; this is what is entailed by their objectivity. By contrast, your atoms and particles are defined *in your own theories* as being non-visible and non-perceivable. I am placing importance not on actually being seen or being perceived but on being in principle visible and perceivable.

Effect But visibility depends, at least in part, upon the viewer. After all, a blind man doesn't lose his sense of an external objective reality.

Cause How do you know?

Effect Look: he gets along, he gets around things somehow. Blindness may be a terrible handicap, but it is not the end of the world.

Cause No, but I'm sure it doesn't help. And of course, loss of *all* perception *is* the end of the world; at least, it must be the end of *the world*. You're right though, the point is that visibility is a *relationship*. The eye, again borrowing the fashionable argot, is an interface. And I will stick my neck out and claim that no *eyes* ever have or ever will be clapped upon this atomic world which you describe in such awesome detail.

Effect Ye-es. So?

Cause So, the conclusion must be that if atoms and particles and the rest are objects at all, they are certainly not objects in the ordinary sense, they are not like tables and chairs. Don't get me wrong, I'm not necessarily suggesting that these things therefore do not exist; the question, as we have now agreed, is: what do they exist *as*?

Effect Well, one thing I do concede: atoms and particles are not like tables and chairs. Obviously our information concerning atomic and subatomic objects comes to us in a different, perhaps less direct way than the information we receive through our senses about perceivable, 'ordinary' objects, as you call them, but I see no great difference in principle between the ways in which we interpret and collate these sets of information into some kind of ordered conceptual-linguistic scheme or, or... objective reality.

Cause You don't? You really don't? You honestly see no difference between deciding whether what you are looking at is an accumulation of dust and dirt and hair on a piece of glass or is a 'genuine' nuclear emulsion photograph and deciding whether what you are looking at in the emulsion is the track of a mu-meson or the track of a pi-meson?

Effect No, I don't. Both decisions involve the interpretation of data, the weighing of the evidence which tends to confirm or deny the rival hypotheses, the application of certain conventional conceptual and linguistic...

Cause What!? Just to see a dirty piece of glass? 'Evidence', 'interpretation', 'the application of concepts'? Look Malcolm, seeing an object is, or at least can be, a perfectly *simple* event, a perfectly... *atomic* experience.

Effect But it's not Andrew, it can't be! Even aside from all the physics and all the neurology, seeing is by no means a simple phenomenon; necessarily, it involves interpretation, conceptualizing, the use of conventional linguistic forms and all that. I thought it was you philosophers who first realized this.

Cause Okay: "I see a red billiard-ball before me", what could be simpler than that?

Effect Oh come on, in making such a statement you are not just reporting a simple visual experience, you are implicitly asserting a whole host of corroborative propositions: propositions concerning evidence from your other senses – that you could touch it; propositions about other people's perceptions – that they could see and touch it too; and propositions about how this object would interact with others. A purely sensory report still leaves us with the question: is this a 'real' billiard-ball, or a projected photographic image, a hologram perhaps of a billiard-ball, or an hallucination of a billiard-ball, or what?

Cause   It's an *imaginary* billiard-ball of course! Complete with imaginary corroboration. We know all this Malcolm: there are many kinds of visual experience and many kinds of visible object, most of which, incidentally, are usually immediately recognizable. This is well understood. In general we have no trouble at all distinguishing between the different sorts of experience and object and no difficulty in appreciating that different sets of corroborative assertions are implied by the associated reports. This is old hat.

Effect   Maybe, but it is always worth talking through. And surely it goes to show that seeing things, whatever else it is, is by no means a simple business. Suppose you discovered of your imaginary billiard-ball that it was not a billiard-ball at all, but was made of red sugar-coated chocolate, was a big red smartie. Wouldn't you then *see it* in a different way?

Cause   I don't know. I might *taste* it in a different way I suppose.

Effect   Yes, I imagine you would. Again, think of our daily experience of seeing the Sun travel across the sky.

Cause   Daily? In England?

Effect   What do you actually *see*? The Sun going round the Earth?

Cause   I see a scientist trotting out a routine argument.

Effect   People used to see the Sun going round the Earth. Indeed in ancient times, men even saw a holed celestial sphere turning in front of a heavenly fire.

Cause   Do you really think that's what men *said* they saw? After all, we don't now say when we look up at the sky that we see the Earth spinning on its axis, that would sound very odd. What we would now say, and I suspect what people have always said, is exactly what you just did say, namely "We see the Sun travelling across the sky", period. The need for interpretation of this phenomenon is recognized.

Effect   Yes, but simply in reporting *that*, in using the words 'Sun', 'travelling', 'sky', you are already engaged in interpretation. Simply by verbalizing, if only to oneself, one is imposing a structure upon one's perceptions.

Cause   But I don't have to verbalize about perception at all, that is the beauty of it! I can be deaf and dumb and still see things. I can be deaf, dumb and illiterate and still see things. I can be deaf, dumb, illiterate and *stupid* and still see things.

307

Whose Duck-Rabbit?

Effect I wonder. Does a stupid or an ill-informed person see what an intelligent or well-informed person sees?

Cause Does a layman see what a scientist sees?

Effect And what can assertions like these *mean*? What are questions like these *about*? You see Andrew, seeing things is not that simple after all. Another example: I remember something in Wittgenstein's *Philosophical Investgations* which caught my eye called a 'duck-rabbit'. It was a very simple line-drawing which could be seen one moment as a duck and the next as a rabbit.

Cause A figure Malcolm, a drawing, an object which characteristically *requires* interpretation. Models, drawings, representations, these are members of a family well-known for their trickeries. We can, after all, distinguish unequivocally enough between ducks and rabbits; at least until such times as the genetic engineers get their hands on them. Just because one can see Wittgenstein's figure *as* a duck or *as* a rabbit, you must not conclude that therefore one sees ducks *as* ducks and rabbits *as* rabbits; we don't, we see ducks and we see rabbits. Indeed, the difference, this extra interpretative element is actually *marked* in our description of what we see, it is made explicit in this case by our use of the word 'as'. Remember, we don't say that we see Wittgenstein's duck-rabbit drawing *as* Wittgenstein's duck-rabbit drawing, we say that w⌣ see Wittgenstein's duck-rabbit drawing.

Effect Ah, no, not true! I didn't know what it was until I had had it explained to me, until I had read the text. Indeed, I seem to remember reading that it wasn't *Wittgenstein's* duck-rabbit drawing in any case, but had been borrowed from some other writer.

Cause Whatever else, you knew that it was a figure printed on a page in a book.

Effect 'A figure'? 'Printed'? 'A page in a book'? Each of these is a highly complex concept, each presupposes a whole history of linguistic usage and understanding. This is it you see: the very act of verbalizing one's perceptual experiences, if only to oneself, if only subconsciously, necessarily confers a kind of logical, conceptual interpretative framework upon them. You said "I see a billliard-ball before me" quite glibly, quite unthinkingly, yet concealed within that apparently simple pronouncement was a complex mass of psycho-linguistic background information, of conventionally established rules for the application of...

Cause Oh rubbish! I saw a billiard-ball before me, full stop! I see a fan heater before me... No, I see a *scientist* before me, no, I see Malcolm Effect, or rather, I see a man. That's it: I see *a man* before me!

Effect   But Andrew, how do you know that I'm a scientist? How do you know my name? How do you know that I am a man? Maybe I'm just a good actress. Saying that you see a man is reporting a load of extremely complex perceptual information, involving an enormous amount of assumption, hypothesis...

Cause   Oh *balls!* Clearly Malcolm, you are confusing a number of different things here. You are confusing the complexity of the physical processes involved in perception with the complexity of the objects we perceive through them, and again with the further complexity of our *knowledge* of those objects and of the various ways in which it can be acquired. What you are persistently, perversely obscuring is the essential simplicity of perception itself, of seeing things. I find myself wanting to say "Look: I am a mind, a thing that perceives. I see physical objects. I see a world. I see a man before me now."

Effect   But that is just a childish response.

Cause   Maybe a childish response is sometimes the right one. Oh, I'm sure that there's a lot of interesting physics and neurology involved in your explanation of the mechanism of sight and that these theories are of great importance to opticians, light-bulb designers, microscope makers and so on, but to me, a well-sighted person, still unpardonably sober, sitting a few feet away from you in a reasonably well-lit room, none of this has any present relevance whatsoever. Again, the business of how a brain 'processes' its incoming streams of perceptual data, visual and otherwise, and 'collates' them into some sort of logical-conceptual-linguistic order, or whatever it is supposed to do, may be very useful to a computer programmer trying to teach a machine how to avoid obstacles or to an academic trying to hold down a job, but it is very boring and quite useless to me, who can already see and classify and describe things quite competently.

Effect   That's a matter of opinion.

Cause   I think Malcolm, that above all you have become confused, 'bewitched' as Wittgenstein would say, by language and all its complexities. And not just by language, but by the whole vogue for philosophy of language which Wittgenstein unwittingly initiated.

Effect   You seem to have a low opinion of the linguistic movement?

Invisible Spectacles

Cause   I fear that people have been bewitched by the very philosophy that was intended to break the spell. I know that in the past some purely linguistic ambiguities have masqueraded as philosophical problems and that an appreciation of the different ways in which language works is very important and illuminating, but I feel that the wheel has now turned, that the movement itself is now throwing up a host of bogus and irrelevant problems and has become a hindrance rather than a help to philosophical understanding. Trust a physicist to latch on to the second-hand gobbledegook of those *quasi*-scientists, the linguistic analysts and semiologists!

Effect   The who?

Cause   It is ironic too that these of all people should apparently find it so difficult to write intelligibly. Why all this semantic navel-gazing, this endless mystification? It makes me suspicious of their intentions... In the end, this modern confusion over the scope and power of language just starts to seem like good old-fashioned perception-scepticism in a subtle, rather dangerous new disguise. Your insistence upon the complex, interpretative nature of perception is edging you into a curiously Berkeleian position, in which the whole notion of an objective external world comes into jeopardy. I suppose that the role of guarantor, in which Berkeley cast his omniscient Employer, would now be played by 'Linguistic Convention' or some such impostor; the Word really is now God.

Effect   But isn't this right, in a sense? We are brought up in language, we live in language and we die in it. We can no more escape language than we can our bodies.

Cause   Oh nonsense, of course we can! We are the masters of our words, not they of us! This is what philosophy is all about!

Effect   Yes, but philosophy is only language again, it is language about language.

Cause   Gbwlljurrrghhh!!

Effect   I beg your pardon?

Cause   Oh Malcolm! *I know* that we interpret the world, our perceptions of the world through language. *I know* that language can therefore seem like some sort of invisible pair of tinted spectacles through which we are all obliged to 'see' things, I am aware of that, that is obvious. But you must not become so mesmerized by this realization that you end up concluding that you can see only coloured glass, that the objects of your perceptions

310

are merely linguistic ones, that there is no world *but* language. It seems to me that the post-war philosophers' obsession with language, their endless search for the invisible spectacles, has actually driven many of them *senseless*! The heirs of empiricism sometimes talk as though ordinary, public physical objects were nothing but their own private intellectual concoctions. The world is in crisis, yet all they do is discuss the meaning of meaning!

Effect   Ahem.

Cause   I suppose the truth is that they've got nothing to say.

Effect   And you think you have? I'll tell you this: one thing today has taught me is that these great philosophical questions of yours *do* seem to be largely linguistic. As far as I can see, your disputes *do* all turn out to concern merely the meanings of words.

Cause   Oh no, you can't say that, surely!? You can't have been listening! Look: it is true that much of our conversation has concerned the ways in which we use certain words and has involved a deal of linguistic analysis, but this doesn't mean that all our speculations have been *about language*. No no, we have been talking about other minds, about non-human personalities, about billiard-ball collisions, about driving laws, about families, about nuclear war, about atomic particles, about all sorts of things. Talking about the ways in which we use words, that is the ways in which we interpret what we see, *is* talking about the world and its objects. What I am trying to do is to *adjust* your invisible spectacles, to improve their perspective, to minimize their distortion, to correct their colour-balance. Although I can only do this in words, only reach you through your spectacles, the aim of my exercise is to rectify the defects in your sight, that is, to change the world you see.

Effect   I thank you for your concern, but doesn't this prove the point: we cannot see an *un*interpreted world; the world we say we see necessarily comes to us already filtered and focussed by our language or, as I guess you would say, by our philosophy.

Cause   I cannot believe my ears! Is this you talking? The scientist? The arch-empiricist? The observation-and-experiment man? The man who a moment ago was insisting that the eye is just an optical instrument, that light is just electromagnetic radiation of wavelengths a, b and c, that the visible world is nothing but a collection of particles arranged in ways x, y and z? Suddenly you have lunged from description of a perfectly objective world where everyone experiences precisely identical optical phenomena, to a hopelessly subjective plurality of worlds, of word-worlds, where literally speaking, no two people can ever see the same thing. What began as an attempt to justify the claim that we can 'see' atoms and atomic particles has ended with the conclusion that we can't even see tables and chairs. What a confusion! You need an oculist mate! I reckon you've got nystagmus, intellectual nystagmus!

Effect   Nystagmus, what's that?

Cause   An uncontrollable oscillation of the eyeballs. I'd have thought you would have known, it's particularly common amongst miners. It comes from working too long underground.

Effect   I've never heard of it.

Cause   Perception verbs like 'see' are richly ambiguous. Seeing can be a purely sensory experience: "I cannot see in the dark, I can see the glowing lightbulb". Seeing can be imagining – seeing, as we sometimes say, 'in the mind's eye': "I can see a day when the world will be free from war". Seeing can be remembering: "I can see it as if it were only yesterday". Seeing can be dreaming or hallucinating: "Is this a dagger that I see before me?" And seeing can be a purely intellectual understanding: "I can see what you mean, I can see the point of the argument".

Effect   I'm not sure I can any more.

Cause   The special, non-ocular senses of 'seeing' are often marked by certain grammatical constructions. We have already observed that an extra interpretative element is signalled by the use of the constructions 'seeing something *as* a so-and-so'. There is also the expression 'seeing so-and-so *in* such-and-such'. Sometimes 'see' is written in inverted commas or is spoken with a certain vocal inflexion. Sometimes there is no special signal at all. On our way to dinner, for example, you casually suggested that in the workings of Nature one can see the hand of God. I guess this is what you would call a 'holy see'.

Effect   Ho-ho. Maybe we should conclude that seeing is always a combination of two elements: an ocular or sensory component and an intellectual or interpretative component. Perhaps seeing is a *marriage* of perception and intelligence, another example of a necessary complementarity?

Cause   Ahh! And God said "Let there be photons". Doesn't have quite the ring to it does it?

Effect   In which case, how can we draw any rigid distinctions? Doesn't the ambiguity of the word demonstrate that this is impossible?

Cause   But Malcolm! The assertion that seeing necessarily involves two elements *implies* that there is a clear distinction, between them. 'Elements', remember? It implies, rightly or wrongly, that there exist two faculties, the senses and the intellect, which are at the very least distinguishable. One cannot suggest that seeing is a marriage if one cannot identify its two partners. There *are* black-and-white distinctions, there have to be borderlines. If seeing atoms and particles is just like seeing tables and chairs, where will you stop, where will you draw the line? Is there no difference between seeing tables and chairs and seeing... the hand of God?

Effect   But...

Cause   What will you say to the clairvoyant who claims to see the future in a crystal ball or to the witch doctor who claims to hear the spirits in the trees? The sense in which you can see atoms is the sense in which a blind man can see them. *But a blind man cannot see!*

Effect   I...

Cause   The whole empiricist empire rests on observation, on the ultimate authority of the five senses. If you lose touch with that, you lose every...

Effect   Okay Okay, but where will *you* draw the line? Where will *you* claim that literal seeing ends and inverted commas 'seeing' begins? At cells, genes, molecules, atoms, electrons, quarks? And where at the other end of the scale? At stars, radio-sources, galaxy-clusters? Where? Why?

Cause   But we have drawn lines, lots of lines. We have crossed dozens of frontiers, spied numerous horizons, outlined plenty of reasons for mistrust of the myths. There is the borderline between visible light and electromagnetic radiation, between X-ray microscopes and electron microscopes, between photographs of things and marks in emulsions, between stars and black radio-sources, between those objects which you claim are, *for your own theoretical reasons* beyond the range of your various detection-methods. "One can extrapolate, one can extrapolate" you keep insisting, but maybe one can't go on extrapolating over horizon after horizon for ever.

Effect   So you tell me then: where do you think physical objects end and... mythical ones begin?

Cause   The fact that distinctions are clear doesn't necessarily mean that the borderlines between them will be sharp. There are grey areas, blurred edges, disputed territories. But, if I may pursue the last analogy, the fact that a frontier between two countries may be uncharted or in dispute in no way implies that their national identities are indistinct. Indeed, a border-dispute usually sharpens the international rivalry and makes it extra-important for the traveller to remember which of the two lands he is presently visiting.

Effect   Hedge! Hedge!

Cause   Okay, so here you are, some categorical distinctions, some white cliffs of Dover, take your pick: atoms and electrons inhabit a conceptually quite different world from that of tables and chairs; tables and chairs are physical objects, atoms and electrons are mythological ones; the words 'atom' or 'electron' and the words 'table' or 'chair' function in logically dissimilar ways in contextually separate language-games; seeing tables and chairs is neurologically a totally different type of process from seeing atoms and electrons; our knowledge of...

Effect   Fair enough, point taken, I concede that we don't see atoms and electrons in the way that we see tables and chairs, of course we don't. But then no-one has ever claimed that we do.

Cause   Ah but that, amazingly, is where you're wrong. It was only fifty years ago that a man as eminent and intelligent as arch-positivist Ayer could write this... hold on, I've got it in my appendix to Hume, here:

> Although scientific objects such as atoms and electrons seem to be fictitious in a way that chairs and tables do not, here, too, the distinction is only a distinction of degree. For both these kinds of objects are known only by their sensible manifestations and are definable in terms of them.

Effect   Hmm, yes, that does seem a bit extreme. It's not simply a matter of degree, I don't think any scientist would pretend that nowadays.

Cause   I don't think Ayer pretended that, latterly. This is the point: people's views about the status of objects can change. Through philosophy one can come to see things in different ways. Through philosophy one can come to see *seeing things* in different ways.

Effect   See seeing things?

Cause   Yes, look: you have interpreted seeing as being a third-person phenomenon, an optical, physical, geometrical process. I, by contrast, have regarded seeing as being a first-person experience, my perception of the external world, my relationship with objective reality. Yet we have been talking about the same thing, we have been seeing the same thing from two different points of view. The aim of philosophy, I repeat, is to achieve a correct perspective.

Effect I am beginning to wonder if there is such a thing as a correct perspective.

Cause There is certainly such a thing as *in*correct perspective, you have only to study a few primitive paintings to discover that... Look at the empty wine bottle Malcolm: from where you are sitting you see one side of the bottle, from where I am sitting I see the other; do we see the same thing?

Effect Well yes... No... I don't know... Oh!

Cause See how easily language can trick us! Words, words, words, they are far more dangerous than any wine!

Effect I'm not so sure. I think I *am* beginning to see two bottles. My head's a bit...

Cause The night air will soon clear it. Come on, let's get out of here, this place gives me the creeps. Let's go and take a look at this new computerized library of yours.

Effect Mm, yes, okay. It's just across the bridge.

✳ ✳ ✳ ✳ ✳ ✳ ✳ ✳ ✳ ✳ ✳

Cause All that glass, it looks like a power station or a swimming pool or something! The lights are on, it must be open.

Effect No, they close at six; it'll be locked. I think they leave them on for security reasons.

Cause Economy. It can cost less to leave strip lights running than to turn them off and on.

Effect Is that so?

Cause Blimey, look at all those books! Rows and rows and rows of print!

315

Tens of thousands of tortured souls trying to get some sleep. A bit spooky in a way.

Effect   One day yours may be there.

Cause   Yes, even if I have to throw it in, attached to a large brick! Oh look, in the window, a model of the city. What a fine piece of work! Let's see how up-to-date it is... Yes... yes... yes... Oh, but this library's not in it, this part is still shown as a meadow. Howabout that!? Now there's a brain-teaser for you!

Effect   This reminds me of something I've been meaning to say Andrew, about the atoms-and-particles business.

Cause   Yes?

Effect   Well, I've been thinking that perhaps all your problems arise because you have been taking the scientific accounts *too literally*.

Cause   Ahh!

Effect   Yes, you are still fighting a battle that was conceded long ago. No scientist nowadays would wish to suggest that atomic particles actually *are* tiny charged billiard-balls whizzing around bashing into one another or that atoms actually *are* like miniature solar systems.

Cause   They wouldn't?

Effect   No of course not. This is merely a primitive picture, an easy-to-grasp representation. The billiard-ball atom is only a model.

Cause   Ohh, a *model*...

Effect   That's right, a model.

Cause   Hmm... Hold on, let's go and sit on those crates over by the entrance there, we'll be a bit out of the breeze.

Effect   Okay.

Cause   Only a model eh? I thought I might hear this disclaimer, sooner or later.

Effect   It's not a disclaimer! No scientist would ever claim that the atom is anything other than a model.

Cause   Uhuh? Dalton? 'Model', 'model', mmm, another word to conjure with... The question now is: what is the billiard-ball atom, or the quantum atom, a model *of*? Normally if you call something a model or a representation, you imply that there exists something else *of which it is* a model or representation, that there exist two objects which display a set of visible correspondences. One thinks of that model of the city or of model trains or model cars or model planes, which are perceivable miniature replicas of their perceivable real counterparts and which are subject to certain clear, testable criteria concerning the accuracy of the modelling they display.

Effect   Ye-es... But one could make a model plane without it necessarily being a model of a particular real plane. Indeed, an aircraft designer will probably build a number of model planes before arriving at his design for a real plane and then perhaps the plane itself may never get off the drawing-board.

Cause   Maybe, but we would still have plenty of reasons for deciding that the designer was playing with model *planes* rather than with, say, model cars. Some sort of object-to-object correspondence is still necessary. The question is: what sort of a thing is your atom a scaled-up replica *of*?

Effect   But... but 'model' doesn't necessarily have to mean 'replica'. Think of the way the word 'model' is used, again with cars, to mean 'design' or 'marque' or 'name'. Here we are thinking of a sort of prototype or blueprint or pattern, a list of specifications to which all the examples of the model conform.

Cause   Like one of Plato's abstract Forms? Or perhaps you are thinking of the word 'model' in the sense of 'fashion model' or 'model prisoner', in which it is used to denote some aesthetic or moral ideal or paragon and the element of correspondence has all but disappeared, residing if anywhere, in one's imagination. In this use incidentally, the meaning of the word 'model' again comes close to that of our old friend 'god'.

Effect   Well that's not how I mean it, no.

Cause   Again, maybe you are thinking of 'model' as in 'Model seeks part-time work'?

Effect   Trust you!

Cause   No correspondence at all here. *Mis*representation more likely. *Mis*representation perhaps. Mind you, I could do with some part-time work myself at the moment, anything.

Effect I'm sure... No, I use the word 'model' because I do wish to assert a correspondence, a real correspondence. I am thinking of the sort of correspondence between an architect's plan and a building or between a survey map and a landscape. Or better still perhaps, of the relationship between a knitting pattern and a woollen jumper.

Cause Okay Malcolm, okay, I can see that things can 'correspond' to one another in a number of different ways, that correspondence need not mean simply the relationship of a replica to its original, but you are repeatedly missing the essential point here: buildings and landscapes and woolly jumpers are on display in the physical world. They can be known and described independently of any supposed models of them. Any alleged correspondence between them and other objects can be tested and verified empirically. The key question remains: what are these atomic models of yours models of? To what do they correspond?

Effect To real atoms of course, to the reality of the atomic world.

Cause And what can you tell me about these 'real atoms', about this 'atomic reality'?

Effect Well... Er...

Cause Exactly, you can tell me nothing, nothing at all, *except in terms of the models.* There is no and there can be no independent, non-model-interpreted knowledge by which the claims you make about the accuracy of your atomic modelling can be verified or falsified. Without necessarily drawing a positivist-style conclusion that statements about atomic phenomena are therefore literally meaningless, I think we must at least accept that there is something very fishy going on here. It may be that your use of the word 'model' is dangerously misleading.

Effect There is nothing fishy or misleading Andrew, it is simply a matter of fact: we *do* have knowledge of the atomic world. Over the years we have accumulated masses and masses of data in thousands and thousands of experiments all round the world. We have learnt a great deal about the patterns, symmetries and asymmetries that exist at the subatomic level. What you do not seem to have understood is that all this knowledge comes to us in an essentially *mathematical* form; the correspondence between the experimental data and the visualizable pictures we have devised to help us interpret the data is a *mathematical* correspondence. What Science provides is a *mathematical* model of the atomic world.

Cause A mathematical model?

Effect   Yes.

Cause   I wonder what *that* phrase can mean... I assume you are not referring to the little cardboard constructions of cylinders, cones, cubes and other polyhedra that are often found gathering dust on classroom shelves in junior schools?

Effect   Obviously not.

Cause   On the other hand, by 'mathematical models' you presumably mean something more than just the abstract figures of pure geometry and calculus?

Effect   You see things in such simple, Euclidean, black-and-white terms. What I am talking about is a model *in* mathematics; a complex of particles and forces and interactions whose behaviour can only be described, or rather expressed, mathematically, in a body of calculus. The billiard-ball model is only a rough and ready way of presenting certain aspects of the mathematical data in an easily visualizable form.

Cause   So what is the model exactly? The billiard-ball picture or the body of calculus?

Effect   They are both models in a sense. The mathematical one is the most accurate though, the least misleading, the one nearest to the truth.

Cause   Then again I must ask: to what do these so-called models correspond? The correspondence in the case of the billiard-ball picture seems to be not between the model and some hypothetical 'real' atom after all, but between the model and the mathematical data, between one model and another model.

Effect   In a way, yes.

Cause   So now the question is: to what does the *mathematical* model correspond? How indeed, can a body of calculus *correspond* to anything? Forgive me and my old-fashioned ideas Malcolm, but I had always thought of mathematics as being a purely abstract, deductive logical system, a language with its own sort of absolute truth and validity and its own set of procedures of proof and verification which are quite different from those of the physical world and the physical sciences.

Effect   You must realize though Andrew, that the logic and the mathematics involved in these high-level particle studies are extremely complex and advanced, way way above my own feeble capabilities, never mind yours. We are talking about the very frontiers of mathematics, as well as of physics.

Cause   Oh now don't try to frighten me with that 'way above your head' claptrap! I don't have to have learnt all the calculus to know that mathematics is mathematics and that physics is physics, however intertwined they may get on occasion. By itself, no amount of mathematics, however complex, can ever add up to *a thing*. No amount of geometry or calculus can ever constitute *a phenomenon*. No amount of logic can ever entail a world. Once again you are trying, under the twin shrouds of mathematical complexity and physical obscurity, to pull the impossible old turning-numbers-into-objects trick. It cannot be done Malcolm! The very phrase 'mathematical model' crystallizes the confusion, clarifies the conceit.

Effect   Look: one can construct a mathematical model of any object, of a table for instance. One can compute its shape mathematically, its orientation in a given framework of time and space, its mass, its physical properties, its...

Cause   Isn't this just a fancy way of saying that you can take its measurements, that you can measure its various physical properties in various ways and can express these observations numerically in terms of certain agreed standards? The art of measurement demonstrates that mathematics is *the language* of any object-object, property-property correspondence. It is in measurement that both the relationship and the distinction between mathematics and physics are at their clearest: without physical substance or physical properties there is nothing that can be measured mathematically; without mathematics there can be no physical measuring. The trouble with the inhabitants of your atomic world is that as their claims to physicality and property-display disappear over our various horizons of observability, it becomes less and less clear what it is that is being measured, what is *the application* of all this mathematics.

Effect   Less clear to you maybe.

Cause   Until all we are left with is just a catalogue of algebraic functions with names, nothing to do with the real, physical world at all. You talk of the patterns, symmetries and asymmetries that have been discovered, but what are these patterns, symmetries and asymmetries *amongst*?

Effect   Amongst the subatomic particles of course, amongst the particle-families, amongst the cosmic forces.

Cause But this is model-talk, billiard-ball-talk! It is post- or pre-mathematical talk! You see, you cannot do without it!

Effect Of course! As you say, one has to have *some* conceptual scheme in terms of which to interpret the mathematics.

Cause Exactly, and yet the mathematics is supposed to come first; the model-making is supposed to come *after* the information-gathering. The trouble is that without some sort of non-mathematical model or picture, there is nothing one can call 'information'. Like your hapless electrons we are going round in circles, in theoretical circles; or rather, we are going down a theoretical vortex.

Effect Oh dear, I'm afraid I haven't expressed myself very clearly over this models business. Perhaps you ought to read that book by...

Cause Uh-oh! None of that 'recommended reading' cop-out if you don't mind! I feel, Malcolm, that the questions I am raising and the points I am putting are all essentially straightforward and simple and I'd prefer to hear your answers to them than to be referred to the doubtless capacious 'philosophy of science' shelves in... there. In any case, it seems to me that what one usually finds on those shelves are attempts by scientists-turned-philosophers to flannel and waffle and fudge their way *out* of their various discomforts rather than genuine criticisms of their positions. Their objections are never *serious*, their doubts are never *felt*. The common paradigm seems to be a massive agglomeration of words and jargon, as though the author hopes that either the problem or the reader will eventually just collapse with fatigue or boredom.

Effect Yes, I know what you mean.

Cause 'Paradigm' is only another pretty Greek word for 'example' or 'pattern' or the one you used, 'model', and 'model' is a perfectly ordinary, good, simple English noun. It is now up to you to defend your use of it, just as it is up to me, a philosopher, to defend the language against *mis*use.

Effect Well Andrew, I think that I have said all that I can say. Your problem, it seems to me, is that all along you have been taking my remarks *too literally*. First, you took the billiard-ball picture of the atom too literally and now you are taking the whole notion of *a model* too literally too.

Cause Ha! That's a good one! Any minute now you'll accuse me of taking the word 'literally' too literally! Honestly, if it's not a physicist's duty to be literal in his language, whose is it? Which brings me to another question: given that the nature of these atomic entities is proving to be so elusive and problematic, what will you now say that words such as 'atom', 'proton', 'electron', 'quark' and so on actually denote? Does 'the electron' signify the unknown 'real' object of which we seem able to say nothing? Is it shorthand for the mathematical model, the body of calculus known only to you experts? Does it refer to the simple common-or-garden billiard-ball picture you are now so anxious to disown? Or what?

Effect I... I think that perhaps it has all of these meanings. As with all words, its precise connotations are determined by the, er, context of its use...

Cause You know Malcolm, it is remarkable how much of what you are now saying about the status of atomic objects echoes what you were saying about the status of gods: the pointed, almost deliberate indecision over whether we are dealing with real objects or with figments of imagination...

Effect Are these the only alternatives?

Cause Historically, the "it's only a model" disclaimer first gained serious currency as a result of the problems of atomic visualizing posed by the quantum theory, yet when you mentioned them, you still spoke of 'the double *nature*' of light and electrons. In truth what suffers from this double nature is nothing in the world but your mythology. You always try to have it both ways.

Effect What's wrong with that?

Cause There is the systematic ambiguity of the words, the names, which now stand for the unknown divinities themselves, and now denote the inadequate little models and representations we make of them; the difficulty in explaining coherently how their world and ours can inter-relate; the exhortation "not to take things too literally" when the philosophical going gets a bit tough. Indeed, the whole retreat you have been beating into woolliness of thought and expression, the "only a model" position, sounds to me very resonant of the retreat that has been beaten over the last couple of centuries by the Christian theologians, who have found the power of their religion steadily being eroded by the advance of yours.

Effect Oh come on, you are just fishing family resemblances out of thin air now! You are seeing them in shadows, glimpsing them in tricks of speech. I mean you cannot seriously be comparing the progress of modern particle physics with trends in Christian theology, this really is stretching parallels beyond endurance. Their subject-matters, their methods, their languages, their histories, their purposes, none of these could be less similar!

Cause   I am not so sure. I think that in many ways the comparison is valid. Notice firstly that in a very broad sense they both fulfil the same explanatory role: they both occur at the same points and for the same reasons in their respective interpretations of the world. Given that the Christian account of the world is an account primarily in terms of minds, purposes and the moral forces of Good and Evil, if one goes on asking a Christian theologian 'Why?' questions for long enough, "Why man?", "Why the world?", "Why should I be good?", he is bound in the end to resort to 'explanations' expressed in terms of the minds, purposes and moral qualities of beings who do not in any obvious way feature in the world: God, the Devil, the Holy Ghost and so on. Similarly, since the scientist's account of the world is an account in terms of physical objects, inanimate forces and causal relations, when the potentially endless asking of 'Why?' questions comes up with apparently meaningful interrogatives like "Why do substances react?" or "Why do objects persist?" he is bound to resort to 'explanations' expressed in terms of objects and forces which are not themselves observable: atoms, electrons, quarks, the colour force and so on. Both sets of fictional entities naturally occur at the points in their respective world-views where first-hand knowledge and explanation in terms of observable phenomena 'run out'. The corollary of this is that the crucial descent into an explanatory myth-world can *appear* finally to bring the endless asking of 'Why?' questions to a halt. It seems peculiarly pointless then to go on asking "Yes, but *why* do like charges repel?" or "Yes, but *why* is God Love?" One might as well ask a mathematician "Yes, but *why* do squares have four sides?"

Effect   But it's the *definition* of squares to have four sides.

Cause   Exactly, and it is interesting that often in arguments for the existence of God or of atomic objects, they too seem to begin life as essentially mathematical or logical entities. I am reminded in particular of Descartes' entirely deductive proofs in his *Meditations* of the logical necessity of God, one of which went roughly like this: everything is caused by something; therefore there must be something that causes everything; therefore God must exist. Similarly, there is a line of thought which goes: everything is made of something; therefore there must be something, some universal substance or set of particles, of which all things are made; therefore atoms or particles or quarks or what-you-will *must* exist.

Effect   But that's abs...

Cause   No prizes Malcolm, for spotting the logical mistake committed in such arguments; a good example of a simple linguistic trip-up, a bad pun on the word 'something': the confusion of 'something' with 'some one thing' or 'some one substance' or 'some one set of particles'. No, the point here is to note how both ideas can begin life as the children of a naïve logic. The trouble starts when the theologians are then tempted to try saying things *about* their God and when the physicists then try to give *an account* of their atoms. When faced with the infinite complexity, subtlety and variety of the world which they are attempting to explain, the theologian and the physicist in no time at all find themselves obliged to indulge in some very long-winded and obscure theorizing in order to keep their account on the road, during the course of which the formerly logical and simplificatory function of the original ideas soon gets forgotten. Before long the mythology, the world-system, becomes an end-in-itself and can even seem to become, to its propagators at least, more important and more 'real' that the everyday experiences or phenomena which it was originally intended to illuminate. Just listen for example, to a theologian trying to explain how it is that suffering and evil can exist in a world created by an omnipotent, all-loving God or how the Holy Spirit can be an immaterial power yet at the same time be 'at work' in the physical Universe.

Effect   Oh I know, I know. I have had many long, troubled conversations with Dogma on these topics. I must admit that he rarely seems to make much sense.

Cause   Dogma again, who is this Dogma?

Effect   You know, Reverend Dogma, the College Chaplain.

Cause   Ah...

Effect   Yes, being a Christian myself, I confess that I find it somewhat saddening that some theologians appear to think it necessary to fight a desperate and ultimately futile sort of rearguard action against the scientists in an attempt to preserve some cosmological role for God. I secretly suspect that much of their learned pronouncements about transcendence, immanence and the rest is just meaningless waffle, empty words merely.

Cause   Well it seems to me that modern particle physics is now going the same way. The mystificatory nonsense of modern theology is now closely parallelled by the absurd, abstruse, abstract web-spinning of modern particle physics. The physicists too have lapsed into gobbledegook.

Effect   Come come Andrew, just because the theories are hard to understand it does not mean that they are therefore nonsensical. Agreed, the

324

highly complex calculus and the difficult, often counter-intuitive concept-ualizing involved in much of the new work is well beyond the intellectual grasp of the layman, indeed much of it is beyond mine, but one must not conclude from this that the theories are the products of abstract specula-tion. They have arisen, unlike those of Christian theology, from years and years of painstaking research, experiment, observation and measurement. Hypotheses about particles and the rest are empirically testable hypotheses that are confirmed or refuted by matters of physical fact; in the end, whether they stand or fall depends, and only depends, upon what happens in Nature.

Cause Ah, but although statements about atoms, like statements about God *appear* to be statements about matters of fact, yet in a way they are curiously immune to disproof, they...

Effect I didn't say that statements about atoms and particles are state-ments about matters of fact, I said that hypotheses about atoms or about particles are confirmed or refuted by empirical observations, which is something very different.

Cause Is it? While there may be details or even important aspects of atomic theory which are open to question or to experimental refutation, just as there are theological issues which are matters of dispute, yet there are also many definitions and hypotheses which have been accepted for so long and have become so deeply embedded in the language of the theory that they have achieved the status of axioms: they are beyond doubt. We have already seen how statements like "Everything is made of particles" or "God sustains the world" can seem to have the self-evidence of laws of logic. But also, it is hard to see how one could now prove or disprove, empirically or otherwise, that statements like "The electron carries a nega-tive charge" or "atoms have nuclei" are true. Compare: "God is all-forgiv-ing", "Christ was the Messiah". Above all, it seems inconceivable that a *physicist* or a *Christian theologian* could now question such assertions. This point reminds me of another, rather more sociological parallel: the way in which ordinary people's beliefs about the atomic world, like their religious assumptions, are handed down to them by an élite. Scientists, like priests, are custodians of a body of expert knowledge and opinion which they dispense to a public of laymen; note *that* word. In short, in political terms, Science operates rather like the *Church*.

Effect Oh come off it!

Cause It does, it does! Think, for a start, how Christianity and Science both agree in seeing man as being systematically condemned, as being born into a situation of disadvantage. Christianity puts man at a moral disadvantage by condemning him to a state of 'original sin'. Man is born 'out of grace'; left to grow up in the wild, naturally, without the benefit of religious education, he is prey to all the forces of evil and wickedness, he will never enter the Kingdom of Heaven. Similarly, Science puts man at an epistemological disadvantage by condemning him, if you like, to a state of original ignorance. Left to grow up in the wild, naturally, without the benefit of a scientific education, he will never come to know anything of the nature of the real world, the world of atoms and subatomic particles and cosmic forces, but will live all his life in the realm of the senses, where all is mere appearance and illusion. The first move of any organized religion is to *cow* the non-believer, to give him an inferiority complex.

Effect   Well you can hardly claim that science does that.

Cause   The second move is to offer him hope, to provide him with a way out of his natural state of sin or ignorance. A man *can* attain a state of grace by, and only by, discovering and following the teachings of Christ and of the Christian Church. A man *can* come to have some knowledge of the real world by, and only by, studying the accumulated body of scientific theory, and in particular, of atomic and particle theory. And of course in these processes of attaining grace and knowledge, the priest and the scientist play special, and closely parallel roles.

Effect   As teachers you mean? Nothing wrong with that, surely?

Cause   They are more than mere teachers Malcolm, they actually accord themselves a special status in their respective scheme of things. Although a Christian priest is human, is as thoroughly mortal and fallible as any layman, yet he is said by the Church to be in a special way *closer to God* than are ordinary men. Priests are God's earthly agents, without whose intercession ordinary men would never attain a state of grace; their job is to guide men to Him. This mysterious, privileged, half-mortal, half-divine status of the Christian priest is parallelled by the special epistemological status of the atomic physicist. Again, although as thoroughly mortal as the next man and without possessing any special intellect or sixth sense which enables him actually to see atoms or electrons, yet the physicist is thought to be in a certain way closer to the truth of things than the ordinary man. He alone knows the reality of the atomic world and he alone is capable of bringing ordinary men to a better understanding of that reality. Scientists stand half-way between the man-in-the-street and the truth; they are the ones in the know.

Effect   Would that it were so! Honestly Andrew, you really do have a chip on your shoulder don't you? You must have had a very hard time at school or something. I mean, why the sneering use of the phrase 'in the know'? Why not just say that physicists know more about physics than non-physicists?

Cause   Because there is more to it than that. The special status of the priests and of the scientists confers upon them significant *political* powers. They establish themselves as being a body of men who are epistemologically indispensible to society. So long as their particular set of mythological pictures and their particular theological jargon retains a hold over the public imagination, so will their position of political pre-eminence go generally unchallenged. It is perfectly natural then, for the priests/scientists to band together, on the one hand as a Church and on the other, more loosely, as the scientific establishment, to form groups which have extremely powerful interests vested in the general acceptance of their mythologies. A maintained public faith in the religion becomes both the source of the Church's power and the end above all to which the Church directs its activity. One will therefore be unlikely to find *a scientist* radically questioning the principles behind the atomic theory, since his own past, present and future depend upon that theory being kept on the road. He cannot afford to air doubts of any great consequence.

Effect   No, I resent this suggestion. It is simply not true. Physicists often air doubts, all sorts of doubts. We are continually questioning assumptions, re-examining arguments, proposing rival hypotheses.

Cause   Yes, but always comparatively trivial doubts, always rather peripheral questions. The great mass of theory, atomic and otherwise, is inherited, is laid down, is embedded so deeply that it is taken as fact. It has become, as they say, part of the language. Is it not odd for example, that in the face of all the difficulties we should have arrived at *an* atomic theory, at *a consensus*? Oh yes the details are disputed, the new quark theory is the subject of much controversy, but no-one now doubts the general correctness of the Rutherford-Bohr model.

Effect   Maybe that is because it *is* generally correct. The experiments have been done. There's no point in repeating them ad infinitum.

Cause   You see! The issue's been settled! An article of faith has been canonized, is now part of the creed. You protest that the scientific establishment does not operate like a Church, but look: the Rutherford-Bohr model

Juggernaut

is not just an abstract theory of atomic structure, it is now a great academic-educational-political juggernaut. Juggernaut, there's another one.

Effect   Another what?

Cause   Another god. The English word 'juggernaut' comes from the Hindi Jagan-Nath, one of the titles of the god Krishna, the eighth avatar of Vishnu and in particular the name of a gigantic wheeled sculpture of the deity in the town of Puri. This monstrous vehicle is annually dragged along in a great procession, crushing everything in its path including, apparently, many of its hysterical devotees.

Effect   It takes all sorts.

Cause   It does. Remember Malcolm, before you assert that controversies are always resolved on purely scientific grounds, when rival theories are vying to explain some new phenomenon, that behind them stand rival scientists, rival laboratories, rival academics, and that behind these stand rival publishing houses, rival universities, rival governments. One must not underestimate the jealousies and powers of the academic institutions, whose interests are vested in keeping *this* theory as the accepted explanation of so-and-so or *that* model as the accepted interpretation of such-and-such or *The Other* University as the recognized centre of bla-bla research. This morning, for example, when you pooh-poohed the 'cold fusion' claims, was I wrong to detect in your tone a hint of good old professional jealousy? Could it perhaps be that the Scientific Establishment finds admitting the waste of all that money and effort on the wrong track just too humiliating?

Effect   The claims have been tested and found wanting, I'm afraid there is no more to it.

Cause   Again, compare the educational imperialism of modern science with the European Churches' recent zealous missionizing: the evangelistic urge to spread its doctrines throughout the 'primitive' or 'backward' peoples of the world.

Effect   Why, don't you think it's right for us to share our new knowledge and techniques with the less fortunate?

Cause   It may be good to share the practical discoveries, to teach the useful techniques, although some might argue otherwise, but certainly it can't be right to inflict on them our atomic mythologies, our gods, our bleak world-view. It is a fine line between teaching and indoctrination.

328

Effect   No-one is *indoctrinated* to believe in the atomic theory!

Cause   Aren't they? They teach the billiard-ball model in *primary* schools nowadays. Science, like any wise church, knows that if you give it a child for the first few years of its life, it will give you a life-long theist. How old were you when you were first told about atoms and electrons?

Effect   Well, er, I'm not sure... I can't remember... It was so long ago...

Cause   Try, try... Come on, let us indulge in a little educational psycho-analysis, unearth a few forgotten memories; this is always valuable. To recall one's first science lessons is also to recall roughly how our various scientific theories historically took root.

Effect   *Very* roughly.

Cause   In both cases it was the original ideas that seemed so clear, and whether or not a child continues to study science to the more advanced levels, it is his first initiations that are the most important. Quiet Malcolm... relax... Shut your eyes... Think back... Think back to your first physics lessons, your first chemistry lessons; I'm sure they were much the same for you as they were for me... We were children, with young minds so thirsty for discovery, so frighteningly anxious to learn. It scared me sometimes, so eager was I to *comprehend* the world. But of course thirsty young minds are vulnerable, are ready to drink of any brew that tastes like knowledge, are too young to question the authority or sincerity of their science teachers, the priests who first offer them the wine... Most clearly of all I can remember the magic, the puzzles, the mysterious experiments and demonstrations...

Effect   Strange magnets with furry iron filings forming curious patterns on sheets of white paper...

Cause   Freshly-used combs that picked up tiny scraps torn from exercise-book pages...

Effect   Balls on strings that flew apart when touched by rubbed rods of amber. Or were they ivory, or ebony...?

Cause   A torch-bulb lighting up when two metal strips were dipped in acid. Something to do with frogs' legs...

Effect   A machine which made long sparks crackle from a silver dome onto our heads...

Initiation

Cause   Classrooms where jars and jars of powders stood on shelves around the walls: white, green, blue, orange, yellow. Crystals and colour-tests, bunsen-burners and bell-jars...

Effect   Silvery metals bubbling in acids, invisible gases that burnt with a pop. Floating sodium fizzing and flashing, a metal that actually caught fire...

Cause   A darkened room into which a ray of sunlight streamed and a mysterious prism which produced a rainbow, a real rainbow glowing on the wall...

Effect   Stories of falling apples and swirling planets, of gravity and energy and friction. It took me a long time, I remember, to understand the difference between mass and weight, but how clear things seemed when I had mastered that...

Cause   I remember dreaming of being able to move through Space, without effort, drifting freely, for ever and ever....

Effect   Astronomy was my special passion. I used to love reading about the Moon and the Sun, about the planets, the stars, the galaxies marking out their ancient orbits...

Cause   As though engaged in some endless heavenly dance...

Effect   And then we learnt of *atoms*, of the tiny solar systems of which everything is made. Perfect patterns of tiny particles, all spinning and spiralling within everything we touch...

Cause   What an initiation! What a revelation! What a picture to flash in the darkness of hungry young imaginations! To discover what the world is made of! At the age of what was it? Ten? Eight? Six?

Effect   Millions of minute billiard-balls, positive, negative and neutral: what lovely, easy sense it made! I can remember the drawings on the black-board, the brightly-coloured charts on the wall and best of all, the films they sometimes showed, where the diagrams actually came to life. I guess it's all on video now... The protons, I recall, were always red, the electrons green and the neutrons white; the colours seemed appropriate somehow...

Cause   A science teacher, like any wise priest, knows that his power comes first from his magic, his myths, his images, from his bewitching of childish imaginations, from his playing upon childhood dreams and fears.

How did the Churches maintain their two-thousand-year stranglehold over men's souls? Do not tell me it was because of the soundness of their theological theories! They did it with magic and with myth! Think of the psychological power of their story of an Almighty Father, of a God who always loved and never punished, who came to you in secret in your dreams and in your prayers... Think of their visions of Heaven and Hell, with their images of boundless wealth and endless torture... Think of their story of a *Son* of God, born of a virgin, crowned a king, crucified and resurrected... Stories of saints and martyrs, miracles and spells... Strange churchly ceremonies and initiations, the rites of baptism and confirmation, the breaking of bread and the taking of wine... God, how I used to hate Chapel! The sickening, stifling, suffocating stench of ancient ritual! I used to *hate* it!

Effect   Really? I never minded going to Church. The whole family went every Sunday. I used to like the hymns.

Cause   I preferred the hers, the few girls who occasionally sat in the visitors' pew, ogled by a thousand frustrated eyes. *Angels* they became, *angels*.

Effect   I suppose it's all a matter of associations. First impressions are so important.

Cause   There is no doubt: it's myth and magic and ritual that are the prime ingredients of any successful religion... Once hooked, there will be those in the congregation who are so inspired by the priests' stories and so fascinated by the priest's games, so quick at mathematics, so adept at handling test-tubes, that they will soon wish to become priests themselves. These few go on to discover the Faith in greater and greater detail, learning by heart its numerous time-honoured catechisms, mastering its many obscure theorems, absorbing its language of explanation so deeply that its jargon actually becomes a way of thought. On and on until by the time the novice priest has grown into manhood and gone to university, it is far too late for him seriously to question the basic tenets of his religion. His world-view, his personal identity and indeed his daily living will all have become so dependent upon his Faith that fundamental doubts are by now unthinkable.

Effect   But this is not so, there are always...

Cause   Oh there are doubts about details, issues of fine interpretation, minor heresies, but no wholesale re-examinations. It is too late for a scientist now to question turnings that were taken fifty, a hundred, two hundred years ago. Yet think again of your own initiation into priesthood... Didn't the magic of those sharp young school-room visions quickly fade? Didn't the bright, clear images soon give way to hazy abstraction? Didn't the view become steadily more blurred, shrouded in an ever-thicker fog of mathematics? As experimental irregularities multiplied and multiplied, didn't ad hoc hypotheses that for a while seemed to fit the facts gradually become instituted as accepted principles? Were not functions of fudge-factors differentiated and differentiated until after a while it became pointless to ask what were now the variables, what were now the objects and what the properties? Did not the language itself sometimes seem to lose its grip upon the world altogether, the meanings of its many new words having more to do with internal theology than with external things? But after all this mystification, what has happened to the simple coloured billiard-balls of your childhood revelation?

Effect   But of course atoms are not *really* like that! Protons and electrons aren't *really* little red and green balls, things were bound to be more complicated! I repeat: you must not take the simple diagrams of the school-books so *literally*!

Cause   Yet *you* once did and every other scientist once did. If the scientists of today had *not* once taken their school-book diagrams literally, had *not* once been inspired by those simple, colourful pictures, they would not have been drawn into the scientific Faith and would never have gone on to become its priests.

Effect   But school-children would not be able to understand the advanced theories, with all their subtleties and complexities and their difficult mathematics.

Cause   So they are told lies?

Effect   Not lies exactly, just...

Cause   Untruths. Untruths in which every schoolchild in every country in the world is now being indoctrinated.

Effect   But the theory has to be made simple so that children can understand it.

Cause   So as to bewitch and fool them you mean, to cast them under a lifelong spell. Ah, you scientists are artful priests: it is only much later, when the school-room magic has done its work, when the chosen student is too deeply immersed in his Faith to turn back, that you then explain to him the 'mistake' of taking the original pictures too literally. And of course once the myths and images of childhood have given way to the abstract theology of priesthood, the mystification begins: the priests retreat into jargon and caballism, the laity into ignorance and awe. One thing, incidentally, we must notice about this hierarchy: most scientists are essentially still only school-children themselves. When an expert starts off "It has been proved that..." or "We already know that..." or "Experiments have shown that..." a hundred-to-one he is only quoting what *he* has read in books, what *he* has been taught, what the scientific establishment has handed down to him. Perfectly respectable scientific scepticism always entitles, indeed obliges us to ask: *How* has it been proved? How *certainly* is it known? *What* experiments showed this, within what margins of error? What alternative interpretations were and are possible? What controversies raged at this theory's inception and how arbitrarily were they 'settled'?

Effect   Of course, and physicists themselves ask such questions all the time.

Cause   Maybe, but their questions can never be very radical, their doubts can never be very drastic. Only small applecarts can be upset and only small boats rocked. The axioms of atomic theory remain inviolable. You advise me now to forget the billiard-ball picture, yet, as I say, there is no question of your now forgetting the Rutherford-Bohr model.

Effect   But what reason could we have for forgetting the Rutherford-Bohr model?

Cause   What reason?

Effect   Yes, why on earth should we abandon such an extremely useful theory?

Cause   Aha, 'useful' you say, not 'true'.

Effect   Useful, yes, useful. Look, we have been through all this: what we are talking about here is a *model*, an aid to understanding. Models are not simply true or false, they are useful, helpful, illuminating.

Cause   Or they are misleading and confusing and dangerous, as the case may be.

Effect   'True' and 'false' are not appropriate predicates here, they do not belong to this language-game. The features which...

Cause   And so the young scientist discovers *philosophy*! You see, it is not

333

usually until university, if at all, in his one-term philosophy-of-science option, that the budding physicist begins to get any inkling of the huge philosophical problems that his theories and his methods and his language generate. And by then of course, not only is his grounding in the Faith sufficiently solid and safe to withstand any tiresome philosophical quibblings about its validity, and his intellect and vocabulary sufficiently 'mature' to grapple with the abstract arguments that are bound to arise, but also the physics itself at this level has become so multi-layered and so fudged and abstruse, that it is impossible to keep philosophy *out* of the ring. The Quantum Theory, Heisenberg's Uncertainty Principle, probability calculus, the waves/particles dichotomy, relativity, the advent of non-visualizable geometries and so on inevitably raise questions about the status of the whole enterprise and its language and its 'objects'. At last the scientist is obliged to dabble in metaphysics.

Effect But what's wrong with that? I'd have thought you would be pleased!

Cause It's all too late Malcolm, far too late! This is not serious critical philosophy but mere self-justification, mugging-up a phrase-book of instant philosophical let-out clauses and mystificatory gambits, rehearsed more as a rudimentary self-defence against nuisances like me than from any genuine interest in or understanding of philosophical problems, scientific or otherwise. There is the 'only models' move, the 'useful rather than true' dodge, the 'have you read that book by...?' feint, the 'unless you know quantum mechanics' parry and an armoury of others.

Effect Hmm. I must admit that I did find the Philosophy of Science option pretty boring and irrelevant. I'm afraid I'm more of a practical physicist by temperament.

Cause Oh yes, and the 'don't bother me with all that waffle, I've got work to be doing' thrust.

Effect But isn't that fair enough? Action not words?

Cause It might be, if it were true. But you are *not* a man of action any more, you *are* a man of words: 'atoms', 'electrons', 'quarks', 'gluons', 'the colour force'.

Effect So what can I do? You are continually asking me philosophically to justify myself, my language of explanation, my theories, yet every argument I put forward you immediately ridicule. 'Let-out clauses' is your latest jibe.

Cause But Malcolm, I have found none of your arguments the slightest bit convincing.

Effect Why not? The suggestion that atoms are models sounds entirely convincing to me.

Cause It has to doesn't it? One would hardly go to a Christian priest for a philosophically objective assessment of Christian theology.

Effect But what do you mean by 'objective'? How can philosophy possibly be objective?

Cause How can atomic physics?

Effect Eh?

Cause This is it you see: none of your philosophical apologies is sincere, you never mean what you say. You scientists merely pay *lip-service* to philosophy. At university you concede that atoms do not in fact exist as minute billiard-ball solar-systems, yet in the schools you continue to tell the billiard-ball stories and display the billiard-ball pictures. You admit to philosophers that your theory is after all only a model of reality, yet you carry on amongst yourselves talking and writing about atoms and particles as though they were everyday objects. You never take the philosophical conclusions literally, seriously. You cannot make this crucial disclaimer about the atom being only a fiction and then just carry on as though nothing important has been said.

Effect So what do you want me to do? Give up my work?

Cause For a start I want you to cut the crap and agree with me that atoms and electrons and quarks and the rest are mythological, are gods, are as *literally* mythological as the gods of the ancient Greeks.

Effect But that is ridiculous! I don't accept it! I don't agree with you! I don't see these family resemblances between Greek gods and atomic particles! And I find your characterization of modern science as a religion altogether too preposterous for words. By all normal lights, the subject-matter, the methods and the purposes of science are diametrically to be *contrasted* with those of religion.

Cause I suppose one sees what one wants to see, what one is predisposed to see. This is the strange thing: one man can refuse to see what another man finds blindingly obvious.

Effect   But I'm not refusing to see anything! The family resemblances of which you speak are just not there!

Cause   Heigh-ho.

Effect   And if you persist in this claim that you find the resemblance between Greek gods and atomic particles blindingly obvious, I can only conclude that you are either mad or lying.

Cause   Neither Malcolm, I assure you. Why should I lie to you? Do I seem mad? I think I *was* mad once, when I used to believe in all that stuff. But then... something suddenly clicked and the mythology of it *did* become blindingly obvious. A spell was broken. A release. I don't know.

Effect   But the very sentence "Atoms are gods" is literally meaningless, it is nonsense. One might as well say "Ideas are yellow" or...

Cause   "Gluons obey the colour force" or "Mythologies can be dangerous"?

Effect   But what would be the point of making such a statement? How is it helpful? How is it useful?

Cause   Ah, well... For the moment, let us at least establish that it is true.

Effect   Of course it's not true! The Greek gods don't exist!

Cause   If you say not.

Effect   And atoms and particles *do* exist, everybody knows that, it's beyond question!

Cause   The cornerstones of religious belief always do appear to be beyond question, to their believers. In the Europe of five hundred years ago, the existence of God was not a subject of opinion as we tend to regard it nowadays, but seemed to almost everyone to be an obvious matter of fact, as certain as that the Sun shone in the sky. To the members of a society which corporately accepts a certain set of philosophical views or religious beliefs, these views and beliefs, however incoherent, do not seem questionable at all, but rather are thought of as being self-evident, axiomatic, and, interestingly, 'common knowledge'. It is therefore the philosopher's first job to unearth, to identify, to lay bare his society's philosophical and religious assumptions. The philosopher is something of an exorcist.

Effect   But our discoveries about atomic structure are not merely sets of beliefs, they are matters of fact. Atoms do actually exist. Experimentally their existence has been proved, conclusively proved. They have finite measurable masses, they occupy finite volumes of space, they have distinctive, observable physical properties, they are real, three-dimensional objects!

Cause   That's funny, a moment ago they were only mathematical models.

Effect   Ah... Oh... Yes...

Cause   So what is it to be Malcolm, physical objects or abstract ideas?

Effect   Ermm...

Cause   The true reality of the world or just some explanatory fictions?

Effect   Oh dear... I'm not sure...

Cause   Figments of imagination or observable facts?

Effect   I... Er...

Cause   Or words maybe, mere words, mere names?

Effect   Ohhh...

Cause   Shouldn't we say that in truth they are gods, that most accurately they are mythological?

Effect   Hell, I don't know, I just don't know any more... Oh dear... Christ! Is that the time? It's half-past nine! I should have been home an hour ago! Connie will be wondering what's happened. I'd better get moving or I'll miss the last train.

Cause   Don't worry. I'll drive you if you like. Is it far?

Effect   About ten miles.

Cause   Come on then. Now which way was the Criminology place? Brrr! Cold!

✻   ✻   ✻   ✻   ✻   ✻   ✻   ✻   ✻   ✻

8

PHYSICS
and
METAPHYSICS

Effect This book of yours Andrew, you say you've been working on it for a long time?

Cause Ten years, more or less, on and off.

Effect Ten years!?

Cause Yes, mad isn't it?

Effect Why? Why all that work? What do you hope to achieve, assuming it ever gets published? One doesn't write philosophy for money.

Cause You're right there. I don't know. Maybe I'd get a crack at some interesting birds.

Effect Tsk. I do wish you'd stop using that word.

Cause What, 'crack'?

Effect No, 'bird' of course, it's, it's so... degrading.

Cause Oh now what's this nonsense? Castrating the language? Time was when four-letter words were taboo, then they seemed to become compulsory and now you're telling me that I mustn't use the word 'b-i-r-d'?

Motivations

Effect   It's so... offensive. The word is 'woman' or 'girl', not 'bird'.

Cause   What prudery! The word, a word is 'bird'. Look it up: 'b-i-r-d', 'b-u-r-d', early Middle English for young maiden or girl; see also 'b-r-i-d-e'. A poetic term a thousand years old, a term of endearment or desire, then as now.

Effect   Is that true?

Cause   Besides, taken literally, birds are creatures to be *worshipped*. They called Bird 'Bird' originally because he ate the things, but later as a sort of deification, because he could *fly*.

Effect   Ah, now, Parker, yes...

Cause   You mean you know... You *do* like jazz?

Effect   Of course, but I always found Coltrane, even his in *Prestige* period, a bit too... religious. I never really got beyond Lester; I guess I never felt the need. He has so much... *humanity*.

Cause   Ah, yes, Lester... such soul, such melancholy, such *time*... But anyway, what about you? Why do you do your fusion research?

Effect   Well... At least it's something practical. It could be useful.

Cause   You mean it pays well?

Effect   No, no. The money's not that good anyway.

Cause   What then, the patent rights? Daylight robbery? Eureka!

Effect   No of course not! I... I simply hope that I can contribute something, can help mankind in some small way.

Cause   Oh claptrap! You don't really believe that do you? Come on, you want to be famous, you want to get into the history books: Sir Malcolm Effect, discoverer of poly-proton-polarity!

Effect   That's your motive is it, celebrity? Or rather, notoriety?

Cause   Hmm. Maybe I should call it 'Leaving Marks'.

Effect   That can't be right though, you're using a nom-de-plume. It doesn't make sense.

Cause It doesn't Malcolm, it doesn't... Let's just say: if you think you've seen a truth, you've got to try to tell it.

Effect How long before it's finished?

Cause Not long. I'm working on the last bit now. It ends with a play.

Effect A play?

Cause Yes, a metaphysical drama.

Effect Really? How odd. No wonder you can't find a publisher... Metaphysical you say. What does that mean exactly, what is metaphysics?

Cause Well originally, it was the name of a book, now you come to mention it, or at least, the name of a collection of writings. Aristotle wrote a number of treatises: *The Ethics, The Politics, The Poetics, The Psychology, The Logic, The Physics*. There were also a number of writings which arose from *The Logic* and from *The Physics* yet which did not seem to belong in either book. These were assembled by Aristotle into an extra treatise he called 'Τὰ μετὰ τά Φυσικά', literally, 'The After The Physics'. Since then we have dropped the 'the's but have kept the 'Metaphysics'. The subject-matter of Aristotle's extra book would come under what we now call 'philosophy'.

Effect So is 'metaphysics' now synonymous with 'philosophy' would you say?

Cause No, metaphysics is a sub-territory, an especially important sub-territory. I think the dictionary definition goes something like: speculation concerning the first principles of things, including substance, essence, being, time, space, cause and identity.

Effect That just about covers it; and that's a *sub*-territory is it?

Cause Yes. Of course the ground has been fought over. Much of the subject is now regarded as being properly the territory of the physicists: meta-*physics* remember. The logical positivists for example, insisted that questions about the ultimate constituents and constitution of the world could not be decided by idle philosophical speculation, but should be left to the no-nonsense investigations of the empirical sciences. Sitting on one's rationalist bum speculating about the nature of things could, they asserted, result only in messy outbursts of meaningless verbal diarrhœa.

Positivism Re-aired

Effect   Quite.

Cause   The trouble is that the positivists and the linguistic philosophers who are their heirs have gone to the other extreme and have concluded that metaphysics, if it is not to be meaningless word-play, must be language *about language*. Result: glottic dysentery!

Effect   But if metaphysics is not about the world and not about language, what is it about?

Cause   It is about both; that is to say, it is about the relationships between the two. The key thing now, it seems to me, is to re-establish the borderline between physics and metaphysics. I would like to hazard a definition: Physics is the study of the objects and phenomena of the physical world. A statement that purports to express a proposition, hypothetical or otherwise, concerning physical objects or phenomena is a statement of physics if and only if certain perceptual observations are directly relevant to the verification or falsification of that statement.

Effect   Echoes of the Verification Principle.

Cause   Yes, but only echoes. This time we have a criterion for deciding what are and are not statements of physics rather than a criterion for deciding whether sentences are or are not literally meaningful. On this account, statements which are not empirically verifiable or falsifiable are not therefore meaningless, they are just not statements of physics; they may be statements of metaphysics or of psychology or of logic or whatever; or they may, of course, be meaningless.

Effect   That sounds reasonable.

Cause   Good. Of course now come the arguments over the meanings of the problem-phrases 'objects and phenomena', 'perceptual observations', 'directly relevant to' and 'verification or falsification'. You, presumably, will still want to maintain that statements about atoms and particles are statements of physics, whereas I will conclude for all the reasons we have already discussed, that they are statements of metaphysics.

Effect   Ye-es, but if you are going to be that strict about the phrases in your definition, will not your 'physics' end up being just a banal, superficial, uncoordinated, purely descriptive account of the physical world?

Cause   No harm in that, I would have thought. There need be nothing *banal* about such a description.

Effect   Maybe not, but if we are to collate, order and pattern our perceptual observations, we *have to* employ some sort of conceptual structure, we
have to adopt what you will probably want to call some 'metaphysics'. I
am thinking not just of our atomic and particle theories but of the perfectly
uncontroversial concepts of macroscopic physics: mass, force, gravity,
energy, pressure and so on. According to your definition, even very familiar notions like these will come within the province of metaphysics rather
than physics since, it could be argued, they are not directly perceptible but
are known only through the interpretation of data.

Cause   Yes, I think that is right. It is important to remember when discussing, for example, Newton's second law – the force acting upon a body
is equal to the product of its mass and its acceleration – that there weren't
forces and masses and accelerations out there in the physical world waiting
to be measured or a relationship existing in Nature waiting to be discovered. Newton was invoking a new way of seeing things.

Effect   Once seen in this new way though, an objective physical relationship, a relationship that existed in Nature was for the first time revealed.

Cause   But Newton didn't discover the existence of masses and forces or
of a relationship between them, he *invented the concepts* mass and force,
concepts which then passed into, indeed became, the language of explanation of classical physics.

Effect   And which have passed, over the years, into everyday language
and understanding too.

Cause   He changed the way people *looked at* the world.

Effect   He changed what they saw.

Cause   He changed the way people talked about the world.

Effect   He changed the world they talked about.

Cause   Ah, no, careful Malcolm, he didn't do *that*. We must be clear:
changing the ways one sees the world or changing one's language is not
changing the world; not directly anyway, not overnight. Again: Newton
recognized the relationship, the mathematical relationship that exists
between the motions of falling bodies here on Earth and the movements of
the planets round the Sun. He named 'the force' responsible for both these
motions 'Gravity', thereby canonizing the relationship in language, but

when we look up at the night sky and when we watch a falling apple, we see no fine strings marked 'gravity', no *perceivable* resemblances.

Effect   The mathematical relationship is there though Andrew, it is objectively, measurably, empirically-testably *there*, in the motions of planets and falling apples.

Cause   Oh I don't doubt it, I don't doubt it.

Effect   So what then? Is the force of gravity a physical phenomenon or a metaphysical concept?

Cause   You tell me.

Effect   Well I don't think it is possible to distinguish, as you wish to, between 'pure' physics on the one hand and 'meta' physics on the other. Heat, sound, light, magnetism, electricity – in each of these branches of macroscopic physics, we have to employ certain 'concepts' as you would call them: temperature, wave-motion, radiation, polarity, force-field, charge and so on, if we are even to *describe* these phenomena with any sort of precision.

Cause   Are you sure that this is true? Have you ever seriously thought about it?

Effect   Take electricity for example: under the heading 'electrical' is included a huge variety of phenomena and effects. In order to relate these phenomena, to identify any patterns amongst them, we obviously need some, some... conceptual scheme or language in terms of which we can describe and classify and measure their various effects. You will say that terms or concepts like 'charge', 'current', 'potential difference', 'resistance', 'capacitance' and so on are metaphysical in origin, yet without them it is hard to see how a physicist could even *denote* electrical phenomena, let alone make any useful discoveries about them.

Cause   Quite so. What went for Newton's second law goes for Ohm's law too: it should be seen not as a discovery about electrical conduction but as a determination to interpret conduction in terms of 'potential difference' and 'current' and 'resistance'.

Effect   So if such 'metaphysics' is necessarily involved in any coherent physics, even at this macroscopic level, what point is there in drawing a distinction between the two? Indeed, *can* such a distinction be drawn?

Cause Of course it can! I repeat: the fact that the borderline between two countries is disputed or undemarcated makes distinction between the two countries more rather than less important.

Effect But what we have here is not a borderline between two different areas of study, but an inextricable entanglement, a necessary inter-relationship between a vast body of purely observational data...

Cause 'Physics'.

Effect And a, a conceptual scheme or language in terms of which this data can be interpreted, described, compared, classified and then, if we are lucky, its patterns identified.

Cause There you are you see! You yourself are drawing the distinction! The very fact that you can speak on the one hand of 'purely observational data' and on the other of 'conceptual schemes' demonstrates that the distinction is meaningful to you. It was the same, we discovered, with the mind/body problem: the fact that the criteria of objects' physicality can only be expressed in terms of their perceivability by minds and that the existence of mentality can be evidenced only by displays of physical behaviour does not in any way blur or weaken or invalidate the distinction between physicality and mentality, what it does is to demonstrate their essential *complementarity*.

Effect Doesn't it also demonstrate that there can be no such thing as *purely* observational data, or *purely* empirical evidence?

Cause Maybe it does. Of course. Perhaps we do not attain knowledge of the physical world, or knowledge of any kind, *just* through the senses or *just* through the intellect. The mind is not just a sensor, nor just a thinker. The senses and the intellect are, again, interdependent, complementary.

Effect A marriage, a working compromise.

Cause I don't however, like your use of the word 'inextricable'. Firstly, even if one accepts that some metaphysical structure or other is bound to be involved in anything that can count as a physics, if only by virtue of being expressed in a language, it is by no means clear *to what extent* metaphysical principles and pictures need be involved. I have a hunch that a great deal of our present physics could in fact get along perfectly well without a great many of the metaphysical structures it presently embodies and that such a 'disentanglement' might in fact prove a lot less painful and less difficult than you seem to imagine.

The Litterbin of History

Effect   Oh yes?

Cause   Secondly, the fact, if it is a fact, that *some* metaphysics will always be necessary must not confuse us by its use of the trick-word 'some' into concluding that *this* or *that* or *the other* metaphysical principle or theory or picture is indispensible, the ones we happen to be employing at the moment for example. The history of science remember, is littered with the wreckage of 'conceptual schemes' and 'explanatory languages' that have been superseded and discarded.

Effect   Well of course Newtonian physics, which strictly speaking has now been superseded by that of Einstein, provides us with a, a classic example of this.

Cause   Thirdly, it must therefore always behove us to try to distinguish, as far as is possible, our physical data from our metaphysical system of interpretation and to examine the latter critically.

Effect   We do though Andrew, we do. Scientists are always in the market for neater explanatory devices, for better conceptual schemes. As you say, history is littered with scientific theories that have been proved wrong or inadequate, or inferior to other theories.

Cause   Fourthly, we must not slide lazily to the conclusion that there are no further frontiers to be marked or distinctions to be drawn or choices to be made *within* this wide-ranging territory we have hastily labelled 'metaphysics'. It is one thing to come up with logico-linguistic schemes which help us to describe, pattern and classify the enormous variety of physical phenomena, it is quite another to start drawing up imaginary landscapes of definitively non-observable particles, forces and what-have-yous. In doing the latter we are embarking, it seems to me, on nothing less than an excursion into purely speculative metaphysics.

Effect   But I thought we had agreed that the distinction between observable and non-observable phenomena is by no means clear-cut, that it is impossible to draw a line?

Cause   What we have agreed Malcolm, is that there are important perceptual horizons, lots of them: microscopes, X-rays, electron beams, particle tracks, you name it. Sometimes, frontiers need to be *policed*... Oh damn! The bastards!

Effect   What is it?

Cause They've put up the barriers! They've put up the barriers in the car-park! They can't do that! They've locked my bloody motor in!

Effect Oh Lord, I'll never get my train now!

Cause Don't worry, don't worry, I'll get out of this somehow.

Effect What? Up a ten-foot wall?

Cause I'll just have to push one of the barriers over.

Effect Oh come off it!

Cause Why not, I've had these sort of buggers down before... Erghhh... Erghhhh...

Effect You'll never do it, they're brand-new.

Cause Erghhhhhhhhh... I know, I'll bend them with the car.

Effect Don't be ridiculous, they're probably set in three foot of concrete, you'll just bend the car; especially that one.

Cause I'll hacksaw the padlock... Oh damn! I gave my blade to that chimp!

Effect Forget it Andrew, forget it. Come back in the morning.

Cause But what about you, how are you going to get home?

Effect I'll have to get a taxi I suppose.

Cause That'll be expensive. I know what: if we walk back to my flat I can borrow my landlord's van. He won't mind, I often use it.

Effect Really? Are you sure?

Cause Certainly. No trouble. I've got some hooch at home as well.

Effect How far is it?

Cause Not far. Ten minutes. Fifteen maybe.

Effect Okay, but one thing: I must phone Constance. She'll be wondering where I am.

Cause   Tell her you're working late.

Effect   Certainly not, I'll tell her the truth... Ah, there's a phone-box on the corner...

＊　＊　＊　＊　＊　＊　＊　＊　＊　＊　＊

Cause   Alright? Is she okay about it?

Effect   She's, er, watching telly. She says she's quite happy.

Cause   Uhuh? And you believe her?

Effect   Of course, why shouldn't I?

Cause   Will Ella be there? I'd like to meet her, see how she's enjoying the course. We may even have crossed paths at some point...

Effect   Don't you dare! She's in enough trouble already.

Cause   Trouble, what do you mean, trouble?

Effect   Oh, er, nothing really... She's aways been a, a difficult girl. She mixes with the wrong sort... It's, it's a worry...

Cause   Ahh! What a beautiful evening! No Moon at all! Great! I love walking in the town at night.

Effect   Mmm, me too... Tell me though Andrew, what is your purpose in drawing this distinction between physics and metaphysics? What do you hope to gain, what are you trying to prove? I mean suppose I were to agree with you, were to concede the metaphysical status of atoms, what then?

Cause   Ah, then I will say and do a number of things!

Effect   Such as?

Cause   Firstly I will say: since it is metaphysics you are into, leave it to the metaphysicians.

Effect   But I thought your point was that we scientists *are* the metaphysicians now? Or perhaps it should be the 'metaphysicists'?

Cause   It doesn't matter who does the metaphysics Malcolm, or what they are called, so long as they get it right.

Effect   Get it right? How do you mean, get it right?

Cause   So long as they deploy at least *some* philosophical understanding of the key metaphysical relationships, such as those between mind and body, causality and probability, freedoms and values, perception and intelligence, physical objectivity and imagination, language and the world, practical knowledge and moral knowledge and so on.

Effect   Everything we have been talking about, in other words.

Cause   So long as they provide a metaphysics which *helps* in some way, a metaphysics which *works*.

Effect   But surely, whatever else you may be able to say about the scientists' atoms/particles/cosmic-forces metaphysics, it has certainly proved to be a metaphysics which *works*! I can see that one could argue over the authenticity of its claims to truth, over its wider moral and religious significance and even over the comprehensibility, plausibility and consistency of its models and its theories, but one thing you simply cannot deny is its extraordinary *usefulness*.

Cause   Usefulness? Useful to whom? Useful for what?

Effect   Oh come on Andrew, one thing no-one can knock, not even you, is the recent remarkable wholesale *technological* advance that scientific theories have brought about. Whatever you may say about the metaphysical inadequacies and incoherence of our atomic and particle theories, they have undoubtedly generated in macroscopic physics an extraordinary number of discoveries of enormously wide practical importance.

Cause   But important physical discoveries can *only* be macroscopic discoveries, and as far as these go, I suggest that atomic theories are neither here nor there. It may be of course, that on some occasions in the past a scientist having in his mind's eye a certain mental model of an atomic world has been inspired to put forward a new hypothesis relating observable phenomena which has subsequently been confirmed empirically, but in these rare cases what the scientist has discovered is not that a particular model of the atom is correct but that a hitherto undiscovered relation exists between certain observable phenomena. What is important as far as physics is concerned is *this* new relation, not any mental model that may or may not have inspired the scientist's discovery. The ways discoveries are arrived at may be interesting, but they are interesting from a psychological, not a physical, point of view.

Effect   What then, do you believe it a mere *coincidence* that the atomic theory has generated so many discoveries?

Cause   I deny that it has, Malcolm, I deny that it has. Cases like that one we are envisaging are in fact extremely rare in the history of science. It seems to me that far more common and important inspirations to discovery-making than any mental picturings are (a) past experience, experimental skill and hard work, (b) intelligent exercise of the imagination in the light of (a) and (c) happy accidents and good luck. As a scientist, you must know that nine times out of ten it is the discovery of a new observable phenomenon, of a new relation between physical events that comes first and the contrivance of an atomic 'explanation' that comes afterwards. In practice, the atomic theory is pretty well incapable of predicting anything in the way of new macroscopic relationships; as far as that goes an intelligent guess, based perhaps upon observations of known phenomena in similar circumstances, is generally more reliable and relied on than any predictions worked out according to the equations of atomic structure. In either case, *it is the experiment that counts.*

Effect   Well at least we can agree on *that*!

Cause   Further, when such a discovery *is* made it rarely even roughly 'fits in with' existing atomic theory. Quite often, atomic predictions are altogether confounded by a series of experiments on some new effect, in which case the theoretical explanations and models have to be further stretched and contorted and fudged in order to fit the new facts. Factors which had before been thought irrelevant are now brought into consideration, or are even invented for the purpose; new hypotheses are proposed or discarded ones retrieved; they get round it somehow; they get round everything somehow, they have to. The archaeology of science reveals a history of fudge-factors layered upon fudge-factors.

Effect   No, this is just not fair. There are many examples of important hypotheses concerning atomic structure being proved true by experiment.

Cause   But remember that we only hear about the successful hypotheses *afterwards*. Surrounding any new mystery at the time there may be a dozen or more rival hypotheses claiming to explain the facts and each may 'predict' a different set of results in certain other experiments. Later, when these experiments have been carried out and the closest hypothesis is hailed as the correct one, it can look as though the results were remarkably well predicted. The point is that later we hear only the story of the hypothesis that won.

Effect   And isn't this the perfectly correct way for scientific investigation to proceed?

Cause   Remember also that there are plenty of patterns and plenty of symmetries in nature, just as there are plenty of surprises and plenty of *a*symmetries, so a necessarily ordered atomic theory is bound to reflect certain of these. Before you marvel, for example, at how brilliantly the Rutherford-Bohr model of the atom can explain the symmetries of the Periodic Table, remember that it was the Periodic Table that came first and that it was a host of practical chemical discoveries that came before that. We must not forget the chronology of our scientific inheritance, the way in which it happens to have happened.

Effect   But it hasn't just *happened*!

Cause   Suppose radioactivity had been discovered before magnetism, or Newton had known of cathode rays... It even occurs to me that this whole atomic-model-constructing game may actually be *counter*-productive, as far as empirical-discovery-making is concerned. There is the danger that in instituting *a* model, a *particular* theory of atomic structure, *the* Periodic Table, although you may thereby be emphasizing certain symmetries and patterns, you may also thereby be *obscuring* certain symmetries and patterns too. If you adopt *a* model, you will become predisposed to expect and seek certain sorts of relationship between certain sorts of phenomenon, you will tend to prejudge certain sorts of empirically-testable hypotheses as entertainable and certain other sorts as non-entertainable, and your scientific eyes will begin to look only in certain predetermined directions. In short, your imagination could easily become over-programmed by too settled an atomic theory.

Effect   But this is ridiculous! You are going on about the atomic theory as though it had been dreamt up on a whim, as though you could propose an alternative model with just a flick of your philosophical fingers! You don't seem to realize that our present knowledge of the atomic world has been acquired only through years and years of infinitely painstaking experimentation, through the careful amassing of enormous quantities of data, through an endless process of testing proposed hypotheses against observed facts, through a gradual but steady evolution of the theory's details and certainties. Many thousands of the most brilliant men and women in history have devoted their lives and energies to this slow and meticulous task.

Cause   Think again of the 'cold fusion' claims: you said you were *always* sceptical of them. Your doubt was *predisposed*, even despite the fact that their suggested explanation is couched within your own scientific, atomic terms. To me however, it seems entirely plausible that the breakthrough should come from an unpredicted, unlikely direction, out of the path of the juggernaut. This 'fits in' perfectly with the history of scientific discovery.

Effect   Though I can imagine it may one day seem crude and sketchy, our present atomic model is a wonderful scientific achievement, a monument to centuries of experimental skill and intellectual insight. And now you come along, not even a physicist but a philosopher, with, as far as I can see, hardly any knowledge or understanding of atomic theory and no experimental evidence whatever, and with little more than a few half-clever arguments and an arrogant wave of the hand you try to dismiss the whole enterprise as some kind of grand mistake or peculiar religious folly. I've never heard anything so absurd and naïve in my life! How can you possibly just *write off* atomic theory like this!?

Cause   Philosophers' prerogative old boy. This is the risk you run when you start messing about with metaphysics, when you try tangling with the gods. After all, it would not be the first time that a culture's brightest intellects had for centuries devoted themselves to theorizing and expounding and preaching a theology that was later to become regarded as irrelevant and valueless.

Effect   Irrelevant and valueless!? How can you seriously suggest that one of the key theories of modern science is irrelevant and valueless!? Its value and its relevance are evident all around us! Look down this street: modern buildings using modern construction techniques and new materials; motor cars, motor bikes, machines of all sorts over there on that building site; listen, up there, an aeroplane; everywhere, electric lighting.

Cause   Technology, Malcolm, mere technology.

Effect   What do you mean, *mere* technology!?

Cause   As far as I am concerned, these things have as little to do with the correctness or otherwise of your metaphysical theories as the architectural pre-eminence of the great European cathedrals has or had to do with the plausibility of Christian theological beliefs. Besides, none of the technological wonders you mention is particularly new anyway. The principles of construction are as old as civilization itself. Building techniques are a good example, I would have thought, of a practical science that has changed hardly at all in thousands of years. Even its materials haven't changed: stone, bricks, mortar, iron, timber, glass. Some improvements in technique and speediness, sure, a plastic gutter here and there, a detail or two, but otherwise nothing in this street is essentially new and certainly there is nothing in it that owes its existence to modern *atomic* theory; indeed I would guess that most of these buildings actually pre-date the theory, and by quite a while. Again, as far as motor cars and aeroplanes go, these innovations owe nothing whatsoever to any *meta*physical speculations, but are the brainchildren of those old and well-established macroscopic sciences Mechanics, Dynamics and Aerodynamics. Our recent practical realization of them is due, above all, to our improved metal-working and engine-building techniques. Think of the modern motor car. Most of the important physical effects it employs are as old as the hills: the function of the piston, the burning of hydrocarbons, the principles of gears and hydraulics, the reduction of friction by lubrication; the Greeks had a pretty good understanding of these ages ago.

Effect   Oh yes? Any minute now you'll be claiming that the internal combustion engine was invented by Aristotle!

Cause   Archimedes more like. And surely Heraclitus had a hand in mine... Seriously though, a motor car is a machine, not a metaphysical theory. I think if one were to draw up a 'top ten' of the most significant technological discoveries that man has made, perhaps six or seven of them would be actually pre*historic*, never mind pre-the-rise-of-modern-science: the use of the wheel; the controlling of fire and the smelting of metals; the development of written languages and later, of printing; the application of mathematics and measurement; the principles of agriculture; construction techniques; the principles of levers, gears, hydraulics. The people who first made these discoveries and started using these techniques as likely as not believed that the world was inhabited by spirits or presided over by gods or consisted of Fire, Air, Earth and Water. It does not matter to the engineer what the metaphysicians tell him about the nature of the world, his concrete, his steel, his petroleum: whether it is sustained by God's Love, consists of charmed and anti-charmed quark triplets or is held together by minute invisible philosophers all digging the music, for as long as he knows *his* stuff, his bridges will continue to stand, his cars will continue to run and his planes will continue to fly, and that of course, is what matters.

Effect   And what about the street lamps? Electric light? The car's spark system and self-starter? What about electric motors and generators?

Cause   I did say six or seven out of the ten. Obviously, the discovery and harnessing of electromagnetism and all its effects has been a recent development of enormous significance and usefulness. But again, it is worth remembering that the initial, crucial discoveries in this field, the production and control of electric currents and of the various effects of conduction, were made a while before any *electronic* theory got going and long before anyone could claim to have 'discovered' the electron. The very word 'current' gives away the game: electricity, like heat, was originally thought of as a *fluid*.

Effect Okay, what about our control and use of electromagnetic radiations – Radio, Radar, X-rays? What about thermionic emission, cathode ray tubes, television?

Cause Wonderful and useful discoveries Malcolm, but all discoveries which arose out of practical electrical experimentation and which owe nothing to particular theories about the nature of matter. Rather it is the other way round: it was the discovery of the various phenomena and effects which these technologies exploit that gave rise to rival theories about the make-up of the atomic world. Did you not yourself admit that some phenomena seem to support a particle and others a wave account of electrons? The various devices of course continue to work whatever the theorists choose to say.

Effect Yes, but how were these devices first perfected? What about the years and years of painstaking research and experimentation and amassing of data?

Cause What about them? Look please don't get me wrong, I am not for one moment decrying all the marvellous practical achievements that physics and chemistry and the other sciences have accumulated over the past two hundred years, what I am questioning is the soundness of some of their metaphysical assumptions and conclusions. Obviously the years of painstaking research to which you refer have expanded enormously our body of physical knowledge and have proved invaluable in our mastering of many new and extremely useful techniques. But we must not be misled by this recent rapid expansion of our physics and technology into imagining that this new knowledge has bestowed upon us any important new *meta*physical insight. Don't be fooled Malcolm, clever priests have always used technological conjuring tricks to impress laymen with the power of their religion. I have even read a theory that Christ himself was trained as a conjuror; apparently in ancient Hebrew the word was synonymous with 'carpenter' – the man who made the magic boxes.

Effect But don't you think the fact that we can now perform these wonderful tricks demonstrates that *we now know more about things*?

Cause   Of course it does. But again we must be careful with this phrase 'know more about things'. The only things we can know about empirically are perceivable things. The achievement of modern science has been vastly to improve our description of how perceivable things behave. It has compiled huge quantities of detailed data, it has greatly increased the accuracy of measurements and the precision of procedures, it has catalogued countless physical phenomena and has identified many of their inter-relationships. But physics, I repeat, can answer only 'What happens when?' questions, never 'Why?' questions. 'Why?' questions, in any case, do not trouble the technologist. Pseudo-questions of the form "Why do things behave as they do?" are of no concern to the engineer who builds bridges or cars or TV sets, for as long as they do, these things will continue to work.

Effect   But in order to build a TV set or an X-ray machine that works, the engineer needs to know why this and that and the other happen, he has to know an enormous amount of electronic theory, he must understand a...

Cause   A specialized language, a particular algebra? He must be able to read circuit diagrams? How much electronic theory do you imagine is known by the printed-circuit stamping-machine operators and the cathode-ray-tube assemblers who *do* actually build our TV sets and our X-ray machines? Isn't skill with a soldering iron in fact a more useful asset?

Effect   But Andrew, you are talking about people just imitating and repeating procedures, copying designs.

Cause   That's right, people doing things, people making things.

Effect   But the question is: how were the designs arrived at?

Cause   That's *a* question, certainly. But I suggest, and in the end this may be impossible to prove one way or the other, that your atoms-and-particles metaphysics has had a great deal less to do with our arrival at these designs than you seem to imagine. One point to make is that far more often than not it is the man engaged in doing or making things rather than the theorist who stumbles upon the important new physical discoveries. It is always the physical discoveries that come first, the metaphysical 'explanations' that come later.

Effect   So you see no link between our 'metaphysical theories' as you call them, and our practical technologies?

Cause   No direct link, no.

Boots on Feet

Effect   An *in*direct link though?

Cause   An indirect link, yes, maybe. Obviously our beliefs about atoms, insofar as they are features of the way in which we see the world, affect in a very broad, subtle, philosophical way how we behave and conduct our lives, the most noticeable symptoms being traits like one's choice of reading matter, certain ways of speaking, odd rituals. This is not to say that such broad, subtle, over-a-period characteristics of behaviour are unimportant, no no, for they can move mountains, can change the world more thoroughly than any of the inventions of physics.

Effect   Seriously though, you see no more direct link than this?

Cause   No, not really. Indeed it seems to me that if anything, this particular boot would fit better on my foot than on yours, for if there were such a link, your metaphysics would be failing miserably to live up to its pretensions. Do you not think it odd that while the particle physicists claim to be learning about the realm of *sub-sub*-atomic particles and talk as though all the questions about the higher realms have long since been understood and solved, most of our practical chemistry in fact still remains largely prehistoric, never mind pre-atomic-theory. Remember, we still have to burn fuel to keep warm, to plough fields for our food, to climb hills on our journeys. We still have to dig the ground for our coal and our iron and our oil; even for our diamonds and our gold.

Effect   What about nuclear power?

Cause   We have to dig the ground for our uranium too, if it comes to that.

Effect   No, I mean don't you think that our harnessing of nuclear energy, in a power station for instance, counts as a significant new technology, a candidate for your top ten?

Cause   Oh most definitely, yes, number ten. Note however the extraordinarily messy and clumsy method we still use, even in nuclear power stations, to turn heat into electrical energy. Does the heat exchanger/steam-turbine/generator/cooling-tower system honestly seem to you like the technology of a metaphysics that's got its finger on the cosmic pulse?

Effect   I agree, but what about the power source, the controlled nuclear reaction? You can hardly deny that *this* is an example of a technology that has resulted directly from the establishment of a particular, nuclear theory of atomic structure. The very name of the process proves that!

Cause   We call the Sun 'the Sun', so what? I don't see that there need be any direct link between the use of this technology and a belief in any particular atomic scenario. What happens happens. Christians and atheists design cars, mend TV sets and build nuclear piles in exactly the same ways; their god-beliefs do not affect the way they *do* things one jot, not directly. I suppose one might go on to suggest that atheists are more likely to be car-designers, TV-repairers and nuclear physicists while Christians are more likely to be social workers, nurses and foreign-aid officials but even a generalization as vague and flippant as this soon proves hopelessly shaky: Christians, it seems, can make perfectly good plasma-researchers too.

Effect   Oh not again! This attempt you are making to equate our knowledge of atomic structure with people's religious beliefs is specious, jejune and insulting. These are two quite different sorts of language altogether, about two quite different sorts of reality.

Cause   Exactly Malcolm, exactly! That is the whole trouble! Do you see no conflict here, do you see no problem? Your two different languages-cum-world-views live side-by-side, yet never meet... Man has an enormous capacity for double-talk and double-think: not only are his claims to knowledge about the nature of matter way behind his practical technologies, but also his fine moral arguments and principles bear no relation at all to the ways in which he actually carries on in the world. Christians apparently, can not only build perfectly good nuclear power stations, they can also drop perfectly good nuclear bombs.

Effect   But look Andrew, Christians can successfully build nuclear power stations only because they have studied and understood the laws, sorry, the principles of nuclear physics. The Christian's nuclear physics is the same as the atheist's. The power stations could not be built without an advanced, coherent, experimentally-validated theory of nuclear atomic structure.

Cause   Nonsense, even illiterate peasants, people who have no words in their own vocabulary for 'atom' or 'nucleus' or 'radiation' can be taught how to build a uranium pile. That is half the trouble. That and the fact that our politicians have a habit of behaving like illiterate peasants.

Effect   Absurd! Men would only be able to build a successful nuclear reactor if they had studied and understood the theories of nuclear physics.

Cause   Learnt to speak the language of nuclear physics, you mean. In the end isn't it all a matter of just reading formulae and repeating procedures?

The Well Now Dry?

Effect   But again the point is that without some detailed insight into atomic structure the formulae would never have been arrived at, such a sophisticated programme of procedures would never have been initiated. Of course not, the idea is preposterous! What do you think Einstein was doing when he came up with his theory of special relativity, ploughing fields?

Cause   Scratching away on bits of paper I imagine, or maybe sitting on a mountainside. I don't know Malcolm, what does it matter?

Effect   Anyway, like it or not, our harnessing of nuclear power is incontrovertibly, undeniably, a clear example of a radically new technology that arose directly from the adoption of a certain nuclear model of atomic structure.

Cause   Hmm... I'm sure you over-simplify the picture, and I suggest that nothing in the case can be proved either way. However, suppose I grant you that these theories *have* helped in one way and another, that your models *have* been useful on some occasions and to some extent and that all this *has* led to a discovery or two; these claims are all in the past tense. The question is: are the old theories of any further use to us *now*, are the old models going to afford us any great *new* discoveries? Or has their metaphysical fertility perhaps been exhausted, their well of fresh physical applications perhaps dried up? Look: since our triumphant harnessing of uranium-fission back in the thirties, what have we had from you? Nothing, nothing, fifty years of nothing!

Effect   What do you mean, nothing? The last fifty years have seen the most extraordinarily rapid technological progress! What about the developments in solid-state circuitry, transistors and semiconductors? What about lasers?

Cause   The discovery of the transistor, the solid-state replacement for the thermionic valve has obviously proved to be a breakthrough of enormous significance in the field of practical electronics, but I believe that this arose as a result more of certain detailed electrochemical experimentation than of any great new insights into the nature of matter. The phenomenon of stimulated emission upon which lasers depend, was known about as long ago as the 1920s. Our new ability to exploit this effect is the result firstly of vastly-improved equipment and secondly of a great deal of patient trial-and-error; I know, I have a friend who's a bit of an expert in the field. He tells me that even for him the phenomenon of atomic lasing is in many respects still quite mysterious and unexplained in terms of the existing theory; the gap between the physics and the metaphysics is acknowledged.

Effect What about space-travel, landing men on the Moon?

Cause Wonderful Malcolm, very impressive, but surely the principles of this technology are as old as Hell? Monstrous great rockets belching fire and molten metal just to get you a mile or two off the ground!? Just so men in baggy suits can go blundering about with spades and spanners and flags? Of course the scale of the engineering is fantastic, the precision of the guidance-systems, the bravery and skill of the astronauts, I don't doubt any of that, but the basic physics seems exceedingly Newtonian and certainly the morality that is fuelling the enterprise is as old as history itself.

Effect But look in these shops: Video recorders! Compact Disc players! Calculators! Computers! Where do you think all this comes from?

Cause Japan, Hong Kong, Korea...

Effect Do you really imagine that all these remarkable machines got here through men meditating in monasteries muttering "cogito ergo sum"?

Cause Careful what you say Malcolm, Descartes was also the father of modern mathematics, of your body of atomic calculus... Look: video recording: the capability of storing encoded information on magnetic tapes or discs is well pre-war, its recent dramatic new applications are mainly the result of our enormous improvements in tape and head engineering. Compact discs: mass-production of laser technology. Silicon chip microcircuits: the product of (a) the astonishing microscopic accuracy of modern semiconductor-etching-machines, (b) circuitry principles as old as steam radio and (c) market, and of course military, forces. Nothing new about adding-up and multiplying; nothing new about saying yes or no; two fingers to decimal counting and off you go! Multiply chips and you get calculators. Multiply calculators and you get computers. Multiply computers and... I suppose eventually you might get a machine big enough to handle the unemployment figures!

Effect I'm not so pessimistic Andrew. I see computers offering us enormous benefits, as having tremendous potential for good. They can relieve us of all kinds of dreary routine drudgeries, in domestic appliances, on production lines, in offices...

Cause On battlefields, in command bunkers... How nice! A drudgery-free World War Three! The ultimate labour-saving technology!

Artifice or Intelligence?

Effect Already with computers we can handle prodigious quantities of information so quickly, so conveniently, so efficiently! My sort of work would be unthinkable without them. Besides, I thought computers were of great interest to modern philosophers in that they provide a model of how our brain processes work, insights into how our intelligence imposes a conceptual framework on the sensory information it receives, a picture of how data is synthesized by the optic lobe into the ordered coherence of an external reality against which...

Cause Oh not again! A.I. radar trying to tell the friendly missiles from foes'? Give us a break! Imagine all the trickeries! Already you've been fooled Malcolm, even by the jargon! Okay, so computer-theory has provided us with some new language-games, some logical fun, a few fashionable phrases, but it hasn't taught us how to *see*! Quite the reverse, by the sound of it. Look in that window, look, there's a computer! What do you see? A tatty plastic keyboard for scribbling on a screen! Artificial Intelligence, pah! Robots' moral rights, pah! *They'll* never have to stand shivering for hours in icy English dole-queues; *they'll* never have to trek for weeks for crumbs of food in the arid African desert; *they'll* never breathe sweet companionship in another's ear or make hot love in sweaty Mediterranean siestas!

Effect Nor they will, but nonetheless computers are extraordinarily useful. Don't you use one for your writing? I find mine a real boon.

Cause I'm sure, I know, my Dad's got one. I still find it quicker with a scalpel and glue.

Effect Well that shows that you're not using it properly. I use computers on a daily basis, for things like tabulating results and writing papers, and they absolutely transform my life. Even my wife who is the most unmechanical being in the world is now writing a book on a word-processor having sworn she'd never touch one. It's so easy to edit things, to correct errors, to rearrange material.

Cause I fear that my problems of error-correction and rearrangement are of another kind altogether; typing is the least of my worries. Besides, I can't afford one.

Effect 'Processing Words', how about that for your book-title?

Cause Not bad, not bad... I am reminded of a recent Queen's Christmas speech in which she extolled the virtues of all our brilliant new communi-

Understanding Matters

cation techniques but then admitted that we seem to be finding it very difficult to work out what to say to one another. Of course the irony was that
her rather touching, bewildered non-message was instantly satellite-beamed
right round the Globe... No Malcolm, marvellous though all these
machines and technologies may be, they tell us nothing about the correctness or otherwise of our metaphysics.

Effect But this is ridiculous! I can see that *whatever* technology or physical discovery we come up with, even if we build a machine which turns
sea-water into sunshine, you will say we know no metaphysics!

Cause That's right! Exactly! You're catching on at last! Since all these
things – the machines, the silicon chips, the sea-water, the sunshine – since
they are all perceivable, since they all feature in the observable world
which your theory of non-observable atoms and the rest has been invoked
to 'explain', they by themselves can get us no closer to any understanding
of the nature of matter.

Effect But as far as I am concerned, 'understanding the nature of matter'
means being able to manipulate it in such ways, what else could it mean?
The fact that we have mastered all these techniques *demonstrates* that we
know a fair bit about atomic structure.

Cause And so we are back with behaviourism again, where knowing and
understanding consist not in storing in one's head or one's library catalogues of facts nor even in picturing in one's mind a particular atomic
model, but in being able to *do* certain things. Once again, positivism has
come up with an awkward inconsistency in its own paradigm.

Effect So what then? Apparently *nothing* I could do would demonstrate
an understanding of your precious 'metaphysics'.

Cause Well you could at least start talking sense... Besides, all the things
you've been mentioning are by-products of physical or technological discoveries that were made long ago. None of them owes anything to this
mass of absurd new particle theory. You still haven't even managed to control simple hydrogen-fusion, something you've been promising us for fifty
years!

Effect We will though, we will. In reactions like this, one is dealing with
enormously high energies, extreme conditions, an extraordinarily complex
balance of critical factors. The research is bound to take time. We are getting there slowly, step by step, experiment by experiment.

361

Down the Wrong Road

Cause   Exactly, experiment by experiment, trial-and-error by trial-and-error. No thanks whatever to any of your grandiose cosmological theories. What about all this high-energy research that's been going on for years now? What have you to show for it? Nothing! Nothing! Not one single quark's worth of useful information! And it's not for want of trying, or of funding: everyone wants to be first with the next bomb. Thanks to Einstein and Co. the scientist himself has become something of a god, research is now an end in itself. But the only great leap forward has been in the size of the machines and of the budgets. Laboratories these days are the size of cities, research costs rival national economies. The new accelerators have become monstrous temples of public sacrifice. And all we get is words, words, words... I tell you Malcolm, we have gone down the wrong road, somewhere we have taken a wrong turning.

Effect   Hey, where *are* we going? Ten minutes you said! We must have been walking for half an hour.

Cause   It was all your gadget-talk, it slowed us down.

Effect   But we've gone right through the town! I'm beginning to suspect this flat of yours is metaphysical!

Cause   It's not much further Malcolm, honestly.

Effect   I'll believe it when I see it... Tell me this then: where does Einstein fit into your definition? Was he a physicist in your opinion, or a meta-physician?

Cause   I don't know. A bit of both I suppose. He was more of a mathematician than an experimenter though wasn't he, more at home in a study than a laboratory? You tell me.

Effect   His theories of relativity were mathematical theories, certainly, but they were not idle algebraic doodlings, they were to be tested in the world, the world where it has been shown experimentally that the speed of light is a finite and universal constant.

Cause   Has it been, conclusively? Couldn't those Michelson-Morley experiments always turn out to have been misinterpreted, or incomplete?

Effect   Yes I suppose so, but until they are... Although Einstein was a geometrician, his new, non-Cartesian geometry predicted certain specific empirically-verifiable and subsequently verified observable effects. Relativity makes various apparently bizarre, counter-intuitive predictions

362

about the behaviour at high speeds of clocks and measuring rods and observers.

Cause   Exactly, of clocks and measuring rods and observers, of physical objects.

Effect   Yes, but of course Einstein's analysis, his model, was all in terms of the behaviour of particles in force-fields. Indeed it was his great hope that he would one day be able to unify the calculi of gravitation and electromagnetism into a single set of equations of particle-interaction, a unified field theory. Unfortunately he never succeeded.

Cause   Huh. And since then, muddle: the fundamental forces have multiplied, the particle families have bred like rabbits, the quanta have become legion. Yet still you dream of your 'grand synthesis'.

Effect   Of course, the more plurality there is in the picture, the greater becomes the need for a unifying model.

Cause   I hereby christen the ultimate fundamental particle 'the Zeno'.

Effect   But the point all along is that in physics the success of any model, the validity of any theory will depend not upon any intuitive or philosophical appeal it may have, but only upon its ability to fit the experimental facts. It is my turn for a quotation. Einstein said:

> I am convinced that the philosophers have had a harmful effect upon the progress of scientific thinking in removing certain fundamental concepts from the domain of empiricism, where they are under our control, to the intangible heights of the *a priori*... This is particularly true of our concepts of time and space, which physicists have been obliged by the facts to bring down from the Olympus of the *a priori*...

Cause   To the insensible depths of the analytic. And where have physicists removed the fundamental concepts of mentality and freedom and moral goodness?

Effect   In other words: you philosophers get on with your philosophy, leave us physicists to get on with the physics. We will decide *empirically* what metaphysical models and explanatory langauges are appropriate. To echo Wittgenstein: don't think, look!

Cause   So the speed of light is finite and constant, so what? I can handle that! I sometimes think I can even visualize your non-visualizable geometry. You talk of relativity's predictions being 'bizarre' and 'counter-intuitive', but what would be an *intuitive* expectation of the behaviour of a clock or an observer travelling at near the speed of light? You stress the word 'empirically' yet you use it in connection with 'models' and 'paradigms' and 'explanatory languages'. Einstein wisely mistrusts *a priori* assumptions yet he uses the phrases "scientific thinking" and "fundamental concepts". You both recognize that there are choices to be made: "under our control" says Einstein, "we decide" say you. And of course these decisions are, at least in part intellectual decisions, rational decisions, decisions about ideas, about concepts, about language. You physicists are involved in philosophy willy-nilly, whether you like it or not. You *need* philosophy.

Effect   Like a hole in the head!

Cause   Like a super-ego, a hand on the tiller. It's no good just intoning this word 'empirically' for ever. Look at what you're now calling 'experiments'! Look at what you're now calling 'evidence'! Don't you see that it is you scientists, you particle-men who have become the rationalists now, the men who dream up the abstract logical worlds, who believe in a higher existence where all is perfectly mathematical, who regard the realm of the senses as being an inferior, third-order reality of mere appearance. This is Plato! This is the Cave! These are the shadows on the wall! What an irony: the positivists' paragons the scientists have actually evolved into their old arch-enemy.

Effect   Okay, particle physics is now extremely complex and mathematical, but it does have experiment and observation as its ultimate validation.

Cause   Can you honestly still say that? Hasn't your whole metaphysical juggernaut got lost, or ground to a halt? Plato, after all, could have claimed that his scheme was validated by experiment and observation too, in a very general way; it was just that his observations went beyond what you call physics to include the experimentally-validated fact that he was a human being, a free agent and possessed of a moral sense. Remember that at the summit of Plato's epistemological hierarchy, above even the truths of logic and mathematics, there shines the Absolutely Good. I mean what's it all about this 'trying to explain' the world? Rationalism must *make sense* of Empiricism, just as Empiricism must keep Rationalism's eyes open and feet on the ground. It is not Empiricism *versus* Rationalism, it is rather that they are essentially...

Effect   *Complementary* by any chance?

Cause   Yes... but no, 'complementary' is too weak, too cosmetic a word. It is more that they form a... a necessary duality. Oh dear, words are so useless... I know, think of sexuality: without *both* of the sexes there can be no offspring.

Effect   Trust you! A *sexist* theory of knowledge!

Cause   Why not, it works, doesn't it? The trouble with you scientists is that you study just science. Science, science, science, and then you *arrive at* metaphysical problems, equipped only with your inherited preconceptions, your inherited language. You start dabbling in metaphysics without having served any apprenticeship. Result: catastrophic failure. You have built a metaphysical castle in the air: no coherent plan, no sound foundations, no longer any solid basis in the real world. A castle which de-materializes as soon as anyone sets foot in it. A castle which in any case is now collapsing internally under the weight of its own over-ornate and over-extended superstructure.

Effect   Okay, so what's *your* metaphysics? Half-baked animism? "The Earth is a person"? That's not going to get us very far is it? Go on, give us a laugh, let's hear Andrew Cause's theory of atomic structure!

Cause   But do we *need* such models any more? This, it occurs to me, is where computers *can* be a big help, where they *can* initiate a philosophical revolution. This whole exercise of trying to concoct atomic and particle models of physical substance, of attempting mathematically to formularize phenomena, of seeking the laws which govern interactions, isn't all this pattern-hunting the only method that has hitherto been available for the storing of empirical knowledge? If we can institute a *law* of gaseous pressures or of gravitational attractions, we can in equations trap and condense huge quantities of experimental information. Never mind that there are exceptions to the rules, that in certain circumstances other factors come into play, that the graphs show strange curves, surprising breaks and unexpected concentrations, that in extreme conditions the 'laws' break down completely, these anomalies will be accommodated in other formulations, in other features of the model, perhaps in other models altogether. And so, as the body of our experimental information has grown and grown, our model-world has become steadily more complex, obscure and unilluminating. But *now*, with our prosect of unlimited computer-memory, all the empirical information can just be bunged on tape or disc, to be recalled at the push of a few buttons. Then if you want to know what happens when x meets y, simply punch in the various measurable conditions and bingo, out come the previously observed results! Let the computer spot the trends and patterns and relationships where it can, let the computer indicate any potentially promising lines of inquiry.

Effect   Something very like this is already happening, certainly in high-energy physics.

Cause   Great, so who needs the models? Who needs any mental pictures? Why embark on this obviously futile task of trying to read into the muddle some coherent metaphysical meaning? Why not just fish around amongst all the information for any phenomena that look as though they might prove useful to us, homo sapiens, and leave it at that? Why not simply *drop* all the atoms-and-particles-and-cosmic-forces talk?

Effect   But you don't understand Andrew! We can't possibly drop all that talk! It *is* the experimental information we feed into the computers, it is the very language of...

Cause   The present language. You see, you are even indoctrinating the computers to think in a certain way, to think atomically.

Effect   But how else can we think? Look: what is it rustling that litter? What is it inflating that tyre? What is it that I breathe in and out? This invisible air must be made of something... Again: what happens when ice melts to water and water boils to steam, and back again? Something must remain the same throughout these changes... What else can we conclude but that air and water are composed of *molecules*?

Cause   Yet already, in the little slip to this apparently innocent conclusion, something very odd has happened: an all-important phenomenon of our own realm, state-change, has been lost in that of our model. Molecules are conceived as tiny objects, are pictured as tiny solids. Somebody who now suggested that perhaps under certain circumstances water molecules themselves can liquefy and vaporize would be making a category-mistake. The implication is that state changes are something of a cosmic aberration and do not mark borderlines of any note in the greater scheme of things.

Effect   Well in a sense that's right. In cosmological terms these are very insignificant changes indeed, involving only the smallest exchanges of energy.

Cause   Yet to me they are borderlines of the very highest metaphysical importance. Firstly because they mark the precise points at which our perceptual hold over the physical world gives way to imagination and hypothesis, at which our descriptions of phenomena involve less in the way of ostensively-defined language and more in the way of metaphysical 'background' assumptions. Secondly because the moves from solid to liquid and from liquid to gas also mark the points at which physical substance itself releases step-by-step its hold upon any sort of identity.

Effect   Eh?

Cause   Physical-object-hood we have seen, is conceptually bound up with perceivability. It is also bound up with certain notions of identity. Identity not just in the sense we mentioned earlier in which no two objects are ever qualitatively exactly the same, but also in the sense that to be a physical object a thing must *persist* in space and time, with all that that entails: it must to some extent *last*. Also we noted, all physical objects age or change with time, so that the general stipulation of an object's persistence must be qualified by various more flexible, more detailed stipulations concerning spatio-temporal continuity. Of course the criteria for deciding at time t_2 whether an X is the same X one had known at an earlier time t_1 will vary greatly from X to X; think of billiard-balls, human beings, games, countries. Sometimes spatio-temporal continuity may not be the only, or even the most important indicator of persistent identity. It might perhaps be a general rule that the more purely physical an object, the more description of it is appropriate in b- rather than M-language, so the more important will be the spatio-temporal criteria. But, one is tempted to say, does not this common persistence of objects, their resistance to change, *in itself* constitute evidence of some sort of atomic personality? Surely nothing could persist that did not have an interest in itself, that was not aware of itself persisting, that did not conceive of itself as something?

Effect   What a load of mumbo-jumbo!

Cause   Ah, there's another one: Mumbo-Jumbo, an African tribal deity, a grotesquely-carved lump of wood they used to worship... But no, the point is that solids, including, I insist, panes of glass, have individual identities while fluids do not. Liquids cannot be counted, they can only be measured by volume or weight although they are still directly perceivable. Gases by contrast are *not* perceivable, they do not have physical properties or identities at all.

Effect   What!? Of course gases have physical properties! Of course they have identities! They have volumes, densities, weights, temperatures, pressures, optical and electrical characteristics, chemical properties! And what do you mean by saying that they are not perceivable? Can you not feel the wind, see a flame, smell a... smell? Of course gases have properties!

An Imaginary Boat

Cause   Hmm, "gases have properties", "Oxygen has properties *A*, *B* and *C*". *What* has properties exactly? And what do we mean by 'having properties' here? Is not all such talk just shorthand, admittedly useful shorthand, for a lot of complex '*Y* happens when *X* happens' information, information which when 'unpacked' into empirically-testable, longhand terms concerns the behaviour of unambiguously physical, that is non-gaseous, objects and substances? In the end are not hypotheses about gaseous existence in the same epistemological boat as all other hypotheses about non-observables, including radioactivity, X-rays, gravitational attraction, telepathy, the Hand of God, spirits in the trees and whatever else?

Effect   Oh come on Andrew! You've said your piece about scientists dabbling in metaphysics. Now see what happens when a philosopher dabbles in physics: Eyewash stuff! No distinction at all between hypotheses which are empirically testable and hypotheses which are not, no recognition of the fact that some relationships have been proved experimentally to exist while others have not.

Cause   No Malcolm, I am not trying to gloss over the empirical facts. I am not suggesting that telepathy does occur or that radioactivity does not, I am simply pointing out that they are in the same epistemological boat. And you should remember that your notion of 'empirical testability' is itself at least partially conditioned by your metaphysical assumptions. *Something* must be causing the TV screen to fluoresce; *something* must be making the geiger-counter crackle; *something* must be making the marks in the emulsions. But what, what? Streams of invisible particles? Waves in a transparent medium? Pulses of energy-quanta? What can such particles be made of and how can they act at a distance? What could such a medium consist of, a universal cloud of yet tinier particles still? What can carry these energy-quanta and how are they transmitted? If I visualize a stream of minute billiard-balls you warn me against taking a model too literally, but what would I be doing if I took it *non*-literally? How can this word 'literally' apply in these contexts? Here's a good one for you: what do you think the word 'plasma' means?

Effect   Well, er, a super-hot gas, er... I suppose there's blood plasma... I, I don't know.

Cause   It's from the Greek again of course: 'πλάσμα' meaning 'form' or 'mould' or 'model'; used, for example, of a wax-work copy taken from an original marble sculpture. Nice eh? Also, you'll be interested to learn, 'image' or 'imitation' or 'fiction' or 'forgery'... Another: the Greek word 'αἰθήρ' from 'αἴθω' to burn, meaning 'the upper, purer air', 'the sky', from which comes our word 'ether'. Reflect for a moment upon the relationships between 'ether' the vaporous liquid, 'Ether' the hypothetical electro-magnetic medium and 'ethereal' as used, say, to describe a piece of music. Ponder on the resemblances between 'methylated spirits', 'high spirits' and The Holy Spirit, or between the Earth's atmosphere and the room's atmosphere, after there has been a row. Think of the different uses of the phrase 'in the air' and of words like 'pressure', 'rarefied', 'sublime' and so on. Are there any grounds for saying, for example, that the first use of the word 'atmosphere' is any more *literal* than the second? Sooner or later, some scientist will 'discover' that the phrase 'good vibrations' as used to describe a 1960s party has a basis in some demonstrable physical phenomenon, or that the expression 'a dog's smelling fear' has some genuine chemical significance.

Effect   It has, it's already been proved. They've discovered that when an animal is afraid it secretes a...

Cause   Of course, of course. And no doubt the war-mongers will soon come to regard pacifism as a biochemical problem and try to treat it accordingly. Maybe, after all, scientists will one day concede that some of the half-believed, half-doubted Eyewash phenomena presently known as the 'para-normal' also have bases in empirical fact and will somehow manage to accommodate them within their established metaphysics. Perhaps even the haunting of houses will be measured on meters!

Effect   Uhoh, more cheap movies, more runaway imagination.

Cause   And perhaps not. Again, what is interesting about this is not that you scientists are sceptical about such phenomena but that you are so fearful of them. Because their existence would cause too great an upset to your established atomic theory.

Effect   If pigs could fly, that would be an upset to our established theories of aerodynamics, so what?

Cause   So... So I wonder about the value of the whole business of atomic model-building, of visualizing gases as swarms of flying molecules, of imagining liquids to be rivers of things. In all this are we not just trying, feebly and clumsily, to draw pictures of the invisible, to see in our mind's eye what can never be seen in the world?

Effect   In a sense, yes, I think that's what we are doing.

Cause   But *should* we be doing it? Isn't *your* imagination now running away with us? Couldn't this exercise turn out to be more misleading than helpful? Are we not in danger of losing our grip upon distinctions that are of the highest significance? Imagine the scene: A coastline. Over the years, the wind and the waves and the rain have pounded away at the rocks, gradually grinding them into the sand of the beach. The sandcastle I make on that beach is an object: it has a shape, an identity. Yet knock the sandcastle over and it becomes just a pile of sand, an amount of a substance. But the sand is still solid; it consists we can see, of numerous tiny grains, each of which is again a solid object with a particular shape and a unique identity. It is easy to imagine, when we watch the dry sand pouring through our fingers, that perhaps this gives us a good model of how the sea-water is constituted and it is tempting to suppose, when we toss the sand into the wind, that the flying grains give us a good picture of the air's composition. But somehow, any model or picture or description of the sea-shore which did not systematically *distinguish between* the rocks, the sand, the sea and the wind would be failing to recognize any of their physically important relationships.

Effect   What is your proposal then? An atomic theory in which the atoms themselves can liquefy and vaporize!?

Cause   Why not? That would be a start.

Effect   But... But this is absurd! The whole point of atomic theory is to explain such changes in terms of things which do not themselves undergo any alteration... Honestly, this is too silly! Where on earth are we? I never knew the town had so many back-streets...

Cause   Again, consider the nature of light: could not the action of light in our own realm, where it is the pre-eminent medium of mind/world inter-action, provide us with a model of how objects can interact at a distance in the atomic realm? Or conversely, could not the postulation of perception in an atomic world provide us with an explanation of the nature of light in...

Effect   Look Andrew, I've *got* to get home! Let's just stop talking about atomic worlds for a moment can we?

Cause   Oh certainly, that would be a pleasure. Okay: atoms do not exist. There! Phoof! Gone, all gone! See: no lightning flash, no thunderbolt. The houses are still standing, we are still breathing, the stars are still shining...

Effect   And there's still no sign of your flat.

Cause   Only a couple more blocks Malcolm, don't worry... How *clear* the stars are tonight! I've never seen them so clear! There's Orion... Perseus... Andromeda...

Effect   No, that's Cassiopeia. *There's* Andromeda.

Cause   Ah yes of course, astronomy's your special passion isn't it... Hmm... Pinprick holes in a celestial sphere you say, that's what men used to believe is it?

Effect   Yes, wrongly.

Cause   Uhuh? That's been proved has it? Forgive me Malcolm, but I confess a woeful ignorance of the subject. Indeed perhaps you could enlighten me a bit, give me a quick resumé of the latest theories?

Effect   I'd love to but honestly, I've got to get back, I...

Cause   Why, what's the hurry? You phoned your wife, she knows where you are... Come on, just a thumbnail sketch.

Effect   Well, it certainly is a beautiful night for it.

Cause   I know, one of those derelict houses over there recently had its roof burnt down by some dossers, it'll make a perfect observatory...

Effect   Heigh-ho... Oh dear, I must be mad!

✳   ✳   ✳   ✳   ✳   ✳   ✳   ✳   ✳   ✳   ✳

Cause   Here we are, this is the one. Errrrumph! Now, watch out for missing floor-boards...

Effect   Pooh! Cats! What a spooky place! Is it safe?

Cause   Probably not. Shoo! Shoo! Follow me, careful on the stairs... There! What did I tell you? Even some armchairs! Now then... tell me about *that*.

Effect   Well, where do I start? With the Earth I suppose. Earth, like Venus, Mars, Mercury, Neptune, is a non-luminous planet orbiting the Sun, a typical luminous star. The Moon, in shadow tonight, is a non-luminous satellite of the Earth. Most of these points of light are nearby stars.

371

A Scale Model

Cause Nearby?

Effect Comparatively, though of course the distances involved are enormous. Already I have taken several quantum-leaps in terms of scale: it is roughly one million miles from the Earth to the Moon, one hundred million miles from the Earth to the Sun and twenty-five *million*-million miles from the Sun to the nearest star. At this level astronomers talk not of miles but of light-years, one light-year being the distance travelled by light in one year, about six million-million miles. The nearest star is about four light-years distant.

Cause The mind boggles.

Effect Yes I know, it's difficult to imagine such vast distances. Perhaps a model will help: if the Sun were the size of a billiard-ball, the Earth would be a grain of sand about twenty feet away and it would be a thousand miles to the nearest star.

Cause From here to the Vatican... And what is a star exactly?

Effect A typical star is a huge sphere of hot gas which emits vast quantities of electromagnetic radiation produced by the large-scale fusion of hydrogen nuclei in its interior.

Cause It's funny how your account of a star is automatically expressed in terms of your *atomic* language. The same metaphysical jargon is used at the opposite ends of the scale, while ordinary language, like the visible band of the electromagnetic spectrum, seems to apply to only a very narrow region of the scientists' world.

Effect Oh no, surely you're not going to suggest that the *stars* are metaphysical? After all, we do actually see the stars' light.

Cause Yes, but that's not quite the same as seeing a huge sphere of luminous gas, or even a bright Sun-like disc, is it? Don't worry though, I'm not suggesting that stars are metaphysical, I'm simply reminding you that astronomy at once presents us with some new perceptual borderlines.

Effect Of course, but we do have a great deal of observational information to go on. For centuries astronomers have been carefully mapping the stars, charting their movements, recording their eclipses, flares, changes in brightness and so on. By using the Earth's orbit as a base-line one can measure the changes in angle of nearby stars relative to the distant 'fixed star' background and calculate their distances. It turns out incidentally,

372

that constellations like the ones you were naming are not in fact groups of neighbouring stars at all, but often comprise stars of very different absolute brightness set great distances apart in our line-of-sight direction. The *constellations* are only apparent and form only a convenient celestial reference-grid.

Cause   So presumably, once we go beyond the nearby stars whose base-line angles can be measured, all our estimations of stars' absolute bright-ness and distance become interdependent? We have to make a number of assumptions, for example about star-uniformity?

Effect   Yes, true, but there is other, corroborative evidence. With pairs or groups of stars which orbit a common centre of gravity in a measurable period, one can calculate their mass-ratios. Then there are certain stars whose luminosity varies with time in an established pattern. And there is the information we get from studying a star's spectrum: the predominant wavelengths or colours of its light and the absorption wavelengths filtered out by its atmosphere tell us a great deal about the star's temperature and composition. From this data we have discovered the existence of relation-ships between a star's size, temperature, composition and colour. Stars, we find, are classifiable into certain well-defined types or families.

Cause   Uhoh.

Effect   The existence of these different star-types, together with detailed observations of our own Sun, have given us a pretty good idea of how stars are formed, evolve and burn out. Stars seem to follow certain clear ageing-patterns. Briefly: a cloud of hydrogen gradually condenses under its own gravitation; during condensation the pressure and temperature rise steadily until H-H fusion begins, producing radiation; when the implosive gravita-tion and the explosive stellar fire reach an equilibrium, the star enters its stable, Sun-like, 'main sequence' state, in which it remains for billions of years; when its hydrogen supply begins to expire, the star begins to cool and expand, entering its 'red giant' phase; finally the cold, spent stellar residue collapses in on itself forming a small, hot, super-dense 'white dwarf' star.

Cause   How can we know any of this? If these processes take billions of years, presumably we can never witness any of the changes?

Effect   Of course, this is only a model, a theory we have deduced from contemporary observations of different stars, that goes without saying. Mind you, there are quite a few stellar events whose progress we *can* witness and monitor: there are solar phenomena like flares and sunspots, there are variable and pulsating stars and there are novae and supernovae, colossal flare-ups which can occur over a few hours and whose resulting gas-clouds can be observed for years, probably caused by stars exploding or colliding.

Cause Okay, but at the end of the day any theory of star-evolution is necessarily of the nature of a guess?

Effect Oh no, a theory, a model maybe, but not a guess, it is a lot better than that. The model has to comply with the known laws of physics. Most astro-physicists agree with the outline of this account, though there are still some areas of ignorance and debate. What, are you now going to suggest that star-evolution is mythological?

Cause Not necessarily no, just testing; just testing the seaworthiness of our epistemological boat... Tell me Malcolm, that faint hazy band of light running across the sky there, is that what they call the Milky Way?

Effect That's right. If you look at it through a telescope you can see that it is in fact made up of millions and millions of distant stars. The Milky Way is our edge-on view through the disc of our own galaxy.

Cause Of course, 'γάλα', the Greek for 'milk', I'd never thought of that.

Effect It is estimated that the Milky Way contains over one hundred *billion* stars.

Cause Christ! So why isn't it much brighter than it is?

Effect Because clouds of dust and gas along the galaxy arms obscure our view. However, if we look out from the plane of our own star-disc into unobstructed space, we can get clear views of other island star-systems from which we can infer a great deal about the shape and size of our own. We are now taking, you realize, another quantum-leap in terms of size and scale: in the model I used earlier, if our Sun and the nearest star are billiard-balls a thousand miles apart, then the Milky Way is a disc of such billiard-balls about twenty-five million miles across.

Cause Twenty-five million miles *in the model*?

Effect Yup.

Cause Well you can forget the model then. It's not really helping any more is it?

Effect   No I guess not. The actual figures are roughly these: distance to nearest star four light-years; diameter of our galaxy 100,000 light-years; distance to nearest galaxy 2,000,000 light-years. Furthermore, our galaxy appears to be one of a small cluster and when one looks beyond this local group, the order of distances increases again, by at least another factor of ten.

Cause   I can't even imagine *numbers* that big!

Effect   Detailed observations have shown that galaxies can be classified into four recognizable types and this, again, has led to a theory of galaxy-*evolution*, according to which...

Cause   Hold on, hold on. I'd like to hear a bit more about the evolution of the galaxy-*idea* first. When and why did this notion of 'island star-systems' originally get off the ground?

Effect   In the mid-eighteenth century. As the resolving power of tele-scopes improved and more celestial bodies were identified, many of the objects in the earlier star-catalogues were seen to be not point-sources of light after all, but hazy, glowing, cloud-like blobs; these blobs were called 'nebulae', the Latin for 'clouds'. Further resolution revealed that while some of these nebulae were indeed clouds of glowing gas, possibly the birth-sites of new stars, others were in fact tight agglomerations of thou-sands of separate stars. Some of these were discovered to be densely-packed 'globular clusters' of stars within our own Milky Way, while others turned out to be true galaxies, at much greater distances altogether.

Cause   How do you mean 'turned out to be'? How was this interpretation confirmed?

Effect   Photography was to provide the great breakthrough here. The trouble was, and is, that even with the best optical telescope in the world, the largest galaxy still appears as just a hazy blob. But with the advent of long-exposure photography it became possible to make out the detail of these nebulae. You must have seen such photographs, the beautiful spiral galaxy M31 in Andromeda for example?

Cause   Yes, beautiful, beautiful, but you mean to say that one can never actually *see* that, even through the most powerful of telescopes?

Effect   Well one can see a fuzzy blob, yes, but...

Cause   But not an island star-system? So when you talk about 'observing

375

galaxies' and 'studying star-systems' what you in fact mean is looking at photographs and studying images? Ah, I never realized that... So how can you tell from photographs that some of these 'nebulae' are outside the Milky Way?

Effect   Ah, well this issue was settled in the 1920s by the identification in the neb... in the photographs of faint variable-brightness stars of a type comparable with ones found in the Milky Way. These provided an independent method of estimating the nebulae's distances and confirmed the distant-galaxy hypothesis.

Cause   So only seventy years ago the nature of these nebulae was still a matter of doubt and controversy and the whole galaxy hypothesis rests on this hazy, photographic evidence of a few faintly variable stars. And I bet there is a myriad of assumptions and interpretations hiding in *that* particular theoretical nebula too.

Effect   Of course there is a lot of theory and interpretation involved, there is bound to be. What would you accept as proof? A personal round-trip to M31!?

Cause   That would help, certainly.

Effect   Oh don't be absurd! We are talking about cosmological distances, of over four million light-years! That's impossible, inconceivable!

Cause   Exactly! Exactly, exactly, exactly! According to your own theory, we are now dealing in statements and hypotheses that are and always will be unverifiable, uncheckable. Much as I enjoy science fiction, in science fact no-one in the foreseeable future is even going to make the fifty-billion-mile round-trip to the nearest pin-prick hole! There's another interesting horizon incidentally: the foreseeable future... What becomes apparent from all this is that, again, although we would doubtless argue about the location of the borderline, we are now well and truly outside the territory of observation and empiricism.

Effect   Ah, but there is another indicator of the galaxies' great distance: the Doppler redshift. You know what it sounds like when a police-car siren approaches you at high speed?

Cause   Only too well.

Effect   Because the speed of sound is comparable with that of a fast car, the pitch of the siren sounds higher when the car is approaching and lower when it is receding: the apparent wavelengths of the sound are distorted. Well, the absorption lines in the galaxies' light nearly all display a distortion towards the red end of the spectrum, indicating that they are receding from us at speeds comparable with that of light. In all directions the Universe appears to be expanding.

Cause   What, with us at its centre?

Effect   No, for wherever one were in the Cosmos one would observe the same recession. You should imagine the galaxies as the raisins in a baking cake: as the cake expands, *all* the raisins move apart from one another.

Cause   You regard this as a fact do you, as being beyond doubt? Is no other explanation for the redshift possible? It seems a bit of a leap to go from police-car sirens to Universal expansion. How do you know that light behaves in the same way as sound?

Effect   There are plenty of other examples. We can observe small Doppler effects at the outer edges of the rotating Sun and in the orbits of some of the planetary satellites; also the spectra of nearby rotating star-pairs show clear blueshifts when approaching and redshifts when receding.

Cause   But how can you know that the same interpretation holds good at the galactic level? How can you be sure you're not being confused by some other, as yet unrecognized effect which only comes into play over these enormous cosmological distances? After all, you have admitted that this involves a whole new quantum-leap in terms of scale. Maybe light starts to slow down after making such marathon journeys, the degree of its deceleration depending upon wavelength. Maybe intergalactic space acts like a very dilute transparent fluid; light, I believe, travels slower in a transparent medium than it does in a vacuum, and refractive index varies with wavelength. Maybe our galaxy itself acts as a special sort of distorting lens. I don't know, there must be lots of possible interpretations.

Effect   Yes, and the galactic-recession theory is the one which best fits all the facts. The 'tired light' hypothesis has been tested experimentally and found wanting.

Cause   Ah, so this galaxy-recession is still only a theory, an idea. You talk of the theory 'fitting the facts', but it seems to me that at this cosmological level there is nothing which can count as a fact any more, there is nothing but a fabric of interwoven assumptions, suppositions and interpretations of interpretations. What, for example, could count as genuine experimental evidence about the deceleration of intergalactic light?

Bending out of Sight

Effect   There are ways Andrew, ingenious ways... But in a sense, I agree. We are only constructing models here, rival models, but what else can we do? The point is that the generally-accepted expanding-universe theory is at present the one which most satisfactorily accounts for our observations in terms of the known laws of physics. Happy?

Cause   No, not really, but go on... So the Universe is expanding. Why? Why is the cake baking, or being baked?

Effect   First, let me again try to correct your overly Newtonian picture of what is happening. Time and space, according to Einstein's general theory, are themselves products of mass-energy and the cosmic forces. It is not that the galaxies are shooting out into empty space, but that with the galaxies' recession, the Universe, that is space-time itself, is expanding. Thus, although the relativistic Universe is expanding with time, it is always infinite in that it never has either an edge or a centre.

Cause   It's funny, when relativitists start talking about the equivalence of mass and energy and about the bending of light and the warping of space-time, one thing that happens is that words themselves begin to run out of control. It is not just that one is trying to imagine odd phenomena of which one has no past experience, nor simply that the predicted relativistic effects are bizarre, but it is also that the very language seems to bend out of sight of the world it is supposed to be illuminating. It is as though your whole explanatory model were itself rushing headlong out into an empty void in a shower of incoherent sounds and hieroglyphs. It's just another picture, I know.

Effect   Well, I'm afraid that whether you like it or not, on all the evidence so far Einstein's geometry fits our cosmological observations a great deal better than Newton's. Just to confuse you further, another observation: not only do all the distant galaxies display a spectral redshift, but also the more distant the galaxy the more exaggerated is its shift.

Cause   Well this proves the 'tired light' theory beyond doubt, surely?

Effect   Nope. it proves that the further away a galaxy is, the greater is its speed of recession.

Cause   So the Universe is not merely expanding but is *accelerating* outwards?

Effect   No, not that. One has to remember that in peering deeper and deeper into space, we are looking at longer and longer light-travel times, we are delving further and further back into cosmological *history*. Incidentally, the discovery of this relation between recession-speed and distance has at last solved a riddle that has baffled astronomers for generations: why the night-sky is so dark.

Cause Eh?

Effect In a Newtonian Universe which was infinite and homogenous, as it would have to be if it were not to collapse under its own gravitation, one would expect the night sky to be uniformly bright, since one should be able eventually to see stars in an infinity of directions.

Cause Couldn't it just be that our view is obscured by intergalactic clouds of dust and gas in the same way that, according to you, our view of the centre of our own galaxy is obscured? Or couldn't it be due to the fact that the stars have finite lifetimes and the Universe a certain stellar density? Again, there must be plenty of alternative explanations.

Effect And again the most satisfactory of them is an expanding, relativistic Cosmos. In such a model the galaxies farthest from ours are receding at such colossal relative velocities, close to the speed of light, that their radiation can never reach us, being redshifted out of detectability altogether. An expanding, relativistic Cosmos automatically recedes into darkness.

Cause Uhuh? So according to your interpretation there is, so-to-speak, a theoretical *horizon*, a finite distance beyond which further observation is impossible?

Effect Yes, that's right.

Cause Thank God for that! And in positivist terms, isn't this just a new way of saying that the Universe is bounded, is finite, that statements about it recede into meaninglessness, into literal insignificance?

Effect Not necessarily, it merely means that wherever one is in the Universe, there is a limit to how far one can observe. The separate question of whether or not the Universe itself is finite has become, in the relativistic model, a matter of whether or not the Universe contains or consists of a finite quantity of mass-energy of whether, for example, the galactic density 'thins out' in deeper and deeper space. And *this*, I am glad to say, is a question that should be answerable by observation.

Cause But Malcolm, how can you know what is or is not happening on the other side of your theoretical horizon?

The Big Bang

Effect Ah, we can get a pretty good idea from what is happening on *this* side of it. At present, most cosmologists go for a *finite* Universe.

Cause Very big of them... Isn't this just the ancient Greeks' infinity problem now in modern dress? In the end aren't all assertions about the finiteness or otherwise of the Universe idle reflections merely upon the scope of our imagination, upon the limitations of our mental model-making?

Effect Not for the modern cosmologist Andrew, they are assertions which have testable, measurable implications in the observable Universe. One assertion, for example, in which nearly all cosmlogists now concur is that the Universe had a finite, determinate *beginning*. If one extrapolates the galaxies' recessions backwards, one arrives at a time when they must all have been closely packed together. The evidence indicates that the Universe was born in a single cataclysmic explosion from which all matter, all space, all the stars and galaxies we are now studying, were expelled: the Big Bang.

Cause And you can place this event at a specific date in history?

Effect Yes, roughly: between ten and twenty billion years ago.

Cause Uhuh? So, one quiet Monday morning, many moons ago...

Effect No mornings and no moons, but something like that.

Cause Yes? Are you sure you're not taking the Old Testament a bit too literally? Hm, I wonder what the preceding Sunday was like? Pretty dull I guess. Still, that figures.

Effect Seriously though, please do try to understand that there was no 'before' and no 'elsewhere' at the moment of the Big Bang. This was an explosion of space-time itself.

Cause Anything you say. But what happened exactly? What exploded, and why? Do your cosmologist friends have any ideas about this 'Bang' shebang?

Effect Yes, they do. Of course all this is the subject of much debate and there are rival theories, but the generally agreed scenario goes something like this: an original, point-like, hyper-dense 'primeval atom' of mass-energy explodes rapidly through a number of stages. Firstly the quark era of the first few micro-seconds, a period of chaos about which we can say little except that the sub-nucleon particles must have been so tightly packed together that all the cosmic forces were roughly equal. Secondly the hadron era, up to one thousandth of a second, during which the 'Strong' nuclear force begins to predominate, resulting in the formation of the nucleons and other heavy hadron particles. Thirdly the lepton era, up to about ten seconds old, in which the lighter electron and neutrino particles explode outwards and simple nuclei begin to form. Fourthly the radiation or 'fireball' era, lasting about one million years, during which the Universe becomes a bath of intense electromagnetic radiation and hydrogen and helium begin to appear. Fifthly our own stellar era in which the stars form, the galaxies evolve and the Universe gradually cools down as they continue to expand outwards. If you want to know more about the actual Bang, there is a book called *The First Three Minutes* by...

Cause   No, I think your sixty-second summary will suffice. I see, so it took three minutes to shoot the film and twenty billion years to write the book... You take this stuff seriously do you? As a good empiricist do you honestly regard such fantasizing as being a valid, meaningful scientific exercise?

Effect   Well it's all highly speculative obviously, but the Big Bang cosmology is certainly the one which best fits the data.

Cause   You surprise me Malcolm, you surprise me. What I find the strangest thing of all, stranger even than these loony stories, is the depth of your own scientific credulity, the power of your faith. Tell me, does this 'Big Bang' myth of yours have an ending? Does the galactic expansion go on ad infinitum?

Effect   There are differing theories about this. Some cosmologists postulate an 'open' Universe in which the expansion continues for ever, while others suggest that the galaxies' mutual gravitational attraction will eventually slow them down and ultimately cause the Universe to contract in upon itself again; this would result in a 'closed' or perhaps even an oscillating Universe. The evidence at the moment is inconclusive. It is hoped that the work currently going on in quasar research will settle the question.

Cause   *Quasar* research?

Effect   Quasi-stellar objects. Objects which look like stars, but aren't.

Cause   Ah.

Effect   I guess it's time I brought radio-astronomy into the picture; most of the great post-war discoveries have come in this new field. Previously, all astronomy had been confined to the visible band of the electromagnetic spectrum, but with improved engineering and electronic techniques we have recently been able to extend our study of the sky to other, non-visible ranges, including microwaves, radio waves, X-rays and so on.

Cause   Please note: a borderline being crossed.

Effect   For a start, radio astronomy has enabled us to map the Milky Way in much greater detail. The 21-centimetre radiation produced by cool hydrogen, great clouds of which extend along our galaxy's spiral arms, is relatively unimpeded by the intervening dust and gas and can therefore be detected and mapped by radio telescopes. Again, Doppler shifts tell us about the galaxy's rotation. The discovery, in the 1960s, of a shifted, low-level residual 'background' radiation added further support to the Big Bang hypothesis and indicates our galaxy's absolute cosmological motion as being in the Aquarius-Leo direction.

Cause   Our galaxy's *absolute* motion? I thought you said that there is no absolute motion, that from wherever one stood in the Universe, everything would seem to be expanding.

Effect   That's right, but of course the original explosion did occur a finite number of years ago, since when our and every other galaxy have been travelling outwards from its site.

Cause   So there is such a site is there? The Universe does have a determinable centre?

Effect   Well, as I say, from measurements of the background radiation one can determine the absolute direction in which our galaxy is travelling and extrapolate back in time to work out the distance travelled, so in a sense there is, yes.

Cause   And what does one see when one looks at this 'site'?

Effect   Oh you don't see anything, of course not, there's nothing there. Space-time *exploded*, that is the point.

Cause   But wherever in the Universe astronomers stood, on whatever galaxies travelling in whatever directions at whatever speeds, they could all make these same measurements and calculations and would all extrapolate back to the same Big Bang site?

Effect   Presumably, if they got the theory right.

Cause And yet there's nothing there, no object, no mysterious radio source?

Effect No.

Cause Nothing? No hamburger stall? No flags?

Effect No hamburger stall, no flags.

Cause Well that proves it doesn't it, there's obviously something wrong with all of this.

Effect How do you mean, something wrong?

Cause Don't you see? Put all this Big Bang theory together with your earlier assertion that there must be other, older intelligent life somewhere in the Universe and you have a real problem: since, apparently, we are all presented with this one absolute reference-point, why has no-one yet marked it in any way? Any human-like, space-travelling civilization that wanted to make contact with others would not be sending out or searching for puny radio bleeps amidst the din of intergalactic space, they would surely by now have posted something at the one spot on which they know all other astronomers should be focussing, the site of your supposed Primeval Atom. They would have signalled it somehow.

Effect You try.

Cause There is a genuine mystery here though, surely?

Effect There are others, more prosaic. Radio observations of our galaxy's nucleus, which is optically obscured, have revealed a number of very energetic sources indeed, whose nature is still something of a riddle. Also, as the size and accuracy of our radio telescopes have increased, it has become possible to pinpoint radio sources very precisely and to correlate them with optically visible objects. One surprising finding is that some of the brightest radio-sources in the sky coincide with distant, optically dim and often oddly-shaped *galaxies*, apparently possessed of extraordinarily high energy-outputs; suggestions of galactic explosions, collisions and matter/anti-matter cataclysms have been mooted. Then there is the discovery of numerous powerful *pulsating* radio-sources or 'pulsars' which coincide with small faint stars. The calculations indicate that in these 'white dwarf' or 'neutron' stars the normal atomic structure of matter has actually collapsed under the force of its own gravity and become a soup of protons and electrons so densely packed together that a star as massive as the Sun would shrink in diameter from 900,000 miles to about fifteen.

Cause   Ouch!

Effect   The quasars are the real puzzle though. They are enormously power-ful radio-emitters coincident with normal-looking, dim or even invisible stars which optically do not resolve into galaxies. Yet their light and radio emissions display very high redshifts, implying colossal recession-speeds, some over ninety percent of the speed of light and indicating that these objects lie at the farthest depths of observable space. Stranger still, some quasars fluctuate in brightness over short periods, suggesting that they are comparatively small objects. All-in-all, with their apparently prodigious power-outputs, small sizes and huge distances, the quasars present us with quite a quandary: *either* we take their redshift recession figures at face-value and place them at enormous cosmological distances, in which case none of our existing physics can begin to explain the workings of such powerful and compact energy-sources; *or* we assume that they are more local objects with more manageable size/power ratios, in which case our whole redshift-equals-recession cosmology goes up the spout.

Cause   Couldn't the problem be solved by postulating a further step-wise collapse in the structure of matter beyond the neutron-star stage, another quantum leap in density?

Effect   I'm afraid it's not quite so easy. The trouble is that if matter takes another step backwards like that, it collapses in on itself altogether and becomes a Black Hole.

Cause   A what?

Effect   A Black Hole. The existence of black holes was predicted some years ago and is implicit in Einstein's theory of gravitation. The equations indicate that if a suitably massive body, a large star say, goes on collapsing under the weight of its own gravity, there comes a point at which it will disappear altogether, being sucked irrevocably into the gravitational vortex set up by its own mass.

Cause   Gulp!

Effect   Nothing, not even light, can then escape from within the hole.

Cause   Sounds like astrophysics vanishing up its own...

Effect   No, seriously, there is now quite a lot of evidence that such objects exist.

Cause   But if not even light can escape from them, if they are by definition invisible, how can there be evidence for such things' existence? How can you even use the word 'object' here? What would Ayer say? Isn't this positivism again being dissolved by its own Verification Principle?

Effect   But there is evidence! We can infer the existence of a black hole from the odd behaviour of other phenomena nearby, from its effects upon the surrounding space-time, matter, light and so on. The theorists claim that black holes may exist in a wide range of sizes. Monstrous supermassive black holes capable of sucking in entire galaxies yet only a few light-hours across may explain the extraordinary power-outputs of the quasars; although no radiation can escape from the hole itself, a spinning hole would act like a gigantic electromagnetic generator. At the other end of the scale, it is possible that the extreme conditions of the Big Bang created minute proton-sized black holes as massive as mountains which may still be wandering freely in the Universe; such a particle would be capable of passing right through the Earth unnoticed.

Cause   Oh come on! If you'll believe that, you'll believe anything!

Effect   Truly Andrew, some scientists are even speculating that one day we may be able to 'tow' a suitably-sized black hole back to Earth to act as an endless energy-supply. At the moment this is little more than a dream obviously, but...

Cause   Uhoh, I told you... And of course everybody will want one, their own personal galaxy-crusher. Tell me Malcolm, what happens to a chap or a particle or a country that accidentally falls or... is pushed into one of these little black hole beauties?

Effect   Well, round the mouth of a spinning hole matter is gradually drawn inwards, as if by a gravitational whirlpool; needless to say, clocks and measuring rods start behaving in some rather strange ways. Spiralling down into the vortex one would cross a critical circle known as the 'event-horizon', from beyond which *nothing* can escape. That, I grant you, really *does* constitute an observability-borderline.

Cause   And then?

Effect   Then down, presumably, to the... the eye of the vortex, to what is called the 'Singularity'. Beyond that there is not much one can meaningfully add. Think what you like.

Cause   Free? Free at last? Free to imagine an animate cosmos?

Effect   I have heard some theorists suggest that supermassive black holes may be 'doorways' into other universes, eventually exploding out into other Big Bangs.

Cause   The gateways to Heaven perhaps, or to Hell?

Effect   Jargon has a theory about a mirror-image universe of ours, where everything is anti-matter and time runs backwards.

Cause   Oh wonderful, wonderful! Physics through the looking-glass! Oh well, they've split the atom, I guess they might as well go ahead and pluralize the Universe!

Effect   Since in relativistic geometry time becomes a fourth dimension and mathematically it can run in either direction, as far as the laws of physics are concerned...

Cause   Ah now this is the stuff I like the best! It couldn't just be, could it, that the idea of reversible time has gained a specious plausibility because of our recent ability to run film and video-tape every which way? We can all now 'watch' a broken cup reassembling and leaping from the kitchen floor to the table, but who will say they can then 'watch' the camera being loaded? Next time this Jargon fellow tries explaining his new theory or tells you about his latest book, just ask him why he bothered: whatever he said was known already.

Effect   I fear that wouldn't stop him.

Cause   And they don't stop at four dimesnsions, do they? I recently heard a young boffin bragging about a ten-dimensional universe travelling through eleven-dimensional space-time! Why so niggardly, I asked, let's have an *infinite* number of universes moving in an *infinity* of space-times! Why not? Go for it!

Effect   That was him, probably.

Cause   Malcolm! Malcolm! Negative time, Big Bangs, Event Horizons, Anti-Matter, Singularities, Gluons, massless force-carrying particles, Gravity waves – surely *Alice* would have been at home here! You know, I think your description of what happens in a black hole may have provided us with a final perfect model of the entire panorama of scientific explanation. Though there seem to be no sharp borderlines either in Nature or in thought between the objects of sense-perception and the objects of imagination, yet it is possible to chart, roughly, one's rabbit-hole descent from the one world into the other, and there does seem to be a critical point from beyond which, one can positively assert, no further light can emerge. We, you, seem to have been sucked into a series of headlong downward spirals of meaningless, pointless, endless questioning: a bottomless, babbling, burbling pit.

Effect   I realize that it may seem so to a layman. It sometimes seems so to me, but scientists are only human Andrew, their theories and their models only human creations. We are doing our best to work things out. You try making sense of... *that*.

Cause   That's the problem isn't it, our craving to comprehend it all, to work it out, to store it in our tiny Earth-bound heads. So we try to reduce it to a few neat sounds and symbols, we play God with words like 'galaxy' and 'constellation'. 'Cosmos'... five letters? Six? 'Universe' is a bit larger of course, with eight.

Effect   But surely this is not the problem, this is the miracle, the greatest miracle of all, that *that* can somehow exist *up there*.

Cause   Can it? You're the scientist remember. We have a lot in common, you and I. We both hate this gravity, this mess, this Earth-bound mortality; so we both try to escape, to fly, to dream of gods. But flying can be dangerous: it is easy to get carried away by one's mythologies. Shoo! Shoo! We must never forget where and what we are.

Effect   Leave it alone Andrew, it's not doing you any harm... Come on, I must be getting back.

Cause   Righto... My flat's just round the corner... There, the blue door next to the Greek Restaurant...

Effect   The Olympus?

Cause   That's the one... Come on up.

❋   ❋   ❋   ❋   ❋   ❋   ❋   ❋   ❋   ❋   ❋

387

9

ABOVE
OLYMPUS

Effect   My goodness, what a shambles!

Cause   Yes I know, terrible isn't it?

Effect   How can you possibly work in such a mess? Clothes on the floor, papers all over the bed, car parts on the desk, books and records everywhere!

Cause   Relax Malcolm, relax, sit down... Clear the stuff off that chair. Just bung the typewriter on the floor...

Effect   What's that in the corner, home-made wine?

Cause   Yes, want to try some? It's not bad actually, and only thirty pence a bottle... I've got Retsina if you'd prefer, or Ouzo, you know, aniseed.

Effect   Oh yes, I'll have some Ouzo please, just a little... This is all you've got then, the one room?

Cause   Er, yes, the bathroom's down the hall... Sorry about the glass... Yamas!

Effect   Yamas! Why don't you get rooms in College?

Prologue

Cause Can't stand the place! I like it out here.

Effect Well why not a bigger flat at least, is the pay that bad in Logic and Linguistics?

Cause Ah, look Malcolm, there's something I think I'd better tell you... I'm, er, not a, a Professor at all. I just said that to, impress.

Effect You impostor! What a nerve! I thought you were a bit young to have made it to Professor! So what then, are you doing a PhD?

Cause No, I'm afraid not. I got kicked out after my second year. Didn't get on with my supervisors; wind-up remarks about Catholicism, politics, you know...

Effect But they can't throw you out for that, surely?

Cause And women in the rooms. The spies found a condom packet under the bed. True! Ghastly business! Pathetic bloody place! I'm glad to be out of it.

Effect So what are you really Andrew? Your name is Andrew is it?

Cause Oh yes... Ah well, I suppose in a strange way I could be called a salesman, like you, a hawker of images, ideas...

Effect Yes yes, but what do you do for a living?

Cause Or a cleaner, a sanitary engineer, a washer of...

Effect Ah, so you're a *cleaner*?

Cause Oh for money, the Dole, a bit of wheeling-and-dealing, the odd neon sign. That reminds me, before I ask Demetrios about the van, there's something I'd like to show you... Excuse my rummaging around...

Effect Go ahead. What are you looking for?

Cause Well... Several times today you have invited me to propose *my* metaphysics, *my* model. "*You* make sense of it!" you exclaimed, "what is *your* theory of atomic structure?" you demanded.

Effect Mm. I can see that in many respects our present models are unsatisfactory, and since we are being honest with one another, I confess that I am as sceptical as you about much of the new particle stuff. Sometimes when I hear Jargon and his pals holding forth, I do wonder whether they know what they're talking about, or rather, I wonder whether they're talking *about* anything.

Cause   They're lost Malcolm, they've lost their way. The inherited model has finally failed, failed completely, failed even you scientists. It has collapsed under the weight of all the new information. Quasars, Quarks, Quantum Numbers, what are these now but just a series of question-marks?

Effect   Okay okay, this may be true to some extent, but the inherited model is the only model we've got, and until somebody comes along with a better one...

Cause   Ah, here we are...

Effect   Until someone comes along with a model that makes better sense *to the scientists,* that is expressed in *scientific* language, that is testable in *scientific* ways, that proceeds from scientific understandings we have already reached... What on earth is that?

Cause   Hold on, you'll see... Okay then, let me try, let me tell you about *my* metaphysical model, *my* 'grand synthesis'. Of course it won't be the kind of model you are expecting; at first you may not find it useful at all, but later, who knows? Anyway, *I* like it, *I* find it helpful... And at least it is a model one can take literally, as literally as one chooses. My trouble was that I wanted a model into which *we* would fit, a model which could tell us something about *us*...

Effect   I don't see how we're going to fit into that little contraption.

Cause   You know, the more I hear this word 'model', the less I like it. It sounds like a toy or an ornament, something one sticks on the mantle-piece... or keeps in a cardboard box under the desk. Excuse me Malcolm, would you mind moving a second, I've just got to get something...

Effect   What *are* you up to?

Cause   No, I prefer the word 'myth'. I wanted a myth that did more than that, a myth that reached out into the heart of things, a myth that got back to a few basics. You remember my statement that your world of atomic particles is literally mythological, as mythological as the gods of the ancient Greeks?

Prologue

Effect   Yes, and I remember asking what could be the purpose, the use of making such an assertion.

Cause   Okay, well now let me tell you, let me try, as they say, to 'cash it in'. First, some observations about the Greek myths. Quite apart from disputes about their bases in fact, about where history ends and mythology begins, there is the point that these stories existed only to be *used*. They served many functions, including entertainment, education, moral guidance, propaganda and so on. They existed only insofar as they were told, sung and written, by people, to people, for people. Our knowledge of the characters and the events in Greek mythology, and again remember how we come by our knowledge of your atomic world, comes to us and can only come to us through the surviving works of the Greek writers. The Greek writers, however, wrote their myths in different ways at different times for different purposes. It is not just that they had individual styles and emphases, but that they often wrote quite different stories and made quite different points. Of course there must be some pattern of common features and resemblances for the various stories to count as different versions of the same myth, but beyond that all was and is license. There is, for example, no definitive, laid down myth of Electra, there are only the different versions of her story told by the different Greek writers Homer, Sophocles, Aeschylus, Euripides and the rest.

Effect   Was there no historical Electra then?

Cause   Of course there must have been, but what can we say of her? Once more we are around that mysterious borderline between history and myth, between observation and imagination. In the end all we have is the writing. The playwright Sophocles, for instance, used the Electra story as a psychological parable, a sort of female version of the Oedipus model. Aeschylus, on the other hand, in his Orestes trilogy, used the tale as a moral argument for the introduction of courts of law and trial by jury to replace punishment by priestly dictat... Excuse my clambering about... Ta... Why, one wants to ask, should there have to be *an* atomic theory, *a* cosmology, an *agreed* particle physics? Why this constant striving for metaphysical consensus? Shouldn't we expect to find different atomic theories, and *non*-atomic theories useful for different tasks, for different reasons, at different times?

Effect   In a sense, maybe that is what is happening.

Cause   Good. Right. I told you, didn't I, that my book ends with a play?

Effect   Yes, why a play though Andrew? Has it got to be a play?

Cause I think it has. Real people before real people. No more images, no more words, no more analogues or models. Real flesh, real swords, real blood, real cries of pain, well, acted pain. That is the point in the end... I know! Why don't we read it together, it's not very long?

Effect I would be interested to see it, certainly.

Cause I've got a second copy somewhere, just a minute... Here. It's not quite finished so it's not properly bound yet. And, er, sorry about all the corrections.

Effect What's it called?

Cause I haven't decided. In case you haven't guessed, it's my version of the Electra story.

Effect Ahhh!

Cause By the way, do you know where the word 'tragedy' comes from?

Effect No, I don't. Greek again presumably?

Cause Yes, it means 'the goat-herds' song'. Another nice reminder is it not? I tell you what: I'll do Electra, you do her brother Orestes, and we'll just use our commonsense over the other parts. Hold on, let me set the scene first... Now, if I stick the Contraption on the table by the window and the control-box on the basin, I can plug it in down... here. Okay, recognize anything?

Effect Oh I see, it's a model of an atom, how clever!

Cause You wait till I get it going.

Effect It actually works does it, it lights up? Good heavens! Where did you get it?

Cause I made it Malcolm, years ago, during my last year at school. I was a scientist myself then, very full of it all. This was my sixth-form project.

Effect You do amaze me. It certainly looks like a fine piece of work.

Cause Of course I got a lot of help from the teachers with the glasswork and with filling the tubes. I remember we had a hell of a job getting the right gas-mixtures and pressures and all that. I worked out the circuitry myself. When it's all adjusted, green-coloured discharges should actually travel around these outer tubes. Excuse the overly classical interpretation.

Prologue

Effect It's Carbon isn't it, C12?

Cause Naturally. The nucleus was comparatively easy, just a cluster of six red and six white bulbs, as you can see. It was the electrons that took the time. And of course the works had to be as invisible as possible: we used the thinnest, strongest glass tube we could find and strands of very fine gut glued with transparent resin to hold it all together. The whole thing's driven round by a geared-down gramophone motor: there are sliding contacts under the turntable. I'm afraid I had to break a few rules on the safety angle; none of the wires is insulated, so once it's switched on whatever you do don't touch anything... Right, I think everything's connected correctly... Now if you could turn the main light off... Ta... Okay, fingers crossed...

Effect I say, that's beautiful!

Cause Hold on, the electrons are not quite right yet... This always takes a little time... A bit more on that one, a bit less on that one, a touch more on number five... Perhaps if I boost up the oscillating fre... Ah, there! All systems go!

Effect Marvellous! With the main light off you can't see the tubes or the wires at all, it becomes just a pattern of glowing lights!

Cause Yes, until your eyes get accustomed to the darkness... No, don't draw the curtains, the night-sky makes a nice back-drop.

Effect It really is beautiful. What lovely patterns of light it throws around the room... What a superb toy, what marvellous workmanship, it must have given you tremendous satisfaction.

Cause In a production of the play, I imagine a large version of this model suspended above the centre of the stage, the lamps in its nucleus providing the stage-lighting. This is an all-electric drama, I tell you! I know, a final touch to the atmosphere: music!

Effect Your beloved John Coltrane I suppose?

Cause No no, we don't want *real* music, just some bland electronic rubbish in the background, something meaningless and repetitive... Here's a tape, this'll do... Right... I hope you can see to read alright; try turning the script more towards the nucleus... Now, at either side of the stage, at the front, two men in modern dress are in conversation. One is seated at a desk piled high with papers. Alternately he peers through a microscope on the desk and through a tripod telescope which is trained on the stars of the night-sky, represented by bright pin-prick holes in the set's black back-cloth. The other man has no props and simply paces up and down. The scientist scribbles notes and operates a calculator; he is agitated, frustrated; his microscopic and telescopic observations appear to contradict and his theories have been thrown into confusion. His interrogator insists that he should go back to first principles and reconsider the model of atomic structure that illuminates all his interpretations. "What about" he asks, "this fundamental Cosmic Principle of yours, the 'Electric Force'? Since this force cannot be seen, does it matter what we call it?"

Effect   How do you mean?

Cause   Well, this Electric Force that is supposed to sustain the atom, this universal attraction between positive protons and negative electrons, in theory can't we call it what we like? I mean, if we chose to call it the 'Axolotl Force' and talked of particles with plus and minus axolotl-values, it wouldn't make any difference to the mathematics, to the physics of your theory would it?

Effect   Er, no, but...

Cause   The force could still obey the same laws and equations?

Effect   Ye-es, but...

Cause   All we would have done is coined a new metaphysical name?

Effect   I suppose so, but...

Cause   And a name is neither here nor there, a name doesn't matter a bent pen-nib?

Effect   Maybe not, but what would be the p...

Cause   And since these supposed objects are beneath the range of light and sight, there is no point in asking what they *look* like?

Effect   That's true, but...

Cause   There's no point in asking what *species* these objects are. Indeed, presumably it is therefore foolish to try to *represent* these things at all?

Effect   Yes, but we have to have...

Cause   ...something to show the kids, we have to have a story to tell, I know.

Prologue

Effect Well, we have to have some way of picturing...

Cause So we draw our pictures and our diagrams but warn against taking them literally?

Effect Y-yes, though...

Cause So in a sense we can draw our diagrams how we like?

Effect But, but...

Cause Right then. I hereby propose that 'Electricity' be renamed 'Sexuality', that 'Positive' and 'Negative' be renamed 'Male' and 'Female', that from now on in our diagrams atomic particles are marked not with plus and minus signs but with men's and women's faces, that instead of a proton we have a protasis...

Effect A protasis?

Cause The prologue to a Greek play. And instead of an electron, we have...

Effect Electra. Of course, of course!!

Cause Now then Malcolm, you read the stage-directions.

Effect At the utterance of the name 'Electra' the lights come up on a group of ten actors moving silently around the stage in measured, circular paths that mirror the movements of the lights in the atomic model suspended above them. There is a 'nucleus' of five men, all dressed in red, rotating slowly at the centre while five women, all in green, 'orbit' around them to produce a complex, ever-changing pattern. The whole effect is of people engaged in some timeless, endless ritual dance, the choreography of which is predetermined; they cannot, it appears, escape from their set paths. The numerical symmetry is completed by two life-size marble statues of Greek Gods: a male figure illuminated in red light at the centre of the nucleus, slightly raised, and a female figure lit green at the rear of the stage, also raised. As the actors move, different combinations come together and drift apart in different areas of the stage. These groups are spotlit in a precise order to provide the sequence of scenes in the play. While each scene is in progress the remaining characters are seen dimly, continuing their monotonous dance. First to appear, front-centre-stage is Electra. With short, rough-cut hair and wearing a simple ragged tunic, she has a certain hard, sad beauty. She is carrying a bunch of freshly cut flowers. She paces to and fro while delivering her prologue, pausing at the end of each verse.

Electra Listen carefully, watch it well, consume, digest the tale I tell.
I interrupt my dirgeful dance to try to trick you from a trance.
When time began and history, when souls were born of sky and sea,
When men were gods and gods were men, my family accursed fell then.
To prove man's power limitless, our ancestor King Tantalus
Held a banquet and invited all who godly parents cited
And served, to test divine pretension, roasted meat   of his own son.

They knew, they knew, of course they knew, once tasted, smelt that evil stew!
How vain and foolish to suppose such hellish stench would go unnosed,
To think our crimes so foul and lewd by gods and demons go unviewed.
So it was that in that seed our curse was born, our fate decreed:
Treachery, adultery and murder, vengeance' law and all disorder.
Fathers flayed their saplings fleshed, sons to chaff their elders threshed,
Whose harvest was the Trojan War, a holocaust for   two men's whore.

The King our Father Agamemnon at Port Aulis massed our force,
A thousand ships all charged with stores, weapons, armour, men and horse.
Troy! they cried with blood imbued, but once again our godly feud
Blew northern winds to foil our fleet, stalled for days at anchor's cleat.
Days turned to weeks, and weeks did weakness, sickness spread amongst the men
Until my Father, fearing ruin, gave his first-born Iphighen.
The Gods had spoken, bartered slaughter, wind for death of his own daughter.

My sister dead, Gods' hunger sated, the ship-confounding winds abated.
The fleet set sail in swift convoy and Greeks at last laid siege to Troy.
As history tells fierce war was waged, for ten dark years the battles raged.
Thousand upon thousand perished, left mothers, wives and babes uncherished.
Yet all the while here in Mycenae plotted our ancestral genie:
Troy's henchman Prince Aegisthus wed my mother Clytemnestra's bed,
And as sham horseman played the stud who dreamed to stirrup Father's blood.

Even now I hear that joy when beacons flared the fall of Troy,
The day the townsfolk celebrated king and heroes long-awaited.
A Sun-bright blaze of singing, cheering, drums and trumpets beating, blaring;
In procession shoulder-high Ag'memnon's gold outshone the sky.
He climbed red-carpeted palace steps, his purple victor's arms outstretched,
Embraced his faithful long-lost queen who kiss-beguiling staged the scene.
But then hosannas were blasphemed by frightful still,   still echoing screams.

Act I

Electra Three times he blurted Murder! Murder! Scared attendants stumbled, faltered.
(cont'd) Our spearmen stormed the room too late, blood flowed from bath to bed to slate.
Her husband's thrice-hacked body lay at his wife's feet a red bouquet.
So once more mocked our ancient curse, new murder-plays now to rehearse.
Orestes, brother in this debt, though mere boy's perceived a threat
And quick to Phocis' friendly state with guardians did abdicate,
Our parting vow that stormy day that we'd our
                                    so-called mother slay.

They say that I am sick or mad, of face perpetually sad;
Hateful of my sex, all sex, its dirty, brutish, faithless tricks;
No family, no love, no friends, my mother's death my sole amends.
My foes want me cast out or killed, my stay's just by my mother willed:
Thus at her tattered conscience cling the hands that final peace will bring.
Here lies the paradox complete, our fearful God-sprung trap is set.
The past and future are my madness, I *chose* not birth
                                    of Father's murderess.

And now I wait and wait and wait for his return,
Tortured, tantalized by hate that impotence keeps taciturn,
Alone but for my childhood nurse, the last here sharing my reverse.
My younger sister Chrysotheme is compromised with sin, unsqueamish,
Mouthing every rumour's breath, some whispering Orestes' death,
Some sneering he's forgot his cause and lives with gamblers, pimps and
whores. These seem more guilty hopes than true, but pray God Orestes
                                    where are you?

Effect Electra fades from sight as three male characters at the centre of the stage appear. They are: Orestes, handsome, auburn-haired and with a small scar on his forehead; Pylades, his friend since childhood; and an Old Man who has been Orestes' guardian throughout his exile. Each wears a red costume appropriate to his status. Orestes and Pylades are armed with swords and daggers.

Cause The three men have been travelling for a long time and are filled with both weariness and excitement at nearing their destination. Orestes looks around as if surveying a landscape that is spread before him.

Orestes At last fair Argos is ours once more! My friends have you ever seen a land so rich and fertile as this our birthplace? The fields reflect the Sun with harvest of ripe corn. The trees weigh down, full with bursting fruit. The animals and birds flock freely, the fish dance in the streams and rivers. Do you remember Pylades, how we would play and hide there by Inachus' banks and how our dear guardian would at nightfall come to bring us safely home to sleep within the bosom of Mycenae, golden city of my father's throne... A *curse* that to so beautiful a land mankind could bear such treachery! That I, its once proudest son

Orestes *(cont'd)*	should now be sworn to cut off life from my own mother! How is it that the Gods can authorize such *shame*?
Pylades	Courage good Orestes, do not criticize cruel Fate, But with a will determined our just purpose generate.
Orestes	This 'just purpose' we determine, parent-murder to requite, Is our cause true righteousness or just revengers' spite?
Old Man	Come now brave Orestes, will you at this hour resign From committed restoration of your father's fractured line? I assure you I will not, I served him every due; I risked my life in war for him and would likewise for you.
Orestes	I know my bretheren, I know, I know what is expected. The killing of my father can't and won't go uncorrected. Fear not my murmurings of doubt, my heart has not grown hollow, It merely beats half-contemplated dread of what may follow.
Pylades	Remember young Electra, amber-haired and honey-flowered, Reflect on all the bitter bane her soul must have devoured.
Orestes	Ah yes, my dear Electra, who would play my other self...
Old Man	You shared a mother, father, nurse, a room, a bed, a shelf.
Orestes	I wonder how her seasons bore sweet budding to fruition... You're right, 'determined will' must be our watchwords in this mission!
Cause	Orestes drinks from a water-flask he is carrying, wipes his lips and passes the flask to the others. Refreshed, they set off again as if towards the city of Mycenae. Suddenly Orestes stumbles over a gravestone, on which are lying Electra's flowers. They stop.
Orestes	What...? Fresh rosaries at such a moss-grown grave? There is some heavy grief here time has failed to unslave.
Pylades	(reading inscription) 'King Agamemnon, Conqueror of Troy'.
Orestes	What!? Is this it, five little words engravèd in such humble stone!? My Father's furtive, scarce-marked grave in land left by for birds and bushes? Shame upon shame! Henceforth I cannot sleep ere this rude slab's transfigured to a mighty mausoleum, a marble palace as befits a *Conqueror of Troy*, which though it had in gold inscription long as books of holy writ could not account yet but one letter of his life... (trembling) What God-inspired irony has brought us here? (falls to his knees and prays) Forgive me Father that I'm not yet proved your son. In such a bed your spirit cannot easy rest, nor mine till all this infamy's redressed. By all the Gods I swear you'll be avenged!

Act I

Pylades   This plot's attended say these flowers,
Most likely by a friend of ours.
Let's lie low amongst those trees
To learn who owes such obsequies.

Old Man   Such use of our good fortune's wise,
But watch, this country's thick with spies.

Cause   They hide, remaining dimly visible near the grave. Shortly, the figure of Electra appears, walking forlornly towards them, as if in a stupor of dejection. Orestes is aghast.

Orestes   Is this Electra? All debased of dress and hair and countenance?
She for whom the spring would bloom and breathless summer blossom
dance?
What grim share of politics can furrow so a maiden's brow
And in a forehead clear as sunshine such a shade of sadness plough?

Electra   (at the graveside)
And so dear Father still we wait; revenge remains a dream's mirage
As every new horizon proves that hope's just bleak fear's camouflage.
The rumours of Orestes' death are growing stronger every hour
Till even my faith saps and falls like petals of an autumn flower.
But have no fear my shivering shade, I will not die a wintered maid
Until I've proof of his demise and seen him ice-cold with these eyes.
I only then will side by side lie with my Lord.

Orestes   (whispering, rising)   What, suicide!?
Quickly, I must free her from tormented, misled martyrdom.

Old Man   (whispering, urgently)
Don't be a fool, two more approach!

Pylades   Stay down, there is more game to poach!

Effect   Chrysothemis, Electra's younger sister, and an old woman, Electra's nurse, approach the graveside. The women are dressed in appropriate green costumes. Chrysothemis is pretty, with curly blond hair; she is carrying a small bronze urn.

Chrysothemis Hello dear sister. What, still nursing sorrow at this so well-trodden graveside? It seems your visits here grow longer day by day. Have you not yet mourned enough?

Electra   (rising, facing her sister, angrily) *Enough?* If I should stay here all my life, my tears to wash away this earth wherein he's buried, even so my mourning would not be *enough* while father-killers yet go free and live!

Chrysothemis Still dreaming of more murders? (She advances, as if to take Electra by
the shoulder. Electra recoils from her sharply)
Electra how it sickens us to see your ill estate,
Consumed like cancer from within by dark revenge and hate.
It brings no good or use humane, our Father will not live again.
Our history is written now but not as yet, pray Gods, our fate.

Electra You shallow girl, your golden curls hide not one thought or passion,
For you life's easiness and peace, a smile, a passing fashion.

Chrysothemis Oh come, today's a feast-day been proclaimèd at the palace,
So why not put aside this grief, for once take up life's chalice?
Come now to the city that together we may dine;
Aegisthus roasts a royal ox, grants music, dancing, wine.

Electra Foul, ignoble celebration! Feeble, fawning, foolish ward!
For food and drink all pride you'll sell, call your father's butcher lord.

Chrysothemis Why should I care for ancient names, for hidden bonds and ties?
The world for me is what I saw when first I bared my eyes.

Electra Silence ill-begotten wretch, else mouth and eyes I'll blind.
I want to see your weeping, kissing, in this tomb enshrined.
(She grabs Chrysothemis by the hair and drags her head down to the
gravestone)

Chrysothemis (crying)
Electra please forgive me please, don't vow to hate me too,
Just because I was too young to know the man you knew.
Ag'memnon's though to me mere name, to you your sov'reign lord,
Pray cannot our true sisterhood to us yet be restored?

Electra (nervous) Get out of my sight before I choke you on this stone!
(She releases Chrysothemis)

Old Woman Peace Electra peace, turn you not upon your sister.
You are right, I share your fight against the foul Aegisthus.
But she's right too, for till he's dead
What good to you's this suffering bred?
Past plots have hatched, their birds have flown.
Pays father's life to wreck your own?

Electra Do even you not understand?
What matters mine while his goes underhand?
She is not wrong because she is not wronged...

Act I

Electra *(cont'd)*	Dear old friend I love you truly, more than any you're my ally. From my birth and from my brother's your love far excelled our <div align="right">mother's.</div>Yet all your wise and kindly words can silence not a suit unheard. No reasonings, however fine, can move the *victims* of a crime.
Old Woman	Your mother Clytemnestra's ill, her spirits jangle hot and chill. Your frigid looks and cold reserve freeze her every vein and nerve. Play not always this wintry part, one smile from you would thaw her <div align="right">heart.</div>
Electra	She is not my mother... Here's proof: She killed my sire ere making love. She killed him ere he reached her vice, Thus making me an orphan twice.
Chrysothemis	Look, she's sent burnt offerings, Her crime still at her conscience stings. All the years of time's complaisance Have not dulled her heart's repentance.
Electra	Heart's repentance, heart's repentance, watch her clutch her heart's <div align="right">repentance!</div>See her help him to her bed, e'en to the path whence I once bled.
Chrysothemis	Troubling visions storm her sleep And toss her bed in sweaty steep.
Old Woman	When we rush in to calm her screams She tells us trembling of her dreams.
Chrysothemis	And though each night she burns ten lamps, Ag'memnon's ghost all-armoured tramps Her soul through corridors and rooms, Unbolting doors, unsealing tombs.
Electra	Good, so Gods remembered Right, Released their Furies: no respite... Go! If her conscience starts to whine She'll have your shoulders, never mine. (She mellows, smiles and takes them by the hand) Don't fret, I'm not irrevocably mad. We'll meet tonight, till then: be glad.

Effect	Chrysothemis and the Old Woman depart. Electra watches as they recede.
Old Man	(aside) Her hatred is implacable, her fire's newly fanned. Quick we must reveal ourselves to plan what has been planned.
Pylades	The youngest spoke such pretty sense I almost thought it true. A pity that girl's innocence can't build the world anew.
Cause	Orestes, Pylades and the Old Man emerge from hiding and face Electra across the grave. She is startled.
Orestes	Sister! (advances to embrace her)
Electra	Orest... (checks herself, recoils)... I do not believe.
Orestes	I am...
Electra	...an actor sent me to deceive.
Orestes	I'm your lost brother, can't you see?
Electra	I see a man. Well, I see three.
Orestes	Don't recognize my auburn hair, The colour that our youth did share?
Electra	My locks are shorn, their stubble's dark, So hair-colour's no certain mark.
Orestes	Our footprints look, their shape's the same, Surely this must stamp my claim?
Electra	A mere coincidence the shape. Besides mine's smaller, less agape.
Orestes	Sisterly you wove this stag; I wear it still, my keepsake flag. (Orestes throws open his cloak to reveal its embroidery)
Electra	Why, perhaps you stole this cloak, Or bought it from some gipsyfolk.
Orestes	(desperate) The scar, the scar here on my brow, You surely will not argue now?
Pylades	While hunting deer he had a fall.
Old Man	You bathed his head, you must recall.

Act I

Electra   That accident I can't deny.
Such signs alone can never lie.
Orestes! Is this really true?
Is this the boy my girlhood knew?
Suppose it is an apparition,
Brother of imagination?
Let me touch you, feel your state
My senses all corroborate.
(She advances to embrace Orestes)

Orestes   (He puts up his hand. She stops, before the grave)
No. I'm not your true brother proved
Until our Father's shame's removed.
Our joy misgotten, premature
Would make this shrine three times impure.

Electra   Speak then, speak to pinch my ears
To swear to me that what I hear's
Orestes's tongue and voice's bow
And not mere memory's echo.

Orestes   I'm no mere image, no mere sound, no spirit immaterial,
No ray of light or trick of sight, no phantasm ethereal.
I'm hard of bone and taut of flesh and red of bloody wound still fresh,
(He cuts his arm with his sword)
Hell-bent on plunging steely shafts in murderers' hot-beating hearts
(He strikes the gravestone with his sword)
With these supporters firm and strong, co-bearers of my pain so long.
(He puts his arms round Pylades' and the Old Man's shoulders)

Electra   Thank Gods that Fate our hour brings.
Orestes, oh my sufferings!

Orestes   I know, we eavesdropped from that wood,
Such sorrow's not misunderstood.
But hush now sister, we must plan
Our scheme as quickly as we can.
Tonight with feasting underway
Their watch will be in disarray.
So tell us of the sentries' rounds,
Their times and changes, codes and sounds.

Pylades   How we'll smuggle in our swords.

Old Man   Judicious bribes should pay rewards.

404

Pylades   Orestes must remain unseen.

Old Man Our plan as blades must needs be keen.

Orestes   And now tell me of Aegisthus and our Mother, ghastly wed:
Do they sleep together?

Electra   They try. In our Father's bed.

Orestes   Then that's where we'll surprise them, oh sickeningly apt!
It will not be the first time in that chamber blood's been tapped.

Electra   They say she does not dare to drowse, her darkness does reveal
Teams of fearful apparitions.

Orestes   This time they'll be real.

Electra   She even feigns repentance, sending proxy-born oblations,
Her guilt itself too guilty to risk any publication.
(She picks up the urn. Her tone changes)
Vile, evil, faithless trash!
A Curse upon your conscience' ash!
(She spits into the ashes and tosses the urn away)

Orestes   (retrieving the urn)
No wait, your spite gives me a clue.
Have they spoke of my death to you?

Electra   Fresh rumours gripped the town today
News of a chariot run away
And your being trampled by its steed;
But I've long learned to pay no heed.
Aegisthus has such myths devised
To keep his realm anaesthetized.

Pylades   These weren't Aegisthus' work but ours.
Goat-herds' gossip has its powers.

Orestes   We'll need liquour and a fun'ral cask,
Can you bring us these by dusk?

Electra   Whate'er you ask me, I will do.

Orestes   Now conscience and a trick or two...

Cause   Orestes licks his hand, dips it in the urn's ashes and wipes it across his forehead, leaving a broad black smear.

Act I

Orestes   With but one stroke of mother's guilt her white-skinned dove's turned
                                                                                          raven:

Cause   Orestes draws his dagger, cuts off a lock of his long hair and lets it fall
              onto the grave.

Orestes   From princely Argive's noble locks to negro slavehood shaven.
               (He draws himself up)
               Rest easy Clytemnestra, your *step*-son shortly will attend you.

Cause   Electra and the three men recede from view, planning together. The fig-
              ures of Aegisthus in opulent red robes and Clytemnestra in green, rather
              rumpled royal dress appear on the opposite side of the stage. Aegisthus is
              near centre-stage facing out towards Clytemnestra who is pacing nervously,
              neurotically to and fro.

Clytemnestra   Stay Aegisthus, stay by me,
                     Alone I fear catastrophe.

Aegisthus   Peace Clytemnestra, all's secure,
                  My guards mind every aperture.

Clytemnestra   I doubt them all, my fancies seize on
                     Shifting shadows, glimpsing treason.

Aegisthus   Calm my Queen, you rest awhile,
                  Let sleep soothe spirits volatile.

Clytemnestra   You know I cannot sleep for dreams,
                     For me Morpheus no bed redeems.
                     Last night my womb a serpent spawned,
                     Which in swaddling soft and warm
                     Sucked softly at my breast adrape.
                     When from his mute milk-sucking gape
                     With sudden fearful snarl there sprang
                     Two-inch long razor-pointed fangs.
                     (She tears at herself)
                     Fiercly clenched they to my teat,
                     Blood-milk spurted, hot and sweet.
                     I could not wrench the thing away,
                     Its jet-black poison forth did spray
                     Till I, my blood all clotted, shed,
                     Sank from the grinning viper... dead.
                     (She collapses, shaking)

Aegisthus   My dear, my dear, hush hush my dear,
             Orestes cannot harm you here.
             I'd rest with you but should away,
             Fresh rumours do his death relay,
             Rumours not of my invention,
             Calling for authentication.
             Anticipating such delight,
             I've ordered for a feast tonight
             Wherein we both shall celebrate
             Our cause at last emancipate.
             So Clytemnestra, sleep in peace,
             That waking from your dreams' release
             This news may radiant reinspire
             True royal dignity's attire:
             Your finest most majestic gown
             With oils, perfumes, jewels, crown,
             That so once more by all you're seen
             To be Mycenae's God-blessed Queen.

Clytemnestra I'll try Aegisthus, I will try
             Though I still ache, I know not why.

Aegisthus   Farewell till evening's bright new raiment,
             Laughter, joy and entertainment. (exits)

Clytemnestra Orestes dead? Do I believe it?
             Still I tremble, sick and fevered.
             The City now's so blind with rumour, fantasies outflood the facts,
             Since Agamemnon's blood we let, all's intrigue, doubts and cataracts.
             What? Hysteria's imagination mothering dreams of child's death?
             A curse that I can *contemplate* the cutting-off of my son's breath!
             Forswear my own, disclaim my boy, Orestes who once nestled there?
             (She cradles her arms, then tears her hair)
             What mad misbegotten morals bring such *bastard* thoughts to bear?

Cause   At rear-centre of the stage, slightly higher than the rest of the male char-
             acters, the light slowly comes up on Agamemnon. He is dressed in a
             red, armoured warrior's costume and is seen, ghostlike, through a muslin
             screen. Simultaneously, at a rear side of the stage, again slightly raised,
             the light comes up on Iphigenia, a beautiful young girl with long black
             hair wearing a simple, flowing pale green dress. She also is seen through a
             muslin screen. Clytemnestra speaks as if in memory.

Act I

Iphigenia   Beloved parents must we part
With our familiarity of heart?
Who seeks this secret marriage tryst
To which I'm suddenly dismissed?

Agamemnon   Come dear girl, your wedding's planned,
To Prince Achilles' noble hand.

Iphigenia   I've no taste for this change of life
To warlord's adolescent wife.

Agamemnon   Iphigenia, please obey,
Let wise diplomacy hold sway.

Clytemnestra   This sounds ill-tuned, I smell a plot.
When men don armour, trust them not.

Iphigenia   (writhing pathetically, as if being held)
Why must I Father, Father, why?
Your soldiers some offence imply!

Agamemnon   You must my child, your country waits,
Your name's with heroes, Gods, the Fates.

Clytemnestra   We're not your Gods' or country's dupes,
Your true aim's to impress your troops!

Iphigenia   (panic-stricken)
Help me Father, quick, I hear the sharpening of a blade!
By which of all the Gods was this severe appointment made?

Effect   Agamemnon unsheathes his sword. He says nothing.

Clytemnestra   Leave her! Leave her! Our own flower! Fruit of love's sweet excellence!
Leave her or take leave I swear, of wife and life and all good sense.

Agamemnon   (weeping) I am sorry pretty one,
I have no choice, it must be done.

Cause   Agamemnon raises his sword-point to Iphigenia's slender white neck.
There is a scream, a crash of cymbals and a black-out. End of Act One.

*   *   *   *   *   *   *   *   *   *   *

Effect   Phew! Steamy stuff!

Cause   It's a fearful story, is it not?

Effect   Mm, yes... I'd just like to go back though for a minute, to this whole business of representing atomic particles as people. Okay, so in a sense you can call the Electric Force what you like, you can call it Sexuality and at first it makes no difference to the mathematics, but, but...

Cause   Yes?

Effect   Well, as soon as you put any flesh as it were, on the bones of such a suggestion, it all goes wrong. I mean, sexuality may be the impulse which sustains human life and sexual desire may be a, or even *the*, most important motivating force in human interaction, but we all know that in practice there is far more to human relations than simple sexuality.

Cause   Nothing simple about sexuality Malcolm, that's another thing we all know. More Ouzo?

Effect   Oh ta. Yes but besides that, as we can see from this, this myth of yours, no two human beings are the same, no two human relationships are the same.

Cause   Go on, go on.

Effect   Human beings are born of parents, they grow up and they die. They have family backgrounds and histories. They belong to social classes, cities, tribes, nations...

Cause   Yes, yes...

Effect   They have different psychological make-ups. They have memories, fears, hopes, dreams.

Cause   Freedoms, tastes, values, aims.

Effect   They have different loyalties, different views of things.

Cause   Different moralities, different philosophies.

Effect   So how can we say any of this in the case of atomic particles?

Cause   How indeed?

Effect   So?

Act II

Cause   And of course human beings believe in gods too.

Effect   Ah yes, the two statues, now where do they come in?

Cause   Act Two, you read.

*   *   *   *   *   *   *   *   *   *   *

Effect   The scene opens with Orestes, whose hair is now cut short, and Electra kneeling
before the male and female statues, which are lit respectively in red and green
light. When the statues 'speak' the other unseen actors on stage, male or female
as appropriate, utter their lines in unison.

Orestes   Great Lord Apollo, golden charioteer of burning Sun,
Mighty archer by whose arrows all life's truth's begun,
Who hot with warlike Ares fought
For ten dark years in Troy's cohort.
Charge us with your fiery will:
Must we our father's murdress kill?

Apollo   Good Orestes, all can see you're fine and young and strong.
Your duty to your family must be to right past wrong.
Your Father, King and hero's slayed; there is no book of morals
That can let this go unpaid, whatever future quarrels.
You are his son, his partisan, you are the instrument of honour,
So take your sword and let these words god-sentenced be your armour.

Electra   Fair Goddess Athene, wise fountainhead of all that's Just,
Source of human morals, laws and civilizing trust,
Greeks' guarantor in peace and war,
Great cities' rock and counsellor,
Tell us the verdict to be drawn
If we fulfill this plan we've sworn.

Athene   Good Electra, all know mother-murder is a crime
Than which there can be none more heinous any where or time.
Although your birthright-duty, for sure you will be doomed
To spend your life with childlessness, in barrenness entombed.
What mortal man or midwife could make matricide a mother?
You'll go fruitless, loveless, bedless, your reward can be no other.

Cause   The lights on the statues dim and Electra and Orestes rise, re-forming a group
with Pylades and the Old Man. A wicker coffin lies open.

Orestes	The die is cast.
Electra	Our fate is sealed.
Orestes	The Gods command.
Electra	Our doom's revealed.
Orestes	So will-determined be fulfilled.
Electra	Here is the coffin you designed and potent liquor long-refined.
Orestes	Our hungry patience let us bury in this fitting sanctuary.
Cause	Orestes takes off his princely red cloak and with it lines the coffin. He and Pylades then carefully place their swords and daggers inside, covering them over with the cloak and replacing the lid.
Pylades	An appetite for feast's deceit that will not leave till filled with meat.
Electra	Ply the watchmen with this drink, that wits may drown and eyelids sink.
Effect	Electra hands Pylades the jar of liquor. He empties Orestes' water-flask and half fills it with the alcohol. The rest he passes to the Old Man.
Orestes	I'll bear the casket on my back, my face will then be double-black.
Old Man	I'll distract the guards' attention, none suspect old men's invention.
Orestes	And now for the dead ashes of my Mother's marriage-vows...
Cause	Orestes pours the ashes from the urn into Pylades' cupped hands, spits on them and rubs the black into his face. Electra picks up the empty urn.
Electra	Tonight by all the Gods I swear I'll toast her from this vase. (She tosses the urn into the coffin)
Pylades	Behold us hapless nation-farers, Tantalus' libation-bearers!
Cause	The lights fade and come up on the other side of the stage where Clytemnestra is now dressed in her most majestic green robe and her finest jewellery. Although still nervous and fretful, she has assumed a certain queenly dignity. She addresses the illuminated statue of Apollo.

411

Act II

Clytemnestra   Another dream still stranger yet
Full stopped my heart with lethal threat:
I saw again King Agamemnon
In sov'reign's garb with gold emblazon
Resnatch his gleaming royal stave
And with it beat upon his grave,
Until the stone slab cracked asunder
To the deafening of thunder
And sprouted from the tomb a tree
So monstrous man did never see.
Its trunk and branches grew and grew,
Its greenery eclipsed the blue,
Till finally the sky was blacked,
All Sunlight stopped, all Earth death-wracked.

Cause   The light on Apollo fades. Enter Chrysothemis.

Chrysothemis   Mother, Mother, I have sad news!

Clytemnestra   (starts) What? Aegisthus?

Chrysothemis   No, no, it is Orestes... He is dead.

Clytemnestra   (She breathes in deeply, wrestling with her relief; distantly) Sad news.

Chrysothemis   Three bearers bring him to the palace
Saying he died by accident, not malice.

Clytemnestra   (aside) At last has Nemesis relented:
Atreid peace is reinvented.

Chrysothemis   (sobbing) Oh Mother, Mother, please explain
Why should the Gods it so ordain
When I Orestes first behold,
It is too late, my brother's... cold.
(She falls into her mother's arms)

Clytemnestra   I know my child, I grieved once too
Ere I learnt fear in every clue.
Just thank the Gods that you were cast
Too late to know your tragic past.
(They weep together)
One moral of this plot I promise:
Your innocence will Nature solace.

Effect	Enter Electra, accompanied by the Old Woman
Electra	(icily) Stop weeping woman. Here's news will surely ease your heart, assuming you have heart to ease: Three weary men await outside, they have a body: Orestes.
Effect	Clytemnestra gently helps up Chrysothemis and straightens herself resolutely, ignoring Electra's hatred.
Electra	Where's Aegisthus, he's not home?
Clytemnestra	He'll soon be here and take command.
Old Woman	He's late, the celebration's planned.
Electra	Then we must start without him. Come!
Effect	Orestes, Pylades and the Old Man appear. Orestes is disguised as a negro slave. Orestes and Pylades are carrying the coffin, which they place upon the ground before the Queen.
Old Man	My Lady, we bring the body of your son.
Clytemnestra	(controlling herself) So I have heard.
Pylades	Will you see it for yourself? (He places his hand on the coffin lid)
Clytemnestra	(recoiling) No no, I take your word.
Electra	It's true, I've seen, my life is lost, all abistinence quite wasted. Now must mutual, jealous grief feed loathing yet untasted.
Clytemnestra	I've long since learnt to live with *that*. Now go, arrange his burial, and pat. Lay him alongside his sire. Nurse, feed our guests as they require. (She turns to go)
Orestes	(unable to control his anger) Madam! Is this the way that here in Argos you greet news of heroes' death? 'Royal Prince get buried hence' without so much as draw of breath? No grief or tears, no priest or prayers, not even pretence of mourning? Just clap your hands and turn your back, in rude dispatch your own son scorning?

413

Act II

Clytemnestra Impudent slave!
How dare you thus dictate a mother-queen's right lamentation!
Do you not know this is no ordinary family, my son no ordinary son?
He would have been a hero, bravest, fairest in the world,
Who beside you would be a god by base and foolish churl.
My son, my son, my only son, whose smile would shine like Phoebus' beam,
Held by these hands, kissed by these lips, thrived by suckling on this cream.
(She tears open her dress to reveal her full white breasts)
Yet from that seed so gently fostered
Grew a hunting, haunting monster
Craving for maternal prey,
Stalking, stealing night and day,
Harrying my briefest thought,
Twisting every nerve-end taut.
Speak not to me of grief and tears
And fitting tributes royal.
What can you know of wifely fears
And husbandly betrayal?
Out boy! You're no Argive,
You are not wanted here.
Heathen, if you'd stay alive,
Be gone, go, disappear!

Pylades But Lady, this poor slave became Orestes' trusted guide,
Together they went everywhere, they shared the day he...

Clytemnestra (softly, her back turned) How did he die?

Orestes (Shaken by Clytemnestra's passionate speech, he starts nervously, haltingly, gradually gaining in confidence)

He was killed in a great race
Held in Mount Parnassus' chase.

The King of Phocis had a daughter,
Fair of face and form and nature.
Her suitors pressed from rival states,
A train of princely candidates.
The King, to settle this division,
Sported a great competition.
A race by chariot to decide
To whom his princess would be bride.

414

Orestes A score of riders made the start.
(cont'd) A whipcrack launched them like a dart.
The Sun burned down, the dust blew high,
The drivers jousted, swords awry.
They lashed and roared stampeding on,
The race became a marathon
Whose men and horses overrun
Fell weakened, wearied, one by one.

At last the course pits unmatched twins,
Orestes and a Trojan prince
Who hurtle on for ten more rounds:
Now Greece succeeds, now Troy rebounds.
Next they jostle, neck and neck:
One fears the very ground must break
From urgent beasts and horsemen straining,
Both for the advantage craning.

The frenzied Phocians shout and scream,
Each spurring on his favoured team:
Look now, Orestes starts to gain
And inch by inch does press his claim!
He is ahead by half a length,
His horses seem to gather strength!
He pulls away look, faster, faster,
The race is his! But then, disaster!

Two iron bolts go Clap! and Clap!
A wheel splits, the axles snap!
Up shoot jagged shafts like staves
An injured horse convulsive raves,
The Trojan's thrown to trampling hooves,
Where wheels churn in bloody grooves.
Orestes tries to hold his reins
As panic grips his horses' manes;
They drag his body to the ground
Where stones and sinews ruts compound.
Round and round... I have to turn...
I hear him shout, I hear him groan.

When finally he comes to rest,
His butchered frame beyond request,
I hold his head in these two arms
Till his last breath his pain becalms.

Act II

Cause	Clytemnestra, whose back has been turned during the story, now slowly faces Orestes and collapses onto the floor in paroxysm of grief. All trace of queenly haughtiness has gone.

Clytemnestra (choking)
Now slave, witness Argive grief in earnest, see how the royal river runs.
See how queens are robbed of daughters, robbed of husbands, robbed of
sons.

(She beats her fists on the ground, wailing)
Oh cruel Gods! That I be robbed even of the chance to beg for his
forgiveness!

Orestes dead? This news brings me no release.
It is fresh sentence on all hope for peace.
Though his dead thoughts are all of matricide,
Take me down O Gods, I would lie at his side.

Orestes (to Pylades) What, slay her now in such sincerity of sorrow?

Pylades It seems more mercy-killing than a settlement of honour.

Electra (aside) How strange that by this fiction the world's turned all inverse,
Blessed mother-love reflecting vengeful Harpy's evil curse.
My anxious mind's eye likewise spins, unsure of what is right.
The Universe itself, I fancy's just a trick of light.

Effect Aegisthus bursts in, with his sword drawn and holding the lock of hair which Orestes had left on Agamemnon's grave.

Electra (aside) Ah, this will surely bring us back, remind us of our purpose.
Our wordy fantasises let fly too easily usurp us.

Aegisthus (to Electra, sneering)
So, unconsummated wretch, your boy-lover's re-entwined:
Orestes' hair once more in Argos. You must be confined.
(to Clytemnestra)
What matter woman, why the weeping?
Who are these men, why have they come?

Clytemnestra Hush good husband, he's dead, sleeping.
They have brought Orestes home.

Aegisthus Can this be true, Orestes dead?
I'll swear this down came from his head.

Orestes	It's true, I held the execution, His last wish for absolution.
Electra	See *King* Aegisthus, all is well, Now must conscience prove your Hell!
Aegisthus	Nurse, take away this speechifier!
Cause	Nobody moves.
Aegisthus	Did you not hear me?
Old Woman	I heard you sire.
Aegisthus	What, servants now make their own laws? (He turns to Chrysothemis) You girl, take her, bolt her doors!
Cause	Chrysothemis bows her head.
Aegisthus	There's mischief here, there is a smell. I shall myself these doubts dispel.
Cause	Aegisthus moves towards the coffin. The Old Man intervenes.
Old Man	I warn you sir, it will affright It is a sharp, unpleasant sight.
Aegisthus	And I tell you sir, by no means, no sight could please me more Than of her brother's mangled corpse laid out upon this floor.
Cause	Suddenly, Orestes and Pylades fling open the lid of the coffin, drawing from it their swords and daggers. Orestes at once advances on Aegisthus, while Pylades covers Clytemnestra. Orestes sheathes his dagger, licks his left hand and wipes the black from his forehead, revealing his scar.
Orestes	Queen, your *heathen's* come at last, We'll soon swap greetings, one another. I've business with your suitor first, An old friend of my Father's. (He prods Aegisthus who steps back and prepares to fight) Fight, Trojan whore'sman!
Cause	For some minutes Orestes and Aegisthus engage in a fierce swordfight around the front-centre of the stage. They inflict several minor injuries on

Interval

Cause one another and their costumes get torn and bloodstained. Finally, a decisive
(cont'd) blow from Orestes strikes Aegisthus on the wrist, sending his sword flying.
Electra pounces on the sword. Aegisthus falls, clutching at his wounded hand,
from which the blood spurts freely.

Orestes Ha! At last your day runs out, time soon to be Apollo's,
Meantime fellow, wander not but mark the act that follows.
(He advances on Clytemnestra, who is trembling, speechless with fear)
Prepare now woman to say your prayers.
The Gods have commanded, this will is theirs.

Cause Orestes raises his swordpoint to Clytemnestra's neck. Simultaneously there is a
crash of cymbals and a blackout. End of Act Two.

* * * * * * * * * * *

Effect Oogh, things are looking pretty grim.

Cause Indeed they are.

Effect I realize that for the ancient Greeks this story must have been a
very powerful moral parable, but honestly I can't see that it has much relevance to us now, with our modern problems and our modern ways of
behaving. People are different nowadays, they...

Cause What!? Just because we don't use swords any more and don't like
the sight of blood? Just because we prefer instead to commit our murders
by push-button, to massacre millions over the horizon? Greece/Troy,
America/Russia, Iraq/Iran, it's the same old story.

Effect Oh yes I know, but... I mean at least we don't believe in this 'will
of the Gods' and 'decreed by the Fates' bit any more do we, this idea that
we are all doomed to run forever on invisible god-given railway-lines.

Cause Don't we? What are your 'causal connections', your 'Laws of
Physics', your 'Cosmic Forces'? What are your 'Quarks', your 'Electrons',
your 'Atoms', your 'Genes'? What is your biochemistry, your neurology,
your psychology? What is your evolutionary necessity? What is... *that*? An
admirable evasion of whoremaster man, to lay his goatish disposition on
the charge of *a star*!

Effect But all this stuff about matricide and the avenging of family dis-
honour, we don't think like that any more, we...

Cause What!? What!? We who would contemplate the murder of ten million mothers, the burning of ten billion babes!? We who even now have our sword-point tickling at the throat of Mother Earth herself!? We who would suffocate her life's breath, who would poison her very placenta!? You're not very good at reading models Malcolm, that's all I can say.

Effect Look, I don't mean...

Cause Oh we've had a reprieve, sure, but nothing's truly changed, has it? The machinery's still there, still ticking away, all over the world. Disarmament is public relations: they dismantle only the *obsolete* vehicles. Meanwhile, the space-war research continues, the new programmes proceed, scientists like you still dream of limitless power... An empire wanes, but nationalism waxes; some old iron is scrapped, but the plutonium stockpile swells. You and your infernal tinkerings, you and your unholy warfare, you and your *inter-national* conspiracies!

Effect But... but...

Cause For how long? Ten years? Twenty years? And then what? Tell me Malcolm, where will you be when the curtain finally goes up? You'll be a top man by then won't you, the fusion expert, you'll be down there in the Bunker, down there in the Cave; the Guardian of Civilization, planning the great leap forward into the Platinum Age; watching the images flickering on the screens, while outside in the fire the shadow-people are being blinded by your thousand counterfeit Suns...

Effect Who are you? Who sent you? Why are you hounding me like this?

Cause Ah Malcolm, I am your alter-ego, your other self, your conscience, your con-scientist, that awkward little philosopher at the back of your mind who says: No! The World is *not* composed of strings of tiny particles, the World is *not* governed by inanimate forces. The World is made of *drops of blood*, the World is inhabited by *souls*, by souls with appetites and desires and dreams and schemes. And some of those souls are human beings, and human beings can be *evil bastards*, given half a chance!

Effect Look, I wish things weren't... it's not my fault that...

Cause And what will happen to your daughters when you're in the Bunker, eh, and to your daughters' children? What will happen to Chrissie, Jean and Ella? Maybe they won't manage to fight their way in... Maybe they won't be lucky enough to cop it straight away...

419

Interval

Effect   Please, I must open the window, I...

Cause   What will your sad Ella say of you, what will she think, out there, as she crawls her way through burning flesh and rubble, as she scratches at the rock-hard ground for scraps of bread? Eh? What will she say when her pretty hair falls out in tufts, when the blisters start to fester on her soft, sweet skin, when the vomit runs choking from her cupid-lips...

Effect   Oh God no, please not that...

Cause   What will she say in a World where the Sunlight is turned black, where cancers are carried on the freezing wind, where the very air is leprous? Eh? Eh?

Effect   Oh dear, oh dear, I don't know, I don't know...

Cause   I tell you Malcolm, in that World when men pick up their swords again, they will not speak of 'Neutrons' or of 'Gamma-radiation' but of *The Vengeance of The Gods*!!

Effect   No, no, it doesn't have to be like that, it doesn't have to happen, no, no, surely...

Cause   Hey, be careful Malcolm, what are you doing?

Effect   I mean there must be a way, there must be... it's... I don't know what, but... Oh hell!

Cause   Sit down, sit down!

Effect   Oh dear, oh dear, I'm sorry, I'm sorry, did I knock the model?

Cause   No no, not the model, the script, the script, you've screwed up the script! That was my only spare!

Effect   Oh dear, yes, I do apologize, I don't know what came over me... I'll, I'll get a copy made for you, I promise, I...

Cause   For now you'll have to share mine.

Effect   Oh, er, yes, erm... shall I turn the tape?

Cause   No, just read.

✳   ✳   ✳   ✳   ✳   ✳   ✳   ✳   ✳   ✳   ✳

Effect	Act Three. The scene is as we left it. Aegisthus is slumped across the coffin, bleeding and guarded by Pylades. Clytemnestra has regained her composure and stands calmly, resignedly. Orestes still threatens her, but his sword is lowered.
Clytemnestra	Hear my children these my prayers ere running your sword through. I once prayed for your sister's life; those ears were deafened too. All they heard was Ares' roar, hounds' howl from Hades' mud, Men's words of war and Greece and gore and tasting Trojan blood.
Effect	The light comes up brightly on the screened figure of Iphigenia at rear-side stage. She is lolling, head back, her throat pierced by a sword and a river of blood flowing from the gaping wound down her pale green dress to the ground. It is a shocking sight and the other characters themselves gasp. The screened silhouette of Agamemnon can be seen dimly at rear-centre stage.
Clytemnestra	What woman in the world could leave this wound uncauterized? His death was branded by the gods, was bounden, authorized.
Effect	The light comes up fully on Agamemnon, who is wearing his victor's purple cloak. A dagger has been plunged into his chest and again a stream of blood flows to the ground. Again there is gasping.
Clytemnestra	Dear sweet sad Electra, deaf as stone and gagged by hate, Hear my words before your orphaned grief you consummate. Long ago I loved him too, pre-war, not yet unmanned, A knight who called his wife to arms, led children hand to hand. But when he turned from man to fiend and slit that girl's soft neck, Then in me swelled battle-cries no loyalty could check. For greed and power and self-esteem they'll wager national slaughters. Men talk of love for motherland then murder their own daughters. But we women bear their soldiers and their victims and their sorrow, We women bear the braves who will their armour briefly borrow. It's you Electra, you who'll pay the price upon my head, You who must decide to bear the children of the dead.
Electra	If ghosts could speak, how would they guide? What counsel pass from Lethe's side?
Old Man	Where they have gone all sides are lost; *Their* country can't be double-crossed.
Pylades	For us Greek heroes fought and died, Our due to them's our national pride.

Act III

Old Woman	Why tender *necro*politics, Young wallowing in ancient Styx?
Chrysothemis	The truth's naïve, the future's ours, Not time itself can disendow us.
Orestes	A phalanx fell in Troy's blockade: Such sacrifice must be repaid.
Electra	Base and vain and putrid struggle! Decade of fist and blade and cudgel. A city razed, a million dead, Then Greek finds Trojan in his bed! What's loyalty but power's whore? Can this be all, is there no more? The dead repaid? Repaid with what, Their moral victories all forgot? War's end is peace, but what of peace If not to prove all war's decease? Why do men fight? Why, to be free – To redefine their enemy.
Orestes	Help us O Gods to see what's right, On dark confusion shed your light.
Cause	The lights come up on the two statues; the pattern of characters is complete. The speakers of the gods' lines are now visible.
Apollo	Children of Argos, honour smeared with family shame, Your line cannot continue till you've cleared your blotted name.
Electra	(gazing at Aegisthus' bleeding body; dully) So Chronos' dreary orbit's turned, with nothing gained and nothing learned. What is the point of all these words if issues end all ways in blood?
Athene	Children of your mother's womb to which all life you owe, If you must kill maternity then barren you must go.
Electra	What now? Our Gods, they contradict, Till to our suicides we're tricked!
Apollo	Your Father's heavy in his grave, his spirit you must heighten.
Athene	Parent-murder's crime most grave, its cost we cannot lighten.

422

Electra   (at Agamemnon's graveside. She struggles to heave aside the stone slab)
What's in this Grave, this Gravity, Earth-spirits' pond'rous hold?
(She kneels at the opening and scoops out a handful of dirt, letting it run
through her fingers)
Why, the *must* that haunts this cavity's mere methylate and mould!

Orestes   I vowed a mausoleum when I saw that rough-hewed stone,
A monument of marble gold-engravèd for his throne.

Electra   A foolish vanity I fear, for dried-up bones and rotten smells.
Better honour good ideas than build more citadels.

Apollo   (tone rising) 'Tis your duty to your Father, your genetic blood-begetter!

Athene   (tone rising) Who will touch a matricide, mix seed with her blood-letter?

Electra   (standing over Aegisthus' body)
Blood, blood, what is this blood? I'd drink this magic fluid,
(She picks up Clytemnestra's urn, now half full of Aegisthus' blood)
This ink that writes us all our lines, this wine so potent brewèd.

Effect   To the shock of the onlookers, Electra gulps the blood, leaving a ghastly
smear around her lips.

Electra   So, Trojan blood and Argive, mixing here within this frame!
See now, am I turned monster, has my breath a dragon's flame?
(She moves, explores her arms and hands, as if for the first time)
My arms move free, my eyes still see, my hands are still my hands!
(She starts to walk freely, for the first time)
I can still walk, I can still talk, the palace wall still stands!

Apollo   (murmuring together,   Your duty to your Father!
Athene   agitatedly, repeatedly)   Who'll touch a matricide?

Electra   (now moving freely around the stage, holding Aegisthus' sword)
I've learned to skip, I've learned to run, I've now learnt how to fly,
I see myself under myself, I do not have to try.
I'm killing now with laughter this Spirit of Gravity,
I'm nimble now and master of the gods dancing in me.
(She stops, looks up and addresses the audience)
Laws of my sex, my family, my race, O hear me now great Zeus,
Is there not a power in me more Godly than *excuse*?

Act III

Effect	Electra strides over to Orestes, breaking the red/green pattern for the first time. She grabs him by the hand, swinging him around to face Athene, as she herself turns upon Apollo. She takes a fierce swipe at the still-murmuring statue and knocks off its head with a crash. Orestes follows her example. There is a terrified gasp from the frozen onlookers as the lights which had been illuminating the statues now flood the stage, eclipsing the effect of the model suspended above and bathing everything in a warm, amber glow. Slowly the characters unfreeze. Orestes runs his fingers through a pile of dust from one of the broken statues.
Orestes	Inanimate and empty atoms, models, idols, imitations!
Electra	Out you Super, Nat'ral Powers, fragmentry imaginations! (They discard their swords and embrace. The pattern now breaks down)
Pylades	I'd trust only a God who moved, who stirred with love's desire. (He runs to Chrysothemis, falls to his knees and kisses her hand passionately. She responds playfully)
Chrysothemis	A God who joked and laughed and wooed, a God who played the lyre.
Clytemnestra	(helping Aegisthus to his feet and bandaging his wound) A God who suffered loss and grief, who knew of hate and blame.
Aegisthus	A God who could forget or pardon all of history's shame.
Old Woman	(turning to the Old Man) I'd believe a God who'd dare to dream a *better* world.
Old Man	A God in whose philosophy old flags stay ever-furled.
Effect	The eight living characters intermingle around the stage. Electra advances.
Electra	Thus our games of gods and names can all our wits entrance, Till in the end they call the tune and lead us *in a dance*!
Effect	Electra and Orestes lead the cast in a gentle, rhythmic dance, joining hands, pulsating in and out to form a series of complex patterns. Curtain.

＊　＊　＊　＊　＊　＊　＊　＊　＊　＊　＊

Cause So you see Malcolm, it's as easy as flicking... a light-switch!

Effect Ouch! Oogh, I feel dizzy, I feel sick!

Cause Yes, yes... I'll open the window, you need some fresh air. Keep your eyes open whatever you do... Now, breathe deeply... That's better isn't it? Wait a moment, I'll switch off the model... There you are you see, just a few bits of gut and glass and glue!

424

Index

Although the choice of names, terms and topics comprising this index is inevitably somewhat arbitrary, it is hoped that it will be of some help. Within entries, sub-entries may be listed in logical or occurrence order rather than alphabetically. Underlining indicates an important source and recommended text. Bold numbering indicates quotation.

Effect   Look, some of the tubes have melted, and we didn't even notice.

Cause   It was always going wrong, never worked for more than five minutes; useless bloody thing... Well, what do you think of the Play?

Effect   I don't know, I don't know, it has set me thinking... I'd have thought it deserves publication. Have you tried the University Press?

Cause   No I haven't, they're too dry aren't they, too academic?

Effect   I hear they're expanding their list. I know a guy in the book trade who runs a little mail-order business from an office over the Market Bookshop. That was who I called on this morning, actually. He tells me the U.P. are keen to get into general publishing, are looking for new authors. I should give them a go.

Cause   I will.

Effect   Listen! What's that music?

Cause   Ah, that's the family downstairs. Sometimes when they've shut the restaurant they get the bouzouki out and have a good old knees-up. Come on, let's go down, they're very friendly and there's no more booze up here... You wait till you see the daughter, she is *de-licious*!

Effect   Oh dear, how am I *ever* going to get home?

Cause   This mail-order friend of yours, do you think he could help at all? Would it be worth sending him the book, or the Play?

Effect   I doubt it; I can ask if you like. What will you call it, the Play?

Cause   Erm, I'm not sure... I think perhaps 'The Children of Electra'. Dunno. Come on.

The two men, their arms around each other's shoulders, stagger wearily but happily down the stairs to join the party going on below. Outside, the wan, expectant, pre-dawn light begins to dim the night's brilliant starshine. Communities of sparrows and starlings start the chorus of their day's business in darkly silhouetted trees. The shadowy blackness of the buildings is relieved only by the restaurant's brightly steamed-up windows, still lit when the milkman clatters by on his lonely round. The sounds of the music and dancing and laughter gradually die away as we drift gently down towards the river and out of the town.

THE END